THEORY AND INTERPRETATION OF NARRATIVE
James Phelan, Peter J. Rabinowitz, and Katra Byram, Series Editors

Copyright © 2018 by The Ohio State University.
All rights reserved.

Library of Congress Cataloging-in-Publication Data
Names: Dwivedi, Divya, editor. | Skov Nielsen, Henrik, editor. | Walsh, Richard, 1964– editor.
Title: Narratology and ideology : negotiating context, form, and theory in postcolonial narratives / edited by Divya Dwivedi, Henrik Skov Nielsen, and Richard Walsh.
Other titles: Theory and interpretation of narrative series.
Description: Columbus : The Ohio State University Press, [2018] | Series: Theory and interpretation of narrative | Includes bibliographical references and index.
Identifiers: LCCN 2017058655 | ISBN 9780814213698 (cloth ; alk. paper) | ISBN 0814213693 (cloth ; alk. paper)
Subjects: LCSH: Fiction—History and criticism—Theory, etc. | Postcolonialism in literature. | Narration (Rhetoric) | Ideology and literature. | South Asian fiction—History and criticism.
Classification: LCC PN3331 .N28 2018 | DDC 808/.036—dc23
LC record available at https://lccn.loc.gov/2017058655

Cover design by Lawrence J. Nozik
Text design by Juliet Williams
Type set in Adobe Minion Pro

Narratology and Ideology

Negotiating Context, Form, and Theory in Postcolonial Narratives

EDITED BY

Divya Dwivedi
Henrik Skov Nielsen
Richard Walsh

THE OHIO STATE UNIVERSITY PRESS | COLUMBUS

CONTENTS

INTRODUCTION
	Divya Dwivedi, Henrik Skov Nielsen, and Richard Walsh 1

PART I   NARRATIVE IN QUESTION
CHAPTER 1   Fractured Tales and Colonial Traumas: Disfigured Stories in Kashmiri Short Fiction
	Patrick Colm Hogan 37

CHAPTER 2   No Center and No Margins: Narrativizing Return Journeys in Works by M. G. Vassanji, Michael Ondaatje, and Rohinton Mistry
	Martin Löschnigg 55

CHAPTER 3   The Legibility of Things: Objects and Public Histories in N. S. Madhavan's *Litanies of the Dutch Battery*
	Udaya Kumar 74

PART II   ZONES OF NARRATIVE (PARA-, META-, INTRA-)
CHAPTER 4   Metanarrative Signs in Ousmane Sembène's *Les Bouts de bois de Dieu. Banty mam Yall*
	Gerald Prince 93

CHAPTER 5   A Contextual Rhetorical Analysis of Audiences in E. M. Forster's Preface to Mulk Raj Anand's *Untouchable*
	Sarah Copland 102

CHAPTER 6   Ideological Ambivalence: A Reading of Salman Rushdie's *Midnight's Children*
	Jan Alber 120

PART III VOICE AND NARRATOR

CHAPTER 7 "We are the people of the Apokalis": Narrative Voice and the Negotiation of Power Structures in Indra Sinha's *Animal's People*
Marion Gymnich — 141

CHAPTER 8 Questioning the Ideology of Reliability in Mohsin Hamid's *The Reluctant Fundamentalist*: Towards a Critical, Culturalist Narratology
Greta Olson — 156

CHAPTER 9 The Immigrant Experience in Jhumpa Lahiri's "The Third and Final Continent": Postcolonial and Rhetorical Perspectives
James Phelan — 173

PART IV STRATEGIES, NARRATIVE AND POSTCOLONIAL

CHAPTER 10 Ideology, Dissidence, Subversion: A Narratological Perspective
Monika Fludernik — 193

CHAPTER 11 The Apocalypse That Will Never Be: Decolonization, Proleptic History, and Satire in India, c. 1946–51
Baidik Bhattacharya — 213

PART V NARRATIVE, THEORY, IDEOLOGY

CHAPTER 12 In the Absence of Post-
Mieke Bal — 231

CHAPTER 13 The Addressee Function, or the Uses of Narratological Laity: Lessons of Khasak
Divya Dwivedi — 251

List of Contributors — 273
Index — 277

INTRODUCTION

DIVYA DWIVEDI
HENRIK SKOV NIELSEN
RICHARD WALSH

THE ESSAYS in this volume all address narratological issues in postcolonial fictions, and as such they participate in what has been called postcolonial narratology, or—more broadly—contextualist narratology. That is to say, the contributors proceed from a narratological perspective, broadly understood, in order to realize the potential interest of narrative-theoretical concepts and methods for scholars and students interested in postcolonial fiction, but also in order to put the adequacy of those theoretical ideas to the test in the crucible of ideologically situated readings.

It is striking that, whatever particular manifestation of contextualism is concerned, the project of contextualist narratology has been consistently framed as both an imperative and a problem (Shen; Kim). The tension to be negotiated here can be felt on two levels: it involves theoretical questions about the relevance of context to form (and vice versa) in narrative, and methodological questions about the commensurability of the goals of criticism and theory. This tension is at the root of a broader disconnect between research in narrative studies and much of the work on narratives that goes under other critical banners—such as postcolonial criticism, for example. Fundamentally, it is a tension between formalism and ideological critique, which are often regarded as antithetical—at least in the larger critical community. Even within narratological circles, where calls for a synthesis of formalist theory and engaged criticism are commonplace (and have been for at least thirty years), the tension remains, and in fact is intensified under the pressure of the imperative to transcend it. The imperative, or set of imperatives, here, derives from principled arguments about the nature and purpose of narrative theory itself: arguments for the accountability of theory to pragmatic and contextual considerations, arguments against the false universalism of theory grounded in a narrow (Western, male) canon. These are staples of postclassical narratology, and indeed the notion of contextualism was one of the most prominent rallying cries for that movement beyond the structuralist paradigm. Yet commentators such as Roy Sommer, Tom Kindt, and Hans-Harald Müller have had occasion to note the disparity between the frequent calls for a contextualist narratology of one kind or another and the relatively meager results of such research (Sommer 66; Kindt and Müller 210). If the impact of contextualism upon narratological practice has been limited, then, it is either evidence of collective bad faith, or of a methodological problem. There are positions on either side of this issue that refuse its messiness, either by reaffirming a strong theoretical formalism or by abandoning the pretensions of theory altogether in favor of the coal-face of particular, situated readings; both of these positions have their adherents, and need to be addressed. The real interest for this volume, however, is in what happens when you attempt to keep both formalism and ideology in play.

FORMALISM AND IDEOLOGY IN NARRATIVE THEORY

The benefits of bringing the theoretical paradigms of narrative theory into relation with an expansive and situated corpus of narrative texts have been rehearsed before, from several perspectives. So, in Susan Stanford Friedman's version of a transnational narratology, the emphasis is upon a comparative and pluralist narrative theory, wary of the false universalism of Eurocentric models and "open to both commonalities and differences across cultures" (5). For Patrick Colm Hogan, on the other hand, the main point of cross-cultural narratology is to set the study of narrative universals upon a proper empirical footing. Hogan takes pains to clarify what universalism on such terms actually means: it does not mean the a priori universalism of analytic narratology, the essentialism of which has made the notion of universals so suspect to cultural criticism; it does not even mean extrapolating from a given corpus (however large and cross-cultural) to claims about all narratives. Rather, it involves the identification of cross-cultural regularities in narrative form that recur with a higher frequency than is consistent with chance (19). There is a tension between the approaches adopted by Friedman and Hogan, but it isn't clear that there is anything problematic about it. For one thing, they both emphasize the point that the study of universals and the study of particulars, of difference, are complementary. For another, they are both primarily concerned with narratological questions, and with a bottom-up inductive methodology.

That inductive model of narratological inquiry is not the only one in play, however. It's worth recalling that Roland Barthes's famous comments on the transcultural ubiquity of narrative, now generally invoked as a celebration of the field's richness and scope, were originally presented in the form of a problem ("Structural Analysis" 237–38). The numberless instances of narrative made empirical inquiry an unfeasible approach to the theory of narrative as such, which therefore called for a top-down, analytic methodology (on the model of structural linguistics, of course). Although much structural narratology was preoccupied with typological empiricism, its methodological foundations were resolutely rationalist, and arguably it is this rationalist methodology at the heart of the classical structuralist project that makes narratology theoretical, not the typological empiricism that nonetheless accompanies it. But neither approach is intrinsically antipathetic to a contextualist narratology of some description. Gerald Prince has argued, in separate articles, in favor of versions of contextual narratology based in both methodologies: the main burden of his defense of feminist narratology, "Narratology, Narratological Criticism, and Gender," was that an inclusive corpus of narrative texts was important to the legitimacy of inductive methods in narratology; his model for postcolonial narratology, on the other hand, explicitly repudiates inductive methodology, basing its engagement with the postcolonial not on particular texts but on concepts associated with the postcolonial (he instances hybridity, migrancy, otherness, fragmentation, diversity, power relations), concepts that are to be considered for their possible relevance as narratological categories ("Postcolonial Narratology" 373).

This differentiation between different models of a contextualist narratology is curious, not least because the best example of the deductive version Prince assigns to postcolonial narratology is probably one from feminist narratology: Susan Lanser's gender-based critique of the concept of narrative voice and its contribution to the scrutiny of the subject as a theoretical primitive in narrative theory. The specificity of each methodology to its assigned context is also somewhat compromised when Prince starts to place in parenthesis the "postcolonial" of "(postcolonial) narratology" (379). At such moments there is justice in the suspicion that such a model of contextualist narratology is no synthesis of the interests of the contextual critic and the theorist, but rather an appropriation of the former by the latter.

Prince, in fact, advocates a restrictive definition of what counts as narratology, contextualist or otherwise, and consistently draws a sharp distinction between the theoretical activity of narratology proper and narratological criticism, or applied narratology ("Narratology, Narratological Criticism, and Gender" 164; "Postcolonial Narratology" 379). Other perspectives on contextualist narratology are more accommodating: Robyn Warhol readily acknowledges that most of what goes by the name of feminist narratology is narratological criticism, tending "to combine the insights of feminism and narratological analysis in developing gender-centred interpretations of individual texts" (162). Monika Fludernik's program for "The Diachronization of Narratology" (which acknowledges the influence of feminist narratology) envisages a narratologically informed literary history, focused upon the development of narrative forms and functions. And Roy Sommer argues for a "both . . . and" model of postcolonial or intercultural narratology, "equally concerned with identifying characteristic and recurrent features of intercultural narrative on the one hand, and with discussing the cultural embedding as well as the transcultural functions of fictional storytelling" (77).

This last "both . . . and" approach raises the question of how well integrated the two kinds of objectives actually are. To what extent is a synthesis between narrative theory and situated cultural criticism possible? There is no doubt that narratological concepts can be, and have been, put to good use in the service of criticism, and that such practice, whether conceived of as applied narratology or as narratologically informed cultural criticism, can in some sense deliver what Mieke Bal characterized as the "point" of narratology: a nuanced and conceptually precise attentiveness to the ways in which specifically situated narrative texts achieve their semiotic, rhetorical, and ideological effects. There is much to be gained from such work, and it shouldn't be the exclusive province of narratologists; so why is such practice not more widespread? One reason is that the implied notion of a narratological toolbox brings with it some methodological problems. Even for the narratologist, the mixed motives of narratological criticism can result in conflicting models of the relation between means and ends: it may be that the project is conceived as the application of a hard-won conceptual apparatus, now in search of the opportunity to bear fruit in the form of critical insight, but it may be instead that the project is more like a testing ground for theoretical concepts—a proof of principle, or a filling out of the theoretical paradigm. For the cultural critic, a narratological toolbox may offer the means to work more effectively upon a particular narrative text or corpus, and the choice of tools can to some extent be justified by their utility, but a certain unease may nevertheless accompany such ad hoc usage, especially if the critic is unwilling to spend time discriminating between those concepts that are tried and tested, those that are blunt with age, and those that are (needfully or needlessly) innovative. On the other hand, should the critic find occasion to challenge theory in the face of the resistance of the text, such a move toward theoretical contestation itself quickly usurps the foreground of critical attention. Narrative theory does not reduce to the typological elaboration of a conceptual toolbox for criticism precisely to the extent that it is theoretical, which is the extent to which it does not take the received terms of narrative description as premises, but as disputable and tendentious, and therefore as fit objects of critique in their own right.

It is considerations of this sort that motivate separatist perspectives, in which theory and criticism are declared to be distinct and incommensurate practices, such that combining them amounts to a kind of category error. Some notable statements of such a position characterized the rear guard of structuralist narratology, including Nilli Diengott's attack on feminist narratology and Seymour Chatman's "What Can We Learn from Contextualist Narratology?" For Chatman, contextualism introduced the pragmatic, contingent, and circumstantial into what was properly the formalist study of the narrative *text*, not the contextual narrative *act*. Failure to abstract from context was simply a failure to be theoretical. For others, including Chatman's main antagonists, Mary Louise Pratt and Barbara Herrnstein Smith, if that was narratology then they were interested in something else—to narratology's loss.

But the tension between theory and criticism is not really between abstraction and contextual specificity; rather, it is between formalist poetics and ideological thematics. Abstraction, as a process, means reducing the density of information in the particulars concerned, on principles of relevance to given ends; it is not identical with idealization, but may equally be an empirical form of generalization. Both formalist poetics and ideological thematics necessarily embrace the interrelation of the general and the particular. The concept of narrative has expanded considerably since Chatman's defense of the text type, and in a sense it has become more abstract—narrative now is more often conceived as a discursive mode or even as a form of cognition. But accompanying each degree of this abstraction is the necessary and constraining role of situated particulars. Narrative, thus conceived, does not transcend but emerges out of contexts: it is situated socially in a context of communication, situated environmentally in a context of intelligible action, and situated biologically in a context of human embodiment.

Ideological thematics, too, necessarily works with relations between the particular and the general, between the representational specifics of the text (and of its referents) and the abstract relations that govern cultural manifestations of power. Ideology, after all, is systematic: its social and political force depends upon a structure of ideas, values, and beliefs that, even if contradictory, must have a sufficient patina of coherence to be collectively embraced as a legitimation of the (perceived) interests of some group (Eagleton 28–30), and of the use of power in defense of those interests. The ideological significance of particular events, acts, or texts involves their relation not just to this systemic frame of reference but also to its internal, structural logic. So yes, the ideological critic may look at the theoretical formalist and see, especially if the formalism is accompanied by a rhetoric of autonomy, not so much a refusal of ideology as an ideological refusal, but equally the theorist may often look at the critic and see an unacknowledged or unarticulated formalism. This is not to suggest that postcolonial criticism has been oblivious to form, or that narratology has disregarded ideology, but only to note the inversion of foreground and background that occurs between the two perspectives.

Narrative itself, taken most fundamentally as a form of cognition, is paradigmatic of this relation of reciprocal and irreducible interdependence. It is intrinsic to a narrative mode of meaning that the sense-making process, whether it is generating or interpreting narrative meaning, must negotiate between the particular and the general. Narrative is a way of articulating particulars on the basis of established general paradigms, but also as a basis for establishing general paradigms. The particular and the general relate to each other reciprocally, each as ground to the other's figure, each throwing the other into relief. The relationship can be oriented either way; what is not possible is to dispense with one or the other, without the result ceasing to signify or ceasing to be narrative. The forms of generality involved are dictated by the frame of reference under consideration, from cognitive templates, scripts, and schemata (Herman ch. 3; Schank and Abelson), to the Barthesian hermeneutic, semantic, proairetic, cultural, and symbolic codes (*S/Z*); and negotiation between the particular and general is differently inflected in fictive and nonfictive rhetorics. So in fiction, prior generality establishes the narrative particulars in relation to (for example) conventions of realism, genre membership, interpretative protocols, plot expectations, and historical and sociological generalizations, while the particulars in turn may produce a posterior generality including revised criteria of realism or of narrative conventions, or reconfigured frames of interpretation. In nonfiction, prior generality constitutes the parameters within which the referential particulars of the narrative are made intelligible and norms and expectations are confirmed, while the recalcitrance of the particulars in certain respects may stimulate the extrapolation of revised general axioms, principles, and narrative logic; historiographical revisionism and counter-histories; even a paradigm shift in a field of knowledge.

Both the fictional and nonfictional cases enact a reciprocal relation between the particular and the general in which neither has logical precedence, and this formal circularity, which has been thoroughly explored and demonstrated by Paul Ricoeur in terms of his threefold model of mimesis (52–87), also puts intrinsically ideological considerations into play. Such a view makes narrative, as such, both a force of conservatism, of the entrenchment of received views, and a means of innovation, critique, and conceptual liberation. The ideological stakes vary according to the kinds and degrees of the particular and general engaged in any given narrative: the respects in which it deals directly with the representation of experience circumscribed within contextual social, political, and ideological conditions, or the extent to which it implicates the reader in the unexamined premises of covert cultural norms by means of its own rhetorical function as a kind of enthymeme, or argument with an implied premise—a process by which narrative discourse always interpellates the subject in the act of interpretation (Frow 77–78; Prendergast 216; Althusser 162).

The point is that narrative, in both its formal logic and its ideological function, is remarkable precisely for the way in which it holds in dynamic equilibrium contrary motions toward the general and the particular. In the context of a view of narrative as fundamental to cognition, there is no getting beyond this feature of its role in thought and understanding, and in that respect narrative marks a horizon to the constitution of meaning and value. In such terms narrative is, on the one hand, an innate endowment with a distinctive and powerful capacity for meaning and affective force, and on the other hand—as such—a problem, since its relations to the real, to social and political conditions, to the complexity of the communicative contexts and purposes it engages, are tendentious and need to be clarified.

It is the role of both formalist analysis and ideological criticism to tease apart the mutuality of the particular and general in narrative, to show its workings, but the methodologies they employ in doing so involve antithetical relations of means to ends. Formalism is indeed aligned with the *process* of abstraction, whereas ideology always finds its meaning, as ideology, in its incarnations—in the material conditions and particular interests, forms and exertions of power, that it legitimates. So while formalist poetics is always oriented toward generalizations, ideological thematics is always moving toward contextual particulars. These are deep methodological commitments, and they are sometimes belied by the surface features of an argument: as, for example, when you work outwards from the particular to the general in order to shore up the foundations of the immediate point, rather than to extrapolate from the particular instance to a general principle. There are false congruencies as well as false conflicts between formalism and contextual criticism.

The formalist orientation of narratology and the ideological orientation of contextual criticism are methodologies that must necessarily engage with the same problematic in narrative, and may be overlain upon each other, but upon close inspection the grain of each runs in a different direction. The two practices are antithetical, but interdependent, each serving as ground to the other's figure. This view actually facilitates dialogue between narrative theory and criticism more effectively than the idea that there is some intermediate ground—the specific terrain of a contextualist narratology—in which a synthesis occurs. The contextualist approach has not provided more than a nominal basis for engagement between theory and criticism, because the synthesis upon which it is predicated is illusory, and felt to be so in practice, and in demarcating a synthetic middle ground, contextualist narratologies have also tended to restrict the overlap between methodologies, and so limited the scope for dialogue. Work that transgresses beyond the bounds of this nominal common ground comes to seem either a return to business as usual or a venture into foreign territory, and to be received on the other side accordingly as either an irrelevance or an impertinence. Conceived as the terrain of a dialogue without the presumption of synthesis, however, the field of common concern is much more comprehensive, and there is much to be gained from the expansion of horizons that occurs when the contrary inflection of formalist and ideological methodologies is not suppressed but brought to the fore. Such encounters between incongruous approaches are always an invitation to reflective practice, but that is not really the point (at least, that would amount to no more than another exhortation); here the nature of the methodological counterpoint has a direct bearing upon the distinctive qualities of the object of study—whether narrative in general, or a particular, ideologically situated narrative—such that a dialogic response, as such, offers the possibility of substantial purchase upon that object, and of reciprocal insights for both theory and criticism. Such a dialogic reciprocity can, and should, operate between scholars working in narratology and those working in specific fields such as postcolonial criticism; it can also operate within the work of a single scholar, or indeed a single essay, and that is the aspiration of the essays in this volume.

POSTCOLONIALISM, LITERARY CRITICISM, AND NARRATIVE

The relevance of narratology to postcolonial literary criticism, as well as the possibility of a postcolonialist critique of narratology, arise in the context of the relationship of literary studies to postcolonialism in general. The limitations of space do not permit a detailed account here of postcolonial studies, which Timothy Brennan has described as "a porous entity rather than a discrete field. It arose in the form of a political metaphorics rather than a bordered space, either 'field' or 'discipline'" (qtd. in Loomba et al. 3). It has multiple genealogies and its definitions have been the subject of much debate (see Young, *White Mythologies*; Mishra and Hodge; Larsen; Brock). The different colonial and imperial histories of various parts of the world and the different anticolonial movements and decolonization processes (see Cooper) are brought together under the title "postcolonial" on the basis of broad thematic and conceptual commonalities regarding the relation between the ruler and the ruled: appropriation of resources, imposition of accelerated means of production on a society, exploitation of labor, erosion of traditional social relations, denigration of native knowledge systems, and cultural hegemony.

While earlier Marxist characterizations of postcoloniality (that is, the state of being postcolonial) dwelt on the political-economic relation between the colonizer and the colonized, later studies emphasized the cultural relations between the metropole and the margin in the form of vectors of knowledge production, representations of the self and the other, and the constitution of colonial subjectivity (see Loomba). The colonization of the psyche and mind that anticolonial thinkers such as Fanon and Gandhi had highlighted was located by theorists like Edward Said in "colonial discourse" (Young, *White Mythologies* 43; Loomba 43–57). Seen broadly, the notion of discourse deployed here took inspiration partly from Foucault's conception of a regime of discourse as a system of acceptability that generates effects of power, and partly from Lyotard's theory of the grand narratives of modernity (see Young, *White Mythologies*). Colonization—and also neocolonialism/neo-imperialism/globalization—proceeded not merely on the material strength of military and economic strategies but also on the moral strength of self-justificatory meta-narratives of modernity, progress, enlightenment, and the attainment of civilization and democracy. Colonial discourse, then, included the institutions of colonial bureaucracy, universities, philology, and cartography, as well as literary canons and popular culture. Indeed, literature and culture have been seen as an integral part of colonialist ideology. For example, Gauri Vishwanathan's book *Masks of Conquest* shows how the teaching of English literature was the main vehicle of British colonial hegemony. To study colonialism is also to read its work in the texts of the colonizer.

By examining the various resources and strategies of resistance to colonialism, postcolonial studies seeks to understand the limited possibilities of decolonization at economic, political, and cultural levels, and also to register the degree to which anticolonial formations, practices, and discourses are necessarily shaped by colonial ones. Postcolonialism draws predominantly from poststructuralist theory and postmodernist aesthetics to propose that the colonizers produced the colonized as their "other" not through a simple form of exclusion, but through inclusion of the figure of the colonized in their discourse as a different entity than the self. In other words, the figure of the oriental, the African, the native or the "third-world woman" was the product of colonial anthropology, linguistics, geography, legislation, travel writing, and, of course, novels. The crux of postcoloniality lies in the fact that anticolonial consciousness and discourse emerge only within the terms of colonial metanarratives whose characteristics are teleological historicism and Eurocentrism masquerading as humanism. Universalist conceptions of politics and ethics, and the very idea of human rights, are seen as complicit in these metanarratives. The condition denoted by the "post" in postcolonial is a product of continuities and discontinuities in the language and ideas that were part of the colonial juncture in post-decolonization societies. Thus, while coloniality is a delimited phase in history (and though many scholars in the field have treated whatever preceded it as an undifferentiated build-up to colonization and termed it "precolonial"), postcoloniality is an indefinite continuation of ideological components of coloniality. This persistence is manifest even in the very language—especially of national and ethnic identity—through which the colonial subject speaks, opposes empire, and writes back (Eaton). Gayatri Spivak invites students and scholars of history and culture to think of this inability to speak from outside that language as a double bind that is a pharmacon (referring to Derrida), that is, both poison and cure. Homi Bhabha finds in postcolonialism a counter-discourse that mimics the metropolitan metanarrative of colonialism and thus interrupts and destabilizes it. This discourse and its subject, who is the third-world migrant in the first world, are marked by hybridization and ambivalence with respect to the master's discourse rather than being a radical alternative to it ("Of Mimicry and Man"; *Nation and Narration*). Textuality, specifically narration, is central to this postcolonial discursive play.

To foreground postcoloniality, then, is also to trace its ideological dimensions in the texts of the colonized and the decolonized. Simon Gikandi calls it "a code for the state of undecidability in which the culture of colonialism continues to resonate in what was supposed to be its negation" (*Maps of Englishness* 14). It has generated narratives and counter-narratives, travelogues, ballads, autobiographical accounts of conversion, of trauma, of political awakening, of liberation, in addition to works of poetry and fiction. It has adapted genres, most notably the novel and the autobiography. Postcolonialist literary criticism is thus a part of postcolonial studies that approaches literature as the locus of validation of postcolonial theory. It is a part, however, that has been criticized by several scholars for dominating the oppositional work that postcolonialism purports to do, to the neglect of material, social, and political transformation, given that it leans toward the cosmopolitan and transnational in its literary-critical enterprise (see Brennan; Lazarus). This also opens the possibility that cultural productions grasped as "postcolonial" in the strict sense are in fact products and harbingers of concerns exceeding postcolonialist theory and criticism. Dalit studies is a prominent field that is characterized by claims and positions that are critical even of the postcolonialist premise of "epistemic violence of colonialism" in that it is found to articulate the cultural anxieties of elite classes and so-called upper-caste intellectuals regarding the loss of their long-held privilege and sense of socially superior identity (Ilaiah; see also Figueira; Mannathukkaren). Dalit literature has occasioned criticism of postcolonial literary criticism and its aesthetico-political principles, and Toral Gajarawala points out that "there has been a Dalit rejection of [the] later critiques of realism, from the modernist and the Marxist to the postcolonial and subaltern" (*Untouchable Fictions* 21). Although this is not the occasion to rehearse the various critiques of postcolonialism, many of which get "ironically absorbed into the field as examples of postcolonial analysis" (Brennan 248), a few main points need to be kept in mind as we reflect on the critical relevance of postcolonial literary studies and narratology to each other.

The term "postcolonial" emerged in the context of political theory in the 1970s—postcolonialism consisting in a historicist thesis regarding the nature and impact of colonialization—but it became established, with the contours sketched above, in the literary academia of both Western and previously colonized countries. Colonial discourse encompassed Western grand narratives of history formulated in Christianity, in the "Enlightenment" and also in Marxism, and postcolonial theory accordingly cast methodologies of historiography up to that point as Eurocentric and inherently imperialistic. Nationalist historiographies were similarly suspect since anticolonialist formations had borrowed the idea of the nation from the West. Anthropology and ethnography were critiqued for their colonial origins and for the Eurocentrist presumption that the other could be understood and inscribed in the categories of the self, which was taken as transparent—and its knowledge, therefore, taken as objective. The literary productions of the colonizers, as well as the very forms of representation that emerged contemporaneously with the rise of colonialism in the eighteenth century, were deemed to be intimately linked with the same epistemological stance and a similar construction of the subject of knowledge, including self-knowledge, one developed in the pages of novels and autobiographies and constituted by the so-called Western realist mode of narration. However, the alternative represented by Bhabha took the "political 'rationality' of nation as a form of narrative—textual strategies, metaphoric displacements, sub-texts and figurative stratagems," and posited the nation as "a form of cultural *elaboration* (in the Gramscian sense), [as] an agency of ambivalent narration that holds culture at its most productive position, as a force for 'subordinating, fracturing, diffusing, reproducing, creating, forcing, guiding'" (*Nation and Narration* 2, 4). In so doing, postcolonial theory after what Meera Nanda calls the "interpretive turn" evidenced a predilection for an ahistorical framework of cultural analysis, since for all its attention to contexts it did not accord history any force beyond that of a deconstructed series of binaries instituted by the event of colonialism ("The Science Wars" 78). As postcolonial contestation became focused upon the compromised ground of cultural discourse, its critique narrowed the horizons of its own capacity for political efficacy.

Crucially, as material dimensions and political agency were increasingly approached in cultural terms and culture was textualized in response to the linguistic and the cultural turns, literature itself was seamlessly absorbed into "cultural practice." Moreover, according to Nicholas Dirks, "much of what we now recognize as culture was created by the colonial encounter" (3). To see literature as a signifying practice, as socially symbolic, then, was to study its role in Eurocentric constructions of the self, its articulation of ideologies of cultural difference, and its "displacements and erasures"; to recover its "effaced historical context and unrehearsed enunciations of the anxieties in the conquering *imagination*, both necessarily repressed by the exigencies of ideological *representation*" (Parry 121). Equally, for the conquered or the decolonizing imagination, according to Helen Tiffin,

> Postcolonial literature/cultures are thus constituted in counter-discursive rather than homologous practices, and they offer "fields" of counter-discursive strategies to the dominant discourse. . . . not seek[ing] to subvert the dominant with a view to taking its place, but . . . to evolve textual strategies which continually "consume" their "own biases" at the same time as they expose and erode those of the dominant discourse. (95)

It has been observed that of the three disciplines that were most engaged by postcolonialism, history remains the most resistant to its impact while anthropology and, even more so, literary studies have confronted their colonialist origins and premises, and have reorganized their disciplinary commitments and methodological orientation (Loomba et al. 29–30).

Perhaps by dint of this very success, the orientation of postcolonial literary studies has undergone a restriction, recognized and criticized by many, particularly with respect to the domain of literary production seen to be postcolonial. The paradigmatic status accorded to literature in the cultural practices analyzed by postcolonial studies has privileged reading as the postcolonial agency par excellence. However, reading continues to be confined to a selective canon of Western, colonial, and Anglophone postcolonial literary works that foreground issues of nation, identity, migration, and multiculturalism, and can be read as political allegories (Mufti; Krishnaswamy, "The Criticism of Culture"). The postcolonial texts are predominantly those produced in the metropole by migrant writers who happen to be the elites of the erstwhile colonies (Dirlik; Mufti). Thus, postcolonial literary studies, despite its commitment to challenging the Western canon and creating new ones, has in fact installed a limited canon that excludes other languages and non-cosmopolitan, non-postcolonial themes (see also Brennan). More importantly, it excludes, or else occludes the different preoccupations of other ideological contestations that cannot and will not be contained within the explanatory ambit of postcolonialism. The example of Dalit writing and Dalit studies (and anti-caste discourse more broadly) has been mentioned above. Another set of contestations concerns globalization, migration within the subcontinent (Gikandi, "Globalization"; Krishnaswamy, "The Criticism of Culture"), the progressive imposition of "Hindu" identity and cultural norms on the diverse religious and cultural practices of other regions in the Union of India (Nanda, *Postmodernism*; Chaturvedi), and the consolidation of Hindu and Islamic fundamentalisms, respectively, in India and in Pakistan and Bangladesh. The formation and cultural assertion of Hindu identity, the development of Hindu nationalism, and the Hinduization of India have historical origins in the colonial juncture, but their evolution belongs to a post-decolonization period (see Dalmia; Jha). Postcolonialist historiography has challenged this ultranationalist discourse and the deconstructivist edge of postcolonial critique has exposed its idealist construction of the past and of national identity as a product of colonial modernity (Chatterjee; Chaturvedi). However, the accelerating phenomenon, in the late twentieth and early twenty-first centuries, of what is effectively a Hindu colonization of southern and eastern regional cultures, religious minorities, tribal populations, and Dalits in India, cannot be comprehended by referring to the epistemic violence of Eurocentrism—both because other, newer sociopolitical processes are involved here (Krishnaswamy, "The Criticism of Culture" and "Globalization"; Chaturvedi), and because Hindu nationalism is itself premised on the notion of epistemic violence, which it attributes to "Muslim rule" (see Young, "Postcolonial Remains"; Yelle; Bose). Postcolonialist arguments have been deployed by proponents of *Hindutva* (Hinduness) to defend and assert Hindu cultural identity as a resistance to

Eurocentrism (see Yelle; Figueira). These recent contexts and the literature emerging in response to them cannot be subsumed by the postcolonialist paradigm since they configure reading itself in other ways. For example, English, the language of colonialism that postcolonialism regards as the pharmacon par excellence, has been hailed by Dalit activists and intellectuals like Chandra Bhan Prasad as the vehicle of their liberation from the native genius of the subcontinent—caste (see Mannathukkaren); their goal is fluency rather than the poststructuralist-postcolonialist virtue of the stammer of minor literature (following an empirical interpretation of Deleuze). On the other hand, Gajarawala proposes "unreading" as a strategy for literary criticism and non-Dalit reading of Dalit writing and of Dalits in literature: "If certain forms of reading overprivilege historical determination, unreading acknowledges other forms of political causality" ("Some Time" 580).

Vilashini Cooppan finds fault with a "predominantly literary postcolonial studies [that] risks reduction to a catalogue of thematics and a canon of fiction and poetry, in which characteristic concepts of hybridity, creolization, and diaspora are not contextualized" and rightly asks postcolonial cultural studies to "recognize the potential of combining textual analysis with historical inquiry to counter the elitism of a cosmopolitan model of intellectual, literary diaspora" (278–79). However, it is also the case that textual analysis has lagged behind even as historical inquiry itself has ventured beyond the postcolonialist framework into globalization theory, trauma and violence studies, urban studies, migration and refugee studies, and Dalit studies, to name a few. Eli Park Sorensen finds that "if there is little interest in literary form within contemporary literary debates, this is particularly the case in postcolonial studies" (3). In other words, colonial and postcolonial discourse analysis is found wanting in the very sphere of its own expertise. As Aamir Mufti recently observed:

> As for South Asian postcolonial criticism, which was intellectually formative for me, it has largely failed, it seems to me, to break out of an area studies mode. This will seem counter-intuitive to many, but I strongly believe it to be the case. Despite all the critique of nationalism that has been produced, the focus remains on the overbearing presence of the national homeland—too many texts, too much history, too much tradition, too much politics, too much memory—rather than its absence. (153)

While there is too much text and textual analysis, it is mostly conducted with a precipitous eye to meaning without attentiveness to the poetological, rhetorical, prosodic, and narratological features, techniques, and devices that mediate and complicate interpretation, nor are these features and their theoretical consideration included as a standard part of postcolonial literary research and pedagogy. The latter mostly combines acquaintance with literary history (usually of the English and European canon) and the history of particular genres with a general kind of close reading that subordinates the formal dimension to content in looking for aesthetic correlatives for concepts like parody, hybridity, liminality, and subalternity. A rare counterexample to this tendency is Spivak's work, for example her analyses of the implied reader in the reading and teaching of European literature in the Indian classroom, or of focalization and its absence in Coetzee; however, these consist in wholesale characterizations of the politics of such features in reading without relating them to other devices in the poetological structure of the work—the way a set of formal features comes into a specific constellation to create specific effects (see *Aesthetic Education*). Other instances are more frequently found in the analyses undertaken by narratologists who have extended their engagement to postcolonial literary criticism, such as Brian Richardson, Marion Gymnich, and Monika Fludernik ("When the Self Is an Other"; see also Sommer), and more recently Laura Buchholz. The constitutive blind spots of postcolonial literary theory and criticism mentioned above contribute to the limitations of postcolonial readings of narratives. Narratology and the narratologically informed study of literature offer a potent opening once we recognize the opportunity to be only secondarily one of enhancing postcolonialist capabilities of textual analysis. Primarily it is an opportunity to examine the ways in which narrative form and ideological content are co-determined. In the course of such examination, not only postcolonialist but other ideological contestations will surface, and new meanings—which are public because they are shared—will emerge in the field of culture.

The notion of co-determination does not imply that form and content are reduced either to each other or to a strict correspondence between the two that would lead to static typologies. Instead, it implies a dynamic in which the formal articulation of ideas, speech, and action in and through the literary work can also be a transformation of meaning. The basic condition of such co-determination is that both form and content find their locus of existence in the words of the literary narrative; however, to use a Bakhtinian distinction, literature is not a primary but a secondary speech genre. Secondary speech genres take up the "immediate relation to actual reality" of primary speech genres or utterances, including their heteroglossia and dialogicity, in complex ways mediated by the highly orchestrated representation of, for example, character-character and narrator-character dialogue in novels (Bakhtin, "The Problem of Speech Genres" 62). The difference between primary and secondary speech genres, as well as between varieties of the latter, helps to show that the interventions literature affords are not seamless with cultural practice/ formation. It is a matter for literary theory and, in the case of narrative texts, narratology, to reflect on the points where the work effects a cut in the fabric of culture without being cut off from the ideological play in the dialogicity of language.

"Form," then, is a (too-general) term for the various levels and dimensions in which the work distinguishes itself within, as well as from, the field of culture with which it communicates and transacts. Formal attention to the work can draw upon the knowledge of genres, which are performed conventions or "relatively stable types" (Bakhtin, "The Problem of Speech Genres" 60) and hence themselves ideological, but this leaves room for much greater theoretical precision in identifying aspects of form beyond genre and the respects in which they determine each other. Indeed, Bakhtin's work is a good example, since his theory of the varieties of double-voiced discourse in the novel depends upon the distinction between narrator and character and upon their hierarchy, as the narrating and the narrated agent, in order to determine the specific orientation of dialogization, whether stylization, parody, or hidden polemic ("Double-Voiced Discourse" 105–8). Sometimes the analysis of voice is a necessary aid to identifying when it is that the narrator speaks and when the character, and when the two mix and overlap (see Aczel). These are narratological categories, not merely linguistic or metalinguistic (in the Bakhtinian sense), and are evidently critical for reading specific narratives. Such distinctions are certainly widespread in postcolonialist criticism, as elsewhere, and predate the birth of narratology, but narratology is precisely the *theoretical* examination of their currency and coherence. Such examination has resulted simultaneously in a sharpening of the distinctions between narrator (and its types) and character, and in a critique of these distinctions, examining their grounds and the psychological or ideological assumptions underlying their anthropomorphism. Narratology returns repeatedly to Plato, Aristotle, James, and Propp, and in the process continues to critique the narrative models derived from them. Narratological distinctions of this kind obtain at the level of narrative form, which is analytically distinct from the forms of specific semiotic media (such as language) or material media (such as print). Narratological assumptions are latent in every analysis that abstracts the plot, the storyworld, the embedded narratives, and the themes of a specific work, and defines the salience of their specific configuration, or indeed annihilation (as in certain postmodernist works). Narratology, then, is not merely the analysis of a specific work or the typologization of abstracted features across a group of works, but the theoretical scrutiny that both posits such features and interrogates their logic and assumptions. This theoretical work is neither purely empirical, since the received terms of discourse about narrative have always informed narrative creativity, nor purely a priori, since innovation in narrative often provokes contestation and revision of established concepts. New narratological objects are born at the intersection of innovative storytelling and narratologically interested reading.

Narrative qua narrative is thus a distinct conceptual entity with respect to text, discourse, communication, semiosis, and culture, which are themselves the objects of textual analysis, discourse analysis, communication theory, semiotic theory, and culture theory, respectively. It draws on each of these as they do on each other, and yet it cannot be reduced to them. This relationship itself demands theoretical study—at what point do specifically narratological questions emerge in the construction of the work that, though cultural, sets itself apart within the single field of ideology-culture? The work is a part of this field and yet it is not a mere record of the forces in this field, neither a metonymy (a higher allegory) nor merely a symptom of fault lines and fissures, an index of sociopolitical change. That would amount to a mimetic or a pseudomimetic approach, as identified by Lubomír Doležel, in which fictional entities are treated in one way or another as imitations of real-world phenomena. Narratology, by contrast, alerts us to the poetics of narrative; it requires attentiveness to the relation between poetics and the cultural, and so to the ideological as it forms and is undone or contested. It demands reflection on specific forms, the variations in their degrees, models, and types, their effects and possibilities, in order that their being put together (poiesis) or being rendered in specific ways by fictional works can become apparent. In other words, narratology involves the study of a vital component of the form-content dynamic that cannot be reduced to matters of content (context, history, culture) alone.

Postcolonialist theory and criticism, even when attuned to form, does not obviate the need for the narratological study of texts, though it often omits it. The questions of nation and narration, of characters being representative, of grand narratives—that is, questions of metaphoric and metonymic displacements in any direction—are questions of narrative mimesis and of anthropomorphism in theory, and must be taken up there. Narratology has a degree of abstraction and formality as well as a diachronicity that is more comprehensive than that claimed by postcolonial theories of history and literature, and this volume, by foregrounding these aspects of South Asian literature in particular, enriches the frame of reference in ways that could be fruitfully extended to other emerging areas such as Dalit studies, migration studies, and refugee studies. Such narratological negotiation with the postcolonialist paradigm of literary studies mitigates its tendency either to confine the literary work to a horizon of reception defined by the cut of colonization as inaugural event, or to extend itself into these emerging fields of study and theorization only to make them appear as merely instances of postcolonialist logic. Narratological enhancement of postcolonialist criticism is possible, as is demonstrated by several essays in this volume, but it is not the only outcome of attending to the elaborate, complex, and understudied (in postcolonialist academia) features of narrative that constitute its logic and even its ideo-logic. Hence this volume aims not to compete with postcolonialist readings but to reveal the interpretative and theoretical importance, in postcolonial contexts, of narrative structures and narratological concepts and frameworks, an undertaking that does not reduce either to formalist analysis, or to the "toolbox" and "typologies" view of narratology.

NARRATOLOGICAL ISSUES FOR POSTCOLONIAL TEXTS

The act of narration raises the fundamental issue of the imposition of narrative form upon material, which at its root is bound up with the affordances of cognition and the nature of experience, but which is neither innocent of, nor even prior to, the imperatives of sociopolitical existence in which all cultural production takes place. The process of narration is a mediated engagement with events or phenomena, and is caught up from the outset in a web of discursive contexts in which the particular becomes intelligible only in relation to the paradigms of narrative schemata, plot prototypes, and genre. Every act of narration intrinsically implies much more than it says, and the implicit is itself a complex and contextually fraught arena of inference, comprising the necessary and tacit, the connotative, subtexts both assertive and passively complicit, the excluded and the negated (a palimpsest combining the negative space of the figure of the narrated, and the positively *disnarrated*). This terrain cannot be critically negotiated, moreover, without attention to the interests it serves, and the ideological investments of such interests are rarely far to seek.

The conceptual framework of narratology embraces every facet of narrative texts and acts, from the local minutiae of a passage of free indirect discourse to the communicative pragmatics and conditions of possibility for the entire discourse. At every level there are current debates around concepts and approaches in which broadly contextualist and particularly postcolonial critical concerns are implicated. The myriad forms of narration itself have, of course, long been a primary focus for narratological inquiry, especially in relation to the elaborately reflexive and recursive permutations that fiction is able to exploit. Fiction, moreover, not only narrates but also represents acts of narration, each of which can itself become the main object of scrutiny. Unreliable narration is a concept that covers a rich variety of rhetorical uses of represented narration, and has been extensively theorized. Such theorization is not always sufficiently attuned to the respects in which unreliable narration is also a foil for the subtle, or not-so-subtle, insinuation of contrasting normative assumptions, and the oblique construction of a tendentious authority that may itself be open to critique.

Narrative voice, therefore, is a much more complex, layered concept than first appears. It is always, first of all, the narrative instance, whatever form the narration may take. But that instance may itself be represented—may be the narration of a character—in which case voice is objectified, no longer just a communicative act but also, perhaps primarily, an idiom that is itself a mimetic product. Beyond this, and whether or not the instance is representationally displaced or doubled, voice is always a communicative gesture implying a source, and an orientation toward a destination. Every narrative act is a construction of narrative identity, the implicit specification of a position from which it is uttered—a position that may be consolidated, or may evolve, in the course of the utterance. This is a fundamental effect of the dual temporality of narrative, its play between the time of the narrated and the time of the narrating, in which much more is at stake than the aesthetic pleasures of an artful disarrangement of chronology. Narrative voice therefore reflects back upon its source, as situated and individual, but also as representative and communal. Voice is also a hailing, an interpellation of its narratee or reader, and delineates a position that is occupied, de facto, in the process of accepting that role (Althusser). The coercive ideological force of interpellation may be very blatant or very insidious, but the task of criticism is always in part to accept it (as a condition of reading) and in part to expose it, to reveal its workings and hold it to account.

Focalization is a specific concept associated with the modality of voice that has received extensive theoretical treatment since its introduction by Gérard Genette. Focalization concerns the possible alignment of narration with the perceptions or assumptions of one or more characters; it has been developed within narratology into a fine-tuned, if not unproblematic, concept involving more than a mere question of point of view—a concept designating the intersection of information access to narrative events and facts on the one hand, and subjective assumptions, values, and attitudes on the other hand. As such, it is a crucial vehicle for foregrounding, or masking, ideological questions (see Bal's essay in this volume). The concept of focalization provides for a rounded examination of the respects in which perspectival orientations shape readers' engagement with a narrative and provides a discriminating way to articulate the entanglement of information, subjective evaluation, and ideological presupposition involved for characters and narrators. The use of internal focalization may serve to expose the perspectival limitations of a character in a way analogous to unreliable narration, but more intimately grounded in experiential subjectivity, and in this respect it participates in a similar rhetorical co-optation of the reader. It may also serve to affirm the contingency of perspectivalism over against the authentication authority of authorial narration, which (in fiction) is constitutive of the "facts" of the case in potentially unhelpful ways. So, heterodiegetic narration can adopt, with or without irony, the idioms, worldviews, and assumptions of characters via internal focalization, including such representational techniques as free indirect discourse, and the point of doing so may have more to do with the inescapable role such perspectives have in the constitution of social and political situations, than with the figment of an authoritative view. Equally, while fictive discourse affords in principle the privilege of an inside view of characters, their thoughts and feelings and the state of their souls, the monologic force of such narration may be refused by the use of external focalization. Focalization is often more importantly about the socially constructed aspects of political situations than the idiosyncrasies of individual subjectivity; it provides for the irreducible role played by beliefs, allegiances, and historical and ideological positionality in the unfolding of social and political struggles.

One of the consequences of classical narratology's investment in structuralism was an anti-intentionalist stance that tended to textualize the communicative axis of narrative. This tendency manifested itself in an ossification of generalized, abstract notions of narrator and narratee that, even in the more rhetorically oriented Chicago School, were only extended as far as the implied author. This problematic concept persists in a range of senses, from a full-blown textual agent to a relatively innocuous shorthand for the inference of authorial purpose behind the explicit text of character narration. But narratological contestation also generated influential conceptualizations of narrative communication that were not subordinate to narrative representation, from Genette's "paratext" to Lejeune's "autobiographical pact." More recent developments have reemphasized the actual authorial communicative act in fiction as well as nonfictional narratives (Walsh; Nielsen). Such approaches to narrative communication stress the continuity between fictive acts and other contributions to cultural discourse, and militate against the classical tendency to idealize the textual encounter and abstract it from the historical and ideological contexts within which it must necessarily take place. A rhetorical approach to narrative theory has been advocated and refined by James Phelan, on the premise that stories, like any other form of communication, have to be understood in relation to assumptions about the occasions and purposes of address from actual authors to actual readers (see Phelan, and his essay in this volume). Rhetorical approaches in general assume that situated communicative agency is a more important consideration than the discrete ontological integrity often attributed to the textual economy of fiction, and that the nuanced engagement of fictive narratives with political and ideological concerns is often best understood through the pragmatic mediation of their context, paratext, and peritext.

Analyzing fictive communicative agency requires a careful discrimination between fictionality and narrativity. These concepts have often been conflated, resulting in a rather indiscriminate and ultimately debilitating consensus characterized by Marie-Laure Ryan as the doctrine of panfictionality. Hayden White famously stated:

> By the very constitution of a set of events in such a way as to make a comprehensible story out of them, the historian charges those events with the symbolic significance of a plot structure. Historians may not like to think of their work as translations of facts into fictions; but this is one of the effects of their work. (92)

In saying so, White was insisting not only upon the artifice inherent in the imposition of narrative form as such, but also that the evaluative, moral significance of such narratives doesn't arise from the events in themselves but from the form of their articulation, the paradigms for which are not found in history, but in literary traditions. But the rhetoric of White's argument overreaches, because fiction is distinguished as such by its overt fictive intent; it is not fictional by mistake. Fictive discourse is overtly, nondeceptively, creative narration, the rhetorical effect of which is not only to suspend its accountability to the actual world but positively to accomplish some real-world communicative purpose in doing so. The panfictionality thesis, then, traduces both nonfictional and fictional narratives. By conflating two common senses of fiction—as construct and as falsehood—it does scant justice to the ethics of nonfictional narration, for example in witness literature. The imperative of testimony is in no way vitiated by due critical skepticism about the difficulties of reducing complex and often traumatic experience to narrative form, and about the tendency especially of emotive narration to draw upon the ready formulae of received plots, motifs, and genres. By figuring fiction negatively, on the other hand, as simply a lapse from truth and factuality, the panfictionality thesis fails to recognize that fictive discourse is a way of meaning. The serious import of fiction does not rest upon the referential truth of its assertions, but indeed depends upon a manifest disavowal of such truth claims. One of the key implications of defining fictive discourse as a rhetorical resource rather than in ontological terms is that it is properly distinguished from the genre of fiction itself (see Nielsen, Phelan, and Walsh). Fictions, then, are texts that generically and paratextually signal that fictive discourse is their dominant mode of signification; this excludes neither the possibility that fictive discourse may be used outside of generic fiction, nor that generic fiction may also make substantial use of veridical rhetoric. Questions about the relation between fictive and nonfictive engagement with postcolonial issues animate several essays in this volume, and rhetorical approaches to fictionality are both enabling for, and illuminated by, such ideological and thematic analyses.

The novel as a genre established itself by gradually naturalizing representational conventions, and more particularly by a cyclical process of consolidation and renewal of the norms of realism. But intrinsic in this reflexive negotiation in fiction is the persistent possibility of refusing realism, or mimeticism more broadly, or the interpretative principles of verisimilar naturalization that underpin them. The pervasiveness of such features of fiction has been highlighted in recent years by the emergence of unnatural narratology, a broad theoretical orientation that contests, in various ways, the assumption that fiction is grounded in a natural paradigm of narrative, whether that is understood in relation to the representational constraints upon nonfictional narrative or the communicative norms of nonfictional or oral narration. The manifest ideological force of notions of the natural, its normative function and its logic of universalizing self-effacement, suggests that here too developments in narrative theory offer points of leverage for critical engagement with the mechanisms of cultural, political, and ideological hegemony, and the power relations of postcolonialism in particular, as negotiated through the resources of narrative fiction.

THE ESSAYS

This volume was conceived as an inaugural project that would bring narratology to postcolonial criticism in a spirit of dialogue and reciprocal contestation, while advancing current debates on the need for, and the difficulties regarding, contextual narratologies. This was a felt need in view of the parallel limitations that the volume editors perceived: on the one hand, the inadequacies of narratology's formalist bent, already being challenged by feminist, functionalist, and diachronic narratologies and the call for postcolonialist narratologies, and on the other hand, the impasse of postcolonial literary criticism, which is usually conducted with little attention to innovative and complex narrative form and its theories. Given that coloniality and postcoloniality are historically specific rather than homogeneous across the colonized parts of the world, this volume concentrates upon South Asian texts in order to conduct a sustained interrogation of multiple narrative theories and narratological concepts with respect to one historical context, rather than strew them arbitrarily across texts and issues pertaining to diverse regions and literary canons. Certainly South Asia itself, and the trajectory of colonialism in the subcontinent, is nonuniform; nevertheless this focus comprises a problematic within which to also contest the nation and very idea of South Asia. More importantly, South Asian coloniality has occasioned a significant, even dominant portion of postcolonial theory (Mufti 152–53), with theorists such as Bhabha and Spivak furnishing paradigmatic concepts (of hybridity, subalternity, epistemic violence) that have transcended their context-specificity (as discussed earlier). This is particularly notable in the invocation of postcolonialism by narratologists seeking to encourage contextualist and cultural narratology (see Prince, "Postcolonial Narratology"; Sommer; and Alber in this volume). The volume's emphasis upon prominent South Asian texts engages an academic context into which the introduction of narratological approaches and debates is particularly valuable, one where postcolonialist literary pedagogy is well established, even somewhat dogmatic, and literary studies is dominated by a social historical approach (see Bose). It also serves as an extended case study for the larger questions of contextualist narratology with which these essays engage. The range of contributors was substantially dictated by the framing theoretical crux of postcolonial narratology itself, both as a live matter of principle concerning the ideological engagement with narrative theory and as the set of theoretical questions that bear upon postcolonial literature and test the contextualist premises of that matter of principle. Most of the contextualist critique of narratology has come from within the field, stimulating its diversification and the readiness of a range of narrative theorists to address postcolonial fiction and criticism. The resulting essays amount to a concerted narratological address to postcolonial fiction and its critical-theoretical contexts, and a reflective examination of the import of postcolonial ideological thematics for narrative theory itself. This is a valuable first step toward a more thoroughgoing dialogue between postcolonial criticism and narrative theory, and it is to be hoped that the volume will stimulate further engagement from students and scholars of postcolonialism, and of South Asian literature in particular.

The contributors were invited to dwell on the pertinence of narratological methods and theories for postcolonial texts, with a focus upon South Asia, not only in order to exemplify the ways in which postcolonial criticism might reap the benefits of those ideas but also in order to draw out the ideological implications latent in the theoretical discourse of narratology itself. This challenging brief, facing in both directions, made no assumption about whether the argument in each case should ultimately resolve upon a theoretical or critical point. Each of the essays stages an encounter between specific narratological and postcolonialist concerns by addressing the relation of content and form. Thematic and ideological analyses of literature cannot be carried out without referring to conventions and techniques of narrative, to genres and their diachronicity, to the complex interactions between the semantics, the intertextuality, and the narrative poetics of literary works, and to their combined role in guiding readers' interpretations. Using narratological concepts and methods of narrative analysis, the contributors read literary narratives pertaining in one way or another to South Asia for the manner in which these texts articulate ideology and intervene at the ideological level. That the texts do so in narrative form, making specific choices of narrational techniques, is of central importance. This narratological engagement with postcolonial texts also tests the limits of narratological abstraction, and of particular narratologies, occasioning considerations of the contextualist scope of various concepts and schools within narratology.

The literary works analyzed by the essays in this volume are drawn from more recent as well as older writings of the subcontinent, including Sri Lanka, Pakistan, and India, and works by expatriate writers in Canada, the United States, and United Kingdom. The only exception, Gerald Prince's contribution on writing from the ex-French colony of Senegal, achieves its relevance to the volume through its focus upon metanarrative signs, and specifically the encounter between languages in postcolonial contexts. Several essays address familiar postcolonial themes of anticolonial resistance, migration, hybridity, and nationhood (see Patrick Colm Hogan; Martin Löschnigg; Gerald Prince; Jan Alber; James Phelan; Baidik Bhattacharya); however, these essays also share with others, like Udaya Kumar's, concerns with trauma and narration, the relation of personal and public memories, and the literary examination of the sources of public histories, which are issues that are not exclusive to postcolonialism. Sarah Copland's essay exposes the shortcomings of a postcolonialist perspective in grasping the power dynamics that play out over the representation of the historical oppression of Dalits, while Monika Fludernik, Greta Olson, and Marion Gymnich treat of narratives engaging with the politics of neo-imperialist capitalism and globalization. Mieke Bal and Divya Dwivedi dwell on ideological issues within narratology itself, with Bal focusing specifically on postcolonial narratology.

The essays have been organized into five sections. In the essays of the first section, "Narrative in Question," matters of narrative form and technique emerge as indispensable in the study of literature that grapples with the ideologies and politics of nationhood, identity, and history. Patrick Colm Hogan's essay finds that emplotment is common to literary works and ideas of nations, and hence narrative structures inform ideologies. The narrative emplotment of nationalism follows prototypes, and distortion or deviation reflect the changing figurations of the past and future of the nation, and also of its action-orienting telos. Hogan identifies three plot prototypes at work in the narrative negotiations of nationhood in Kashmir: heroic action, sacrifice, and revenge. He combines insights from the theory of emotional memory and trauma studies to analyze Kashmiri narratives in the context of traumatized societies undergoing a crisis of national versus subnational definition. Martin Löschnigg's essay uses Monika Fludernik's cognitive-narratological model based on experientiality to analyze narratives of return journeys by Ondaatje, Vassanji, and Mistry. The immigrant perspective is composed of simultaneous frames of experiencing and reflecting that make the nation an incomplete and continuously imagined construct. A number of complex narrative techniques, like metalepsis and self-undermining intradiegetic narration, combine to create a postcolonial narrative identity that departs from the hegemony of Western autobiography. Udaya Kumar focuses on the status of objects in narratives, showing that fictions can interrupt public memory where public histories and museology are insufficient. Through the Malayalam writer N. S. Madhavan, he interrogates some basic distinctions of classical narratology, such as that between object and character, and examines postcolonial theorization of memory and location. The novel effects a breaking off of both narration and remembrance from the interiority of character, thus thwarting postcolonial allegory since postcolonial memory itself exceeds the individual. Kumar proposes that narrative permits a "delectation of memory" that other discourses do not, and Madhavan achieves this, not through conventional methods of focalization, but through narrative abduction of other forms and genres like litany, natakam, poetry (both European and South Asian), and conversation.

The second section, "Zones of Narrative (Para-, Meta-, Intra-)," dwells on the narratological issues that arise with respect to paratexts, metanarrative layers, and problems of levels and their transgression within narratives. Gerald Prince finds that metanarrative signs, which abound in narrative and have the function of mediating, glossing, and explaining, are ideologically charged in the way they control meaning and communication. He explores the affinities between such signs and writings about colonial and postcolonial situations that are multilingual, where the interplay of languages in a single communication occurs also along economico-political and cultural axes, to which narrator and narratee are linked. Prince shows this to be the case with Ousmane Sembène's *Les Bouts de bois de Dieu. Banty mam Yall*, even in its very title, and demonstrates that the narrative is organized by a double concern, both with its own legibility and the legibility of the postcolonial situation. Sarah Copland's essay draws upon rhetorical narratology, demonstrating its efficacy in grasping the power structures embedded in the text-paratext relationship of specific narratives. Rhetorical narratology emphasizes authorial agency and the choices of form and technique made by authors with a view to the impact on readers, including the reader's ideological transformation. Paratext adds another layer of complexity to this relationship because of the possibilities of appropriation, contestation, and resistance, but also reinforcement, that open up in that threshold space. Copland explores the dynamics of real and authorial audience in relation to both Mulk Raj Anand's *Untouchable* and E. M. Forster's preface to it, dynamics that have been neglected in simplistic and programmatic misreadings of the colonizer's preface and the colonized's text. Her choice of a text whose very publication was obstructed is apposite, since Dalits faced oppression directly from upper-caste South Asian elites, and since one of the sharpest criticisms of the ideology of postcolonial theory itself has come from Dalit studies. She shows how issues of caste do not map on to those of race and coloniality. Jan Alber's essay undertakes the difficult task of a thoroughgoing narratological analysis of *Midnight's Children*, which has generated a mountain of critical literature, in order to identify the clashing ideological workings of its form. Attending closely to its use of multiple beginnings, homodiegetic narration with zero focalization, hybrid and multifarious characters, various intertextual references, and numerous different styles, Alber arrives at a fundamental conflict between the narrative discourse and the fabula of the novel, which complicates the allegory of nationhood critics have hailed and later novelists have imitated. His analysis raises a problem: how do the gaps—in knowledge, in narration—contribute to an understanding of the politics of ideology when Sinai uses his telepathic powers in a totalitarian way, and when he displays an impotence that undermines the idea of democratic pluralism constructed by the novel's postmodernist aesthetic? The second section as a whole alerts the student of ideology in literature to the way zones of narrative function with respect to each other: the identification and isolation of these zones requires an attention to the logic of narrative discourse.

The third section is devoted to issues of narrative voice and the narrator. Who speaks, who is unable to occupy this subject position, and what is the constitution of this position in the first place, cannot be decided through postcolonial theory alone or through the generalizations and essentialisms that pervade the idea of "colonial discourse"—orientalism, for instance—its poststructuralist inclinations notwithstanding. Marion Gymnich explores the negotiation of power, specifically the power to represent the muted victim and the exonerated oppressor, in a novel about the Bhopal Gas tragedy, the exemplary case of neo-imperialist depredation of the third world in the era of globalization. In Indra Sinha's *Animal's People,* Gymnich finds that the use of certain techniques of narrative voice raises questions about the politics of remembrance and the possibilities opened up by fictionalized narratives in contrast to nonfictional, scientific, legal, and journalistic accounts. Political and ethical questions regarding disaster, victimhood, and empathy are shown to turn upon who tells and how that telling is set up. In the process, Gymnich takes the discussion of memory beyond the questions of culture, identity, and history typically posed by postcolonialism. Both James Phelan and Greta Olson devote their essays to reliability and unreliability, the narratological feature that makes its way most frequently into postcolonialist literary scholarship. Olson goes through the scholarship on the concepts of reliable and unreliable narration to expose the ideological underpinnings of the very model of reliability within which unreliability emerges as a shortcoming. These rhetorical models start with the assumption of an equality of culture and power between the author and the reader that does not in fact obtain in specific contexts. She finds in Mohsin Hamid an appropriation of unreliable narration coupled with ambiguous use of second person by a migrant Muslim in the United States to speak to and against the ideology of terror. Hamid's novel offers mimicry à la Bhabha and a hybridized discourse constructed through specific narratological features whose analysis, according to Olson, suggests that narratological models, here the model of reliability, need to be historicized. Narratology can contribute to the study of literature's political power only when it becomes more contextualist and critical of its own models' ideologies. Phelan's essay, on the other hand, suggests that rhetorical narratology offers tools to discern the specific narrative communication staged by a narrative. Registering the power dynamics of communication, he proposes to redress the neglect of character-character dialogue in the rhetorical model. Phelan theorizes the possibilities of layering this communicational channel with reliable narration and mask narration to show how Jhumpa Lahiri's play with the possibilities of un/reliability ceases to constitute an aesthetic, as in Rushdie, and instead illuminates real-life communicational challenges in migrant experiences. These narrational techniques complement the postcolonial thematics (here, of multiculturalism in the metropole) since both comprise the functions of reporting, interpreting, and evaluating.

The two essays in the fourth section, "Strategies, Narrative and Postcolonial," compare and weigh the value of narratological and postcolonial critical insights into the strategies of literary works. Monika Fludernik points to the absence of connections between ideological criticism and classical narratology, on the one hand, and the preponderance of such connections in applications of postclassical narratology to postcolonial literatures on the other. She provides a useful survey of ideology in the history of narratology, and cautions against an easy alignment of narrative techniques with ideological content (here, postcolonialist agendas of resistance and "writing back"), given that the same narrative features can be found equally in conservative and radical literary articulations of ideology and power. A novel about postcoloniality by Nayantara Sahgal and another by Mohsin Hamid about eco-imperialism are analyzed by Fludernik to demonstrate this crucial nonequivalence and to foreground the specific architecture of each text instead. She outlines the task before scholars at the intersection of postcolonialism and narratology as one of investigating the pertinence of existing narratological frameworks to native non-European traditions, as well as the theoretical implications of moving beyond such categories as "non-Western" literature. Baidik Bhattacharya's essay conducts a meticulous analysis of the narrational strategies in Bengali satires written at the time of Indian independence, in which the possibility emerges, if ever so fleetingly, of decoupling the postcolony and the nation in imagination. Attention to this moment also offers theoretical instruction, according to Bhattacharya, to those critics of postcolonialism who point to the demise of the nation-state in order to dismiss the relevance of the category "postcolonial." He finds that the postcolony is rescued as a space pregnant with possibilities of a "coming community" and of nonlinear postcolonial history in the works of Paraśurām (Rajshekhar Basu), where it is figured in an apocalyptic mode, as an event yet to come. This narrative relation is established specifically through the techniques of historiographical metafiction and prolepsis.

The last section, "Narrative, Theory, Ideology," offers broader theoretical reflections on the relation between narratology and ideology. Mieke Bal provides an aesthetic-critical sketch for a postcolonial narratology based on focalization, albeit one predicated on the absence of the "post," which she calls a "vexed preposition." Offering a critique of the terms "perspective" and "gaze," which are often confused with focalization, she explains afresh the latter and its potential in combination with visual analysis, which she illustrates with analyses of a short story by Jhumpa Lahiri and the visual artworks of Nalini Malani. A meditation on Spivak's proposal of counter-focalization (built on Bal's theory) serves to highlight the special relevance of this focalization for postcolonial narratology since it is a trigger for the imagination particularly when it is absent. However, Bal goes on to narrativize Spivak's own writing style to indicate the point where postcolonial narratology should give way, in fact, to migratory aesthetics and even further, to what she proposes as "critical narratology." Finally, Divya Dwivedi exposes the ideology of reading in various narratological and postcolonialist approaches, thus opening the way for an interrogation of the very concept of reading that is so easily taken for granted. To do so, she proposes the concept of the "addressee function," which obtains for both narratologies and narratives but in different ways. Much like Foucault's concept of the "author function," the addressee function is ideological in that it operates as a control over the proliferation of meaning. She shows how in cognitive and rhetorical narratologies, as well as in Gayatri Spivak's deployment of narratological concepts in her postcolonial theory of reading, this function appears in the way each model contains an implicit pedagogy. Pointing to the leakage of meaning through the addressee function, Dwivedi reads O. V. Vijayan and isolates a distinct technique in his *Legends of Khasak*, which she calls "dispersive focalization."

While it should be acknowledged that only a few of the literary works analyzed here are in translation or in a non-Anglophone language, and to that extent this volume repeats the concentration of attention toward the metropole within the erstwhile colonies, it does not aspire to representativeness or exhaustiveness. It is intended as a provocation to link the fields of narratology and ideological analyses of textual form and textual power vis-à-vis postcolonialism, and to provide an approach to pursuing the question of contextualist narratology. It will have served its purpose if the essays contained here can attract students of literature to pay greater attention to the narratological construction of what literary criticism often takes for granted—namely, voice, characters, emplotment, storyworld, perspective, authorial intention, readings, unreliability, and dialogue—and perhaps to extend critical narratological analysis (rather than application of models) beyond postcolonial studies to the areas of globalization studies, migration studies, subaltern studies, and Dalit studies, for instance, and indeed to nonliterary, nonfictional works, as well as informal, oral narratives, including those produced before colonialism in South Asia and elsewhere.

WORKS CITED

Aczel, Richard. "Hearing Voices in Narrative Texts." *New Literary History* 29.3 (1998): 467–500.

Althusser, Louis. *Lenin and Philosophy and Other Essays.* Trans. Ben Brewster. London: New Left Books.

Bakhtin, Mikhail. "Double-Voiced Discourse in Dostoevsky." *The Bakhtin Reader: Selected Writings of Bakhtin, Medvedev and Voloshinov.* Ed. Pam Morris. London: Arnold, 2003. 102–12.

———. "The Problem of Speech Genres." *Speech Genres and Other Essays.* Trans. Vern W. McGhee. Eds. Caryl Emerson and Michael Holquist. Austin: University of Texas Press, 1986. 60–102.

Bal, Mieke. "The Point of Narratology." *Poetics Today* 11.4 (1990): 727–53.

Barthes, Roland. "An Introduction to the Structural Analysis of Narrative." 1966. Trans. Lionel Duisit. *New Literary History: A Journal of Theory and Interpretation* 6.2 (1975): 237–72.

———. *S/Z.* Trans. Richard Miller. London: Jonathan Cape, 1975.

Bhabha, Homi. "Of Mimicry and Man: The Ambivalence of Colonial Discourse." *October* 28 (1983): 125–33.

———, ed. *Nation and Narration.* London: Routledge, 1990.

Bose, Sugata. "Post-Colonial Histories of South Asia: Some Reflections." *Journal of Contemporary History* 38.1 (2003): 133–46.

Brennan, Timothy. *At Home in the World: Cosmopolitanism Now.* Cambridge: Harvard University Press, 1997.

Brock, Richard. "Framing Theory toward an Ekphrastic Postcolonial Methodology." *Cultural Critique* 77.1 (2011): 102–45.

Buchholz, Laura. "Unnatural Narrative in Postcolonial Contexts: Re-reading Salman Rushdie's *Midnight's Children.*" *Journal of Narrative Theory* 42.3 (2012): 332–51.

Chatman, Seymour. "What Can We Learn from Contextualist Narratology?" *Poetics Today* 11.2 (1990): 309–28.

Chatterjee, Partha. *Nation and Its Fragments.* New Jersey: Princeton, 1994.

Chaturvedi, Vinayak. "From Peasant Pasts to Hindutva Futures? Some Reflections on History, Politics, and Methodology." *South Asia: Journal of South Asian Studies* 34.3 (2011): 402–20.

Cooper, Frederick. "Postcolonial Studies and the Study of History." *Postcolonial Studies and Beyond.* Eds. Ania Loomba, Suvir Kaul, Matti Bunzl, Antoinette Burton, and Jed Esty. New Delhi: Permanent Black, 2006. 401–22.

Cooppan, Vilashini. *Worlds Within: National Narratives and Global Connections in Postcolonial Writing.* Stanford: Stanford University Press, 2009.

Dalmia, Vasudha. "The Only Real Religion of the Hindus: Vaisnava Self-Representation in the Late Nineteenth Century." *Representing Hinduism: The Construction of Religious Traditions and National Identity.* Eds. Vasudha Dalmia and Heinrich von Stietencron. New Delhi: Sage, 1995. 176–210.

Diengott, Nilli. "Narratology and Feminism." *Style* 22 (1988): 42–51.

Dirks, Nicholas. *Colonialism and Culture.* Ann Arbor: University of Michigan Press, 1992.

Dirlik, Arif. "The Post-Colonial Aura: Third World Criticism in the Age of Global Capitalism." *Critical Inquiry* 20 (1994): 328–56.

Doležel, Lubomír. "Mimesis and Possible Worlds." *Poetics Today* 9.3 (1988): 475–96.

Eagleton, Terry. *Ideology: An Introduction*. London: Verso, 1991.

Eaton, Richard Maxwell. "(Re)imag(in)ing Otherness: A Postmortem for the Postmodern in India." *Journal of World History* 11.1 (2000): 57–78.

Figueira, Dorothy. "Aryans and the Brahminization of Theory: Identity Politics East and West, Past and Present." *Comparative Studies of South Asia, Africa and the Middle East* 32.3 (2012): 511–22.

Fludernik, Monika. "The Diachronization of Narratology." *Narrative* 11.3 (2003): 331–48.

———. "When the Self Is an Other: Vergleichende erzähltheoretische und postkoloniale Überlegungen zur Identitätskonstruktion in der (exil)indischen Gegenwartsliteratur." *Anglia* 117.1 (1999): 71–96.

Friedman, Susan Stanford. "Towards a Transnational Turn in Narrative Theory: Literary Narratives, Traveling Tropes, and the Case of Virginia Woolf and the Tagores." *Narrative* 19.1 (2011): 1–32.

Frow, John. *Marxism and Literary History*. Oxford: Blackwell, 1986.

Gajarawala, Toral Jatin. "Some Time between Revisionist and Revolutionary: Unreading History in Dalit Literature." *PMLA* 126.3 (2011): 575–91.

———. *Untouchable Fictions: Literary Realism and the Crisis of Caste*. New York: Fordham University Press, 2012.

Genette, Gérard. *Narrative Discourse*. 1972. Trans. Jane E. Lewin. Oxford: Basil Blackwell, 1980.

Gikandi, Simon. "Globalization and the Claims of Postcoloniality." *South Atlantic Quarterly* 100.3 (2000): 627–58.

———. *Maps of Englishness: Writing Identity in the Culture of Colonialism*. New York: Columbia University Press, 1996.

Gymnich, Marion. "Linguistics and Narratology: The Relevance of Linguistic Criteria to Postcolonial Narratology." *Literature and Linguistics: Approaches, Models, and Applications (Studies in Honour of Jon Erickson)*. Eds. Marion Gymnich, Ansgar Nünning, and Vera Nünning. Trier: Wissenschaftlicher Verlag, 2002. 61–76.

Herman, David. *Story Logic: Problems and Possibilities of Narrative*. Lincoln: University of Nebraska Press, 2002.

Hogan, Patrick Colm. *The Mind and Its Stories: Narrative Universals and Human Emotion*. Cambridge: Cambridge University Press, 2003.

Ilaiah, Kancha. "Productive Labour, Consciousness and History: The Dalitbahujan." *Subaltern Studies IX*. Eds. Shahid Amin and Dipesh Chakrabarty. Delhi: Oxford University Press, 1996. 165–200.

Jha, D. N. *Rethinking Hindu Identity*. London and New York: Routledge, 2009.

Kim, Sue J. "Introduction: Decolonizing Narrative Theory." *Journal of Narrative Theory* 42.3 (2012): 233–47.

Kindt, Tom, and Hans-Harald Müller. "Narrative Theory and/or/as Theory of Interpretation." *What Is Narratology? Questions and Answers Regarding the Status of a Theory*. Eds. Tom Kindt and Hans-Harald Müller. Berlin: De Gruyter, 2003. 205–19.

Krishnaswamy, Revathi. "The Criticism of Culture and the Culture of Criticism: At the Intersection of Postcolonialism and Globalization Theory." *Diacritics* 32.2 (2002): 106–26.

———. "Globalization and Its Postcolonial (Dis)contents: Reading Dalit Literature." *Journal of Postcolonial Writing* 41.1 (2005): 69–82.

Lanser, Susan S. *Fictions of Authority: Women Writers and Narrative Voice*. Ithaca: Cornell University Press, 1992.

Larsen, Neil. "Postcolonialism's Unsaid." *Minnesota Review* 45.1 (1995): 285–90.

Lazarus, Neil. *Nationalism and Cultural Practice in the Postcolonialist World*. Cambridge: Cambridge University Press, 1999.

Lejeune, Philippe. *On Autobiography*. Minneapolis: University of Minnesota Press, 1987.

Loomba, Ania. *Colonialism/Postcolonialism*. London: Routledge, 1998.

Loomba, Ania, Suvir Kaul, Matti Bunzl, Antoinette Burton, and Jed Esty, eds. *Postcolonial Studies and Beyond*. New Delhi: Permanent Black, 2006.

Mannathukkaren, Nissim. "Why Claim Reparations Only from the British?" *Tehelka* 35.12 (2005): n. pag. <http://www.tehelka.com/2015/08/why-claim-reparations-only-from-the-british>.

Mishra, Vijay, and Bob Hodge. "What Was Postcolonialism?" *New Literary History* 36.3 (2005): 375–402.

Mufti, Aamir. "The Predicaments of Postcolonial Thinking." Interview with Ato Quayson. *Cambridge Journal of Postcolonial Literary Inquiry* 3.1 (2016): 143–56.

Nanda, Meera. *Postmodernism and Religious Fundamentalism: A Scientific Rebuttal to Hindu Science*. Pondicherry: Navayana, 2007.

———. "The Science Wars in India." *Dissent* 44.1 (1997): 78–83. Nielsen, Henrik Skov. "Natural Authors, Unnatural Narratives." *Post-Classical Narratology: Approaches and Analyses*. Eds. Jan Alber and Monika Fludernik. Columbus: Ohio State University Press, 2010. 275–301.

Nielsen, Henrik Skov, James Phelan, and Richard Walsh. "Ten Theses about Fictionality." *Narrative* 23.1 (2015): 61–73.

Parry, Benita. *Postcolonial Studies: A Materialist Critique*. London: Routledge, 2004.

Phelan, James. *Narrative as Rhetoric: Technique, Audiences Ethics, Ideology*. Columbus: Ohio State University Press, 1996.

Pratt, Mary Louise. "The Ideology of Speech Act Theory." *Poetics Today* 7 (1986): 59–72.

Prendergast, Christopher. *The Order of Mimesis: Balzac, Stendhal, Nerval, Flaubert*. Cambridge: Cambridge University Press, 1986.

Prince, Gerald. "Narratology, Narratological Criticism, and Gender." *Fiction Updated: Theories of Fictionality, Narratology, and Poetics*. Eds. Calin-Andrei Mihailescu and Walid Hamarneh. Toronto: University of Toronto Press, 1996. 159–64.

———. "On a Postcolonial Narratology." *A Companion to Narrative Theory*. Eds. James Phelan and Peter J. Rabinowitz. Oxford: Blackwell, 2005. 372–81.

Richardson, Brian. *Unnatural Voices: Extreme Narration in Modern and Contemporary Fiction*. Columbus: Ohio State University Press, 2006.

Ricoeur, Paul. *Time and Narrative, Vol. 1*. Trans. Kathleen McLaughlin and David Pellauer. Chicago: University of Chicago Press, 1984.

Ryan, Marie-Laure. "Postmodernism and the Doctrine of Panfictionality." *Narrative* 5.2 (1997): 165–87.

Schank, Roger C., and Robert P. Abelson. *Scripts, Plans, Goals and Understanding: An Inquiry into Human Knowledge Structures*. Hillsdale: Lawrence Erlbaum, 1977.

Shen, Dan. "Why Contextual and Formal Narratologies Need Each Other." *Journal of Narrative Theory* 35.2 (2005): 141–71.

Smith, Barbara Herrnstein. "Narrative Versions, Narrative Theories." *Critical Inquiry* 7.1 (1980): 213–36.

Sommer, Roy. "'Contextualism' Revisited: A Survey (and Defence) of Postcolonial and Intercultural Narratologies." *Journal of Literary Theory* 1.1 (2007): 61–79.

Sorensen, E. P. *Postcolonial Studies and the Literary*. London: Palgrave Macmillan, 2010.

Spivak, Gayatri C. *An Aesthetic Education in the Era of Globalization*. Cambridge: Harvard University Press, 2012.

Tiffin, Helen, "Post-Colonial Literatures and Counter-Discourse." *The Postcolonial Studies Reader*. Ed. Bill Ashcroft, Gareth Griffiths, and Helen Tiffin. London: Routledge, 1995. 95–98.

Vishwanathan, Gauri. *Masks of Conquest: Literary Study and British Rule in India*. New York: Columbia University Press, 1989.

Walsh, Richard. *The Rhetoric of Fictionality: Narrative Theory and the Idea of Fiction*. Columbus: Ohio State University Press, 2007.

Warhol, Robyn. "Feminist Narratology." *The Routledge Encyclopedia of Narrative Theory*. Eds. David Herman, Manfred Jahn, and Marie-Laure Ryan. London and New York: Routledge, 2005. 161–63.

White, Hayden. *Tropics of Discourse: Essays in Cultural Criticism*. Baltimore: Johns Hopkins University Press, 1978.

Yelle, Robert A. "Comparative Religion as Cultural Combat: Occidentalism and Relativism in Rajiv Malhotra's *Being Different*." *International Journal of Hindu Studies* 16.3 (2012): 335–48.

Young, Robert J. C. "Postcolonial Remains." *New Literary History* 43.1 (2012): 19–42.

———. *White Mythologies*. London: Routledge, 1990.

PART I
NARRATIVE IN QUESTION

CHAPTER 1

Fractured Tales and Colonial Traumas

Disfigured Stories in Kashmiri Short Fiction

PATRICK COLM HOGAN

IN EARLIER work, I have argued that the emplotment of nationalism—prominently including anticolonial nationalism—commonly follows a limited number of story prototypes. Those prototypes operate to explain past and current events and to orient nationally identified individuals toward future goals. The following essay continues this exploration of the implications of narrative theory for (postcolonial) nationalism by considering a somewhat unusual case—Indian Kashmir.[1] Specifically, it argues that the ongoing colonial occupation of Kashmir has led to a situation of such traumatic intensity that for many Kashmiri writers, the usual operation of nationalist emplotment is undermined. This results in a sort of disfiguring of what might otherwise be nationalist stories. This is particularly evident in stories that are aimed at other Kashmiris, rather than appealing to an international readership, with its possible influence on policies regarding Kashmir. The essay begins with a theoretical account of the disruption of nationalist emplotment by trauma. It then turns to an exploration of a number of Kashmiri stories, written in the Kashmiri language and therefore aimed at other Kashmiris.

---

1. This essay is adapted from *Affective Narratology: The Emotional Structure of Stories* by Patrick Colm Hogan, by permission of the University of Nebraska Press. Copyright 2011 by the Board of Regents of the University of Nebraska.

EMPLOTTING THE NATION

A link between nation and narration has been recognized in postcolonial theory since at least the time of Homi Bhabha's influential collection. But the precise nature of narrative and the precise relation between narrative and nation is not always entirely clear in this work. For instance, Bhabha writes that "nations, like narratives . . . only fully realize their horizons in the mind's eye" (1). This is a suggestive comment, surely, but one that it is difficult to turn into a precise theoretical analysis. Simon During more helpfully links stories with the modeling of behavior (see 144), but the algorithmic details of this connection are perhaps less clear than they might be.

One main argument of my *Understanding Nationalism* is that the cognitive and motivational consequences of group identification are not simply a matter of beliefs. Such consequences are inseparable from narrative structures, which shape our comprehension of the world and orient our feelings toward it. The narrative structures prominently include the cross-cultural prototypes of heroic, sacrificial, and romantic tragi-comedy, as well as family separation and reunion, and other less frequent genres (on these structures, see Hogan, *Affective Narratology*).[2] *Understanding Nationalism* also sought to isolate some general principles guiding which prototypes would tend to dominate nationalist thought at different times and places.

Initially, one would expect these principles and prototypes to apply in Kashmir as they do elsewhere. In a sense, they do. For example, the heroic emplotment is central to both the standard Indian and standard Pakistani accounts of the current "crisis" in Kashmir. Specifically, the standard heroic plot has two components, a usurpation component and an invasion component. In the usurpation component, the rightful leader of the home society is displaced by a usurper; in the invasion component, the home society is invaded by the national enemy, sometimes with the collaboration of the usurper. In the standard Pakistani view, the maharaja of Jammu and Kashmir was a usurper who initiated the enemy invasion of Kashmir by India in 1947. The official Indian view draws on the same structure, but with a different mapping of the prototype onto historical events. Specifically, in that case, the initial aggression of 1947 came from a Pakistani invasion (see, for example, Jha 2–3 on the Indian emplotment). This emplotment recurs in subsequent events, such as the Kargil war, as can be seen from the film *L. O. C.*

The heroic prototype is the default form of emplotment for national identification. In other words, other things being equal, a national group tends to

---

2. Of these genres, the relation of romantic stories to nationalism had been productively treated, in a different theoretical context, by Doris Sommer.

imagine itself and its relation to other national groups in terms of the heroic prototype. This is true independent of the degree to which the home society is actually under threat of invasion or usurpation. However, there are conditions in which other sorts of emplotment may rise to prominence. For example, the romantic plot involves two lovers who are separated and (in the comic version) subsequently reunited. This tends to become a salient form of national emplotment when the home society is internally divided. We see this to some extent in Indian emplotments of the Kashmir crisis, such as the film *Yahaan*. The family separation and reunion plot is often found in the context of national divisions as well.

The sacrificial narrative involves some national devastation, often including drought, hunger, or disease. This devastation is understood as the result of some national sin, either by the populace as a whole or by some national representative (e.g., a leader), often due to some seduction. The devastation is ended by the sacrifice of some innocent victim. This narrative tends to become prominent in nationalism when the condition of the home society is so weak that it precludes the possibility of any full military confrontation of the heroic type. More precisely, in nationalist contexts, the sacrificial narrative tends to be integrated into a more extended heroic emplotment. The sacrifice of the innocent victim is, then, what enables the struggle to advance toward a heroic confrontation. This is a component in some Indian narratives—for example, in the story of Mohd Maqbool Sherwani, who sacrificed his life to the Pakistani invaders, thereby allowing the Indian army to arrive and partially defeat the invasion. A recent version of "the martyrdom of Sherwani" may be found in a 2005 *Times of India* story by Rahul Singh, "Who Changed the Face of '47 War?"

The sacrificial emplotment is more common on the Pakistani side, particularly among militants, such as Maūlana Muhammad Azhar of Jaish-e-Muhammad. Specifically, jihādi leaders commonly specify the sacrificial narrative in terms of the ideal of the shahīd or martyr. For example, early in his commentary on verses treating jihād, *Fat-hul-Jawwād,* Azhar writes that Jews and Christians are seeking "to mislead the Muslims" (26). This places Jews and Christians in the seducer role of the prototypical sacrificial plot. He goes on to state that due to their imitation of Christians, "Muslims have grown weak" (34). This is the standard preface to a sacrificial emplotment, one that indicates the reason an ordinary heroic emplotment is not possible: the weakness of the home society will not lead to heroic victory. Azhar immediately supplicates Allāh, writing that it is "a great blessing . . . to be slain in Your way" and imploring Allāh to make "us" martyrs (34). Azhar's claims are fairly general. But Jameel stresses the particular focus of Azhar on "the Hindu oppressions to the Muslims of Kashmir" (518–19).

Other cross-cultural forms of emplotment turn up as well, particularly the revenge and criminal investigation prototypes. The revenge structure typically involves a criminal violation of some attachment relation (e.g., the murder of the protagonist's spouse), followed by acts of retribution. The retribution commonly involves misrecognition, thus the death of innocent people; it also frequently leads to the death of the protagonist. This is found in some Indian representations of Kashmir. For instance, in *Dhokha* a Kashmiri woman becomes a suicide bomber in order to take revenge for her rape and the killing of her father. An innovative (if ultimately not very successful) combination of the revenge and heroic prototypes may be found in *Madhoshi*, where a young woman from a Kashmiri Hindu family has hallucinations of the world being saved from terrorism by a secret antiterrorist militia. The hallucinations follow her sister's death at the hands of terrorists.

Of course, emplotment does not operate on its own. It is inseparable from the use of cognitive models for aspects of the nation. Prominent models include THE NATION IS A PERSON, THE NATION IS A FAMILY, and THE NATION IS THE LAND AND ITS CITIZENS ARE PLANTS WITH ROOTS IN THE LAND.[3] Indeed, these cognitive models are often embedded in narratives as metaphors. When this integration is consistent throughout a particular emplotment, we have an instance of national allegory. Given the importance of both modeling and emplotment to nationalism, it is unsurprising that national allegory should be a recurring literary form during periods of nation building. The general point is given its most famous formulation in Fredric Jameson's (rather grossly overstated) claim that "all third-world texts are necessarily . . . to be read as . . . national allegories" (70).[4] Indeed, we see some allegorical elements in the cases mentioned above. For example, in *Madhoshi*, the point of the film is not that a particular Kashmiri Hindu might have a particular hallucination. It is, rather, that a segment of traumatized Kashmiri Hindus (represented by a single character) might have the political delusion (represented by the character's hallucinations) that a particularly powerful military response (represented by the hallucinated antiterrorist militia) will rescue them by wiping out terrorism.

---

3. It is a convention in metaphor analysis to use uppercase for the large, conceptual structure shared by particular metaphors. For example, Uncle Sam and John Bull are instances of THE NATION IS A PERSON.

4. On the excessive breadth of Jameson's claim, see chapter 3 of Ahmad. In the following analyses, I will emphasize allegorical elements. In a situation where nationalist feeling and conflict are intense and highly consequential (often a matter of life and death), it is unsurprising to find personal stories developed in such a way as to comment on larger social trends. That is exactly what we find in Kashmir. Of course, even here, not all stories involve national or related allegories. Moreover, even stories that do involve such allegories are open to non-allegorical interpretations as well.

The preceding examples indicate that the Kashmir crisis—a crisis of national or subnational definition and conflict—is emplotted in predictable ways by non-Kashmiris. But what about Kashmiris themselves? Unsurprisingly, we can find all these versions of emplotment among Kashmiris. Kashmiri mujāhideen are likely to emplot their struggle in heroic or sacrificial terms along Pakistani lines. Kashmiri officials are likely to adopt the heroic emplotment of the Indian government. In *Imagining Kashmir*, I consider how Hindi-language films treating Kashmir have taken up heroic, romantic, revenge, and other narrative structures to emplot the conflict in ideologically consequential ways. I also examine the more complex heroic, sacrificial, and other emplotments found in Anglophone novels written by Kashmiris (specifically, works by Naseer Ahmed, Bharat Wakhlu, and Mirza Waheed). Though they differ in their political orientations and their precise uses of narrative structures, all these works organize the conflict in ways that at least to some extent make sense of the situation and seek to orient practical responses to it.

In contrast, a reader of work by Kashmiri-language writers is likely to be struck by the degree to which the usual genre-based expectations of emplotment are not merely complicated but profoundly violated. Specifically, many writers from the valley itself, writers who have experienced the "crisis" in their homes and are writing for other Kashmiris, often do not have the same sense of optimism that is suggested by nationalist emplotments of heroism, romance, or sacrifice. Nor do they necessarily stress revenge. This is not to say that the cross-cultural genres are missing or that national issues are absent. The cross-cultural genres are still prominent and they are taken up by these individual writers for national or subnational topics. But these genres often appear in strangely distorted forms, bereft of their usual national functions. To understand why this is the case, we need to consider some aspects of the operation of emotion and what happens to emotion in trauma. (Note that this is trauma experienced by individual writers. It is not some sort of supra-individual trauma, though it is the result of widespread, largely public events, such as military crackdowns or explosions in markets, rather than more simply private events, such as a relative having heart disease.)

EMOTION, TRAUMA, AND DISFIGURED NARRATIVES

In the sacrificial emplotments mentioned in *Understanding Nationalism*, the sense of social impotence was widespread. Moreover, there was a clear relation to the prototypical cases of devastation, such as famine. But the experience of devastation was limited and often indirect. Consider, for example, the case of the Irish Easter Uprising in 1916—a paradigmatic instance of political action based on sacrificial emplotment. The terrible nineteenth-century famine in Ireland, though imaginatively prominent, was not experienced directly by the poets and revolutionaries who, in 1916, engaged in what they thought of as a blood sacrifice (see Lyons 89–92). In contrast, there are societies in which devastation is widespread and immediate. Kashmir is one of those cases. It is a place where ordinary life has become highly threatening and uncertain. In short, it has become traumatic. Indeed, the "traumatic stimuli" have been particularly intense and consequential because "the degree of predictability and controllability" have both been very low (Başoğlu and Mineka 184, on the two key variables bearing on the long-term effects of trauma; Başoğlu and Mineka are speaking generally and not about Kashmir). The point is not metaphorical. When Basharat Peer arrived at the *Kashmir Times*, a "veteran reporter" explained to him that "thirty-seven words is all you need to know to be a reporter here." These words are mostly obvious—"arrest, prison, torture," as well as "Indian security forces, separatists," and so forth. But they also include "fear . . . anxiety . . . despair . . . rage" and "trauma" (91). More significantly, Kazi cites a study that found "40 per cent of children in the age group of 4–18 years suffer from post-traumatic stress disorders, fear psychosis and panic" (188, fn. 113). Habibullah notes that after the insurgency began, "annual outpatient visits to the psychiatric hospital in Srinagar soared from 3,000 to 18,000" (140).

"Trauma theory" has become an important area in literary study today. Writers such as Cathy Caruth have explored the consequences of traumatic experience using psychoanalytic principles. However, it is not at all clear that psychoanalysis is the best approach to trauma, considering that it has been largely surpassed by cognitive and affective science. Both a psychoanalytic and an affective scientific account would agree, however, that memories are at the basis of trauma. In a cognitive account, these are specifically what are now called "emotional memories" (see LeDoux). Emotional memories are memories that may or may not call to mind particular "episodic memories," thus specific sensory images of or information about the past. However, when activated, emotional memories revive the relevant emotion. A fundamental feature of post-traumatic stress is the repeated, intrusive, and uncontrolled experience of strong emotions from emotional memories (see, for example, Banich et al. 621, 624–25). In some ways, trauma produces a disorder of emotional memory. As Kirby and colleagues point out, "Impaired regulation of emotional memory is a feature of several affective disorders, including . . . post-traumatic stress disorder" (527; see also Haas and Canli).

Here we might try to work out some details of this general connection. The usual function of emotional memories is preparatory. The activation of emotional memories motivates one to anticipate possible outcomes of current events and to engage in relevant actions to exploit opportunities or avoid threats. Suppose I nearly have an accident when driving quickly on a dangerous curve on a particular road. When I approach the place again—or when I approach a similar curve elsewhere—the conditions activate the emotional memory. The emotional memory causes fear of the repeated outcome, motivating me to reduce my speed before actually encountering the danger. The operation of emotional memories may be embedded in larger, more narrative trajectories as well. Someone who has had bad romantic experiences may avoid initiating a romantic relationship, while someone else is encouraged to imagine a love story unfolding in the future. The same point holds for the range of individuals that constitute nations. It was a commonplace that the "Vietnam Syndrome" discouraged Americans from emplotting wars as heroic comedies leading to the triumph of (national) good.

In sum, I would argue that if we put together research on trauma with research on the operation of emotion, we may draw some illuminating conclusions. To begin, we may conclude that functional emotional memories have three properties. First, they are activated in narrow circumstances—the ones that are close enough to the initial condition that they are likely to present similar threats or opportunities. Second, they are integrated into causal sequences that enable relevant sorts of action—avoiding threats or exploiting opportunities. Third, they are strong enough to motivate action. However, we might add, they are weak enough to be overridden in cases where they are irrelevant and they are not so strong as to prevent appropriate action (e.g., disordered panic rather than avoidance of danger).

Trauma can produce dysfunction at each of these three points. First, the emotional memories of traumas may be activated widely, thus in irrelevant circumstances. Second, they are commonly removed from causal sequences since it is difficult to make causal sense of the traumatic occurrence in any predictive way. Putting this second point differently, we may say that traumatic threats tend not to be regular, but anomalous, without clearly categorizable causal precedents. Finally, the feeling tends to be overwhelmingly strong, thus producing panic rather than action-motivating fear and overriding attempts at cognitive modulation. It should be clear how an insurgency/counterinsurgency war, leaving tens of thousands dead (see, for example, Widmalm 131), could produce trauma, particularly in the conditions prevailing in Kashmir. Severe harm, including death (e.g., of a close relative), has been sudden, unpredictable, seemingly random. It could come from any quarter. As Salman

Rushdie put it, "It was getting to be a characteristic of the times that people never knew who had hit them or why" (286). As Rushdie indicates, there has been no clear way of anticipating or avoiding the blows. The harm has not been confined to certain places or times, or to certain groups. In keeping with this, the emotional memories might be activated at any moment in virtually any context. Moreover, these memories cannot be integrated into predictive structures that would allow relevant actions. The interviews reported by Kazi present a picture of a widespread sense of utter helplessness, an inability to take any effective action whatsoever (see, for example, 104). Finally, these memories could not be overridden by reasoned inferences to likelihood.

Trauma might in principle give rise to a compensatory affirmation of reassuring predictive structures, including story prototypes. However, its fundamental nature is such that it tends to undermine the validity of such structures. The heroic prototype seems pointless, even ludicrous. The sacrificial structure is, if anything, worse. It holds out the hope of divine salvation through suffering, when experience seems to suggest that sacrifice and suffering are likely to be the prelude only to yet more sacrifice and suffering. Indeed, what might have been imagined as sacrifice is now simply a desire for death. As Kazi notes, "In 1980, Kashmir had the lowest suicide rate in India; presently, it is among the highest in the world" (119). In traumatic conditions, then, the usual functions of emplotment—particularly its organizational and predictive qualities—seem to be lost. In consequence, the use of story prototypes may be highly distorted.

This distortion is just what we find in many Kashmiri short stories, as well illustrated in one of the very few collections of Kashmiri-language writings available in English.[5] It is what I am calling "disfigured narrative." This is a sort of extension in the sense of Lakoff and Turner—a highly unusual or innovative use of a standard structure. But unlike the cases discussed by Lakoff and Turner, disfigured narratives violate the fundamental function of the structure in question, even reversing it. One striking feature of some Kashmiri short fiction is that it takes up the prototypical story structures in relation to national identification,[6] but it so radically distorts the prototype that it is barely recog-

---

5. Though there are roughly five and a half million Kashmiri speakers, the literacy rate has not been terribly high (see Government of India and "Jammu") and that literacy has often been in Urdu (or Hindi or English) rather than Kashmiri. This means that Kashmiri-language literary production has been less than one might have expected. In addition, very little of that has been translated into English. Mattoo's 1994 book is probably the most widely accessible selection.

6. Needless to say, this does not mean that there are no other concerns in Kashmiri narratives. However, in this period of intense national conflict, national identification is a highly prominent concern.

nizable, and its national function is more like a cry of despair than an imagination of nationhood. Note that this is not simply a matter of, for example, presenting nonheroic characters in a heroic structure. It involves a more pervasive undermining of the sense-making function of emplotment. (Of course, there is no strict dividing line here; a heroic narrative including only nonheroic characters certainly moves in the direction of a disfigured story.)

Unsurprisingly, this disfiguring occurs not only with stories per se but also with metaphors or models. Indeed, I have drawn the name "disfigured" from one story that takes up THE NATION IS A PERSON. Anees Hamadani's "The Burnt-Out Sun" concerns a man who, though apparently healthy, is suddenly taken away by two men in an ambulance and confined to a cell. Eventually, surgeons come and divide his face in two, removing half. He is allowed to leave. But he finds that he cannot see anything anymore, because "my eyes had gone with the part of my face that had been removed" (Mattoo 137). THE NATION IS A PERSON is commonly used to present the unity of the nation. Here, however, it is used to present precisely the disunity, the division. Moreover, it does so in a way that makes no sense. A person does not survive if his face is cut in half. But this is not a lack of skill on the part of the author. Rather, it is a use of the standard metaphor that expresses one aspect of the trauma of Kashmir since 1947. The two men in the ambulance represent forces that are in some sense pretending to "save" the speaker, thus Kashmir. These men suggest India and Pakistan—the former in its "rescue" of Kashmir from the Pakistani invasion, the latter in its "rescue" of Kashmir from the maharaja. The detention further recalls the many Kashmiri nationalists imprisoned over the years. Finally, the man is cut in two, just as Kashmir was divided between India and Pakistan. The ludicrous conclusion announced by the two men is that the speaker is "free now" (137)—just what Pakistan and India in effect announced to their respective parts of Kashmir.[7] We find many examples of this sort of distortion in relation to narrative genre.

FRACTURED TALES

When I was a child, there was a cartoon program called *Fractured Fairy Tales*. It presented rather distorted versions of common stories. I now imagine that

---

7. In a more literal treatment of the story, one in keeping with the poststructuralist orientation of much postcolonial theory and criticism, Kabir sees the surgery as manifesting "the orthopedic regimes of the modern state" (*Territory* 150). As this suggests, this story and others like it are open to non-allegorical readings, though it seems that important features of the work are lost if the allegorical significance is not recognized.

the irony of these works was aimed at entertaining parents even as the vivid and strange tales themselves entertained the children. There is an element of that in some Kashmiri fiction. They too are, in a sense, fractured fairy tales—though in this case the fairy tales concern national identification. They are also pervaded by irony. However, the irony, though sometimes humorous, is most often too despairing even to rise to the level of tragedy. In these fractured tales, I have come upon examples of all the usual genres in disfigured forms, except the heroic. Perhaps a heroic emplotment is simply inconceivable for ordinary Kashmiris (as opposed to Indian or Pakistani officials), even in a disfigured form. In keeping with this, the sacrificial emplotment—the emplotment of the militarily weak—is most common, though romantic, revenge, and other genres turn up as well.

Akhtar Mohi-ud-din's "The Second Meeting" presents a nice instance of a disfigured romantic plot. It concerns the long separation of a Kashmiri man and an Indian (specifically, Bengali) woman. They had met once. She was the "Eternal Beloved" (Mattoo 110), and "fear and doubt had been reduced to ashes, burnt down like the effigy of Ravana" (110). Twenty years later, the man "happened to visit that country again" and "met her for the second time" (111). It was now a time of "fear and mistrust" (110). Now she is old and lacks the charm of two decades before. She does not even remember him. They are both embarrassed when he discovers and reads "the superlatives [he] had chosen to describe her qualities and her beauty" two decades before (112).

The story takes up the separation of lovers, reunited at last after their separation (inevitable in the genre). But the reunion is pathetic. There is no longer any feeling between the two, and their earlier enthusiasms now seem ludicrous. The significance of the story is suggested in the reference to her country and the burning of "fear and doubt" like "the effigy of Ravana." In the context of Kashmiri history, this hints that the first meeting was the initial response of many Kashmiris to the events of 1947, with fear and doubt arising due to the threat posed by a Pakistan-supported invasion (see Akbar 106). (Pakistan is often explicitly or implicitly associated with the demon Rāvaṇa in Indian views of Indo-Pakistan wars, such as that in 1947.) The enthusiasm and love are the feelings of that early postindependence moment. But after decades, "fear and mistrust" have grown between Kashmir and the rest of India. Even those who were formerly enthusiastic about the association are only embarrassed by those feelings in retrospect.

While "The Second Meeting" recounts a Muslim Kashmiri's return from Kashmir to another part of India, Avtar Krishna Rehbar's "Anguish" presents the story of a Hindu émigré's return to Kashmir. The protagonist recalls a time when he had lost "his head and heart" on the steps of the Veth river, whose "running water would move him to ecstasy" in his youth (Mattoo 141). Here, the love story is more clearly allegorical and the beloved is more clearly the nation, though in this case Kashmir rather than India. Here too, the former beauty is lost. This is not a joyous reunion of lovers. Now the river is "toxic, polluted" (145)—an ecological fact, but also a metaphor in the story, for the people too have changed; their "hearts have grown cold" with "fanaticism and greed" (144). The story ends with an allusion to the well-known myth of how the god Śiva saved the world by sucking up a vast poison that would have destroyed everyone. The protagonist plunges into the filthy water, praying that he be given the power to suck up all the poison—the pollutants in the river, but also the poison in the hearts of the people—or that he die. There is no reason to expect that he will be able to drain the poison. Thus the end is a sort of lover's suicide, an integration of the romantic and sacrificial structures. But it is a suicide for a beloved who is "cold" and who is, in any case, not really a beloved anyway. Whether he dies or not, neither nature nor Kashmir will be restored; no one will be redeemed. In short, it is not a tragic sacrifice, but a senseless, pseudo-sacrifice.

The criminal investigation genre receives some minimal treatment in Nazir Jehangir's "The Boy Is Guilty." In the usual genre, it is not uncommon for there to be some miscarriage of justice. But the conclusions of the investigation are rarely entirely arbitrary. In this story, a boy faints, then explains that his pocket has been picked. Two factions form, proposing slightly different explanations for how this occurred. In a prototypical criminal investigation narrative, an examination might have led to the discovery and conviction of the pickpocket. It might have temporarily imprisoned an innocent man, but it would be likely to find the true culprit in the end. Here, however, there is no investigation of the crime. Rather, the two groups proposing different explanations form different parties and engage in battles against one another. One party connects the theft with attempts "to tamper with the sanctity of Article 370" (Mattoo 105; as Mattoo explains, this is "an Article in the Indian Constitution which guarantees a special status to Jammu and Kashmir State" [151]). This leads the police to fire on the crowds. In the end, the boy himself is "arrested on the charge of having started a riot" (105).

Here, again, we see both allegory and disfigurement. The parties represent conflicting political groups in Kashmir. The boy stands for the ordinary Kashmiri people. The different political parties claim to have the interests of the Kashmiri people at heart. But they do not examine the causes of Kashmiri problems and try to solve them. Rather, they turn those problems into occasions for political sloganeering. The only punishment is exacted on the victims themselves. The entire criminal investigation structure leads not only to injustice but to the precise reversal of justice—and not for any comprehensible reason.

The revenge prototype is found in Amin Kamil's "The Grave Robber." In this story, someone repeatedly defiles new graves. Finally, the perpetrator, Gana Baba, confesses his crime "in his dying declaration" (Mattoo 119). The crime fits with the revenge prototype in that it violates an attachment relation, the relation of the mourners to their dead relative or friend. But it is strangely unmotivated. We are never told why Gana Baba did this. This is what we would expect, however, from the traumatically disturbed processes of death and mourning in Kashmir. The bodies of loved ones may be returned in pieces, or only in part, or (in the case of the disappeared) not at all. The murders by the military and the militants are a sort of defilement of the grave as well, a defilement that renders the grief of the bereaved all the more troubled (e.g., when it is accompanied by uncertainty, in the case of the disappeared). What follows in the story introduces further disfigurement. In the prototypical revenge plot, the revenger may mistakenly punish one or more innocents before finding the true culprit. Here, however, the reverse happens. Gana's grave is defiled, presumably by someone who "had taken revenge" (119). But then, following this revenge, graves continue to be defiled. The revenge does not stop with the culprit. Revenge against the criminal is, rather, only the beginning of an evidently endless series of defilements. The point makes gibberish of the revenge structure. However, it fits the situation in Kashmir all too well.

The family separation and reunion prototype is taken up in Abdul Gani Beg Athar's "The Enemy," though this work also draws on the sacrificial prototype for an embedded story. "The Enemy" concerns a man who is separated from his brother due to the establishment of a border between Pakistani Kashmir and Indian Kashmir. The allegorical significance of this is too obvious to require comment. Hearing that his brother is dying, the protagonist decides to cross over into Pakistani Kashmir. He is arrested and beaten by the Pakistani military.[8] He tries to object, "I am not an Indian. Neither am I a Pakistani. I am only a Kashmiri" (Mattoo 30), but the soldiers torture him as an Indian spy. Ultimately, his brother dies. He tries to get permission to see the corpse. But in a Kafkaesque ending, no one can ascertain who has the authority to grant such permission. So the man is never able even to see his brother's corpse. The family separation prototype is in some ways more ambivalent than other prototypes. It reunites the family, but commonly in a way that is

---

8. Here, too, Kabir takes a more standard poststructuralist and postcolonial approach, linking such events with the Foucauldian idea of "biopolitics" ("Cartographic" 61).

temporary and troubled. But here the reunion is not only never realized—it is actually impossible to determine what would have allowed the reunion to occur. The allegorical suggestion is that there is not even a way of imagining how Kashmiris could be reunited.

Again, there is a sacrificial plot embedded in "The Enemy." Specifically, when the protagonist is beaten unconscious, he dreams that his brother is about to die and, like Jesus on the cross, asks for water. The protagonist is manacled and cannot reach water. However, he is bleeding. He gathers the blood in his hands. He will revive his brother with his own blood—suggesting that the Kashmiris in Indian Kashmir will help to revive the Kashmiris of Pakistani Kashmir through the sacrifices of their own blood, presumably so that both can struggle for an independent, united Kashmir. But this is all too absurd. The brother dies when the protagonist cannot reach him. Moreover, drinking his brother's blood is at least as sinister an image as it is salvational. Finally, this blood sacrifice is, in any case, simply a dream that would have no real effects anyway. Once again, the prototype is rendered ludicrous, multiply false. The point is only enhanced by its embedment in an equally ludicrous and multiply false family reunion prototype.

A particularly effective use of the sacrificial prototype may be found in Nayeema Ahmad's "I Am Still Alive." This story begins with a woman asking passersby where they are going. They do not know what to say, for everything was "chaos and anarchy" and all these people were "adrift, cut off from one another" (Mattoo 73). This clearly represents the traumatized condition of the Kashmiri people. They do not know where they are going in the sense that they do not know what their goals are or what they can possibly achieve (separate nationhood, autonomy within India, union with Pakistan, or something else). But who is the woman? She is the narrator's "own lost self" (75). When the narrator meets this woman, she suddenly feels her "life . . . return." She says to herself, "This is she—yes—the one in whose search I have been lost for so long" (74). The woman is evidently the "self," not in the personal and individual sense, but in the collective sense. She is the group identity, what they are all together. In that sense, she is Kashmir or some aspect of Kashmir, what would foster identity and direction for these people who are "cut off" and "unaware of their own selves" (73). That is why she can later address all the people, pleading, "Why are you all mourning your individual losses? Why don't you all raise one collective cry?"

Shortly after the woman's admonition, the "gaunt skeleton of an old man" rises "from a grave" (75). Far from a saving sacrifice, the old man—perhaps recalling the dead nationalist leader Sheikh Abdullah—merely laments that "crows and vultures feed upon my body" (75). If the old man is indeed linked with Sheikh Abdullah, the crows and vultures would appear to suggest what has happened to his nationalist legacy after his death—its self-interested use by those who, so to speak, feed off its remains.

What occurs next is very much in keeping with the incomprehensible developments that particularly marked the time of this story (written in 1992)—prominently including protestors being killed as soldiers and police fired into crowds of demonstrators (see, for example, Jamal 136 and Peer 118–19). Specifically, "a throng of people" runs "blindly, as though chased by armed marauders" (Mattoo 76). Then, just as suddenly as the near-riot, everything stops. The man is dead once more. All the people are motionless, "two-dimensional bodies that lay plastered on the roads where thousands of vultures had gathered" (76). Clearly, the crowd has been shot down by the army or police, a scenario wretchedly familiar to readers at the time. As Peer explains, referring to a time shortly before the story was written, "Srinagar was a city of massacres" (120). He goes on to explain that "the men who had been killed by the Indian forces . . . were no ordinary dead. They were seen as martyrs" (121). In the story, too, this "throng" has become a group of martyrs. Their martyrdom is made clear by the woman's comment, "Those you imagine to be dead, are alive. They are the people who are condemned to live for a thousand years" (Mattoo 76). But their sacrifice has not revived society. Indeed, the story goes on to present death not as a sacrificial salvation, but as a possible release from the damnation of life. At the end, the speaker wishes that she "could live on for thousands of years" (76). But we have just learned that living for a thousand years means having died (as a martyr). In short, she wishes that she too had died. In keeping with this, she too "wanted to lie there in peace" (76). On the other hand, even this "peace" is troubled. The martyr is not blessed with, but "condemned to" an extended life. As in Hamlet's famous soliloquy ("in that sleep of death what dreams may come" [III.i.67]), it is not clear that even death will bring peace, despite the speaker's apparent assurance. In this story, even despair is disfigured.

Given the importance of the sacrificial prototype in Kashmir today, it is unsurprising that a disfigured version of that prototype is such a prominent feature of Kashmiri short fiction. Again, most of these disfigured narratives are utterly despondent about possibilities for understanding and possibilities for action. We may conclude with another strange and affecting sacrificial story, which nonetheless points at least toward some possible comprehension, if not action—"The Voice" by Ghulam Rasool Santosh (in Mattoo). Like "The Enemy," this story too combines family separation and reunion with sacrifice, both of course disfigured. The story concerns a man named Karima who had been abandoned as a child and raised by a man who, in turn, abandoned him.

This sets us up for two possible family reunion stories—Karima with his birth parents and Karima with his foster father. Then Karima discovers another abandoned child. Here we have a third family reunion possibility. None of the three comes to anything. Indeed, rather than being reunited with his birth parents, this boy is brutally separated from Karima as well—when Karima kills him.

That killing brings us to the sacrificial narrative. In contrast with the usual sacrificial structure, there is no society and no devastation. Karima and his foster son seem to live an almost ideal life. But, just as Ibrahim in the Qur'ān heard the voice of Allāh asking for the death of his son, Karima begins to hear a voice calling on him to kill the boy he has raised from infancy. Eventually, like Ibrahim, he agrees. However, unlike in the Qur'ānic story, he is not stopped by Allāh (see 37:104–5), but goes through with the act. After the boy is dead, he cremates him and smears his own body with the ashes. Sitting in meditation, he recalls the ash-covered god of yoga and destruction, Śiva, the primary deity of Kashmiri Hindus.

The story clearly undermines the pretense to salvation that is part of the sacrificial narrative. As such, it may at least suggest that sacrificial killing involves a sort of delusion. This is where some glimmer of understanding may enter. Specifically, the story hints that, by its appeal to a higher principle than human compassion and affection, religion—Muslim or Hindu—can drive us to do things that are not only immoral, but that we ourselves do not even wish to do. Though still disfiguring the sacrificial prototype, the story seems thus to have a positive element in this respect. It suggests a way of understanding some of the violence that has become so commonplace in Kashmir. On the other hand, it is a positive element that hardly suggests any possibility for concrete action. It still does not point toward any enabling emplotment that would somehow overcome the traumas of this "postcolonial" colony and its disfigured stories.[9]

---

9. One referee asked about the relation of these disfigurations to medium. In this connection, it is worth referring briefly to Tariq Tapa's fine 2008 film, *Zero Bridge*. The film is largely in Kashmiri, though with parts in Urdu and English. It too exhibits narrative disfigurement. Specifically, it concerns a youth who was abandoned by his mother and who falls in love with a physics student eleven years his senior. The film suggests the possibility of a mother-son reunion, while simultaneously indicating that the mother and son have no real bonds that would make such a reunion meaningful, and neither of them seriously pursues it. (This is despite the boy's understated, but clear and deeply moving desire for such a reunion.) The romantic connection of the youth and the physics student is, if anything, even less comprehensible. The youth had earlier stolen her passport, which has led to a situation in which she is likely to be married off to a cousin. The youth and the physics student plan to escape to Delhi (where the youth's mother happens to be). But the plan does not work out. Here too, then, the characters' goals and actions—and the story trajectories they imply—seem muddled

CONCLUSION

In sum, the imaginative and emotional engagements of nationalism are inseparable from narratives, prominently narratives guided by cross-cultural genres. Nationalist narratives—including anticolonial, nationalist narratives—operate in part by making sense of the past and projecting a desirable and attainable future, thereby motivating pursuit of national or putatively national goals. Trauma produces an emotionally, thus motivationally disabling condition in which it is difficult to make sense out of past events or to pursue or even envision an appealing future. When the trauma is broadly social, this is likely to affect national emplotments, producing disfigured versions in which the national stories are not merely tragic, but senseless. This is what we find in many stories from the troubled state of Kashmir, subject as it is to the "postcolonial colonialism" of both India and Pakistan. These disfigured narratives seem particularly common in the work of Kashmiris writing in the Kashmiri language, thus largely without concern for a foreign (Indian, Pakistani, Euro-American, or other) readership.

WORKS CITED

Ahmad, Aijaz. *In Theory: Classes, Nations, Literatures.* London: Verso, 1992.

Akbar, M. J. *Kashmir: Behind the Vale.* New Delhi: Viking, 1991.

Azhar, Maūlana Muhammad Mas'ūd. *Fat-hul-Jawwād Fe-Ma'ārif Āyāt-il-Jihād (Detailed Discourse on Verses on the Topic of Jihād).* Trans. Rasheed Mas'ūd. Lahore: Maktaba Irfān, n.d.

Banich, Marie, et al. "Cognitive Control Mechanisms, Emotion and Memory: A Neural Perspective with Implications for Psychopathology." *Neuroscience and Biobehavioral Reviews* 33 (2009): 613–30.

Başoğlu, Metin, ed. *Torture and Its Consequences: Current Treatment Approaches.* Cambridge: Cambridge University Press, 1992.

Başoğlu, Metin, and Susan Mineka. "The Role of Uncontrollable and Unpredictable Stress in Post-Traumatic Stress Responses in Torture Survivors." In Başoğlu, *Torture* 182–225.

Bhabha, Homi, ed. *Nation and Narration.* New York: Routledge, 1990.

Caruth, Cathy. *Unclaimed Experience: Trauma, Narrative, and History.* Baltimore: Johns Hopkins University Press, 1996.

During, Simon. "Literature—Nationalism's Other? The Case for Revision." In Bhabha, 138–53.

---

and pointless. In the end, nothing is clear, except that the characters have few if any options for the future. The story's events are related to the political situation in Kashmir by the characters' appeal to achieving freedom. But none of the options available to them seem to promise freedom—or to make sense of their miserable, alienated (and even abusive) conditions.

Government of India. "Abstract of Speakers' Strength of Languages and Mother Tongues—2001." Web. 19 May 2013.

Haas, Brian, and Turhan Canli. "Emotional Memory Function, Personality Structure and Psychopathology: A Neural System Approach to the Identification of Vulnerability Markers." *Brain Research Reviews* 58 (2008): 71–84.

Habibullah, Wajahat. *My Kashmir: Conflict and the Prospects of Enduring Peace*. Washington, DC: United States Institute of Peace Press, 2008.

Hogan, Patrick Colm. *Affective Narratology: The Emotional Structure of Stories*. Lincoln: University of Nebraska Press, 2011.

———. *Imagining Kashmir: Emplotment and Colonialism*. Lincoln: University of Nebraska Press, 2016.

———. *Understanding Nationalism: On Narrative, Cognitive Science, and Identity*. Columbus: Ohio State University Press, 2009.

Jamal, Arif. *Shadow War: The Untold Story of Jihad in Kashmir*. New York: Melville House, 2009.

Jameel, Muhammad. "The *Āmir-ul-Jihād* and *Fat-hul-Jawwād*." In Azhar, 516–22.

Jameson, Fredric. "Third World Literature in the Era of Multinational Capital." *Social Text* 15 (1986): 65–88.

"Jammu and Kashmir Population Census Data 2011." Web. 19 May 2013.

Jha, Prem Shankar. *Kashmir, 1947: Rival Versions of History*. Delhi: Oxford University Press, 1996.

Kabir, Ananya Jahanara. "Cartographic Irresolution and the Line of Control." *Social Text* 27 (2009): 45–66.

———. *Territory of Desire: Representing the Valley of Kashmir*. Minneapolis: University of Minnesota Press, 2009.

Kazi, Seema. *In Kashmir: Gender, Militarization and the Modern Nation State*. Brooklyn: South End Press, 2010.

Kirby, E. D., et al. "Basolateral Amygdala Regulation of Adult Hippocampal Neurogenesis and Fear-Related Activation of Newborn Neurons." *Molecular Psychiatry* 17 (2012): 527–36.

Lakoff, George, and Mark Turner. *More Than Cool Reason: A Field Guide to Poetic Metaphor*. Chicago: University of Chicago Press, 1989.

LeDoux, Joseph. *The Emotional Brain: The Mysterious Underpinnings of Emotional Life*. New York: Touchstone, 1996.

Lyons, F. S. L. *Culture and Anarchy in Ireland 1890–1939*. New York: Oxford University Press, 1979.

Mattoo, Neerja, ed. and trans. *The Stranger Beside Me: Short Stories from Kashmir*. New Delhi: UBS Publishers' Distributors, 1994.

Peer, Basharat. *Curfewed Night: One Kashmiri Journalist's Frontline Account of Life, Love, and War in His Homeland*. New York: Scribner, 2010.

Rushdie, Salman. *Shalimar the Clown*. New York: Random House, 2005.

Shakespeare, William. *Hamlet, Prince of Denmark*. *The Complete Works of Shakespeare*. Ed. David Bevington. 4th ed. New York: HarperCollins, 1992, 1060–116.

Singh, Rahul. "Who Changed the Face of '47 War?" *Times of India* 14 Aug. 2005. Web. 1 Sept. 2012. <http://articles.timesofindia.indiatimes.com/2005-08-14/india/27857480_1_baramulla-srinagar-infantry-day>.

Sommer, Doris. "Irresistible Romance: The Foundational Fictions of Latin America." In Bhabha *Nation*, 71–98.

Tapa, Tariq, dir. and screenwriter. *Zero Bridge*. New York: Artists Public Domain, 2008.

Widmalm, Sten. *Kashmir in Comparative Perspective: Democracy and Violent Separatism in India*. London: RoutledgeCurzon, 2002.

CHAPTER 2

No Center and No Margins

*Narrativizing Return Journeys in Works by
M. G. Vassanji, Michael Ondaatje, and Rohinton Mistry*

MARTIN LÖSCHNIGG

MIGRATION AND (dis)location are ideologically freighted phenomena, especially in a postcolonial context. As Ashcroft, Griffiths, and Tiffin emphasize in their "classic" *The Empire Writes Back,* "It is here that the special post-colonial crisis of identity comes into being; the concern with the development or recovery of an effective identifying relationship between self and place" (8). While postcolonial theory has largely conceived the spatial associations of self in terms of an axiomatic distinction between "center" and "margin," recent accounts of (postcolonial) migration and travel in literature have frequently expressed an ideologically significant shift away from such binaries to a new, self-confident transculturalism or cosmopolitanism. As it seems, the rendering of transcultural selves in these accounts depends to a great extent on narrative technique, and narratological analysis may thus be fruitfully applied to reveal the ideological underpinnings of these texts. These ideological issues, in turn, reflect back on narrative theory in that they bring to mind the necessity to acknowledge the cultural and historical dimension of narrative structures and strategies. According to Ansgar Nünning, narrative structures are highly semanticized, which calls for a "context-sensitive and diachronic approach to narratives" (356), in contrast to the synchronic and text-centered orientation of structuralist narratology. As a consequence, narratological categories may have to be expanded and modified to accommodate the cultural-historical and ideological dynamics of narratives. Since these dynamics are especially vibrant in postcolonial narratives, such texts underline the importance of a cultural and historical narratology in a particular manner.

The present essay analyzes the ideological implications of migrancy and of "return journeys," and the narrative strategies employed to convey these implications in works by three writers of South Asian origin or ancestry who now live in Canada. These works are M. G. Vassanji's *A Place Within* (2008), Michael Ondaatje's *Running in the Family* (1981), and Rohinton Mistry's *Tales From Firozsha Baag* (1987). I have chosen these texts not only because of their chronological stratification and because they represent different genres—a travelogue in the case of Vassanji, a fictionalized memoir[1] in that of Ondaatje, and a short story cycle whose locations and themes are based on the author's life in that of Mistry—but mainly because they all show themselves highly conscious of the role of narrative in the rendering of their themes. Ranging from nonfiction to fiction, these narratives represent explorations of alternative versions of "self," constructing and revising concepts of postcolonial selves and (migrant) identities. According to Michel Foucault, literature is a means by which individuals make sense of and define their existence through historically and culturally constituted "subject positions" (cf. Foucault), such as, in the case of the writers in question, that of the migrant, exile, and temporary returnee. Since these subject positions are expressive of power relations, narratives of migration and return, whether fictional or factual, reflect the discursive formations that justify, rationalize, and reproduce migrant or diasporic identities. However, the texts I shall be discussing explore, modify, expand, and often reject such discursively construed "subject positions" by creating narrative versions of self that seem to oppose definition and/or limitation. Indeed, these narratives portray selves that display the openness and processual nature of identities, especially in the sign of migration as postulated by theorists like Stuart Hall (see, for instance, "Cultural Identity and Diaspora" and "The Question of Cultural Identity"), Homi Bhabha, or Iain Chambers. In particular, these narratives render the experiential dimension of such identities by showing how migrant identities are lived and experienced by people in particular (social) locations and over certain time periods. It follows, therefore, that narratological models that emphasize the experiential dimension of narrative, beside narratologically grounded approaches to the question of identity, appear of particular relevance to the analysis of "migrant literature."

---

1. *Running in the Family* represents a mixture of genres as well as a combination of autobiographical and fictional elements. The "I" of the text is Ondaatje's, and the narrative is mostly about real members of his family; their stories, however, are explicitly marked as—possible—fabrications (see below).

As Ellen Oxfeld and Lynellyn Long have emphasized, "provisional returns to homelands also may be understood as modern day pilgrimages to affirm or redefine . . . cultural traditions . . . [and] the return visit often prompts a reevaluation or even a confrontation with past cultural practices and traditions" (9–10). In particular, such "modern day pilgrimages" to one's place of origin or ancestry represent searches for self and for cultural identities, emphasizing the autobiographical element in travel. Narrative renderings of return journeys are characterized by a specific chronotope, as the discourse oscillates between the narrator's past and present, and the spaces associated with them. My analysis will therefore concentrate on three parameters, the chronological, spatial, and identitary, and will attempt to point out how narratological categories can be aligned with concepts of postcolonial theory to grasp the ideological dimensions of these texts.[2] The narratological categories I shall be using are derived from Monika Fludernik's cognitively based model of a "natural narratology." Drawing on Jonathan Culler's concept of "naturalization"—that is, the reader's integration of a text into the framework of real-life experience—Fludernik distinguishes between five cognitive frames that "relate to basic perspectives on human experience and its narrative mediation" ("Cognitive Parameters" 246) and that therefore become functional in narrative discourse: action, telling, experiencing, viewing, and reflecting. Basic to Fludernik's understanding of narrative is the concept of "experientiality," which is described as an individualized rendering of experience as reflected in human consciousness: "[consciousness] both mediates narrativity and constitutes one of its signifiers" (*Towards* 374). The continuity of experience and narration that is thus central to Fludernik's narratological model seems to be particularly well suited to capture the characteristics of the kind of narratives discussed here, whose chronological fragmentation and blurring of diegetic and ontological levels frequently undermine clear-cut distinctions between narrating and experiencing selves or between authors and fictional narrators.

Concerning the autobiographical and/or autofictional narratives of Vassanji, Ondaatje, and Mistry, the three narrative parameters identified above are expressive of culturally determined forms of "self-fashioning" and of changing conceptions of the self. On the chronological level, the merging of "then" and "now" as "old" and "new" world identifications and allegiances interact and are mutually modified, creates a dynamic that counteracts static divisions into earlier (and possibly colonial) and later selves. This dynamic in turn may be conceived in terms of an interaction of the frames of "expe-

---

2. For a lucid survey of the interfaces between narratological analysis and postcolonial theory, see Birk and Neumann.

riencing" and "reflection," as proposed by Fludernik. Regarding the second parameter (space), her model offers a narratological complement to concepts of "embodied space," that is, of space as a location where human experience and consciousness take on material form, as topographical places acquire meaning according to the desires of those who inhabit it. In terms of Michel de Certeau's theory of lived space, for instance, spaces are "practised places," since "space occurs as the effect produced by the operations that orient it, situate it, [and] temporalize it" (115, 117). In the same way, and with regard to the third parameter, the emphasis on the experiential in narrative correlates with theoretical approaches to life-writing and especially to autobiography since the 1980s (cf. Löschnigg). These approaches have emphasized the role of narrative as a constituent factor in the creation of a sense of self, underlining either the cognitive function of narrative, which enables the subject to impose coherence on contingent experience (cf. Bruner, *Acts of Meaning, Making Stories*), or the fact that experience itself has a (pre)narrative structure, which makes the temporal dimension of experience a referent of autobiographical discourse (cf. Eakin, *Touching the World, How Our Lives*). In both cases, this means that narratives of self may no longer be regarded as the mimetic rendering by a previously constituted subject of itself as object, but as a staging of the construction of identity. As identity is created in narrative, it appears not as stable, but as processual and open.

M. G. Vassanji's *A Place Within* (2008) describes the author's several journeys to India since his first visit in 1993. Vassanji, who now lives in Toronto, was born into the Indian community of East Africa and grew up in Dar es Salaam and in Kenya. His "return journeys" as described in the book are thus not to a personal, but an ancestral homeland.[3] Significantly subtitled *Rediscovering India*, *A Place Within* renders Vassanji's explorations of what had been unknown and intimately known to him, through family traditions, at the same time:

> The India I would find, on this and later trips, seemed at once so startlingly familiar and yet so alien; so frustrating and yet so enlightening and humbling; so warm and friendly and yet so inhumanly cruel and callous. But above all, it spoke to me. It was as if a part of me which had lain dormant all the while had awakened and reclaimed me. (xvi f.)

---

3. In this sense, Vassanji's book may be compared to an earlier Indo-Canadian travelogue, Clark Blaise's and Bharati Mukherjee's *Days and Nights in Calcutta* (1977), their joint account of a one-year stay in India in 1973 and 1974. For Indian-born Mukherjee, this provided an opportunity to reconnect with her childhood; for her husband, an American raised in Canada, a chance to encounter his wife's origin.

As Vassanji makes clear, his motivation for "rediscovering" India is a search for identity, an identity in which the ancestral past and the writer's present appear to be inextricably intertwined:

> Why this obsession with the past? I can only conclude that it reflects the deep dissatisfaction of unfinished, incomplete migrations, a perpetual homelessness in my life. My colonial existence—in which memory and the past were trampled upon in a rush to better our lot—and the insecurities of an unorthodox communal culture, in the process of extinction and reinvention by the exigencies of globalized living and modern politics, have both created an uncontrollable and perhaps vain desire to know and record who I am. (53)

This passage emphasizes the sense that identity, whether individual or communal, is continuously in flux, as has been mentioned in the introductory part of this essay. Vassanji is looking for the Indian side or part of his identity, conscious that his multiple, transcultural self also comprises his Indian inheritance. As he tries to construct for himself this "Indian" identity that will also comprise a new self-confidence about the past, this process can be grasped in the "fluidity" of the narrative, its oscillating between past and present, and between different spaces—Canada, East Africa, and the various regions of India visited during the years. Moreover, *A Place Within* is suffused with the author's awareness that from the first time, his visits have been an ongoing search for a "real" spiritual home:

> A country you've seen in films; you're linked to by tradition, culture, language. "Where is it?" I asked myself, and kept asking throughout that visit. (xv)

> India ... seemed to do something to the soul; give it a certain ease, a sense of homecoming.... During each visit I sought it more, as intensely as ever. There was no satisfaction. (x)

Instead of positioning himself as a detached observer, Vassanji's attitude is characterized by an intensely personal, affective response to the country and its people: "What I did not understand, I was curious about; what was familiar comforted me; what seemed to disturb, I filed away for contemplation. In return I was treated like a long-lost cousin, a genuine returnee" (4).[4] Vassanji's narrative amounts to a dialogue with India, which is carried out through a

---

4. In any case, Vassanji is aware that he cannot keep up a distanced point of view: "On one hand I stood at an objective distance, watching and observing; and yet everything I saw I took

frequent changing of perspectives and through the constant interpenetration of the experiential and the reflective:

> There is so much of India, I tell myself. How does one get to it? I would like to reach out and touch it, it feels so close and familiar, yet there seems a glass cage around me. (7)

> [There are] moments when I feel pushed away; on one hand I receive the confidences and treatment due to an insider, one of them; then I become the outsider, someone who doesn't know and has to be protected. (10)

As Vassanji's narrative progresses, it engages with the outer and inner dimensions to which travel writing is continuously directed, aligning the "I" and the "eye" (cf. Moore-Gilbert 83) of the traveler in a discourse that firmly locates the emerging image of India in the consciousness of the author/narrator. Thus, in accordance with its title, the book truly renders India experientially as "a place within."

Vassanji's account is not structured chronologically, from his first Indian journey to the last within the time frame of the book, but according to individual regions and cities of India as visited and revisited by the author over the years: Delhi, the destination of the first trip, Simla and the Himalayas, Kerala, and Mumbai and Gujarat. Although there are indications as to the succession and dates of individual journeys, these are rather infrequent and unsystematic, which makes it difficult to establish a precise chronology. As a result of this blurring of chronological boundaries, however, the book's subject emerges as an "experiential" traveler, whose awareness of the diversity of India is continually enhanced as he "lives" and "relives" the places described.[5] The telescoping of past and present that results from Vassanji's identitary and cultural longings is thus enacted within wider and narrower "circles of identity" (cf. Lützeler 95): wider, as the author tries to recover his ancestral past, narrower as circumscribed by Vassanji's actual Indian experiences. In both instances, Canada serves as a vantage point, and a vanishing point in which spatial and chronological axes converge.

While the book contains a number of extensive historical excursuses, Vassanji also reminds the reader of the subjectivity of his notes: "My India was

---

personally, conscious all the time, This is India, this is the homeland, to which I am returning on behalf of my family after seventy, eighty, a hundred years" (3).

5. An interesting detail in this connection is that Vassanji's "recurrent visits to tombs [and other historical sites] alternate with travels by train, creating a dynamic of myth and modernity, stasis and movement" (Hornung 549).

essentially my own creation, what I put of myself in it" (ix f.) In addition, the book is full of stories and anecdotes about other people, and of references to other books, thus creating a web of lives and of texts that engulfs the narrator's individual experience. The resulting decentering of the narratorial self is reflected, on a concrete social level, by the fact that his ancestral background and command of Indian languages allow Vassanji to blend rather naturally into the mosaic of Indian society: "I am anonymous, for most people assume that I am from another part of India, this diverse subcontinent. I am as strange or familiar as anyone else" (162). This oscillation between proximity and distance, between Vassanji's identification with India and his East African and North American selves, accounts for the strong self-reflexive element of his discourse, a meta-narrative dimension that also includes an awareness of generic frames that might or might not apply: "a return after three generations, if one wanted to lend it epic proportions, an element of drama" (xiv). Whatever its generic associations may be, Vassanji's text subverts conventional first-person discourse through its chronotope, that is, its cyclical time structure and overlapping spaces, and the multiple intradiegetic voices. *A Place Within* is by no means the narrative of the temporary returnee flaunting his cosmopolitanism, as the self-consciously ironic toying with this notion indicates, but a narrative that disintegrates the narrator's self, as well as notions of center and margin, by delineating a communal past and present. Narratologically speaking, this disintegration of a unified narrative voice and the resulting chronological, spatial, and perspectival implications are effected through an interaction of frames of experiencing, telling, and reflecting.

A vital factor that enables Vassanji's perceptive approach to the multiplicity of India is the multicultural element in his Indian ancestry itself. Nominally a Muslim, Vassanji is a descendant of Gujarati Khojas, themselves "heirs to a syncretistic, mystical tradition uniting Hindu and Muslim elements" (303).[6] As he claims, it is the Khoja community's "syncretism, a happy combination of mystical and devotional Hinduism and Islam, without a thought to internal contradictions or to the mainstream traditions, [that] inevitably defined my relationship with India" (xii). Before this background, the deep-reaching religious and cultural divisions within India are experienced by Vassanji as particularly painful: "I imagined India as my ancestral homeland; to

6. In an interview, Vassanji commented on the "multiple cultural and racial ancestries" in his work: "It was natural because people are syncretistic, and there are various kinds of Islam, various kinds of Hinduism. On the east coast of Africa, you have the Bantu culture and the Arab culture, and the Swahili culture that was a mixture of these two. You have stories from the Middle East, from China, which were spawned within the local context. Plus we had English-style education, and our influence from American films, Hindi films, and so on. For me, that is really a wealth of experience that I treasure" (Ball 203–4).

witness, upon my arrival, its divisions running so deep was unsettling. It was to be asked to carry an open wound where perhaps only an itch had existed; to accept difference at the profoundest level" (83). The body imagery clearly expresses empathy and the narrator's identification with the predicaments of Indian society; indeed, Vassanji describes himself as someone "to whom the concept of the Partition comes as an offence on the self, because it asks me to choose, and it invites others to put a label on me" (200). Previously unaware of the extent of the divisions (as he states, in Africa all Asians were simply called "Wahindi," or Indians [238]), Vassanji is especially shocked by the extent of the religiously motivated violence and grieved by the fact that Gujarat, his ancestral home, has been one of its focal points (cf. the chapter "Gujarat: Down Ancestral Roads, Fearfully").

In an essay entitled "The Postcolonial Writer: Myth Maker and Folk Historian," published eight years before his first visit to the subcontinent, Vassanji emphasized that "in many instances, [the] reclamation of the past is the first serious act of writing. Having reclaimed it, having given himself a history, [the writer] liberates himself to write about the present" ("The Postcolonial Writer" 63). Giving "himself a history," however, enables Vassanji not only to write confidently about contemporary India but also to engage with "the ancestral mythical memory of India" (xi) and to put both aspects in perspective. In this context, the significance of the many historical and biographical narratives included in *A Place Within* becomes apparent, as they render the "social autobiography" (Schmidt 393) of India, its projections of national history and processes of self-ascertainment. Indeed, Vassanji's multilayered book illustrates that the construction of sociocultural identities rests to a large extent on memory-based narratives, which enable collective experiences in the sense of a transfer and appropriation of individual experiences among members of the community. The book renders a "multiplicity of histories" (Loomba 13), also in the sense that the author speaks as the representative of a family that has lived outside of India for many decades, and a transgression of binaries of "self" and "other" and of "center" and "margin" in the sense of a new "polybridity" (Bennett).[7] However, this "polybridity" does not signify rootlessness, as the desire to reconnect with India and thus to belong remains the motivation of the author's journeys.

---

7. Bennett uses the term "polybridity" to refer to the transcultural identities that are constituted through the interrelation of past and present and of various cultural spaces. With regard to Canadian literature, she argues that renderings of polybridity are enhanced by Canada's institutionalized multiculturalism, which "encourages individuals to see their identity simultaneously in terms of place of origin and of place of residency" (10).

Vassanji's multifaceted narrative in *A Place Within* results in a disintegration of the boundaries of the narrative instance, counteracting the subject-object relation of traditional travel writing and autobiographical discourse. It thereby also "challenge[s] the resolution of conflicts of identity which is traditionally understood to structure western male autobiography" (Moore-Gilbert xxii), rejecting a stable subject position in favor of an ongoing process of identity formation. In narratological terms, the blending of the experiential and of the reflective in Vassanji's book counters their distinction in traditional autobiography and travel writing, undermining projections of an autonomous and homogeneous self. With regard to ideological implications, especially in a postcolonial context, this commingling of frames and the resulting chronotope undermine the hegemonic significations of Western autobiographical discourse. If narratives of travel and migration normally render a quest for self in alien surroundings, and the attempt to achieve a sense of self-understanding,[8] the return journeys described by Vassanji blur the boundaries of self, emphasizing instead that the creation of a sense of identity is by nature continuous—in the words of Homi Bhabha, that "identity is never an a priori, nor a finished product; it is only ever the problematic process of access to an image of totality" (51). In Vassanji's text, postcolonial ideological concerns that are manifested in the narrator's refusal to position himself with regard to a "center" or a "margin" are not explicitly stated. Rather, they are conveyed through narrative technique, and can thus be grasped through narratological analysis. In particular, this refers to the way in which Vassanji subverts conventions of autobiographical discourse: the temporal and epistemological distance between narrating self and experiencing self becomes blurred as linear chronology is broken up and Vassanji's past and present mingle. In the same way, notions of causality (of one event leading to the other) and of teleology (approaching India with a purpose, namely that of "explaining" or even "appropriating" it) are undermined. As the narrator's self seems to blur in the communality created by multiple voices, the narrative voice becomes integrated into its object, as it were, experiencing India in its multiplicity rather than providing an individualized report. Thus, the text creates a continuity of experience and narration that can be grasped theoretically in terms of the cognitively based framework provided notably by Fludernik.

"Return journeys," although of a fictionalized nature, also figure prominently in the works of Michael Ondaatje. Born in Colombo, Sri Lanka, into a family of Dutch, Tamil, and Sinhalese descent in 1943,[9] Ondaatje went to Eng-

---

8. Cf. Holland and Huggan 12.

9. The plurality that characterizes the world of the author's family circle in the 1920s and 1930s is emphasized in the following passage: "Everyone was vaguely related and had Sinhalese,

land in 1954 in order to join his mother, who had gone there upon her separation from her husband. In 1962, he went to study in Canada, where he has since lived. *Running in the Family* (1981) explores Ondaatje's Sri Lankan family background in an imaginative and highly experimental manner, combining anecdotal family history, poems, and photographs in a search for the author's roots.[10] Chronologically, "the book is a composite of two return journeys to Sri Lanka, in 1978 and 1980," as the author states in an appendix ("Acknowledgments"; Ondaatje 205). In *Anil's Ghost* (2000), a novel on the civil war in Sri Lanka, the protagonist is a forensic anthropologist who, after having studied and worked in Britain and the United States, returns to her native island on a UN mission. Ondaatje's most recent novel to date, *The Cat's Table* (2011), renders events during a passage from Sri Lanka to Britain, and a youthful protagonist whose migration is clearly based on the author's own.

Ondaatje's fiction is characterized by multiple perspectives and a fragmented, nonlinear style, and this also applies to his fictionalized memoir *cum* travelogue, *Running in the Family*. The author's focus is on his father, Mervyn Ondaatje, and his drunken antics, and the book may ultimately be seen as an attempt to reconcile himself with the father he scarcely knew, as well as the father's world:

> I realised I would be travelling back to the family I had grown from—those relations from my parents' generation who stood in my memory like frozen opera. I wanted to touch them into words. . . . In my mid-thirties I realised I had slipped past a childhood I had ignored and not understood. . . . I was running to Asia and everything would change. (22)

Ondaatje's text does not refer to itself as an autobiography, yet the search for the father is also a search for self;[11] however, *Running in the Family* undermines conventional patterns of self-narration by ostensibly creating "authenticity," for instance through the photographs, while at the same time dissolving the contours of the autobiographical subject through the centrifugal tendencies of its discourse: "while obviously employing the discourse of (auto)biography, *Running in the Family* shades off into history, legend, myth, poetry—ultimately to become a poetics of the imagination" (Verhoeven 182). Ondaatje's narrative is

---

Tamil, Dutch, British and Burgher blood in them going back many generations" (Ondaatje 41).

10. Smaro Kamboureli refers to *Running in the Family* as a combination of "oral history, memoir, collection of anecdotes, historiographic metafiction, and biography" (80); on generic questions with regard to the book, see also Russell.

11. See Kamboureli: "Perhaps Ondaatje's ultimate autobiographical act is that he names his father as his other" (88).

based on sources, and the accounts of people listed in the "Acknowledgments." However, as Ondaatje adds: "While all these names may give an air of authenticity, I confess that the book is not a history, but a portrait or 'gesture.' And if those listed above disapprove of the fictional air I apologize and can only say that in Sri Lanka a well-told lie is worth a thousand facts" (206). As it is, the book blurs the borderlines between memoir, history, and fiction with a view to "an imaginative reconstruction of the past which insists that history *could have been* as Ondaatje presents it" (Heble 100).[12] If Ondaatje's text claims at one point that "history is always present" (85), it has been stated earlier that, on the other hand, "truth disappears with history" (53). As a specific rendering of the interrelation between the past and present in accounts of "return journeys," the present in *Running in the Family* functions as the site of a continuous reconstruction of the past: "No *story* is ever told just once. Whether a memory or funny hideous scandal, we will return to it an hour later and retell the story with additions and this time a few judgments thrown in. In this way history is organized" (26).

The blurring of boundaries in the book occurs also in the sense that it seems to question established notions of authorship: "A literary work is a communal act. And this book could not have been imagined, let alone conceived, without the help of many people" (205). Accordingly, *Running in the Family* (like Vassanji's *A Place Within*) features a plurality of voices by introducing a number of intradiegetic narrators (especially in the chapters "Lunch Conversation" and "Dialogues"), which means that the narratorial self, while it remains tangible as an integrating consciousness, is at the same time also subject to decentering and to being relegated to the periphery.[13] Another effect created by Ondaatje's rendering of an "unauthorized" and polyphonic world is the foregrounding of the process of writing and the projection of a "fictionalized" self that is changeable and open to revision.

---

12. I should still hesitate, however, to regard *Running in the Family* as a novel, as Birgit Neumann does. According to her, the book is a "metamnemonic novel" that reflects on the workings of memory. Neumann is certainly right about the "metamnemonic" dimension, and also when she argues that the book undermines an "autobiographical pact," for instance through paratextual "disclaimers." However, and in spite of the emphasis on anecdote and the "tall tale," *Running in the Family* remains moored in the realm of nonfiction, since Ondaatje's imaginative recovery of family history is essentially different from the intentional projection of a "possible world."

13. As Jeanne Delbaere has emphasized, this antihierarchic indeterminacy and obfuscating of a discursive center leads to a decidedly anarchic quality of Ondaatje's text: "Freed from the limitations of the individual point of view and of a controlling authorial voice [the text] bursts out in a carnivalesque plurality of voices which tell and retell *their own* stories without any inhibition" (99 f.).

If the formation of an individual sense of identity is based on the continuity established by narrative(s), then Ondaatje's fragmented and hybrid text points to the instability of self and the permeability of its boundaries. Combining and contrasting oral and written modes and traditions, and continually shifting between genres, *Running in the Family* becomes a self-conscious narrative that rejects the form of traditional autobiography, a form that for the postcolonial writer represents a "master narrative of Western hegemony" (Smith and Watson 59). Instead of construing the image of an autonomous and homogeneous individual, the book's heterogeneous structure serves to create a "subtle interplay between the singularity of perception and the archive of cultural representations" (Spinks 110). It thus also renders the "double temporality," wedged between a history of extraneous definition and present self-assertion, which Homi K. Bhabha has considered as characteristic of postcolonial experience (153). Rather than being conceived, however, as a clear-cut differentiation between the past and the present, this "double temporality" is rendered by Ondaatje in more dynamic terms, as both dimensions continuously interact and influence one another. The identitary implications of this interaction can therefore hardly be grasped in terms of the structuralist division into an "experiencing" and a "narrating" self. In contrast, Fludernik's category of the "experiential," which plays down the structuralist polarity between experiencer and narrator, seems more suited to accommodate the epistemological implications of an autobiographical narrative that, like Ondaatje's, transgresses discursive and generic conventions.

As is the case with Vassanji, the journeys to Sri Lanka in search of the past create in Ondaatje's narrative persona alternating feelings of proximity and distance ("I am the foreigner. I am the prodigal who hates the foreigner" [79]), and a cultural ambivalence that is suspended through the (poetic) imagination. Thus, for instance, the imaginative identification with the "Cinnamon Peeler" who is given a ride in Mervyn Ondaatje's car and also becomes the subject of a poem in his son's book also enables empathy and identification with the father, illustrating "the impossibility of spelling out the self in a monologic way" (Kamboureli 86). As one aim of the book is to investigate this self "in all its multiplicity" (Kanaganayakam 35), the narratorial self of *Running in the Family* is multidimensional and fragmentary at the same time, its components becoming visible in its interaction with others and with the past. Ondaatje's narrative thus deals with "alternative ways of inventing oneself, one's past, one's family—and of finding, or failing to find, a space between others' words, others' fictions, others' languages" (Huggan 117). As Ondaatje's/the narrator's "Canadian" identity is lost in the Sri Lankan family chronicle, the discourse suspends binaries of present and past, and of here and there (of "center" and "margin"), in an imaginative attempt at reclamation: "We own the country we grow up in, or we are aliens and invaders" (81).

Rather than struggling with the colonial past of Sri Lanka, and with the way this may have affected the writer's family, Ondaatje embraces cultural hybridity and the dual perspective of "prodigal" (or returnee) and "foreigner." The nonlinear, polyphonic discourse of *Running in the Family* "reproduces the dislocation of a subject unable to recognize itself in the received forms of colonial historiography" (Spinks 112). In the postcolonial context of the book, therefore, the decentering of the autobiographical subject also appears as subversive and empowering, as it undermines notions of Eurocentric dominance that have been associated with Western autobiographical discourse. Also, Ondaatje juxtaposes his own (fictionalized) portrait of Sri Lanka to the fictions of Ceylon as created by the colonizers. Narratological analysis, and especially the alignment of cognitively based frames of the "experiential" with concepts of the narrative constitution of a sense of identity, will bring to the fore the ideological implications of the book's structures and techniques.

The theme of alienation, which Ondaatje thus renders as an ultimately productive force, also figures prominently in Rohinton Mistry's short story "Swimming Lessons," the last in his collection *Tales from Firozsha Baag* (1987). The story is narrated by Kersi Boyce, a young Parsi from Mumbai who has recently immigrated to Toronto, and it captures very powerfully the sense of disorientation and the subliminal desire to return that may characterize the situation of the migrant. Like his narrator, Rohinton Mistry was born into the Zoroastrian community of Mumbai/Bombay in 1952 and immigrated to Canada in 1975, where he has lived in Toronto. In the linked short stories of *Tales From Firozsha Baag*, he connects both cities by making his fictional alter ego Kersi the "author," as it were, of the whole collection. In this sense, the stories represent Kersi's (and Mistry's) return journey, here an entirely imaginative one, to his place of origin. In "Swimming Lessons," the newly arrived Kersi leads an isolated life in an apartment complex similar to the one inhabited by his family back in India. The plot of the story centers on Kersi's attempt to take swimming lessons at a nearby gymnasium, a highly symbolic activity suggesting his attempts at "staying afloat" in his new surroundings. Initially, these attempts seem to fail as Kersi meets with a number of obstacles (in one instance, he is confronted with outward racism) and seems to be unable, at first, to open himself up to his new life. Eventually, however, he wins through from an emigrant perspective, or a perspective whose main focus is backward to his origins, to an immigrant perspective, or a readiness to adapt to his new sociocultural environment. Kersi's in-between state during much of the story is rendered by the many shifts of the narrative between the present and the past, that is, between Toronto and Mumbai, where his parents are eagerly awaiting news from their son. What they eventually receive is a book of his stories, the very *Tales from Firozsha Baag,* a metalepsis that strikes home the intimate connection between fact and fiction in much immigrant writing:

> The last story they liked the best of all, because it had the most in it about Canada, and now they felt they knew at least a little bit, even if it was a very little bit, about his day-to-day life in his apartment; and Father said if he continues to write about such things he will become popular because I am sure they are interested there in reading about life through the eyes of an immigrant, it provides a different viewpoint; the only danger is if he changes and becomes so much like them that he will write like one of them and lose the important difference. (Mistry 248)

Rendering the perspective of the young man's parents, this passage reflects on the complexities of immigrant writing through its ironic play on difference and acculturation, on integration and opposition and on self and other. As in the books by Vassanji and Ondaatje, Canada provides a point of departure from which Kersi transcends places and chronological strictures, looking back on his old world to see how it intersects with Canada.

As in Vassanji and Ondaatje, the ideological implications of Mistry's fictional "return journey" to Mumbai in the *Firozsha Baag* stories are mediated through narrative structures, through the interrelation of past and present and of highly semanticized spaces like the multicultural apartment complex or the swimming pool, whose sterility and discipline provide a stark contrast to the dirt, anarchy, and richness in ritual associations of Mumbai's Chaupatty Beach, where the narrator's first unsuccessful attempts at learning how to swim took place. In "Swimming Lessons," Mistry illustrates the effects of hegemonic discourse, namely stereotyped conceptions of the "other," and the reduction of individuals to representatives of their ethnicity or race. According to Frantz Fanon's well-known argument, these stereotyped projections are internalized by the subaltern subject, who is thus alienated from himself and is in consequence driven to assimilation with the dominant culture (cf. Fanon 109). However, Kersi breaks out of this cycle as he comes to reconcile, on the basis of a newly won self-confidence, his past and present. As a writer, he has imaginatively re-created and thus reclaimed his past through the preceding stories. On this basis, he is also shedding stereotyped notions of his host country. The "experiential" interconnection of then and now, and of related spaces, makes for an overlap in which essentializing or dichotomous concepts of identity and alterity are dissolved, and identity is continuously formed anew. As in Vassanji and Ondaatje, narrative technique thus prevents the creation of binaries that may help to further ideologically motivated compartmentalizations. The image of self that emerges in these texts is not that of a hyphenated identity ("Indian-Canadian," in the case of Mistry), but a hybrid, transcultural one. Again, the ideological implications of Mistry's narrative, and the fact that narrative structures are not inconsequent with regard to such implications, can be shown by means of narratological analysis. Such analysis rests on the conception of autobiography as the construction of a version of self through narrative. Whatever version emerges, be it the image (!) of a homogeneous self, as in "classical" Western autobiography, or the projection of fluid, changeable, transcultural selves, as in the texts analyzed, the "construction process" can (and should) be analyzed in narratological terms in order to understand better the conceptions of self behind it. In the case of my postcolonial texts, the suitable categories, I argue, are not those of structuralist narratology so much (narrating vs. experiencing self) as models of cognitive frames proposed by "natural narratology" (Fludernik) sketched in the early portion of the essay.

Emphasizing the continuity of experience and narration through the chronotope of their texts, and through the interpenetration of frames of experiencing and reflection, Vassanji, Ondaatje, and Mistry suspend the representational function of autobiographical discourse, which rests on the privileged position of a narratorial subject as against its object. In accordance with Edward Said's argument that "human identity is not only not natural and stable, but constructed, and occasionally even invented outright" ("East Isn't East" 3), their texts render selves that are open to revision and reconstruction. One may also want to draw a parallel to Said's essay "Permission to Narrate," where Said distinguishes between what he refers to as "vision" on the one hand and the temporal dynamics of narrative on the other. "Visions," according to Said, are those representations of other cultures that emphasize the static and homogeneous, projecting the image of an unchanging nature of these societies. In contrast to such "essentializing" "visions," Said argues, narrative represents a mode that actively engages with history and thus underlines the possibility of change. The works here discussed reject static and categorizing "visions" (in the sense of Said) for the dynamic of (again, in Said's sense) "narrative," as the narrators of Vassanji, Ondaatje, and Mistry seem to be moving within circumscriptions of identity that the transcultural subject may leave, replace, expand, or diminish. Identity thus becomes the result of a conscious positioning, and the search for roots takes place within an enriching intercultural context. What characterizes the texts here analyzed is an experiential reliving of the past, which is manifested in the successive abandoning and resumption of "identities" as the temporary returns, actual or imaginary, to individual or ancestral homelands enable new histories and trajectories of self. Narratological analysis will help to profile the inward and outward relocations and (re)definitions involved by providing a framework to capture their temporal dimension. In particular, the category of experientiality appears congenial to the continuity of these processes, and will therefore cast some light on what Iain Chambers refers to as "the making of identities in movement" (82).

Transcending binaries of "center" and "margin" through the chronological structures as well as spatial and identitary associations of their narratives, Vassanji, Ondaatje, and Mistry establish identitary parameters that subvert and reject hegemonic discourses, in particular the ideological implications of "traditional" Western autobiography and travel writing. Circumscribed along narrative lines, identity in their works is not representational but performative, and is characterized by a transcultural dimension that results from the fact that identity is conceived simultaneously in terms of the narrators' "old" and "new" worlds. As I have tried to show, this transculturality and its ideological significance, which are constituted through narrative, can be grasped through narratological analysis, in particular through the application of cognitively based models like Monika Fludernik's, which emphasize the experiential dimension of narrative. Rendering experientiality through the interconnectedness of experience and reflection, the texts here analyzed represent "return journeys" in search of a self that is continuously to be (re)discovered. In any case, it is never confirmed or stable, as the conventional structure of autobiography or of observational travelogues would imply. For the postcolonial pilgrim through time and place, "the truth is elsewhere: the true place is always some distance, some time away" (Bauman 20). Indeed, as Vassanji says, "the journey is endless" (*A Place Within* 3).

What I have tried to show in this essay is that postcolonial theory (in particular its conceptions of self as fluid and processual) and narratological approaches that emphasize the narrative construction of self and the experientiality of narrative are in fact congruent and mutually supportive, and that bringing these together will highlight the ideological significance of texts. The multifaceted and fragmented narratives here discussed emphasize the fact that narrative structures as such may act as cultural and ideological signifiers. In particular, this applies to autobiographical discourse and its chronotope. In contrast to conventional autobiography or travelogues, which are marked by linear chronology, causality, and teleology, the narratives by Vassanji, Ondaatje, and Mistry undermine traditional expectations as to structural coherence or "authorship." Ideologically, therefore, they may be seen as countering the hegemonic implications postcolonial critics have associated with "Western" self-narration. Narratologically speaking, postcolonial writing on travel and migration often challenges a universalist and ahistorical understanding of narrative structures (as characteristic of structuralist narratology), implying the necessity to accommodate cultural and historical (and the resulting ideological) dimensions. With regard to the texts here analyzed, narratology may thus assume the role of an interface between textual analysis and context-oriented approaches by proposing "models that are jointly formal and functional—models attentive both to the text and to the context of stories" (Herman 8).

WORKS CITED

Ashcroft, Bill, Gareth Griffiths, and Helen Tiffin. *The Empire Writes Back: Theory and Practice in Post-Colonial Literatures*. 2nd ed. London: Routledge, 2002.

Ball, John Clement. "Taboos." Interview with M. G. Vassanji. *The Power to Bend Spoons: Interviews with Canadian Novelists*. Ed. Beverley Daurio. Toronto: The Mercury Press, 1998. 200–209.

Bauman, Zygmunt. "From Pilgrim to Tourist—Or a Short History of Identity." *Questions of Cultural Identity*. Ed. Stuart Hall and Paul du Gay. London: Sage, 1996. 18–36.

Bennett, Donna. "Getting Beyond Binaries: Polybridity in Contemporary Canadian Literature." *Moveable Margins. The Shifting Spaces of Canadian Literature*. Ed. Chelva Kanaganayakam. Toronto: TSAR Publications, 2005. 9–25.

Bhabha, Homi K. *The Location of Culture*. London: Routledge, 1994.

Birk, Hanne, and Birgit Neumann. "*Go-Between*: Postkoloniale Erzähltheorie." *Neue Ansätze in der Erzähltheorie*. Ed. Ansgar Nünning and Vera Nünning. Trier: WVT, 2002. 115–52.

Bruner, Jerome. *Acts of Meaning*. Cambridge: Harvard University Press, 1990.

———. *Making Stories*. Cambridge: Harvard University Press, 2003.

Chambers, Iain. *Migrancy, Culture, Identity*. London: Routledge, 1994.

Culler, Jonathan. *Structuralist Poetics. Structuralism, Linguistics and the Study of Literature*. London: Routledge & Kegan Paul, 1975.

de Certeau, Michel. *The Practice of Everyday Life*. Trans. Steven Rendall [*Arts du faire*]. Berkeley: University of California Press, 1984.

Delbaere, Jeanne. "Magic Realism: The Energy of the Margins." *Postmodern Fiction in Canada*. Ed. Hans Bertens and Theo D'haen. Amsterdam: Rodopi, 1992. 75–104.

Eakin, Paul John. *How Our Lives Become Stories: Making Selves*. Ithaca: Cornell University Press, 1999.

———. *Touching the World: Reference in Autobiography*. Princeton: Princeton University Press, 1992.

Fanon, Frantz. *Black Skins, White Masks*. 1952. London: Pluto Press, 1986.

Fludernik, Monika. "Natural Narratology and Cognitive Parameters." *Narrative Theory and the Cognitive Sciences*. Ed. David Herman. Stanford: Center for the Study of Language and Information, 2003. 243–67.

———. *Towards a "Natural" Narratology*. London: Routledge, 1996.

Foucault, Michel. "Afterword: The Subject and Power." *Michel Foucault: Beyond Structuralism and Hermeneutics*. Ed. H. L. Dreyfus and P. Rabinov. London: Harvester Wheatsheaf, 1982. 208–64.

Hall, Stuart. "Cultural Identity and Diaspora." *Identity: Community, Culture, Difference*. Ed. Jonathan Rutherford. London: Lawrence and Wishart, 1990. 222–37.

———. "The Question of Cultural Identity." *Modernity: An Introduction to Modern Societies*. Ed. Stuart Hall, David Held, Don Hubert, and Kenneth Thompson. Malden: Blackwell, 2011. 596–632.

Heble, Ajay. "Michael Ondaatje and the Problem of History." *Clio* 19.2 (1990): 97–110.

Herman, David. "Introduction: Narratologies." *Narratologies: New Perspectives on Narrative Analysis*. Ed. David Herman. Columbus: Ohio State University Press, 1999. 1–30.

Holland, Patrick, and Graham Huggan. *Tourists with Typewriters: Critical Reflections on Contemporary Travel Writing*. Ann Arbor: University of Michigan Press, 2000.

Hornung, Alfred. "Transcultural Life-Writing." *The Cambridge History of Canadian Literature*. Ed. Coral Ann Howells and Eva-Marie Kröller. Cambridge: Cambridge University Press, 2009. 536–55.

Huggan, Graham. "Exoticism and Ethnicity in Michael Ondaatje's *Running in the Family*." *ECW* 57 (1995): 116–27.

Kambourelli, Smaro. "The Alphabet of the Self: Generic and Other Slippages in Michael Ondaatje's *Running in the Family*." *Reflections: Autobiography and Canadian Literature*. Ed. Klaus Peter Stich. Ottawa: University of Ottawa Press, 1988. 79–91.

Kanaganayakam, Chelva. "A Trick with a Glass: Michael Ondaatje's South Asian Connection." *Canadian Literature* 132 (1992): 33–42.

Loomba, Ania. *Colonialism/Postcolonialism*. London: Routledge, 1998.

Löschnigg, Martin. "Postclassical Narratology and the Theory of Autobiography." *Postclassical Narratology: Approaches and Analyses*. Ed. Jan Alber and Monika Fludernik. Columbus: Ohio State University Press, 2010. 255–74.

Lützeler, Paul Michael. "Vom Ethnozentrismus zur Multikultur: Europäische Identität heute." *Multikulturalität: Tendenzen, Probleme, Perspektiven*. Ed. Michael Kessler and Jürgen Wertheimer. Tübingen: Stauffenburg, 1995. 91–105.

Mistry, Rohinton. *Tales from Firozsha Baag*. 1987. London: Faber & Faber, 1992.

Moore-Gilbert, Bart. *Postcolonial Life Writing. Culture, Politics and Self-Representation*. London: Routledge, 2009.

Neumann, Birgit. "Der metamnemonische Roman: Formen und Funktionen der Metaerinnerung am Beispiel von Michael Ondaatje's *Running in the Family* (1982)." *Metaisierung in Literatur und anderen Medien: Theoretische Grundlagen—Historische Perspektiven—Metagattungen—Funktionen*. Ed. Janine Hauthal, Julijana Nadj, Ansgar Nünning, and Henning Peters. Berlin: de Gruyter, 2007. 303–20.

Nünning, Ansgar. "Towards a Cultural and Historical Narratology: A Survey of Diachronic Approaches, Concepts and Research Projects." *Anglistentag 1999 Mainz: Proceedings*. Ed. Bernhard Reitz and Sigrid Rieuwerts. Trier: WVT, 2000. 345–73.

Ondaatje, Michael. *Running in the Family*. 1982. London: Picador, 1984.

Oxfeld, Ellen, and Lynellyn D. Long. "Introduction: An Ethnography of Return." *Coming Home? Refugees, Migrants, and Those Who Stayed Behind*. Ed. Lynellyn Long and Ellen Oxfeld. Philadelphia: University of Pennsylvania Press, 2004: 1–15.

Russell, John. "Travel Memoir as Nonfiction Novel: Michael Ondaatje's *Running in the Family*." *ARIEL* 22.2 (1991): 23–40.

Said, Edward. "East Isn't East: The Impending End of the Age of Orientalism." *Times Literary Supplement* 4792 (1995): 3–6.

———. "Permission to Narrate." *Journal of Palestine Studies* 13.3 (1984): 27–48.

Schmidt, Siegfried J. "Gedächtnis—Erzählen—Identität." *Mnemosyne: Formen und Funktionen kultureller Erinnerung*. Ed. Aleida Assmann and Dietrich Hardt. Frankfurt a. M.: Fischer, 1991. 378–98.

Smith, Sidonie, and Julie Watson. *Reading Autobiography: A Guide for Interpreting Life Narratives*. Minneapolis: University of Minnesota Press, 2010.

Spinks, Lee. *Michael Ondaatje*. Manchester: Manchester University Press, 2009.

Vassanji, M[oyez] G[ulamhussein]. *A Place Within: Rediscovering India*. 2008. [Toronto]: Anchor Canada, 2009.

———. "The Postcolonial Writer: Myth Maker and Folk Historian." *A Meeting of Streams. South Asian Canadian Literature*. Ed. M. G. Vassanji. Toronto: TSAR Publications, 1985. 63–68.

Verhoeven, Wil. "(De)Facing the Self: Michael Ondaatje and (Auto)Biography." *Postmodern Fiction in Canada*. Ed. Hans Bertens and Theo D'haen. Amsterdam: Rodopi, 1992. 181–200.

CHAPTER 3

The Legibility of Things

Objects and Public Histories in N. S. Madhavan's Litanies of the Dutch Battery

UDAYA KUMAR

THE FORTUNES of things in the novel have been a matter of interested discussion among narratologists. Roland Barthes tried to comment on their presence through his concepts of "functions" and "indices," as well as through a further, finer distinction between "indices" and "informants" ("Structural Analysis" 88–97). Objects, attached to smaller functional units of action or nuclei, may contribute to the advancement of the plot, as in the chance appearance of a material piece of evidence in a detective story, or serve as indices to participate in building up an atmosphere where fog lights or an overcoat work as indices of weather. Objects crop up in Barthes's analysis of the sequencing of functional units, where his favorite examples are from Ian Fleming. The offer of a light from a cigarette lighter may be a mere element in "a logical succession of trifling acts which go to make up the offer of a cigarette," but James Bond's declining it may open it up to the plane of meanings by signaling his instinctive suspicion of a booby-trapped device (102).

Barthes shifted his gaze from these instrumentalities of the object to recognize a dimension of their existence that has little to do with the plot or atmosphere. In "Structural Analysis," he had already identified a set of elements that he called "informants"; distinct from functions and indices, these were narrative units that did not refer us to signifieds but merely offered us information, authenticating the "reality of the referent" and thus embedding "fiction in the real world" (96). Later, in his essay "The Reality Effect," Barthes suggested that most narratives include a number of "useless details" that resist assimilation into economies of meaning; these were there precisely to produce a sense of reality (141–48). The barometer in Flaubert's description of Mme. Aubain's room in "A Simple Heart" or the "gentle knock at a little door," mentioned by Michelet in his account of Charlotte Corday's execution were elements of this kind. Their ultimate function, for Barthes, was to signify the "real" without explicitly announcing it:

> Flaubert's barometer, Michelet's little door finally say nothing but this: *we are the real*; it is the category of "the real" (and not its contingent contents) which is then signified; in other words, the very absence of the signified, to the advantage of the referent alone, becomes the very signifier of realism: the *reality effect* is produced, the basis of that unavowed verisimilitude which forms the aesthetic of all the standard works of modernity. (148; emphasis in original)

It is clear that in focusing on "Reality Effect," Barthes was highlighting a commitment that the novel from its inception displayed toward a sense of reality where the semiologically undigested stuff of the world made its indispensible presence felt. Things appearing in their material tangibility, devoid of symbolic value, make up much of the "stuffness" in novels. It is perhaps not accidental that the emergence of the novel coincided with an unprecedented expansion of objects in people's everyday lives. Baudrillard, in *The System of Objects*, notes a shift from an older symbolic system to a new functional system in the modern configuration of objects. Commodity exchange has been an inevitable frame for understanding the modern proliferation of objects; foregrounding the structure of the commodity makes possible a new form of visible existence for objects. However, the move from an analytic of the object to the logic of commodity and consumption may be too quick: this may attenuate the material presence of objects and regard them solely in terms of circuits of value and exchange. Conversely, it is possible to suggest that an unassimilable remainder that escapes analysis is intrinsic to the commodity structure; the mysticism of the commodity, one may argue, works precisely by producing illegible excess as a dimension of the object.

Does this story hold globally? How about postcolonial societies with a different historical relationship to capitalist production, commodity culture, and novelistic narration? Could it be the case that the history of the novel—a form that developed in the context of the colonial encounter—reveals a different locus for objects, a different grammar for their legibility?[1] This essay is about the presencing of objects in a contemporary novel from Kerala and its complex negotiation with questions of narrative significance. N. S. Madhavan's Malayalam novel *Lanthanbatheriyile Luthiniyakal* (2003; English translation: *Litanies of the Dutch Battery,* 2010) sketches an archaeological scene where fictional lives, public histories, intersect with a world of objects and documents.

The novel in Malayalam, right from its inception, had close transactions with a history of contemporary objects. In early novels, things appeared as vital tools for differentiating characters and attitudes. O. Chandu Menon's *Indulekha* (1889) contrasted a rich, unintelligent Nambutiri Brahmin landlord's collection of things made in gold with the educated Nayar heroine's intelligent and tasteful restraint in the choice, arrangement, and use of objects. While the Nambutiri surrounded himself in public by the dazzling glow of gold, the heroine reduced gold to no more than a border on the impeccably white clothes she wore, fresh and clean, every day. The heroine's favored things were not clothes or ornaments: they were printed books, the piano, the tools of embroidery work, and tastefully chosen modern pieces of furniture. At first this may appear as a distinction between tradition and modernity, but for Chandu Menon the dazzle of the Brahmin's gold was no true representation of traditional object culture at its best; it stood for the decay and dissipation of tradition and its values. The vanity in owning and showing off personal possessions was matched by the Brahmin's ignorance about those objects, their cultural value and proper use. The novelist placed opposite to this the educated upper-caste young woman's knowing, tasteful, distinctive use of things. This did not involve a rejection of traditional objects: the heroine wore Indian clothes, played not only the piano but also the violin in a south Indian classical style. The contrasting attitudes of dazzle and restraint had deeper, more extended resonances: in *Indulekha* they allegorized opposed attitudes to sexual desire and marital practices.[2]

Things that appear in the fictional world of *Indulekha* and other early novels in Malayalam may not merely be a revelatory prosthetic attached to character subjects. In fact, we might more usefully regard characters as props in the overall narrative machinery of novels. In the world conjured up for experience and judgment in *Indulekha,* modern objects are associated with a sense

---

1. For a discussion of objects in the postcolonial context, see Appadurai. For a discussion of representations of interiors and objects in the nineteenth-century Bengali novel, see Chaudhuri.

2. For a detailed discussion of objects and various modes of seeing them presented in the novel and how they could be linked to themes in contemporary debates on sexual desire and marital practices, see Kumar, "Seeing and Reading."

of joy and marvel. Late nineteenth-century Kerala, with its relatively weak commodity culture and its sense of the provincial, appears in early novels as an inegalitarian world of things: modern objects are endowed with the talismanic power of modernity; they are harbingers of a larger, busier world. It is the modern commodity, rather than the Nambutiri Brahmin's golden things, that dazzle the narrator. Descriptions of things in the new cities of colonial India send the narrative into paroxysms of pleasure. When *Lakshmikesavam*, a novel written in the wake of *Indulekha*, describes a family from Malabar enjoying the sights of the Madras city, shops, with their plethora of commodities, serve as the primary pleasure point:

> In shops—some forty metres long and twenty-twenty five metres broad and thirty metres high, constructed in three or four floors—one floor has very expensive cloth of diverse kinds and colours piled up bundle after bundle; on another floor, various sorts of clocks, watches and timepieces in one section, soaps such as Turbin, Pears, Glycerine and Carbolic, and peppermint cakes, biscuits and sweets, and different kinds of paper, pens and pencils piled up in another section, painted mirrors, plain mirrors, wall shades displayed beautifully and globes of many colours and beautiful lustres hung from ceilings in yet another section. (P. Menon 139)

Description whirls into a dizzying vertigo of objects. The shop is a sort of exhibition of modern things, and its primary curatorial principle is excess and disorder: things appear replicated, diverse, piled up. Their dizzying proliferation makes narrative lose its grip on syntactic structures: sentences, like the shop, begin to expand and burst at their seams. The valorization of Indulekha's personal study with "a few English objects, beautifully arranged" as a picture of delightful order has its background perhaps in the mind-boggling magical plenitude of mass-manufactured things offered for sale.

This disordered abundance, classified but not arranged, is itself the image of what may be called a "historical" experience. It marks a time of modernity, measured in terms of the effective distance between the colonial city and the province. These objects acquire their dignity and value in a space of newness and proliferation. "Each 'sight' is as novel as the next; each as valuable," says G. Arunima, "And in that lies the fact that despite colonialism, large parts of India were entirely unaware of the commodities of western everyday life. This allows for the same kind of breathlessness while seeing peppermint sweets, biscuits or soaps to teak furniture and precious jewellery."

An experience of shops as a space for promiscuity of objects appears part of the experience of modernity and the design of realism in colonial metropolises in the West as well. It is not always under the sign of newness that objects are contemplated. The opening chapter of Balzac's *The Wild Ass's Skin* shows the protagonist entering an antique shop, intending to give a treat to his senses and spend the interval till nightfall in bargaining over curiosities:

> At first sight the show-rooms offered him a chaotic medley of human and divine works. Crocodiles, apes and stuffed boas grinned at stained-glass windows, seemed to be about to snap at carved busts, to be running after lacquer-ware or to be clambering up chandeliers. A Sèvres vase on which Madame Jacquetot had painted Napoleon was standing next to a sphinx dedicated to Sesotris. The beginnings of creation and the events of yesterday were paired off with grotesque good humour. A roasting-jack was posed on a monstrance, a Republican sabre on a medieval arquebus. Madame du Barry, painted in pastel by Latour, with a star on her head, nude and enveloped in cloud, seemed to be concupiscently contemplating an Indian chibouk and trying to divine some purpose in the spirals of smoke which were drifting towards her.
>
> Instruments of death, poniards, quaint pistols, weapons with secret springs were hobnobbing with instruments of life: porcelain soup-tureens, Dresden china plates, translucent porcelain cups from China, antique salt-cellars, comfit-dishes from feudal time. An ivory ship was sailing under full canvas on the back of an immovable tortoise. (34)

Jacques Rancière drew special attention to this passage not only as a space where heterogeneous objects came together but also as revealing a new configuration of signs and signification:

> The mixture of the curiosity shop made all objects and images equal. Further, it made each object a poetic element, a sensitive form that is a fabric of signs as well. All these objects wore a history on their body. They were woven of signs that summarized an era and a form of civilization. And their random gathering made a huge poem, each verse of which carried the infinite virtuality of new stories, unfolding those signs in new contexts. It was the encyclopaedia of all the times and all the worlds, the compost in which the fossils of them were blended together. (162)

Rancière saw in this new habitat of objects a fundamental feature of literature in the modern sense of the term, the sense in which we understand this discursive institution now. This new conception of literature, which emerged alongside the realist novel, rested on the convergence of three things: a writing that was indifferent to subject matter and status of addressees, a practice of symptomatic reading that interpreted the muteness of the writing by focusing on the things made perceptible through that silence, and the opposed ways of political reading this practice gave rise to. Rancière suggested that in this new mode, literature appeared as a "historical mode of visibility of writing, a specific link between a system of meaning of words and a system of visibility of things" (155).

In this new regime of writing, things acquired a new salience. In their muteness, they "wore on their very bodies the testimony of their own history. And that testimony was more faithful than any discourse" (160). Rancière identified this propensity at the core of the realist novel. "Its principle," he says, "was not reproducing facts as they are, as critics claimed. It was displaying the so-called world of prosaic activities as a huge Poem—a huge fabric of signs and traces, of obscure signs that had to be displayed, unfolded and deciphered" (162). The realist novelist is somewhat like the natural historian Cuvier:

> He displays the fossils and hieroglyphs of history and civilization. He unfolds the poeticality, the historicity written on the body of ordinary things. In the old representational regime, the frame of intelligibility of human actions was patterned on the model of the casual rationality of voluntary actions, linked together and aimed at definite ends. Now, when meaning becomes a "mute" relation of signs to signs, human actions are no longer intelligible as successful or unsuccessful pursuits of aims by willing characters. And characters are no longer intelligible through their ends. They are intelligible through the clothes they wear, the stones of their houses or the wallpaper of their rooms. (163)

The reading of mute things ushered in by the realist novel and the new regime of literature in France may fail to account for the enchantment of new objects found in early postcolonial novels. While characters, as we saw in the case of *Indulekha*, are revealed through economies of objects, muteness of things does not strike us as a prominent feature: objects are incorporated into a rhetorical system, and often placed in the limelight of narrative attention and comment. The proliferation of commodities and their accelerated consumption were the preconditions for the existence of the shop of antiquities in Balzac; there, amidst haphazardly arranged objects from diverse civilizations, the protagonist finds the magic talismanic skin that combines the promise of fulfillment of all desires with an irrevocable threat of death. In the weak commodity culture from which novels like *Indulekha* and *Lakshmikesavam* emerged, the magic resides not in the unique object hidden in the disorderly profusion of the antique shop; it is to be found in the modern shop where not merely the objects but their piling up, their sheer excess, conjures up a moment of magic fulfillment. Not singularity but recursiveness and multiplication marks the marvelous economy of new objects. In these novels, history appears not in the survival of objects from earlier times and in the eloquent marks they bear on their mute bodies; its presence is felt rather in the newness, the unmarked surface of modern things. In their disconnection from an older thing-scape, these new objects announce their having come from another world. Historicity appears less as trace than as advent.

The novels considered so far were written more than a hundred years ago, at the dawn of new commodity culture in places like Kerala. Let us now turn to a later moment, when such modern objects no longer gleam in their newness, having accumulated on their surfaces inscriptions of use and affect. What happens when they have acquired a history, and that too a history that does not rehearse the trajectory of objects in the Western world? In other words, what is there between objects and postcolonial memory? These questions take us to N. S. Madhavan's *Litanies of Dutch Battery* (hereafter, *Litanies*).

Like Balzac, Madhavan too presents a shop—in fact, two shops—that helps us sense the grammar of things in the novel:

> Lonan's grocery was in the first room. He sold miscellaneous goods in small quantities in miniscule wraps, to daily wage labourers and fisherfolk. The shop stank of jute strands, with which he tied the wraps. School kids used to crowd Wilfred's shops in the next room. Besides the supplies of ink tablets, four-lined books and shiny nibs for dip pens, the shop had a bunch of glass containers filled with crescent-shaped orange candies sprinkled with white flour and dark molasses candies, sold at four per anna. (68–69)

Two shops, two kinds of objects, two sorts of customers. The first shop does not particularize things—they remain miscellaneous goods, hidden from our sight by the miniscule wraps and the jute strings with which these are tied. In fact, the wraps and strings are the only objects we get to see there. Wilfred's shop next door, in contrast, spurs naming and description: ink tablets, four-lined books, shiny nibs, dip pens, and glass containers. These culminate in the lingering invocation of "crescent-shaped orange candies sprinkled with white flour" and "dark molasses candies." The poetry of things in the Dutch Battery is different from that in Balzac's antique shop. Lonan's and Wilfred's shops are not storehouses of antiquities: things there are not repositories of time; they are ordinary objects of everyday use. Yet the narrative tarries over them with tacit affective attention. Interestingly, this attention is not a result of internal focalization: narration here is not determined by the perspective and feelings of any character.[3] Jessica is the ostensible narrator of *Litanies,* but the narration is not always focalized on her as character. It often moves beyond the limits of narrative information available to her to serve as a site of more generalized documentation and recall. We need to differentiate this from the more "mimetic" passages in which Jessica appears as a child growing up in the late 1950s and early 1960s. The gentle suffusion of affect in the description of things in Wilfred's shop appears to belong to the plane of diegesis. Where, then, does this special tone of recollected descriptions in *Litanies* come from? What do we make of its existence as a diegetic principle?

The answer to this question is enmeshed with the practices and principles of remembrance and location in *Litanies*. The novel names itself by its location: Dutch Battery is a fictional island—a miniscule landmass imagined into the confluence of Periyar river and the Arabian Sea near Fort Kochi, but vividly pointed out to the reader in a map at the beginning of the novel. Yet this is not really a matter of geography; place is more deeply a matter of time, history. Surrounded by water on all sides, everything that was originally not in Dutch Battery, including its inhabitants, had to arrive from outside. History too belongs to this list of imports, yet it permeates the island and acquires a strange sense of materiality, a sort of thingness. The island, however, is also a site of premature archaeology:

> Our delta, called Dutch Battery, was young. Its soil not hardened yet. With a bit of digging one would find shards of clams and shells of not-so-primordial marine organisms. Dig a little deeper and you would find brackish water and soggy sea sand. Not many people dared to excavate further. If they did, they might have found chests filled with Venetian ducats guarded by ghosts of black slaves, baby dragons crawling out of Chinese silk pennants, enamelled dinner china that had belonged to Carmelite priests, burnt altars of chapels set on fire by the Dutch, and other such things. History was the most important commodity that our delta imported. (2–3)

Not only natural history, but human incursions into the island too, acquire texture and taste to be remembered with one's mouth. Three colonial rules, each a hundred and fifty years long, like rings on the island's body, but also like three slices of a pie, each with a different taste: "the first piece had the hot peppery bite of the Portuguese, the second had the tangy sourness of the

---

3. For an initial formulation of the concept of narrative focalization, see Genette (189–94). For further discussion, see Bal; Niederhoff.

Dutch, and the last piece, that of the English, could conjure up nothing but the bland taste of drinking water" (15).

Macrohistories are an important resource for marking time in *Litanies*. Jessica's carpenter father demonstrates the materiality of history to her in the annual rings inscribed on the cleanly cut trunk of an anjili tree: on this ring the First World War began and the German ship *Emden* appeared in the Indian Ocean, on this ring India became independent, Jessica is told in her apprenticeship in historical chronology (13). A deliberate mapping of intimate events of a local or personal character onto larger public histories through chronological correspondence has been used in autobiographies from Kerala, especially those written against the backdrop of changing times.[4] Two moves reside in this gesture: the individual life at the center of autobiographical narration acquires context and meaning from the times; equally importantly, historical narration is provincialized in its encounter with registers of the vernacular and the local. This is particularly relevant for personal histories from marginalized communities. The public histories on which they pegged stories of their lives referred to new archives and unrecognized marginal publics. Dominant idioms of public history in Kerala have over the past half century assimilated many of these archives under the sign of democracy. Dalit archival historians have shown that the absorption of little stories into a happy holdall of public history has its own sleights of hand.[5] Madhavan's *Litanies* simultaneously extends and interrupts the consolidated archive of Kerala's public memory.

Although the novel presents history self-consciously through a first-person narrative voice, it becomes very clear that the "I" of narration cannot be anchored in structures of personal recollection or witnessing. Jessica's early childhood is entirely made of history as hearsay, as voices that came to displace the darkness of those years; this makes it difficult to establish parallels between national history and the protagonist's life, as in some of the well-known idioms of postcolonial allegory.[6] Jessica says: "All that I am writing is born out of what I saw, heard or experienced. . . . Oh chumma! I am kidding. I made up some of them. I didn't have enough playthings in my childhood. I had to invent stories to kill time" (3). In *Litanies,* the narrators and transmitters of history, the bearers of the archive, are the islanders. In toddy shops and libraries and boats, the islanders thematize history, they mobilize repositories of traces and enact scenes from the historical past.

---

4. For a discussion, see Kumar, "Autobiography."

5. See, for example, Ramadas.

6. See, for instance, Holden, "Other Modernities." See also Holden, *Autobiography and Decolonization* and Arnold and Blackburn.

Three interconnected series emerge through these invocations. The first connects things on the island to the sea that surrounds it. Seemingly narrow in places, making Ernakulam town from the mainland almost a neighbor, the sea nonetheless contains powerful currents beneath its surface, connecting the island by its sheer force to the wide expanse of the ocean and the continents beyond. Jessica's grandfather as a young man had experienced a free transoceanic passage on these currents to the shores of Africa. A ship rescued and transported him all the way to Nigeria, and decades later a transcontinental network of missionaries brought him back to Fort Cochin as an old, blind man. Such passages were not propelled by Christianity alone; migration, exile, flight, trade, and slave trade—the sea was the medium of plural connections. The trope of the undercurrent in *Litanies* connects with stories of labor and production. Jessica's grandfather was a boat maker, the son of a legendary carpenter who had in his time fled from his foreigner master, having stolen the shipbuilder's jealously guarded table of measurements.

The transcontinental as a supplement of the vernacular—early lower-caste conversion novels in Malayalam had already proposed this link. Dilip Menon perceptively highlighted the importance of oceanic geographies for narratives of slavery resonant beneath the surface of lower-caste Christian novels written in the late nineteenth and the early twentieth century. *Sukumari*, written by Joseph Muliyil in the 1890s, contains the biography of a slave who finds his free life in Australia and who returns to Kerala in a strange act of homecoming. When *Litanies* invokes transoceanic voyages more than a century later, slavery is not its immediate context, but the predecessors of the inhabitants of the Dutch Battery were slaves who found their freedom through Carmelite missionaries. After the Dutch conquest of Cochin in 1663, they had fled into the uninhabited delta of the novel's imaginary island in order to escape the persecution meted out to Catholics.

Accompanying oceanic trajectories, making them possible, a geological series appears in the novel through Robert Bristow's writings and public speeches, and their later recollection by the islanders.[7] In this narrative, around 1341, a configuration of natural forces resulted in a transformation of the coastline of Cochin and paved the way to ships securing anchor there. "A gigantic struggle was being fought by the natural forces," Bristow declaimed in one of his public speeches in the 1930s, reenacted on several occasions by his former cook Edwin. The geological event of creation and destruction anticipates a latter day mythical moment of human agency, the deepening of

---

7. For an account of Bristow's experiences as a harbor engineer in Cochin, see his *Cochin Saga*.

the harbor and the production of a new landmass in the form of Willingdon Island by Bristow.

A third series in *Litanies,* which may seem to arise from the first, moves in a different direction, orienting itself to imagination and ecstatic creativity. This is the story of the Cavittunatakam, a form of dramatic performance that draws on Ariosto's *Orlando Furioso.* The epic most likely reached the shores of Kerala through Carmelite priests from Portugal. The voyage of culture, like that of boatbuilding, is prone to deviations and betrayals. The story of Charlemagne of the eighth and ninth centuries transformed itself on the shores of Kerala to defy chronology: in the narrative of Cavittunatakam, Charlemagne is a glorious hero of the Crusades, which took place more than two and a half centuries after his death! In the novel's present too, Cavittunatakam is a site of fresh innovations and appropriations. For the actors, who work in a factory during the day, it offers an escape from the drudgery of their present. Sponsorship is uncertain and difficult to obtain, and when it arrives from the church, one priest would like to see the story of Jesus performed instead of that of Charlemagne; another would indeed have Charlemagne but would like to have the play perform the story of his reconquering Jerusalem! Eventually, Cavittunatakam comes to have a fragmented life; snippets are performed in festivals of folk art forms, as indices of regional cultures that have survived within the modern nation. For Jessica, the grand performance form appears ludicrous in its new surroundings, like a whale trapped in the shallows.

If these three series mark history as it came down to Jessica's childhood, her life and experiences produce fresh series, which have subsequently become history for the readers of the *Litany.* Jessica's life as it unravels in the novel creates a space for housing traces and marks from everyday life, making them acquire a resonance in their afterlife that is contemporaneity. Two of these deserve special mention: the early history of Malayalam cinema as it shapes the idioms of narrative and affect in the island and the history of communism and anticommunism.

The stories of films like *Jeevitanauka* told by the mother to the child in bed, which for Jessica becomes the first apprenticeship of desire, the early film songs, and the Kundan music club dedicated to the legendary singer K. L. Saigal—these refer to archives of the everyday and the popular that do not find a place in the developmental history of the region. These invocations are accompanied by a display of what may be called an impulse to "collect." The songbook, the cinema notice, the old announcements—the novel becomes their repository through Jessica's almost tactile, corporeal memory of them. The songbooks, story synopses, and handbills are cited and materialized on the pages of the novel.

The preoccupation with objects in *Litanies* appears oriented toward collections rather than metonymies. Walter Benjamin proposed an illuminating contrast between the allegorist and the collector. According to Benjamin, while the allegorist "dislodges things from their context and, from the outset, relies on his profundity to illuminate their meaning," the collector "brings together what belongs together; by keeping in mind their affinities and their succession in time he can eventually furnish information about his objects" (211). Benjamin also highlights a secret meeting point between these two divergent approaches to objects. The collector's task always remains incomplete and the allegorist can never have enough of things as he cannot foresee "what meaning his profundity may lay claim to for each of them" (211).

Elaine Freedgood in her reading of Victorian thing culture draws on Benjamin's distinction to make the case for a non-allegorical reading of objects in fiction, tracing like a collector their prior histories of ownership, circulation, and use. Through this she attempts to disrupt allegorical readings anchored in character subjects and track down a moment of split in the novel that makes possible for her a thematization of the text's unconscious. After performing this function, the non-allegorical reading seems to give way to a new allegorical recognition of character subjects.

The object world of *Litanies* is powered by a collector's attitude. The lingering descriptive gaze we saw in the description of objects in Wilfred's shop appears to be that of a collector, who moves from the ink tablet to the gleaming nib to the glass jars of candies to the flour that covers them, animated by that desire for placing things together and seeking a sense of completion. "For the collector," Benjamin wrote, "the world is present, and indeed ordered, in each of its objects. Ordered however according to a surprising and, for the profane understanding, incomprehensible connection. This connection stands to the customary ordering and schematisation of things something as their arrangement in the dictionary stands to a natural arrangement" (207). Although the narrative voice is Jessica's, no protocol of realist narration, including focalization, permits us to attribute the collector's voice to her. The objects seem to exceed anchoring in character subjects, plots, or even the designated redundancy—in Freedgood's words, "insignificant notation" (9)—that marks Barthes's "reality effect." They offer no metonymic relationship to the interiorities of characters. Their presence in the novel is predicated upon an implied possibility of historical commentary and retrieval. With the little commodities of childhood that mark a small provincial culture, commodities that have disappeared long before the time of the novel's composition, Wilfred's shop becomes a space of historical resonance and the delectation of memory. The medley of things in the shop turns into a constellation of objects of remembrance, not anchored in any subject except the author-collector, making the tiny room into the staged space of an ethnographic museum.

This narratorial commitment to objects is in tune with a tendency displayed throughout *Litanies* to regard objects as repositories of historical affect and information. The making of dum biryani for Jessica's baptism feast moves from a detailed list of ingredients and a narrative of the steps in its making to a discussion of the lines of circulation through which biryani came to the Kerala coast and variants of the dish. The culinary narrative intersects with the histories of colonialism: even spices like pepper, native to Kerala, became a gustatory ingredient through the experience of trade and, later, colonialism. And it was Vasco da Gama, the cook reminds us, who introduced the large onion and the dry red chili into Kerala cuisine.

One can cite any number of examples of this kind from *Litanies* of objects or practices being presented with the presupposition of a space of historical resonance. The "historical" dimension of things does not invest them with a resonant muteness as in Rancière's account; it is rather a matter of eloquent elaboration in passages inadequately anchored in characters. Sometimes such passages appear with some narrative alibi, as in the cook's explanations on dum biryani, but often they float above or in between character subjects. Since the overall narrative of the novel is presented in the voice of a character, Jessica, the construction of historical resonance in the novel involves a strange temporal structure. Objects contemporary to Jessica and that form a part of her unreflective relation to the world are often presented as if they are recalled in a world from which they have disappeared. In other words, contemporary objects of use in Jessica's world already foresee their eventual residence in a space of conservation and resonance. Jessica's experiences acquire the strange resonance of an anticipatory recollection that seems to precede and determine the recording of her fresh impressions.

If the strands of relations mentioned above stand for an innocent ecumenism, another series of the history of the communist movement, the ban imposed on it, its coming to power in 1957, and its dismissal after violent agitations in 1959, traces a more difficult history in Jessica's childhood and adolescence. In tracking this, the novel yet again seeks to become a repository of traces: celebrations of the swearing in of the communist ministry, the textual reconstruction of a popular narrative form—Bhagavan Macaroni kathaprasangam—used in the anticommunist agitation, Father Vadakkan's fiery speeches, the reports and recollections of the first police firing.

Litanies makes an interesting attempt to house these traces and objects in Jessica's body and its experiences. When the three actors of Cavittunatakam, pretending to be emperors, visit infant Jessica in a mock repetition of the visit of the three magi, her sex is revealed to them, and the text breaks into a litany:

> "Forgot to ask, is it a boy or a girl?" Santiagu asked.
>
> "A girl," replied Anniyamma. She removed the cloth covering me. All three looked at the space between my legs.
>
> My body's wound in the middle; my wisdom; my shyness that grows the palm of my hand; my taboo; my purity; my transgression; my discernment; my confessional; my punishment; my silence; my impurity; my hinterland; my chalice; my gill; my chapel; my lame lamb; my temperate zone; my Golgotha; my pennant; my third eye; my sandbar; my salt's sourness; my comet; my intercession; my equator; my magnetic needle; my vineyard; my wonder; my portal; my joke; my faith; my multiplication table; my mountain pass; my harbour mouth; my chronometer; my anchor; my blessing; my vulva. (52–53)

At its first exposure, the body is an already written space. However, it is not written over by the familiar idioms of vernacular poeticization. The language of the litany displays a decisive, exuberant, cosmopolitan modernism that in Kerala transformed poetic idioms through an encounter with translations from Pablo Neruda and Cesar Vallejo, Bertolt Brecht and Paul Eluard. The language of modernist poetry in Malayalam from the 1960s to the 1980s may be seen as becoming an intertextual repository of translated locutions that entered into fresh alliances and collisions with the vernacular and the more evidently literary. In the space of that translated, cosmopolitan, urban Malayalam, Madhavan's *Litanies* constructs the body as the space of historical archiving. In this sense, the collector's impulse in *Litanies* is overrun by an archival principle, that is an attempt to turn narration into a house for archival traces.

I focused on Madhavan's *Litanies of the Dutch Battery* because it stages in striking fashion the strange predicament in which the discourse of the novel stands vis-à-vis things and documents as historically marked up, and beyond or alongside them, the domain of collections and archives. Fort Kochi is presented in the novel as a special topos of promiscuous transregional connections through the constant invocation of diverse histories—be they the complex transregional travels of the performance form of the Cavittunatakam or the natural and artificial transformation of geography or the transactions in the domain of cuisine. At the same time, *Litanies* also tries to become a repository of objects and locutions of everyday life in Fort Kochi during the late 1950s and 1960s. However, it offers no uninscribed space, not even the body, to hold or contain these marked-up traces. The container is well within the world of inscription and documentation. Everything has a date. Even the geological transformation of the Cochin harbor has a date: 1341. Even the immemorial is within the ambit of memory and recording. As this pushes *Litanies* decisively into the world of prose, it does not attenuate the novel's investment in affective recall. The geographical feeling that links *Litanies* to a sense of location comes from a desire for public history. Such a desire had marked Kerala's modernity right through the late nineteenth and the early twentieth centuries, and extends beyond the archival validation of the professional historian or the curatorial gloss of the professional museologist.

Madhavan's *Litanies* comes with its own distinctive organization of historical markup. Characters in whose lives the objects make their appearance at times appear as no more than props in the curatorial work of the novel's cultural historical collections. The preponderance of historical narrators—from the cook to the carpenter to the communist—underlines this. History is embedded not in mute objects or life events; the narrators are the real witnesses and transmitters of public histories. However, even as they live their lives and tell their stories, they are framed by the quadrangular shadow of the collection's display case and shaped by the impulse to conserve and document. Characters are spaces of citation: their utterances are part of the curatorial apparatus of the novel. One may see an interesting reversal of allegorical readings of realism, which understood objects in relation to characters; here characters may need to be understood as functioning in the service of a curatorial imagination of objects.

What kind of museum does *Litanies* curate for its public? In its ecumenical inclusiveness and criticism, it mirrors a secular, post-left, yet-left cosmopolitan consciousness in Kerala's civil society, where history—in spite of its injustices and barbarities—still reassures the remembering subject, despite its own imminent annihilation at the end of the novel, about the legibility of the past. Madhavan's novel demonstrates, in its ways of saying and showing, how this reassuring consciousness depends on an archival and museumizing relation to the past. In this, *Litanies of the Dutch Battery* displays the increasing unviability of location as a space of unmediated belonging and embodied remembrance. Location appears here as a museum ruled by the future anterior, where lives are lived, the world inhabited, and things made present in a documented collection that will find its existence in the future—a future that is the present of the book's writing.

WORKS CITED

Appadurai, Arjun, ed. *The Social Life of Things: Commodities in Cultural Perspective*. Cambridge: Cambridge University Press, 1986.

Arnold, David, and Stuart Blackburn, eds. *Telling Lives in India: Biography, Autobiography and Life History*. Delhi: Permanent Black, 2004.

Arunima, G. "Fantasies, Phantoms and Funny Jokes: The 'City' and Colonial Modernity." Paper presented at workshop on "Cultures and Empires," Stanford University, February 1999.

Bal, Mieke. *Narratology: Introduction to the Theory of Narrative*. Toronto: University of Toronto Press, 1985.

Balzac, Honoré de. *The Wild Ass's Skin*. Trans. Herbert J. Hunt. London: Penguin, 1977.

Barthes, Roland. "The Reality Effect." *The Rustle of Language*. Trans. Richard Howard. Berkeley: University of California Press, 1989. 141–48.

———. "Towards a Structural Analysis of Narratives." *Image-Music-Text*. Ed. and trans. Stephen Heath. London: Fontana Press, 1977. 79–124.

Baudrillard, Jean. *The System of Objects*. Trans. James Benedict. London: Verso, 1996.

Benjamin, Walter. "The Collector." *The Arcades Project*. Ed. Rolf Tiedmann. Trans. Howard Eiland and Kevin McLaughlin. Cambridge: Belknap Press, 1999. 203–11.

Bristow, Robert. *Cochin Saga*. Cochin: Paico Publishing House, 1959.

Chandu Menon, O. *Indulekha*. 1889. Kottayam: Sahitya Pravarthaka Co-operative Society, 1978.

Chaudhuri, Supriya. "Phantasmagorias of the Interior: Furniture, Modernity and Early Bengali Fiction." *Journal of Victorian Culture* 15:2 (2010): 173–93.

Freedgood, Elaine. *Ideas in Things: Fugitive Meaning in the Victorian Novel*. Chicago: University of Chicago Press, 2006.

Genette, Gérard. *Narrative Discourse: An Essay in Method*. Trans. Jane E. Lewin. Ithaca: Cornell University Press, 1980.

Holden, Philip. *Autobiography and Decolonization: Modernity, Masculinity and the Nation-State*. Madison: University of Wisconsin Press, 2008.

———. "Other Modernities: National Autobiography and Globalization." *Biography* 28.1 (2005): 89–103.

Kumar, Udaya. "Autobiography as a Way of Writing History: Personal Narratives from Kerala and the Inhabitation of Modernity." *History in the Vernacular*. Eds. Partha Chatterjee and Raziuddin Aquil. Delhi: Permanent Black, 2008. 418–48.

———. "Seeing and Reading: Early Malayalam Novels and Some Questions of Visibility." *Early Novels in India*. Ed. Meenakshi Mukherjee. New Delhi: Sahitya Akademi, 2002. 161–92.

Madhavan, N. S. *Lanthan Batheriyile Luthiniyakal*. Kottayam: D. C. Books, 2003.

———. *Litanies of Dutch Battery*. Trans. Rajesh Rajmohan. Delhi: Penguin, 2010.

Menon, Dilip M. "A Place Elsewhere: Lower Caste Malayalam Novels of the Nineteenth Century." *India's Literary History: Essays on the Nineteenth Century*. Ed. Stuart Blackburn and Vasudha Dalmia. Delhi: Permanent Black, 2004. 483–515.

Menon, Padu. *Lakshmikesavam*. 1892. *Nalu Novelukal*. Ed. George Irumbayam. Thrissur: Kerala Sahitya Akademi, 1985.

Muliyil, Joseph. *Sukumari*. 1897. *Nalu Novelukal*. Ed. George Irumbayam. Trissur: Kerala Sahitya Akademi, 1985. 271–395.

Niederhoff, Burckhard. "Focalisation." *Living Handbook of Narratology*. 24 September 2013. Web. 3 July 2015.

Ramadas, Cherayi. *Ayyankalikku Aadarathode* [*To Ayyankali, Respectfully*]. Ernakulam: Upardodham Books, 2009.

Rancière, Jacques. "Politics of Literature." *Dissensus: On Politics and Aesthetics*. Ed. and trans. Steven Corcoran. London: Continuum, 2010. 152–68.

PART II

ZONES OF NARRATIVE (PARA-, META-, INTRA-)

CHAPTER 4

Metanarrative Signs in Ousmane Sembène's *Les Bouts de bois de Dieu. Banty mam Yall*

GERALD PRINCE

AMONG THE many signs that make up a narrative, metanarrative signs are those that refer explicitly to one of the numerous codes or subcodes in terms of which the narrative signifies. In this acceptation, therefore, metanarrative signs do not comment on the narrative in which they occur. Rather, they shed light on the codes framing that narrative: the (linguistic) code through which the narrative is represented, for example; the proairetic code or logic governing the sequence of narrated actions and their folding into larger actions or unfolding into smaller ones; or the cultural code, the body of cultural knowledge relied on by the narrative in making sense. For instance, should an utterance like "*Gregarious* means *sociable*" occur in a narrative, "sociable" functions as a metanarrative sign and, more specifically, as a metalinguistic sign. Similarly, should an utterance like "In that society, touching one's nose means surrendering" occur in a narrative, "surrendering" functions as a metanarrative sign and, more specifically, as a metacultural one.[1]

Metanarrative signs are found in all kinds of narrative. However, because of their mediating, glossing, or explanatory function, there may exist affinities between them and texts exploring multilingual and multicultural situations, identity and alterity, separation and integration, intercommunal conflicts, ten-

---

1. On metanarrative signs, see Prince, "Remarques" and *Narratology*; on codes, see Barthes.

sions, and accommodations: regionalist fictions, for example, or cosmopolitan ones, tales of travel and adventure, science fiction novels, spy stories, and, generally speaking, postcolonial narratives, given that they often feature at least some such explorations.

Like other sets of signs found in narratives, metanarrative signs can perform various functions. They can illustrate a theme (that of knowledge, that of explanation, that of translation); they can serve as a characterization device (with some characters but not others formulating or requiring them); they can contribute to the definition of the narrator, the narratee, and their relationship; and, in general, they help to constitute and foreground the text's ideology. After all, who glosses what, for whom, how, where, when, and why—all these elements combined establish and highlight differences and (power) relations between characters (or communities), while embodying (certain kinds of) mediation and drawing attention to the narrative components that are glossed. This is the case in Ousmane Sembène's 1960 *Les Bouts de bois de Dieu. Banty mam Yall (God's Bits of Wood)*, a novel about the strike by the railroad workers on the Dakar-Niger line to get the same rights and benefits as their counterparts in France. The strike lasted more than five months—from October 10, 1947, to March 19, 1948—and ended in the workers' victory.[2]

There are nearly one hundred and fifty metanarrative (sets of) signs in Sembène's novel (more than one every three pages) and about eighty of them are metalinguistic (more than one every five pages). They are distributed fairly evenly and, though most of them are deployed by the narrator (*22, 28, 35,* et passim; 18, 24, 27), a few appear in a character's utterance (e.g., *53; 111*; 43, 94). One group among them specifies the (social) identity of various characters or their relation to one another (*42, 50, 75,* et passim; 33, 41, 60). The metaproairetic ones summarize sets of events by providing a phrase or term designating and subsuming them (*38, 41, 126*; 29, 32, 108). The metacultural ones shed light on certain sites, conditions, or practices (*18, 77, 147,* et passim; 15, 62, 126). The metalinguistic ones, which are mostly found in footnotes rather than in the body of the text, usually explain the meaning of terms in Wolof or Bambara (*16, 19, 22,* et passim; 14, 16, 18), but one or two provide glosses for French expressions (e.g., *111*; 94) and some, instead of dealing with signification, deal with pronunciation, characterize the nature of a speech act,

---

2. Parenthetical page references will provide page numbers first—in italics—for the French edition (Sembène, *Les Bouts de bois*) and then for the English translation (Sembène, *God's Bits*). Though readable, the latter is not very faithful, which is why I have chosen to use my own renditions of the original version. For instance, it eliminates most of the metalinguistic signs in the novel. Still, the page references provided can help to contextualize relevant passages.

or give reasons for a particular lexical choice (*15, 87, 134, 162*; 13, 72, 114, 140). As for the words and phrases translated or commented on, they generally pertain to kinship terminology (e.g., *16, 19, 28*; 14, 16, 24), foodstuffs (*19, 84, 88*; 16, 69, 73), clothes (*26, 37, 75*; 22, 29, 60), everyday objects (*93, 117, 144*; 77, 100, 124), and the like.

As this quick description suggests, however else metanarrative signs in *Les Bouts de bois de Dieu* may operate (as stylistic flourishes, say, reality effects, markers of Africanness), they unsurprisingly seem to be linked to the novel's concern with its own legibility. Implied by Sembène's avoidance of technical pyrotechnics and narrative eccentricities (odd focalizations, contradictory descriptions, capricious chronology), this concern is emphasized by several textual features like, for instance, the list of (prominent) characters supplied at the very beginning and indicating their city of residence, their area of employment, and/or their familial status; the chapter titles ("The Judgment," "The Apprentices," "The Women's March") and the table of contents too; the reliable narration and straightforward narratorial commentary, of course; and the preamble to the narrative proper: "Les hommes et les femmes qui, du 10 octobre 1947 au 19 mars 1948, engagèrent cette lutte pour une vie meilleure ne doivent rien à personne, ni à aucune 'mission civilisatrice,' ni à un notable, ni à un parlementaire. Leur exemple ne fut pas vain: depuis, l'Afrique progresse" [The men and women who, from October 10, 1947, to March 1948, started this struggle for a better life owe nothing to anyone, neither to any 'civilizing mission' nor to any notable or any parliamentarian. Their example was not in vain: since then, Africa has been progressing]. Sembène obviously wants to make certain that the meaning and point of the situations and events recounted are clear.

But the novel's concern with legibility raises a number of questions with regard to its use of non-French terms and metalinguistic commentary. It should be noted that several non-French terms are not (explicitly) glossed, perhaps because they are easily recognizable as common expletives (*71, 80, 102*, et passim; 57, 65, 86) or perhaps because an implicit or indirect clarification seems sufficient, as in: "—Va me chercher le *nguégué*, dit Assitan en posant son van. Un instant plus tard, la fillette revint portant une cravache" [Go bring me the *nguégué*, said Assitan, putting down her fan. A moment later the little girl came back carrying a whip] (*22*; 18).[3] It should also be noted that some non-French terms are used several times but glossed on first men-

---

3. Significantly, the term *toubab* (person of European descent; white person), which is by far the most frequently used African term in the novel, is elucidated only through its various contexts and through the gloss supplied for *toubabous-dyions* (slaves of the Europeans) (*15*; 12). Perhaps it is a term whose meaning can simply not quite be rendered in French.

tion only. Now, this may not affect legibility very much when a new mention of a given term occurs within a few lines (or even a few pages) of the gloss (e.g., *m'ba,* grandmother, *16* and *17* or *Baillika mou vahe,* Let him speak, *335;* 14, *296*), but it can prove more problematic when the new mention occurs many pages later, as is the case with, say, *banco,* hard clay (*22, 145;* 18, *124*), *soungoutou,* girl (*23, 162;* 19, *141*), or *tapates,* fences (*35, 76;* 27, *62*). Similarly, glosses provided in footnotes rather than in the body of the text are likely to affect legibility in more significant ways and yet they are largely favored by Sembène (compare, for instance, *15* and *35;* 12, *27*). Besides, as the published English translation of *Les Bouts de bois de Dieu* shows again and again, many of the metalinguistic signs could have been altogether avoided had the non-French terms calling for them not been used. For example, Sembène writes, "Quand quelqu'un ne voulait pas s'asseoir, on le tirait par son *boubou*" and provides *tunique* as a gloss (*26*) as opposed to simply using *tunique* instead of *boubou,* as the published translation suggests: "When someone refused to sit down, the others pulled him by the tunic" (*22*). Maybe Sembène's preference for non-French terms accompanied by (footnoted) metalinguistic commentary does not primarily relate to a concern with legibility. Maybe it is better explained by the various ways they illustrate a particularly important thematic complex in the novel, that of language and such related topics as translation or communication.

The thematic complex of language-related matters manifests itself in the very title of the novel, *Les Bouts de bois de Dieu. Banty mam Yall.* Repeated in the dedication ("A vous, Banty mam Yall, à mes frères de syndicat et à tous les syndicalistes et à leurs compagnes dans ce vaste monde, je dédie mon livre" [To you, Banty mam Yall, to my union brothers and to all unionists and their female partners in this vast world, I dedicate this book], the second half of that title, in a reversal of the usual pattern in the novel, constitutes a translation from French into Wolof of the first half and, as the text later reveals in a footnote, is a way of referring to human beings: "Une superstition veut que l'on compte des 'bouts de bois [de Dieu]' à la place des êtres vivants pour ne pas abréger le cours de leur vie" [Superstition has it that one counts '[God's] bits of wood' in place of living beings in order not to shorten the course of their life] (*77; 62*). Rather than bridging a distance by providing an explanation, the Wolof phrase represents an obstacle for the narratee, which the textual metalinguistic signs characterize as not knowing African languages. Moreover, the literal meaning of the phrase in French is not particularly meaningful in itself, and this underscores the gap between the language of the narratee and the languages of the narrator and the African characters, much as non-French terms and their corresponding metalinguistic commentary do.[4]

The fact that different languages are used is emphasized by the novel's attributive discourse, the discourse accompanying the characters' discourse and specifying their identity, the nature of their speech acts, and/or various aspects of the latter's makeup and context, including the language adopted (192, 196–97, 211, 282, et passim; 169, 173, 184, 251). This fact is also emphasized by what some of the characters themselves say about language and languages. When, for example, at the very beginning of the novel, young Ad'jibid'ji uses the French world *alors* (so), her traditionalist grandmother, old Niakoro, who finds the word vulgar, screams at the child: "—Aloss, Aloss! . . . Je te parle en bambara et tu me réponds dans ce langage de sauvages" [Aloss, Aloss! . . . I speak to you in Bambara and you answer me in this language of savages] (20; 17). Much later, musing about the different languages she knows (and the arbitrariness of linguistic signs!), Ad'jibid'ji asks the old woman: "—Grand-mère, pourquoi dit-on en bambara *M'bé sira ming*, 'je bois du tabac'? *Ming* veut dire absorber tandis qu'en oulofou 'avaler de l'eau' se dit *nane* et 'aspirer la fumée' *touhe*. Il y a donc deux mots, comme en français. Pourquoi nous, les Bambaras, nous n'avons pas aussi deux mots?" [Grandmother, why does one say, in Bambara, *M'bé sira ming*, "I drink tobacco?" *Ming* means to absorb whereas in Wolof "to swallow water" is *nane* and "to inhale smoke" *touhe*. So there are two different words, like in French. Why do we Bambaras not have two words also?] (162; 140). The language difference is further emphasized by one of the characters in the novel being an interpreter who, like the narrator through metalinguistic signs, elucidates African speech for those who do not understand it.[5] Most obviously, the language difference is foregrounded by the characters' widely differing linguistic knowledge. If Ad'jibid'ji knows Bambara, French, and (some) Wolof, and if Bakayoko, the soul of the strike, knows these three languages as well as Hasounké and Toucouleur, neither Dejean, the French director of the railroad company, nor Mr. Edouard, the work inspector, seem to know any African language. In fact, during the negotiations between the strikers and the management, Bakayoko pointedly foregrounds the disparity: "Je ne suis pas seul dans cette grève, mais, étant donné que votre ignorance

---

4. The uses of linguistic intelligibility and obscurity in postcolonial writing have been extensively discussed. See, for example, Dasenbrock; Vakunta. See also Gayatri Chakravorty Spivak's translator's preface, translator's note, and afterword in Devi. On language in *Les Bouts de bois de Dieu*, see Joseph; Nzabatsinda. On Sembène's novel in general, see Harrow; Jones; Makonda; Njoroge. On Sembène, see Sikoumo.

5. Like Francis Price, the translator of the published English version of the novel, the interpreter takes liberties with the utterances he translates (123; 105).

d'au moins une de nos langues est un handicap pour vous, nous emploierons le français, c'est une question de politesse. Mais c'est une politesse qui n'aura qu'un temps" [I am not alone in this strike, but, given that your ignorance of any of our languages is a handicap for you, we will use French, it's a matter of courtesy. But it is a courtesy that will not last for long] (277; 247). In a way, the very title of the novel had foreshadowed Bakayoko's last point: there will come a time when French is translated into Wolof (or another African language) rather than the reverse.

As Bakayoko's remark more than suggests, languages are associated with the colonial situation and the power relations it institutes and promotes. Particularly telling in this regard is the characters' relation to French.[6] Some characters do not know French (18, 334, 364; 16, 295, 320) and, furthermore, some do not want to know it. Thus, Niakoro tells her granddaughter: "A quoi sert le toubabou pour une femme? Une bonne mère n'en a que faire. Dans ma lignée qui est aussi celle de ton père, personne ne parle le toubabou et personne n'en est mort! Depuis ma naissance—et Dieu sait qu'il y a longtemps—je n'ai jamais entendu dire qu'un toubabou ait appris le bambara ou une autre langue de ce pays. Mais vous autres les déracinés, vous ne pensez qu'à ça. A croire que notre langue est tombée en décadence!" [What use is Toubabou [the white man's language] to a woman? A good mother has no need of it. In my tradition, which is also that of your father, no one speaks Toubabou and no one has died of it! Ever since my birth—and God knows that was long ago—I have never heard that a Toubabou had learned Bambara or another language of this country. But you rootless people, you think only of that. As if our language had fallen into decline!] (18; 15–16). Other characters speak what is at best broken French (123–24, 189, 223, et passim; 106, 166, 195). Still others, like the assimilationist N'Deye Touti, who has never read a book by an African writer because she is sure that it cannot be of any value (101; 84–85), speak it as if it were their native language (109, 192; 92, 169). Finally, characters like Bakayoko, who know French just as well, prefer not having to use it and not yielding to the French imposition of it as a sign of their dominance. Indeed, when he addresses the big meeting attended by the strikers, their supporters, and the authorities, he does it in Wolof first and only then repeats in French important parts of his speech (336, 338; 297, 298).[7]

However, Bakayoko understands the value of knowing French. He not only speaks it but also reads it and writes it, and he encourages others, like Tiemoko, one of the leaders of the strike, to do the same. But Bakayoko also

---

6. On this topic, see Joseph. On (post)colonialism and linguistic power relations, see, among many others, Ashcroft, Griffiths and Tiffin; Dubreuil; Ngugi wa Thiong'o.

7. Note that Sembène became a filmmaker in part to reach a wider African public.

understands that no language is inherently better than any other and that no language is anyone's property or has any special affinity with particular groups or individuals. Like Tiemoko, who borrows *La Condition humaine* (*Man's Fate*) from him and finds that novel inspiring even though it was written by a white man, Bakayoko believes that languages and books, principles, machines can transcend differences (144; 122).[8]

Times have changed. The strikers' action is making new human beings out of them (63; 52). Women too now address the assembled crowds (289; 255) and it is no longer demeaning for men to seek water for their families (290; 256). Acting as a veritable school (*140, 147*; 120, 126), the strike and the principles it represents overcome differences of gender, class, ethnicity, generation, without minimizing or ignoring them and without hatred (*295, 367*; 260, 324). Old Mamadou Keïta understands that one should not confuse respect for tradition with knowledge (30; 25), and Bakayoko's father thinks that he should perhaps learn French (213; 185). N'Deye Touti begins to fetch water for her community, and when there is no paper with which to light a fire, she uses some of her notebooks (347; 307). Masons and carpenters, fishermen and dockers, policemen, civil servants, and office workers come to realize that the strike is their strike too (338; 298). So do the workers in Dahomey, Guinea, and even France (288; 254). Indeed, instead of trying to break the strike, white men send the strikers money to go on with it (74, 262; 59, 232). Similarly, the differences indicated by metanarrative signs as well as by the many words in italics (*82, 163, 267, 274,* et passim; 67, 141, 237–38, 243), for instance, or by the many expressions in quotation marks (*100, 116, 248, 333,* et passim; 84, 99, 218, 294) are surmounted. The heterogeneity they represent and point to is subsumed by the unity of the text. Sembène's art shows difference, preserves it, and goes beyond it.

The various questions raised about metanarrative signs in *Les Bouts de bois de Dieu* are (or should be) standard narratological questions and can be raised, more or less profitably, with regard to any narrative. They help to shed light on specific aspects of Sembène's novel, on the latter's general thrust, and on the novelist's view of his own art and its role. Other narratologically driven questions—about the novel's plot, for example, or the novel's character configuration—would likewise help to clarify the thematic or ideological functioning of *Les Bouts de bois de Dieu*. The events in the novel take place in Bamako, in Thiès, on the road from Thiès to Dakar, and in the latter city, and just as it goes from one language to another, the narration goes back and forth between the different places to evoke the role of the railroad and to underline

---

8. On the place of *La Condition humaine* in Sembène's novel, see Joseph; Ojo.

the fact that the strike involves much more than one particular location. Similarly, rather than a single protagonist, and just as it has many languages, the novel has many prominent characters—Bakayoko, Tiemoko, N'Deye Touti, Maïmouna the blind woman, Penda the prostitute, Ramatoulaye—to stress the collective nature of the strike and of its success. Conversely, through its thematic or ideological concerns and the way it deploys metanarrative signs, the novel helps to suggest that the latter are not necessarily or primarily instruments of legibility and it helps to appreciate the diverse ways in which they can function—in *Les Bouts de bois de Dieu,* as markers of (transcended) difference. In other words, if narratology can illumine specific works of literature, it can also be illumined by them.

WORKS CITED

Ashcroft, Bill, Gareth Griffiths, and Helen Tiffin. *The Empire Writes Back: Theory and Practice in Post-Colonial Literature.* New York: Routledge, 1989.

Barthes, Roland. *S/Z.* Trans. Richard Miller. New York: Hill & Wang, 1974.

Dasenbrock, Reed Way. "Intelligibility and Meaningfulness in Multicultural Literature in English." *PMLA* 102 (1987): 10–19.

Devi, Mahasweta. *Imaginary Maps: Three Stories.* Trans. Gayatri Chakravorty Spivak. New York: Routledge, 1995.

Dubreuil, Laurent. *Empire of Language: Toward a Critique of (Post)Colonial Expression.* Trans. David Fieni. Ithaca: Cornell University Press, 2013.

Harrow, Kenneth W. "Art and Ideology in *Les Bouts de bois de Dieu*: Realism's Artifices." *The French Review* 62 (1989): 483–93.

Jones, James A. "Fact and Fiction in *God's Bits of Wood.*" *Research in African Literatures* 31 (2000): 117–31.

Joseph, George. "Identité, intertextualité et langues nationales dans *Les Bouts de bois de Dieu* d'Ousmane Sembène." *JALA* 3 (2008–2009): 91–110.

Makonda, A. *Les Bouts de bois de Dieu de Sembène Ousmane—étude critique.* Paris: F. Nathan and Nouvelles Editions Africaines, 1985.

Ngugi wa Thiong'o. *Decolonising the Mind: The Politics of Language in African Literature.* London: J. Currey, 1986.

Njoroge, Paul Ngigi. *Sembène Ousmane's* God's Bits of Wood. Nairobi: Heinemann Educational Books, 1984.

Nzabatsinda, Anthère. *Normes linguistiques et écriture africaine chez Ousmane Sembène.* Toronto: Editions du GREF, 1996.

Ojo, S. Ade. "André Malraux et Sembène Ousmane: Créateurs des romans prolétariens historiques." *Peuples Noirs Peuples Africains* 17 (1980): 117–34.

Prince, Gerald. *Narratology: The Form and Functioning of Narrative.* Berlin: Walter de Gruyter, 1982.

———. "Remarques sur les signes métanarratifs." *Degrés* 11–12 (1977): e1–e10.

Sembène, Ousmane. *God's Bits of Wood*. Trans. Francis Price. Garden City: Doubleday & Company, 1962.

———. *Les Bouts de bois de Dieu. Banty mam Yall*. Paris: Le Livre contemporain, 1960.

Sikoumo, Hilaire. *Ousmane Sembène: écrivain populaire*. Paris: L'Harmattan, 2010.

Vakunta, Peter W. *Indigenization of Language in the African Francophone Novel: A New Literary Canon*. New York: Peter Lang, 2011.

CHAPTER 5

A Contextual Rhetorical Analysis of Audiences in E. M. Forster's Preface to Mulk Raj Anand's *Untouchable*

SARAH COPLAND

ACCORDING TO Indian writer Mulk Raj Anand's story of the genesis of *Untouchable*, when he told Mahatma Gandhi in the late 1920s or early 1930s that he had written a novel about a day in the life of a sweeper and latrine cleaner, Gandhi asked him, "Why don't you write a straight-forward pamphlet about Harijans [that is, members of the untouchable caste]?" ("On the Genesis" 94).[1] Anand recalled that the remark put him "on the defensive" and that he replied, "That is your job. . . . I feel I want to tell the story" (94). He did not deny the ideological work that *Untouchable* was doing, expressing much later, in 1991, his hope that by then the novel had "perhaps evoked empathy for the hero-anti-hero in several places where there are other[s] insulted and injured" (95). He went on to reference D. H. Lawrence's claim that a novel can "start a flow," "open[ing] the windows of the reader's consciousness towards a vision of reality, of understanding of a whole world and stir[ring] the chords of sympathy" (95). Nevertheless, the now famous tale of the editorial advice Gandhi gave Anand indicates that while the young Anand intended to do ideological work, he wanted to do it through narrative.[2]

---

1. I am very grateful to James Phelan and the volume's editors for their feedback on this essay. I am also grateful for the questions posed and insights shared by members of Aarhus University's Narrative Research Lab, where I first presented my work on this subject in May 2013.

2. Suijit Dulai notes that "as a progressive writer, Anand firmly believed that literature had a social purpose. But he also believed with an equally sure feeling about the nature of literature

Important to understanding the ramifications of Anand's choice of a narrative over a pamphlet are both the fact that narrative theory, across its range of approaches, maintains a distinction between narrative and that which is not narrative[3] and the fact that even in 1935, the year of the novel's publication, long before *Untouchable* became arguably the most famous work of Indian modernism, two influential reviews expressly noted that Anand's choice of a narrative over a pamphlet was particularly effective in engaging and "mov[ing]" (Scott-James 89) his readers. In the *London Mercury,* R. A. Scott-James praised the novel as "a rare example of the manner in which material that lends itself to propaganda can be so treated as to produce the pure effect of art. It achieves with no appearance of effort the end proper to fiction; in simply telling its story and drawing its picture it moves us as no didactic work could do" (89). In *Left Review,* John Sommerfield admiringly declared *Untouchable* "a very different kind of book" from F. Le Gros Clark's *Between Two Men,* also being reviewed, for in the latter "the ideas are more important than the story" (423). While Sommerfield agreed with the book jacket's description of *Untouchable* "reflect[ing] the struggle of the masses of India against the ancient forces that enslave them," he pointed out that Anand "doesn't mention it, he leaves it to you to work it out" (424).

Nevertheless, although Anand chose to do his ideological work by means of a novel rather than a pamphlet, he ultimately needed a pamphlet to accompany the novel as a condition of publication—a pamphlet not, however, about the issue of untouchability so much as about the very idea of a novel on this subject. After rejections by nineteen publishers, revisions under the advice of

---

that this purpose was achieved better by a faithful portrayal of authentic experience and by imaginative and esthetic integrity than by a bald enunciation of social theory thinly masked in fabricated stories" (188).

3. While different approaches within narrative theory develop different definitions of narrative, they all maintain a distinction between narrative and that which is not narrative. For example, rooting his conception of narrative in research into the mind-narrative nexus, David Herman defines narrative as a blueprint for world construction, designed by creators of stories and "prompt[ing] interpreters to construct worlds marked by [among other things] a particular spatiotemporal profile, a patterned sequence of situations and events, and an inventory of inhabitants" (Herman et al. 17). "Narrative" is a text type to be distinguished from other text types, such as "description," or "list," which engage "in a non- or antinarrative listing of locales that do not add up to a world" (224). Approaching narrative as an act of communication, rhetorical theorists James Phelan and Peter Rabinowitz define narrative as "somebody telling somebody else on some occasion and for some purpose(s) that something happened" (Phelan, *Experiencing Fiction* 3), with narrative thereby distinct from other communicative acts that do not possess these features. As Herman notes, the difference between these two seminal approaches in narrative theory is a difference stemming from emphasis on the semantic or world-creating properties of narrative, in his case, and emphasis on the transactional or communicative aspect of narrative, in the case of Phelan and Rabinowitz (Herman et al. 232).

Gandhi, and a recommendation by E. M. Forster, Anand's novel was finally published in 1935 by Wishart & Company on the condition that a preface by Forster (essentially a pamphlet for the novel) would be published along with it. Anand's intended readership was English colonials, and those associated with Bloomsbury in particular, as well as the few Indian students, professionals, and civil servants in the United Kingdom (Baer 585; Karunanayake 73). As the publishers' rejections and private correspondence between Anand and Forster and Anand and other British writers reveal, the barriers preventing access to this readership were the novel's subject matter and the fact that Anand was both unknown and a foreigner. A preface by Forster was expected to surmount these barriers, and Wishart's editor Edgell Rickward expressed his confidence that the preface would do just that. In a letter to Anand, dated 30 November 1934, Rickward praised the preface as "from every point of view . . . just what we wanted. It is a little masterpiece of suggestion and understanding, and will be the book's *passport* through the latent hostility of the ordinary reviewer" (qtd. in Nasta 163). Scott-James, reviewing the novel in the *London Mercury*, confirmed Rickward's judgment: "knowing India, having taste in literature, and being artistically incorruptible Mr. Forster is a welcome intermediary between ourselves and an author whose work might easily have escaped attention" (89). Since then, many Anand scholars have referred to the preface's role in facilitating the novel's publication and reception by both reviewers and the reading public.[4]

Even in 1935, Forster's preface and its relationship to the novel were starting to become subjects of critical analysis in their own right. In his *Left Review* piece, Sommerfield devoted one paragraph of seven to Forster's preface, agreeing with Forster that only "an Indian who observed from the outside could have written this book," but disagreeing with his claim that "an Untouchable would not be able to write about his class because he would be too involved in indignation and self-pity" and pointing out that Forster's "tone" primes the reader for "the most detailed excremental descriptions, which actually do not occur at all" (424, 425). In contemporary scholarship, however, only Amardeep Singh undertakes a textual analysis of the preface. He maintains that while modernist allographic (nonauthorial) prefaces foreground "a scene of exchange between Europe and non-European writing" and help "to *push modernism outside of itself,*" "Forster blurs the line between himself and Anand, [and] . . . this blurring is absorptive rather than equalising" because "the preface describes the subsequent literary text largely in terms of the preface-

---

4. See Baer; Berman, "Comparative Colonialisms" and "Toward a Regional Cosmopolitanism"; Nasta; Pontes; Ram.

writer's own work" (2, 3; emphasis in original). Furthermore, Singh argues, "Forster provides a *finish* (ie [sic] a reading) to Anand's text before the reader holding the book *Untouchable* even starts to read it" (3). Singh in fact argues that Forster's preface—like the other two Western writers' prefaces to non-Westerners' texts that Singh examines[5]—"reinscribes the political order of colonialism and leaves the coevalness of the [colonial writer's text] in question" (2). His reading, rooted in postcolonial theory, depicts the relationship between Forster's preface and Anand's novel in terms of the theory's construction of the colonizer-colonized dynamic.

In *Paratexts: Thresholds of Interpretation* (published as *Seuils* in 1987 and in English translation in 1997), Gérard Genette's synchronic, structuralist theory of the paratext, which remains the seminal and definitive work in the branch of narratology known as paratext studies, Genette describes allography as "a separation between the sender of the text (the author) and the sender of the preface (the preface-writer)" and the allographic prefacer as a "literary or ideological 'godfather'" (263, 273). To the original authorial preface's functions of promoting a work and guiding a reading of it, the allographic preface adds two specifications "attributable to the change in sender": "high praise of the text becomes a recommendation, and information about the text becomes a presentation" (265). Allographic prefaces are, according to Genette, by their very nature "inseparable from the routines of protection and patronage—as well as—sometimes— . . . those of highjacking and interception" (293) relative to the novels they accompany. Singh elaborates on the dynamics of allography in the colonial context, arguing that the "line between preface and text, the split between the two is . . . extended and enhanced in the colonial context, where the distinction between preface and text can be the very site of enforcement of colonial authority" (3).[6] Although they approach the allographic preface-text relation from very different angles—ideology and form, respectively—postcolonial theory and structuralist narratology conceive it in strikingly similar terms. In my view, however, Singh's analysis inadequately characterizes the ideological effects of Forster's preface, and structuralist narratology provides an inadequate guide to its actual workings. In the rest of this essay, I will substantiate this claim by deploying the tools of rhetorical narra-

---

5. W. B. Yeats's 1912 preface to Rabindranath Tagore's *Gitanjali* and André Breton's 1943 preface to Aimé Césaire's *Notebook of a Return to My Native Land*.

6. Surveying "the surprisingly narrow and often polarized critical landscape surrounding evaluation of Anand's fiction," Susheila Nasta argues that Anand "has been all but invisible in British literary histories," "seldom described as a dynamic activist, or as a key contributor to the refashioning of Britain as a crucible for international modernity, but as a colonial outsider 'lifted up' by the patronage of Forster's liberal humanist cosmopolitanism" (153).

tive theory to unpack both the formal strategies and the ideological work of Forster's preface, at the same time challenging the conception of prefatorial allography assumed by both postcolonial theory and structuralist narratology.

More specifically, because the preface uses narrative centrally and is explicitly persuasive, rooted in a specific occasion, and directed at a particular group of readers, I draw on rhetorical narrative theory's construction of the communications between the author and two of his audiences, the flesh-and-blood reader and the authorial audience. The flesh-and-blood reader is the actual reader reading the text; when I read Forster's preface, I, Sarah Copland, am the flesh-and-blood reader. The authorial audience is "the author's ideal reader," "the hypothetical, ideal audience for whom the author constructs the text and who understands it perfectly" (Phelan, *Experiencing Fiction* 4; *Narrative as Rhetoric* 215). As James Phelan and Peter Rabinowitz argue, flesh-and-blood readers "typically join (or try to join) the authorial audience," meaning that they take on (or try to take on) "the knowledge, values, prejudices, fears, and experiences that the author expected in his or her readers and that ground his or her rhetorical choices" in the construction of the text (Herman et al. 6). In other words, when I, Sarah Copland, a flesh-and-blood reader, read Forster's preface, I try to join Forster's authorial audience by taking on the knowledge, values, prejudices, fears, and experiences that he expected his mid-1930s, mainly British readers would possess, including hostility and skepticism toward Anand's subject matter, as well as—and this is crucial—openness to persuasion about the novel's merits. Phelan and Rabinowitz offer the example of Mark Twain's authorial audience for *Huckleberry Finn*: "the book is written for an authorial audience prepared to question at least some of the givens of standard nineteenth-century Christianity, and . . . failure to join the authorial audience is a . . . barrier to appreciation of the novel" (Herman et al. 142). Likewise, Twain has a "set of expectations with regard to the ethics of race relations: the novel simply will *not* work for a reader who is ethically incapable of endorsing the friendship between a runaway slave and a young white boy" (142). "Put all these things together," Phelan and Rabinowitz say, "and you are beginning to understand what it *feels like* to read *Huckleberry Finn* as a member of the authorial audience" (142). Returning to Forster's preface, in order to understand Forster's design, I, Sarah Copland, flesh-and-blood reader, must try to understand and inhabit the authorial audience for whom his rhetorical strategies were originally crafted.

For the purposes of my analysis of Forster's preface, the authorial audience is a particularly useful concept for understanding not only what we do when we try to participate in the reading experience Forster has created for us but also the impact of historical and cultural circumstances on Forster's "constructive choices" (Phelan, *Reading the American Novel* 28).[7] To put this in Phelan's terms, "the concept of the authorial audience provides the bridge between history and rhetorical form, because it taps into what a historically situated author will assume about her audience's knowledge of the period and other raw material and into how she uses those assumptions in the shaping of her material" (28). In other words, an author's understanding of her actual flesh-and-blood reader's knowledge, values, prejudices, fears, and experiences has a significant impact on her creation of the authorial audience *and* on her selection of rhetorical strategies used to appeal to flesh-and-blood readers to join that audience.

As is the case, then, in all narrative communications, the opening narrative in Forster's preface is a multifaceted rhetorical appeal, directed at a flesh-and-blood reader—a skeptical prospective reader of Anand's novel—and designed to invite him or her into the authorial audience. Understanding the moves Forster makes in his rhetorical appeals requires both a recognition that this preface was quite simply not written for us (us contemporary readers) and, consequently, a conception of the flesh-and-blood reader for whom this preface was written and upon whom its invitations to join the authorial audience were based.[8] In a highly contingent paratextual communication, the rhetorical moves by which an author invites his contemporary flesh-and-blood reader into the authorial audience will not function in precisely the same way for later flesh-and-blood readers in very different historical and cultural circumstances, possessing different knowledge, values, prejudices, fears, and experiences.[9] Assertions about the appropriative or colonizing nature of Forster's preface relative to Anand's novel—and, indeed, about allographic prefaces relative to novels, especially those with preface writers from colonizing countries and writers from colonized countries—may, then, be rooted not in (or not only in) a theoretical commitment to the often universalizing, essentializing constructs of structuralist narratology's paratext studies or postcolonial

---

7. Rhetorical narrative theory makes further distinctions between flesh-and-blood reader, authorial audience, narratee, and narrative audience, as well as distinctions between author, implied author, and narrator, but, in tune with the approach's emphasis on pragmatism, I draw only on the author, flesh-and-blood reader, and authorial audience, as only these concepts bear sufficient interpretive weight for analysis of Forster's preface.

8. My search for the historical authorial audience in Forster's preface, irrespective of theoretical assumptions governing prefatorial allography, aligns with Arun P. Mukherjee's search for the historical untouchable (not) in Anand's novel, irrespective of what he calls the "nationalist historiography" of the relationship between untouchables and Gandhi and other nationalist leaders.

9. The paratext in general is by its very nature much more in flux than the text itself in the course of its publication history, so it is much more closely tied to contingent historical and cultural circumstances and to actual readers from specific times and places.

theory but rather in a problem of reference: reference to a mismatched pairing of contemporary flesh-and-blood reader and original authorial audience.

Consequently, I frame my inquiry independently of preconceived ideas from structuralist narratology's paratext studies or postcolonial theory about the role an allographic preface writer must be assuming simply by virtue of being an allographic preface writer (especially one from a colonizing country). I thus have no assumptions about what it means, for example, to begin an allographic preface with a reference to one's own work, not automatically concluding that such a move is a self-aggrandizing domination of the prefaced text, but instead examining the move's rhetorical functions in the specific context of the occasion and purpose for the preface. In other words, attending to the occasion of Forster's writing, that is, the fulfillment of a request to supply a preface that would ensure the novel's publication, I am more committed to exploring the specific, local context in which his preface's rhetorical strategies unfold than to assuming the general, global dynamic existing between author and allographic preface writer or colonized and colonizer. Openly acknowledging how lamentable and shameful it is that an English writer's preface was a precondition for the publication and reception of an Indian author's masterpiece, I am committed to analyzing the preface's rhetorical appeals within the context of its publication and thus to a contextual narratological enterprise.

NARRATIVE, THE FLESH-AND-BLOOD READER, AND THE AUTHORIAL AUDIENCE

Forster opens his preface with a story about the time he discovered an indignant colonel's notes in a library copy of his novel *A Passage to India* (1924). The notes read "burn when done" and "has a dirty mind, see page 215," the page on which Forster makes a passing reference to sweepers and latrines (Preface v). While we might conclude, as Amardeep Singh does, that this opening anecdote subordinates Anand's work to Forster's, historicizing the flesh-and-blood reader and Forster's rhetorical strategies for inviting that reader into his authorial audience leads to a more nuanced appreciation of the story's role in the preface. Forster uses this anecdote to epitomize a flesh-and-blood reader's (the colonel's) refusal of an author's invitations to join his authorial audience in a narrative concerning material that is similar to the material that prospective readers of Anand's novel will shortly encounter. In other words, knowing that he is responding to "the latent hostility of the ordinary reviewer [and, by extension, the broader reading public]" (Rickward qtd. in Nasta 163),

Forster captures and attempts to alter the dynamic he knows will likely be present even if he manages to convert potential flesh-and-blood readers into actual flesh-and-blood readers of Anand's novel. Indeed, as Susheila Nasta demonstrates, the British reading public was truly skeptical: "to many, the central focus of this novel, concerning a day in the life of Bakha, one of India's untouchables (a sweeper and latrine cleaner) seemed to be too 'vulgar,' even too 'dirty'; too inappropriate a subject to be admitted easily into the 'supposedly' respectable world of 1930s' British fiction" (151). Reading in a different time and place, neither skeptical about nor hostile to Anand's novel, likely curious and open-minded about it, and having perhaps been exposed to colonial and postcolonial literature and to postcolonial theory, we (contemporary flesh-and-blood readers) should not lose sight of the impact that the original flesh-and-blood readers' knowledge, values, prejudices, fears, and experiences had on Forster's construction of his authorial audience and his selection of rhetorical strategies to appeal to his actual readers. Keeping the original flesh-and-blood readers in mind and understanding the constraints they placed on Forster's rhetorical choices will help us to negotiate the skepticism and hostility we (contemporary flesh-and-blood readers) may feel toward not the novel but the preface itself, conditioned as we are by the constructions of prefatorial allography inherent in postcolonial theory and in structuralist narratology's paratext studies.

Aware that he needs to prime actual flesh-and-blood readers of Anand's novel for acceptance of Anand's invitations to enter his authorial audience, Forster tells a story that positions the flesh-and-blood reader of the preface in his own authorial audience right away. Rickward's decision to include a preface by Forster presupposes that potential readers have heard of Forster and esteem him, either because they have read his work or by reputation. Such readers would have either joined Forster's authorial audience when reading *A Passage to India* or assumed that they would do so, were they to read the novel. They would, in other words, see themselves responding to Forster's novel very differently from how the colonel responded to it. To aid those who have not read *A Passage to India* and are responding to Forster on reputation alone, Forster implicitly characterizes the colonel as a narrow-minded and ridiculous figure, one whose judgments the reader of the preface would not want to share. Although Forster does not say so explicitly, the continued existence of the book proves that the colonel has obviously failed to fulfill his commitment to burning it, and, even if his injunction is directed at other readers rather than at himself, his reference to the specific page on which the dirty material is found ("see page 215") reveals a perverse commitment to having others share this reading experience, a move greatly at odds with the ostensible claim that such material is subliterary, offensive, and polluting. Forster himself, on the other hand, makes an appeal to ethos, appearing, both in terms of the way he reacts to this discovery and in terms of the way he recounts the tale, to be reasonable, good-humored, and urbane. He recounts that he "turned to page 215 with pardonable haste" (Preface v) to find out what he had written there that had so offended the colonel's sensibilities. Forster copies in full the offending sentence, "The sweepers of Chandrapur had just struck, and half the commodes remained desolate in consequence" (v), emphasizing the disjunction between the relative harmlessness of the material and the extremity of the colonel's reaction to it. Forster then concludes, wittily and equally hyperbolically, "This light-hearted remark has excluded me forever from military society ever since" (v).

Having drawn readers into his own authorial audience by creating a position for them relative to *A Passage to India*, Forster goes on to use the story to contrast the colonel's hypothetical response to Anand's novel with his (Forster's) own actual response, which he sets up as the response of a flesh-and-blood reader who has accepted the author's invitations, who has tried to take on "the knowledge, values, prejudices, fears, and experiences that the author expected in his . . . readers and that ground his . . . rhetorical choices" (Herman et al. 6). Posing the rhetorical question about what the colonel "will . . . think about *Untouchable*" "if [he] . . . thought *A Passage to India* dirty" (Preface v), Forster implies that the colonel would refuse Anand's invitations to join his authorial audience, just as he refused Forster's. Because Forster has already positioned his readers in opposition to the colonel relative to *A Passage to India* and relative to his own preface, he need only take a few more steps to position readers in opposition to the colonel relative to Anand's novel too. He starts by declaring his own decision to accept Anand's invitations to join his authorial audience on the basis of the classic rhetorical distinction between material and treatment, here applied to the dirty material of excrement and Anand's clean aesthetic treatment of the subject. Attributing Anand's "success" to "the directness of his attack," Forster concludes that Anand's novel is not a "dirty book" but a book that is "indescribably clean": "avoiding rhetoric and circumlocution, it has gone straight to the heart of the matter and purified it" (v).

Forster's story about the indignant colonel thus establishes a kind of outgroup of readers, a "them," in comparison to the "us" group of readers, those who are willing to accept an author's invitations to enter the authorial audience, whether those invitations are Forster's relative to *A Passage to India*, Forster's relative to his own preface, or Anand's relative to *Untouchable*. Narrow-minded, prudish, repressed readers who dismiss Anand's subject matter outright find themselves lumped in with the indignant colonel. A more hypocritical, ridiculous, and bigoted fellow reader can scarcely be imagined, and Forster sets himself up against the colonel to invite readers into his own camp, entry consisting simply of willingness to read Anand's novel and accept Anand's invitations to think open-mindedly about hitherto unnarratable subject matter.[10] Forster does not, however, simply expect his readers to take his word for it that Anand's novel is worth reading and his authorial audience worth joining. In the rest of the preface, following the opening narrative and the aforementioned distinction between material and treatment, Forster explains how and why he joined Anand's authorial audience.

CLASSIC RHETORICAL APPEALS

Having used the narrative to create an analogy between one reader's reaction to reading his own novel and potential readers' reactions to reading Anand's, contrasting these reactions with his own acceptance of Anand's invitations to join the authorial audience, Forster turns to a more overtly persuasive mode of engagement with his readers, using classic rhetorical appeals to logos, pathos, and ethos. The bulk of the preface, though not written in narrative form, essentially tells the story of Forster's reading experience, which is pitched not as the story of an individualized, subjective, idiosyncratic response but as the response that shares the authorial audience's knowledge, values, prejudices, fears, and experiences.

Forster's appeal to logos is rooted in an analogy between English and Indian forms of mental "knots" (Preface v), which one might think of as kinds of mental constipation. Forster argues that the English suffer from psychologically damaging reticence and prudishness about the process of excretion, while Indians suffer from a ritual aversion to the product of excretion, which has given rise to the untouchability taboo, in which handlers of human waste, such as latrine cleaners, are considered, according to a metonymic logic, literally untouchable. Neither civilization has fallen prey to the other's

---

10. Furthermore, while the average flesh-and-blood reader of Forster's preface has no way of knowing this, Forster's decision to begin with the anecdote about finding the colonel's note in a library copy of *A Passage to India* is also a rhetorical strategy that appeals to a smaller audience, members of the Bloomsbury Group who can appreciate the allusion to *Untouchable*'s genesis story: Anand later reported that he heard Forster's anecdote during a conversation with Forster and Leonard and Virginia Woolf and that it gave him the idea for the novel, which he then wrote over a long weekend (Pontes 128–29). Forster thereby enlarges the "us" group to include other modernist writers who share Anand's and Forster's opinions about the importance of broadening readers' minds.

"knot," but each is very much caught up in its own "tangle" (v, vi). In this argument based on reason, Forster demonstrates the relevance of seemingly irrelevant subject matter for an English readership, suggesting that their own relationship to the human body's functioning is problematic and, by implication, that confronting the subject matter of Anand's novel is a healthy step in the right direction.

He then appeals to pathos and to ethos, the former via a description of the plight of the untouchable: "The sweeper is worse off than a slave, for the slave may change his master and his duties and may even become free, but the sweeper is bound for ever, born into a state from which he cannot escape and where he is excluded from social intercourse and the consolations of his religion" (vi). Forster's appeal to ethos is an account of Anand as ideally and uniquely suited to writing a book on this subject. Anand, an Indian but not an untouchable, has "the right mixture of insight and detachment" (vii). He "played [as a child] with the children of the sweepers attached to an Indian regiment" and grew "fond of them," gaining an understanding of "a tragedy which he did not share" (vii). Anand's background in philosophy gives him "depth" without "vagueness—that curse of the generalising mind" (vii).

Each of the last three paragraphs of the preface also contains responses to objections or criticisms Forster can imagine the flesh-and-blood reader making, either before or during the reading experience: about the opinion that the untouchable is "so degraded that he doesn't mind" the discrimination he faces, about the possibility that Bakha is an abstraction, and about the relationship between the "closing section of the book," possibly "too voluble and sophisticated," and "the clear observation which has preceded it" (vi, viii). At times, Forster allows other voices to respond to these imagined questions and objections, perhaps to modulate the authoritative position he must, given the purpose and occasion of the preface, assume. He draws on the words of one of Anand's characters to describe untouchability's metonymic logic—"They think we are dirt because we clean their dirt"—and refers to "the opinion of those who have studied [the untouchables'] . . . case" in addition to his own "slight testimony" regarding the plight of untouchables in India (vi). While the middle section of Forster's preface is a much more overtly persuasive discourse than the narrative opening, its purpose is the same: to encourage the reader not only to read Anand's novel but also to join his authorial audience by dropping some deep-seated cultural prejudices and opening himself or herself to a new view of Anand's subject matter, in turn becoming more receptive to Anand's treatment of that subject matter—just as Forster has done but the indignant colonel would refuse to do.

MODELING RHETORICAL READING

The preface's final paragraph, far from providing a finish to or a reading of the novel for the reader in a dominating or appropriative way, as Singh claims, takes the reader back, full circle, to the opening anecdote, but this time models or enacts—as opposed to simply referring to—rhetorical reading, a practice antithetical to the indignant colonel's response. Rhetorical reading is "the critical approach that attends both to the journey and to the destination" and whose "method is to analyze both the what and the how of the reading experience" (Phelan, *Reading the American Novel* 23). Forster's assessment is, unlike the colonel's, based on treatment as well as material, on the aesthetic whole and the role of its component parts, and on the progression of the reader's engagement with the narrative. He finds that the work as a whole involves action occupying "one day" in "a small area" with "the great catastrophe of the 'touching' occur[ring] in the morning, and poison[ing] all that happens subsequently"; then, "after a jagged course of ups and downs, we come to the solution, or rather to the three solutions, with which the book closes" (Preface vii).

If we extend to Forster the same effort to understand his "scheme" (viii) that he does to Anand, we see that although Forster gives away the ending of the novel, describing each of the three solutions to the untouchables' plight and Bakha's responses to them, the purpose of this disclosure is pedagogy rather than spoiling. He has positioned his readers in his own authorial audience relative to *A Passage to India* and his preface and in Anand's authorial audience relative to *Untouchable,* but now he must model interpretation and evaluation based on an appreciation of the author's scheme and of how the parts of that scheme function together. He does so in his reading of the novel's conclusion, which, he writes, may seem too voluble and sophisticated in comparison with what has come before, but is in fact "the necessary climax, and it has mounted up with [the] triple effect [of the three solutions]" (viii).

The preface's final sentence signals a return to its opening reference to *A Passage to India,* this time to implicitly acknowledge that Anand's novel goes much farther than Forster's and, therefore, that being in Anand's authorial audience is a more challenging and potentially more rewarding experience. The preface ends with the sentences: "Bakha [the central character] returns to his father and his wretched bed, thinking now of the Mahatma, now of the Machine. His Indian day is over and the next day will be like it, but on the surface of the earth if not in the depths of the sky, a change is at hand" (viii). This statement recalls the final sentence of Forster's *A Passage to India*:

> But the horses didn't want it—they swerved apart; the earth didn't want it, sending up rocks through which riders must pass single-file; the temples, the tank, the jail, the palace, the birds, the carrion, the Guest House, that came into view as they issued from the gap and saw Mau beneath: they didn't want it, they said in their hundred voices, "No, not yet," and the sky said, "No, not there." (306)

Susheila Nasta writes, "There is no doubt that, when Forster first drafted his short preface to *Untouchable* in 1934, he was already aware that Anand was extending his reach well beyond a simple recounting of a day in the life of his untouchable anti-hero, Bakha" (161). She argues that the preface's final sentence points "perhaps to the possibility of resolution not realizable at the time he [Forster] penned his own novel" (161). Forster does more than point; he makes a direct intertextual reference via the repetition of "the earth" and "the sky," but the difference between the two passages is significant. No one and no thing, neither in human civilization nor in nature, is ready for change at the end of Forster's novel, but Forster recognizes that there is indeed change at hand in both human civilization and nature—"on the surface of the earth"—by the end of Anand's.

Stepping outside Anand's storyworld, in which Forster sees change at hand, we can readily see that two of the changes on the surface of the earth are the very existence of a novel on the subject of untouchability and the possibility that this novel might engage readers in ways that Forster's own novel could not. After all, the difference between what Forster's novel asks of the reader and what Anand's novel asks of him or her is striking. Forster's novel asks for the reader's interest in and affective and ethical engagement with the affairs of a cast of British colonials and comparatively middle- and upper-class Indians, Anand's for a cast of untouchables. Forster's preface plays a small but critical role in bringing this change about: he provides the groundwork for Anand's actual flesh-and-blood readers to accept Anand's invitations to join the authorial audience. That he moves them through his own authorial audiences for *A Passage to India* and his preface in order to get them there is a rhetorical strategy selected to suit the historically and culturally contingent occasion and purpose of his writing.

CONTEXTUAL RHETORICAL ANALYSIS AND REPRESENTATIONS OF UNTOUCHABILITY

A historically and culturally inflected formal analysis is ideally suited to recovering the historical authorial audience inscribed in and the historical flesh-and-blood reader addressed by Forster's preface and thus to parsing the preface's appeals, both the opening narrative, the subsequent appeals to logos, pathos, and ethos, and the model of rhetorical reading. The treatments of untouchability in both *Untouchable* and *A Passage to India* are particularly helpful as means of conceptualizing the rhetorical analysis I have undertaken in this essay. Just as my analysis conceives the preface's rhetorical strategies as context-dependent, based on occasion, purpose, and audience, so the two novels feature episodes that represent untouchability as a context-dependent phenomenon and serve as contrasts with the central events, which feature context-independent, highly coded and regulated untouchability taboos. In *Untouchable*, the inadvertent physical contact between Bakha and the Lalla in the street constitutes the central event, with other important events, such as the priest's molestation of Bakha's sister Sohini, also centering on the issue of untouchability. In *A Passage to India*, the central event is an incident in the Marabar caves, possibly involving physical contact, deemed transgressive, between the Muslim doctor Aziz and the English visitor Adela Quested.

Despite the binary construction of touchable and untouchable inherent in the concept of untouchability and maintained in the aforementioned central incidents of both novels, the novels also include other incidents depicting untouchability as a context-dependent phenomenon, operating differently among different groups of people in different settings. In *Untouchable*, the untouchable caste is untouchable from the point of view of caste Hindus, but so are Muslims, and, for Brahmins, so are the British (Cowasjee 202), whereas for the Christian missionary Colonel Hutchinson and for the Hindu children during their field hockey game, no one is untouchable. At different points in the novel, the untouchables alternately ignore and enforce an etiquette of touch amongst themselves. In the group of three untouchable friends, Ram Charan is "of the higher caste" because he is a washerman, Chota "next in the hierarchy" because he is a leather-worker's son, and Bakha, the sweeper and latrine cleaner, "of the third and lowest category"; however,

> among the trio they had banished all thought of distinction, except when the snobbery of caste feeling supplied the basis for putting on airs for a joke. They had eaten together, if not things in the preparation of which water had been used, at least dry things, this being in imitation of the line drawn by the Hindus between themselves and the Mohammedans and Christians. Sweets they had often shared together, and they handled soda-water bottles anyhow, at all those formal hockey matches they played once a year. (96–97)[11]

---

11. This paragraph's references to *Untouchable* are taken from the 1990 Penguin edition.

Dejected by a day of humiliations, Bakha forces his friends to become aware of his subjection even in their own social group, refusing to take his sugarplum from Ram Charan's hand and instead insisting that Ram Charan throw it to him. Bakha's friends are "surprised" and concerned because "never before ha[ve] they seen Bakha behave like that" (96)—and because they have never really enforced the rigid rules of the untouchability taboo amongst themselves.[12] As it is in some of *Untouchable*'s episodes, the binary construction of touchable and untouchable inherent in the concept of untouchability is also entirely context-dependent in one of *A Passage to India*'s episodes: after the car accident, Adela's hand touches Ronny's in a way that is welcome and thrilling to both parties, but she responds viscerally, with revulsion, to that touch in the caves. While Ronny does not, of course, literally touch her in the caves, as he is not part of the expedition, when she is touched or imagines herself to be touched, what she is thinking about is her relationship with him and, very probably, about being touched by Ronny, Ronny whom she knows she does not love.

My hope is that the kind of contextual rhetorical analysis I have undertaken in this essay, which I find helpfully conceived in terms of the two novels' secondary representations of untouchability, will lead to a long overdue critical edition of *Untouchable,* featuring an introduction, notes, and other scholarly apparatus presenting the preface as a historical artifact. Such a presentation of the preface would offer readers contextual information helpful to understanding the rhetorical strategies by which Forster and Anand each appealed to their flesh-and-blood readers, created their authorial audiences, and did so in light of the appeals and creations the other was making. In 2008, Susheila Nasta noted that "only one edition of *Untouchable* . . . does not conform to the pattern of retaining Forster's preface without comment and that is the Bodley Head edition, published in 1970, which adds a revealing 'Afterword' by Saros Cowasjee, one of Anand's most perceptive critics and biographers, providing details of the novel's troubled publication history" (164). In January 2014, however, Penguin released a new edition of the novel, featuring an introduction by Ramachandra Guha that mentions neither the text's publication and reception histories nor Forster and his preface. The preface itself has been relocated to the end of the edition and labeled "Afterword."[13]

---

12. Anand's own life experiences also reflect context-dependent practices of untouchability. On a ship en route to England, Anand, a caste Hindu, found himself untouchable from the point of view of the English (qtd. in Pontes 131). In Gandhi's ashram, however, no one was untouchable, and Anand himself was asked to clean the latrines once a week ("On the Genesis" 94).

13. The Longman Study Edition, published by Dorling Kindersley India in 2007, omits the preface entirely.

So much time has passed since the publication of *Untouchable* that modern readers are likely to be familiar with colonial and postcolonial literatures, as well as (possibly) postcolonial theory, making it potentially difficult to read Forster's preface in ways other than those assumed by structuralist narratology and postcolonial theory, which dominate scholarship on prefatorial allography. That is, it is potentially difficult to read Forster's preface as anything other than self-serving and appropriative. Lamentably, Penguin's editorial decisions endorse such a (mis)reading. One might argue that the preface is no longer necessary, as modern readers do not share the knowledge, values, prejudices, fears, and experiences of Anand's original readers and therefore would have far less difficulty in or resistance to joining Anand's authorial audience. From this perspective, the preface is surely not necessary; if, however, the preface is presented as a historical artifact, in the context of information about the novel's publication and reception histories, it would be invaluable for modern readers' understanding of the what and the how of the work the novel performed in its own time and the magnitude of its eventual success, against all odds.[14] As David Herman notes, just as "norms shape the kinds of stories people tell," so "the telling of particular kinds of stories in particular contexts provides scaffolding for the construction of normative frameworks" (Herman et al. 169). In other words, norms relating to acceptable subjects for narrative fiction and acceptable means of depicting these subjects help us to build narrative worlds, but, particularly when "what goes on in a storyworld disrupts normative or canonical situations," these narrative worlds can, in turn, change our norms about what kinds of stories are imaginable and tellable. Forster's preface, as a historical artifact, shows us in the clearest possible terms just how unimaginable and untellable Anand's story once was, giving us an index for assessing how much has changed since then—and how much remains to be changed.

Returning to the issue of the practice of literary criticism, I note that one of the things that a contextual rhetorical analysis of historical artifacts like Forster's preface might change is the way in which we engage with prefato-

---

14. As an anonymous reviewer of this essay insightfully noted, *Untouchable* might still be regarded as a controversial text today, not because of the issue of colonialism but because of caste politics and debates about high-caste writers' appropriation of Dalit voices. This reviewer noted that a new preface to the novel would need to address caste and appropriation. If we regard Forster's preface as important precisely because of the historical and contextual inflection it contributes to one's reading of the novel, a new preface, offered alongside Forster's, would further—and productively—illuminate the core issues my essay attempts to address: a new preface, juxtaposed with Forster's, would illuminate the very different rhetorical choices a preface writer today would make in order to construct his or her own authorial audience and to appeal to a very different body of flesh-and-blood readers to join that audience.

rial allography in colonial-era and even postcolonial productions. Based on analysis of Forster's preface, I do not conclude that relations of "protection and patronage" "highjacking and interception" do not obtain in cases involving a Western allographic prefacer and a non-Western writer, simply that they do not obtain in this case, when this case is viewed from a historically and culturally situated perspective (Genette 293). The only way to make a textually grounded assessment of the preface-text relation is to adhere to an a posteriori methodology of the kind pursued in rhetorical narrative theory: to enter the feedback loop of textual phenomena, authorial intentions, and reader response at any point—and all three are readily available to us in this case—and to assess multileveled author-audience relations according to the evidence provided, rather than undertaking analysis with preconceived ideas about the author-audience relations and the narratological hierarchies or ideological agendas they manifest. An a posteriori rhetorical analysis of prefatorial allography in colonial and postcolonial productions is textual, contextual, historical, pragmatic, and intention- and reader-oriented. In contrast to the gesture of spatiotemporal deferral at the end of *A Passage to India*—"No, not yet, . . . [n]o, not there" (306)—this approach says, "Yes, now, but also then. Yes, here, but also there."

WORKS CITED

Anand, Mulk Raj. "On the Genesis of *Untouchable*." *South Asian Review* 15.12 (1991): 94–95.

———. *Untouchable*. 1935. London: Penguin, 1990.

———. *Untouchable*. 1935. Delhi: Dorling Kindersley (India), 2007.

———. *Untouchable*. 1935. London: Penguin, 2014.

Baer, Ben Conisbee. "Shit Writing: Mulk Raj Anand's *Untouchable*, the Image of Gandhi, and the Progressive Writers' Association." *Modernism/Modernity* 16.3 (2009): 575–95.

Berman, Jessica. "Comparative Colonialisms: Joyce, Anand, and the Question of Engagement." *Modernism/Modernity* 13.3 (2006): 465–85.

———. "Toward a Regional Cosmopolitanism: The Case of Mulk Raj Anand." *Modern Fiction Studies* 55.1 (2009): 142–62.

Cowasjee, Saros. "Mulk Raj Anand's *Untouchable*: An Appraisal." *Literature East and West* 17 (1973): 199–211.

Dulai, Suijit S. "Practice Before Ideology: Mulk Raj Anand's *Untouchable*." *Journal of South Asian Literature* 27.2 (1992): 187–207.

Forster, E. M. *A Passage to India*. London: Penguin, 2005.

———. Preface. *Untouchable*. By Mulk Raj Anand. 1935. London: Penguin, 1990. v–viii.

———. "To Mulk Raj Anand." 5 May 1934. *South Asian Review* 15.12 (1991): 93.

Genette, Gérard. *Paratexts: Thresholds of Interpretation.* Trans. Jane E. Lewin. Cambridge: Cambridge University Press, 1997.

Herman, David, James Phelan, Peter J. Rabinowitz, Brian Richardson, and Robyn Warhol. *Narrative Theory: Core Concepts and Critical Debates.* Columbus: Ohio State University Press, 2012.

Karunanayake, Dinithi. "The Empire Writing/Righting Itself?: A Reading of Mulk Raj Anand's *Untouchable.*" *The Sri Lanka Journal of the Humanities* 36.1/2 (2010): 69–85.

Mukherjee, Arun P. "The Exclusions of Postcolonial Theory and Mulk Raj Anand's *Untouchable*: A Case Study." *ARIEL* 22.3 (1991): 27–48.

Nasta, Susheila. "Between Bloomsbury and Gandhi? The Background to the Publication and Reception of Mulk Raj Anand's *Untouchable.*" *Books Without Borders: Perspectives from South Asia.* Ed. Robert Fraser and Mary Hammond. Vol. 2. Basingstoke: Palgrave Macmillan, 2008. 151–69.

Phelan, James. *Experiencing Fiction: Judgments, Progressions, and the Rhetorical Theory of Narrative.* Columbus: Ohio State University Press, 2008.

———. *Narrative as Rhetoric: Technique, Audiences, Ethics, Ideology.* Columbus: Ohio State University Press, 1996.

———. *Reading the American Novel 1920–2010.* Hoboken: John Wiley & Sons, 2013.

Pontes, Hilda. "Anand's *Untouchable*: A Classic in Experimentation of Theme and Technique." *Studies in Indian Fiction in English.* Ed. G. S. Balarama Gupta. Gulbarga: JIWE Publications, 1987. 128–41.

Ram, Atma. "A Reading of Mulk Raj Anand." *Poetcrit* (2010): 4–7.

Scott-James, R. A. "An Indian Out-Caste." Rev. of *Untouchable,* by Mulk Raj Anand. *The London Mercury* 32.187 (1935): 89.

Singh, Amardeep. "The Lifting and the Lifted: Prefaces to Colonial Modernist Texts." *Wasafiri* 21.1 (2006): 1–9.

Sommerfield, John. "Two Novels." Rev. of *Between Two Men* by F. Le Gros Clark and *Untouchable* by Mulk Raj Anand. *The Left Review.* 1.10 (1935): 423–25.

CHAPTER 6

Ideological Ambivalence

A Reading of Salman Rushdie's Midnight's Children

JAN ALBER

THIS ARTICLE addresses the ideological ramifications of Salman Rushdie's novel *Midnight's Children* (1981).[1] As I will show, the novel as a whole displays a rather ambivalent attitude with regard to its first-person narrator and his vision of postindependence India.[2] Saleem Sinai states that he would like to initiate a "journey into newness" (Rushdie, *Midnight's Children* 376) where the "multiple faces of the Bharat-Mata" (392) can be freely expressed. He argues that he is directed against qualities such as uniformity,

---

1. I follow Louis Althusser's use of the term "ideology." For him, ideologies are "imaginary . . . world outlooks," that is, worldviews that do not "correspond to reality" (1498). As examples of such imaginary distortions, Althusser mentions the belief in God, Duty, Justice, the Family, the Trade Union, the Party, and so forth. These beliefs are ideological because there can be no absolute reason why one should take them for granted. In contrast to Terry Eagleton, Althusser is not only interested in "organizing social forces" that aim at "the general reproduction of the social order" (Eagleton 223). For Althusser, ideologies may also call the existing social order into question. Furthermore, in contrast to Karl Marx, Althusser assumes the existence of numerous different ideologies that interpellate (and speak through) human subjects, thus turning them into networks of ideologies.

2. Other critics speak of the "implied author" (or perhaps even "the author") rather than the "text as a whole." Since I do not think that one can easily know the implied (or real) author's intentions, I try to avoid these two terms. Instead, I resort to hypothetical intentionalism, a cognitive approach in which "a narrative's meaning is established by hypothesizing intentions authors might have had, given the context of creation, rather than relying on, or trying to seek out, the author's subjective intentions" (Gibbs 248). I want to acknowledge the fact that my reading is based on hypotheses and speculations about authorial intent.

egotism, power, and hierarchies. Instead, the narrator claims to be interested in a "loose federation of equals, all points of view given free expression" (215) and believes that "it's a dangerous business to try and impose one's view of things on others" (208). The novel shares Sinai's pluralist vision of an India where different ethnicities, religions, and local communities peacefully coexist—at least it does not argue in favor of the despotic principles represented by Sinai's opponent, Shiva. But *Midnight's Children* also demonstrates that the forces of a homogenizing nationalism make it impossible to implement Sinai's vision. Furthermore, the narrator is not immune to these forces: his actions repeatedly violate his ideological beliefs.

This essay seeks to contribute to the further development of a "postcolonial narratology" (see Alber; Birk and Neumann; Fludernik "Narrative Forms"; Prince; Sommer). As Roy Sommer has shown, the primary goal of such a narratology is "the exploration of relationships between narrative structures and the core concepts of postcolonial studies" (68). Narratives typically merge different ideologies. This mingling of standpoints is often what makes it difficult to critically read the overall text. In order to determine what the narrative as a whole is doing or wants us to do, it is important to deal with the functions of the individual strategies that the text deploys. Monika Fludernik argues that postcolonial narratologists "describe how the choice of specific narrative techniques helps to transmit underlying orientalist or patriarchal structures and how the narrative, by its choice of focalization, plot structure, or use of free indirect discourse, sometimes resists these structures, undermines or deconstructs them" ("Histories" 45). In this essay, I look at the specific ideological functions of the narrative strategies used in *Midnight's Children*. I want to show what individual techniques do to me during the reading process, and how these strategies add up to an ideological whole. My goal is not to falsify or critique existing postcolonial interpretations of Rushdie's novel. Instead, I want to show what kind of reading a narratological analysis of *Midnight's Children* might produce, and I shall compare my own analysis to readings by others (including postcolonial critics). I believe that this approach can be illuminating for both postcolonial criticism *and* narratology. Like Sommer, I am interested in "a lively dialogue and mutual exchange between . . . critical traditions" (71). In what follows, I will try to determine the ideological ramifications of narrative techniques such as the use of multiple beginnings, the novel's allegorical structure, the narrator's telepathy, Sinai's invocation of the "Third Space" and the multifariousness of the characters, the intertextual references, and the different styles and registers. All of these choices matter with regard to the novel's underlying ideology.

Specifically, I will show that some narrative strategies invite us to identify with Sinai's vision, while others expose the impossibility of implementing his ideas. *Midnight's Children* implicates its readers in Sinai's democratic pluralism; after all, we never leave his consciousness and his voice dominates the narrative up until its end. At the same time, however, Sinai's actions consistently contradict his own moral standards. The narrative exposes Sinai as an idealist dreamer who is unaware of the discrepancy between his vision and his actual behavior. As a Western reader who has lived in (more or less) functioning democracies all his life, I am highly sympathetic to Sinai's political ideas. It is therefore important to look at gaps, breaks, and contradictions by closely scrutinizing Sinai's position and his interactions with other characters.

MULTIPLE NARRATIVE BEGINNINGS

Midnight's Children is a highly digressive narrative. Rushdie points out that the novel is based on the model of oral narrative because it is

> not linear. An oral narrative does not go from the beginning to the middle to the end of the story. It goes in great swoops, it goes in spirals or loops, it every so often reiterates something that happened earlier to remind you, and then takes you off again, sometimes summarizes itself, it frequently digresses off into something that the story-teller appears just to have thought of, then it comes back to the main thrust of the narrative.... So it's a very bizarre and pyrotechnical shape. ("*Midnight's Children* and *Shame*" 7)

Because of his numerous digressions, Sinai does not stick to one fixed beginning. Instead, he presents us with a whole series of beginnings. He immediately denarrates his first statement ("I was born in the city of Bombay . . . once upon a time") by stating, "No that won't do" (Rushdie, *Midnight's Children* 11), and he then begins his narrative again.

One page later, he presents us with yet another beginning and moves back from 1977 to 1915. This analepsis, which involves a new start, takes us to the point at which his Kashmiri grandfather Aadam Aziz "resolved never again to kiss earth for any god or man" (12). While his grandfather decides to no longer submit to religious entities or human leaders, Sinai's game with multiple beginnings likewise involves freedom and self-determination. By transcending the idea of the singular beginning, which often involves absolute ideas about the world, he denies essentialist conceptualizations of identity and nationhood, and welcomes multiplicity into his thinking. In the narrator's words, "all games have morals" (140), and his games with beginnings are expressive of his pluralist worldview and the tolerance of heterogeneity.

Throughout the novel, Sinai uses the lexeme "beginning" in the plural: he mentions "my beginnings" (95), "false starts" (107), and he states that he wants to "begin with beginnings" (214). It is also difficult to pinpoint the "beginning" of the character of Saleem Sinai. His birth is subject to so many forces that it is better to speak of a variety of beginnings. Biologically speaking, he is the son of William Methwold, an English colonizer, and Vanita, a Hindu street performer. In addition, the Christianized Indian ayah Mary Pereira wants to impress her lover Joe D'Costa, a radical communist: in a microscopic version of the revolution, she changes the name tags of Saleem and Shiva, born to Muslim parents, thus causing the former (whose parents are Hindu) to grow up in a well-to-do Muslim family (116). After this quasi-"changeling birth" (136), the narrator is brought up in the household of Ahmed and Amina Sinai. For Gaura Shankar Narayan, "Saleem is not 'really' Hindu or Muslim, just as he is not 'really' Indian or English. He is a bastard child who combines various points of origin and accomplishes a wholly paradoxical relationship to the notion of national legitimacy" (143). Indeed, Sinai's identity does not only challenge the colonizer versus colonized dichotomy; it also cuts across religious differences.

In Sinai's vision of postindependence India, the country lacks a fixed origin or beginning as well. For the narrator, India is "a mass fantasy shared in varying degrees by Bengali and Punjabi, Madrasi and Jat" (111). It goes without saying that such a multilayered entity requires "the efforts of a phenomenal collective will" (111). From Sinai's perspective, India is a country "which is itself a sort of dream" (117). In contrast to Marc C. Conner, who detects a "quest to establish both familial and national origins" (293), I argue that Sinai rejects the very idea of origin: he does not share the "genealogical obsession" (Rushdie, *Midnight's Children* 379) of his uncle Mustapha Aziz. Among other things, the narrator makes this point by using multiple beginnings. Hanne Birk and Birgit Neumann write that Sinai's rambling digressions challenge the Western notion of history as a linear and teleological process (140, fn. 51). I agree with this reading but feel that it has to be counterbalanced by looking at Sinai's political failure as well as the deviations from his own democratic and egalitarian principles.

THE NOVEL'S ALLEGORICAL STRUCTURE

Like the other midnight's children, Sinai is born at the point at which the British Raj (1858–1947) comes to an end, that is, during the first hour of August

15, 1947.³ All of the one thousand and one children of midnight are endowed with magic powers (Rushdie, *Midnight's Children* 195, 222). Shiva and Sinai, who are born exactly at midnight, are the most powerful magical children. While Shiva (a proud, egotistical, and power-driven individual who feels that everybody should submit to his will) dooms India to "flounder endlessly amid murder rape greed war" (290), Sinai follows a different approach: he advocates a pluralist India and sees others as allies rather than competitors.

Shiva and Sinai are allegorical figures who do not only represent themselves; they also represent two diametrically opposed visions of India.⁴ At the beginning, Sinai's fate is "mysteriously handcuffed to history" (11). A fictionalized version of Jawaharlal Nehru, the first prime minister of postindependence India, informs us that Sinai's life is a "mirror" (122) of the country. Toward the novel's ending, however, Sinai states that "the connections between [his] life and the nation's have broken for good and all" (382). The rivalry between Shiva and Sinai reaches a brutal climax when Major Shiva, "the warlord of tyranny" (415), sends Sinai to the Widows' Hostel, where he and the other midnight children are (irreversibly) sterilized (423). At the allegorical level, the will to power (represented by Shiva) here makes democratic pluralism (represented by Sinai) impotent.⁵

By seeing Shiva and Sinai as allegorical figures, I do not follow Fredric Jameson's claim that "all third-world texts are necessarily . . . allegorical." For Jameson, "the story of the private individual destiny is always an allegory of the embattled situation of the public third-world culture and society" (69).⁶ *Midnight's Children* is an allegorical text but I disagree with Jameson's claim that *all* "third-world" texts are allegorical, and I also have problems with the term "third-world literature." Robert Bennett seeks to move beyond Jameson's model by showing that "Rushdie's novel does more than simply allegorize some organic, collective national identity." Bennett writes that *Mid-*

---

3. India's independence and Partition, that is, the division of the former British Indian Empire into the Dominion of Pakistan and the Union of India, happened at the same time.

4. Depending on one's perspective, one can argue that "allegories turn abstract concepts or features into characters" or, alternatively, that allegories "transform people and places into conceptual entities" (Mikics 8).

5. Shiva may also be identified more immediately with the Hindu right-wing vision and its violent attempts to shape India up until today. More specifically, the figure of Shiva might represent the fusion of Shaivism and Vaishnavism into the modern notion of a unified Hinduism through various conjunctures including colonial administration. Sinai, on the other hand, may be associated with Jawaharlal Nehru (1947-64), whose vision of a multiparty democracy Sinai often represents, especially given his long nose and Kashmiri origin. The charge of impotence plays a role because at the time, many people believed that the Congress Party was incapable of achieving anything in the areas of economy and politics.

6. For a comprehensive critique of Jameson's claims, see Ahmad.

night's Children "creates a polyphonic narrative that gives utterance to India's diverse, heteroglot voices" (177, 192). However, like many other critics, Bennett focuses exclusively on Sinai's vision while ignoring the other (and ultimately predominant) force of Shiva. Instead, I argue that the novel illustrates that post-independence India is dominated by two conflicting visions, namely the intolerance and brutality of Shiva and Sinai's pluralist approach.

What does the novel have to say about these two ideologies? How does it negotiate the relationship between the two? *Midnight's Children* seems to share Sinai's ideas about a democratic India rather than Shiva's principles, which involve "the sharp aroma of despotism" (Rushdie, *Midnight's Children* 409). This might have to do with the incredible cruelty of the power-driven characters. For instance, we learn that after the sterilization of the midnight children, "certain ectomized parts were curried with onions and green chillies, and fed to the pie-dogs of Benares" (424). From this perspective, the novel appears to construct Shiva and Sinai as diametrically opposed characters that represent radically different visions of postindependence India.

At the same time, however, Shiva prevails, whereas Sinai disappears by exploding into "(approximately) six hundred and thirty million particles of anonymous and necessarily oblivious dust" (38). Also, again and again, we are confronted with "the sanctification and renewal which can only be provided by rituals of blood" (111). Indeed, the novel contains fictionalized versions of the following violent historical events or periods: the Jallianwala Bagh (or Amritsar) Massacre on April 13, 1919 (36); the Sino-Indian War of 1962 (247–86); the dispute over Kashmir and the resulting Indo-Pakistani War of 1965 (327) (during which Sinai's family is eliminated and the amnesiac Sinai decides to fight India on the side of Pakistan); and the first administration of Indira Gandhi (1966–77), which involved a rather ruthless political style (402). During the state of emergency (1975–77), for example, everyone is arrested who "had ever made the mistake of sneezing during the Madam's speeches" (404) and the constitution is altered to give Indira Gandhi "well-nigh-absolute powers" (409) (see also Galler).[7]

Furthermore, one can associate many of the novel's characters with Shiva because they are also power-driven individuals. The career-minded Mustapha Aziz, for example, hands his own nephew over to the agents of Indira Gandhi's

---

7. *Midnight's Children* represents blood in rather ambivalent ways. The blood that drops when Aadam Aziz hits his nose against the Kashmiri earth, for instance, is described in terms of "rubies" (Rushdie, *Midnight's Children* 142). Second, when Aadam Aziz finds himself in Amritsar in 1919, his clothes are covered in mercurochrome so that his wife believes that he is bleeding. A few days later, he happens to be at Jallianwala Bagh when General Dyer kills numerous civilians. He returns home with blood on his clothes and this time his wife believes that it is mercurochrome (24ff.).

regime (412). Also, Ahmed Sinai seeks to inculcate "the eternal verities of the master-slave relationship" (322) wherever he is. As we learn earlier on, he does not only mimic the colonizers' strategies of submission; he also tries to imitate their language: "in the presence of an Englishman," he speaks in "a hideous mockery of an Oxford drawl" (96). Further, when Sinai's beloved sister Jamila becomes a famous singer in Pakistan, her personality becomes dominated by essentialist notions of self and nation: the narrator speaks of "the exaggerations and simplifications of self which are the unavoidable side-effects of stardom" and a kind of "right-or-wrong nationalism" (304).

Midnight's Children as a whole deplores Sinai's political impotence, that is, the fact that his vision of India is never put into practice. However, since Sinai's "much-trumpeted existence" actually turns out to be "utterly useless, void, and without the shred of purpose" (152), the novel highlights the impossibility of implementing his vision. The novel as a whole is ideologically ambivalent: it sympathizes with the idealist Sinai while it also illustrates that his approach is killed by the forces of a homogenizing nationalism. In other words, its approval of Sinai is undercut by its disbelief that he represents a viable political alternative to Shiva. Interestingly, Sinai repeatedly gives in to Shiva's principles so that he might—from a certain perspective—be seen as Shiva's (hypocritical) alter ego.[8]

THE NARRATOR'S TELEPATHY

Midnight's Children is a rare example of what Genette calls homodiegetic narration with zero focalization. In such cases, the information provided by the first-person narrator is unrestricted (which is, strictly speaking, impossible because every narrative has a certain focus that implies some sort of restriction). What Genette has in mind is that the narrator says "more than any of the characters knows" (189). This narratological classification, which in a sense fuses first-person and omniscient narration, applies to *Midnight's Children*: like all first-person narrators, Sinai is part of the story, but like omniscient narrators, he has access to the minds of the characters.[9]

---

8. The narrator is interpellated by different ideologies, and he is not consciously aware of this process. In this context, Stuart Hall explains that "we are spoken by and spoken for, in the ideological discourses which await us even at our birth, into which we are born and find our place" (109).

9. Henrik Skov Nielsen has a different take on Genette's statement that in some cases, the narrator says "more than any of the characters knows" (189). Nielsen looks at narratives (such as Bret Easton Ellis's *Glamorama* [1999]) in which the first-person narrator reports something that he or she cannot possibly know as a character in the storyworld. While Nielsen defines the

After a nose-related accident, the nine-year-old Sinai realizes that his head is full of voices: "I heard, at first, a headful of gabbling tongues, like an untuned radio" (Rushdie, *Midnight's Children* 161). From this point onward, the narrator has access to the thoughts of others: "I was a radio receiver, and could turn the volume down or up; I could select individual voices" (162). When Sinai discovers that he can also broadcast messages by the other midnight children, he founds the "Midnight Children's Conference" (M. C. C.), and acts "as a sort of national network, so that by opening [his] transformed mind to all the children [he] could turn it into a kind of forum in which they could talk to one another, through [him]" (221). Since the possibility of telepathic communication coincides with India's independence from the British colonizers, it seems to serve a specific thematic purpose, namely as an opportunity for mutual understanding among different groups and mentalities. Sinai himself describes the M. C. C. as being "the embodiment of the hope of freedom" (295), and Patrick Colm Hogan likewise argues that Sinai's "telepathic mind allows a place for all the hopes and dreams of the new India, all its classes and persuasions, all its talents and ideas and histories, jostling and disagreeing like so many parliamentary representatives" (513).

Other textual clues, however, suggest that what the narrator calls his "miracle-laden omniscience" (149) is a much more ambivalent phenomenon. The novel does not only celebrate Sinai's telepathy as a form of mutual understanding because the narrator immediately begins to use his superhuman ability as an instrument of power. For example, the nine-year-old boy picks crucial information out of the minds of his schoolteachers and clever classmates to be in a more powerful position (169). At a later stage, he spies on the thoughts of his aunt Pia Sinai and finds out that she has an affair with Homi Catrack (243). Some characters are even annoyed by Sinai's presence inside their minds. At one point, the American Evie Burns, whom the narrator becomes infatuated with, explicitly tells him to "get out" of her mind (188) when Sinai wants to inspect her thoughts to find out how to best impress her.

The narrator of *Midnight's Children* gives in to the lure of power. When he observes Amina Sinai's meeting with Nadir Khan, her former husband, the narrator even announces that he will use his "telepathic powers . . . as a *weapon*" (251; emphasis added) to teach his mother not to engage in adultery.[10]

---

narrator as one of the characters, I see the narrator as being in a special (extradiegetic) position in relation to the characters.

10. The use of telepathy as a weapon is reminiscent of Mark Seltzer's claim that the omniscient narrator of the realist novel is a tyrant who enjoys "an unlimited authority over the novel's 'world,' a world thoroughly known and thoroughly mastered by the panoptic 'eye' of the narration" (54). To my mind, various different types of omniscient narrators exist, and they are

In this segment of the novel, Sinai enters the mind of Commander Sabarmati and causes him to shoot his wife (Lila Sabarmati) and kill her lover Homi Catrack (who also has an affair with Sinai's aunt Pia).[11] The unintended consequence of this forced assassination is that Sinai's beloved uncle Hanif, a writer of film scripts, commits suicide because he depended on the income from the film magnate Homi Catrack (263). With regard to this episode, Sinai's actions violate his ethical principle that one should not impose one's ideas on others.

In addition, Sinai undermines his vision of a "loose federation of equals, all points of view given free expression" (215) because his actions are based on a resolutely patriarchal understanding of gender differences. While the narrator has absolutely no problem with his father's "fantasies of secretaries taking dictation in the nude" (173), he finds the idea that his "shameless mother" (160) engages in adultery extremely unsettling: while watching his mother undress, Sinai says explicitly that such "emotions . . . have no place in family life" (160).[12] Sinai is incapable of acknowledging his mother's sexuality, and this patriarchal character trait introduces a hierarchy among men and women that clearly goes against his proclaimed idea of equality and the free expression of the "multiple faces of the Bharat-Mata" (392).[13]

Moreover, despite the high hopes concerning a form of mutuality, the M. C. C. remains but a moment of miraculous potentiality. The group is put under threat by "fantasies of power" (223) both from the inside and the outside: Sinai admits that he "was not immune to the lure of leadership" (222), and we learn that the group "finally fell apart on the day the Chinese armies came down over the Himalayas to humiliate the Indian fauj" (247). The other midnight children notably accuse Sinai of "secrecy, prevarication, high-handedness, egotism" because he conceals "Mary's secret" (289), that is, the fact that he is not actually the biological son of the rich Sinais. At the same time, "the prejudices and world-views of adults" (248) take over the minds of the

---

not all tyrants. Nevertheless, it is interesting to note that the telepathic first-person narrator in *Midnight's Children* at times behaves like an authoritarian spy.

11. This crime of passion initiated by Sinai is based on *K. M. Nanavati vs. State of Maharashtra*, a court case from 1959, which dealt with K. M. Nanavati, a naval commander, who had killed Prem Ahuja, his wife's lover. I would like to thank Divya Dwivedi for pointing this out to me.

12. As we learn later on, the narrator is completely mistaken: Sinai only thinks that his mother has an affair with Nadir Khan (212).

13. As Hans-Georg Erney has shown, Sinai's thinking is not only binary with regard to men and women. The narrator also reproduces the binary thought system of colonialism in his representations of Pakistan: he uses the Otherness of Pakistan ("the land of the pure" [301]) to construct his Indian identity. See, for example, the derogatory description of the city of Karachi (300) or the claim that in order to be "a citizen of Pakistan," one has to learn "the arts of submission" (340).

midnight children so that religious rivalries and class snobbery determine their interactions. The M. C. C. disintegrates as power relations destroy this platform of common understanding, and *Midnight's Children* ends with a pessimistic outlook due to the persistence of hierarchies and domination.

The novel highlights that Sinai uses his "frequent psychic travels" (176) to radically different ends: the narrator founds the M. C. C., while at other times he deploys telepathy for purely personal gain. These two approaches are expressive of different ways of engaging with alterity. Sinai uses his "mental peculiarity" (167) to connect with others, but he also uses it to wield power over them. One might see the narrator's ambivalent take on telepathy as well as the related creation and collapse of the M. C. C. as ways of mocking the slogan "unity in diversity," which played a crucial role in postindependence India. This slogan was supposed to shore up a fragile and contended union that was won first by the British and later by the Indian Army in Goa and Hyderabad. The novel illustrates that mutual understanding and parliamentary conversation are only options: postindependence India also involves tenacious fights between communities, castes, and regions that are not contained by the parliamentary form.

THE THIRD SPACE AND THE MULTIFARIOUSNESS OF THE HUMAN SUBJECT

The narrator of *Midnight's Children* is rather fond of the idea of the "Third Space," and he is also taken by the multifariousness of the human subject. Since Sinai and the M. C. C. do not actually achieve anything in political terms, the novel can be seen as foregrounding the impotence of the poststructuralist concepts on which their visions of India are based. This ineffectiveness has to do with the fact that their rather abstract ways of conceptualizing identity constructions are somewhat alienated from the social realities. These ideas do not address the full extent of the colonialist and neocolonialist forces in India as well as the power relations they imply. Sinai and his vision are too detached from the average Indian citizen to have a political effect.

Homi K. Bhabha defines the "Third Space" as an in-between space that "makes it possible to begin envisaging national, anti-nationalist histories of the 'people.'" Furthermore, Bhabha believes that "by exploring this Third Space, we may elude the politics of polarity and emerge as the others of ourselves" (38–39). The Third Space plays a central role in Sinai's thinking: he consistently highlights that "a third possibility must be kept in mind" (Rushdie, *Midnight's Children* 221) and that there can be a "third way" (249) beyond the polarity of "us" versus "them." Most importantly, Sinai states that the M. C. C. should speak from the Third Space: "We . . . must be *a third principle*, we must be *the force* which drives *between the horns of the dilemma*; for only by being other, by being new, can we fulfil the promise of our birth" (248; emphasis added). Sinai also highlights the hybridity of other existents in the narrative world: Aadam Aziz, for example, is a Kashmiri doctor who was educated in Germany. Among other things, we learn that he "was caught in a strange middle ground" (13), and he is described as being "neither this nor that" (19). The inhabitants of the storyworld watch "eastern Western[s]" (49) in the cinema, and they dance "a new style of dance by fusing Western ballet with bharatanatyam" (239), a form of Indian classical dance.

Michael Tratner reads *Midnight's Children* as "a powerful critique of hybridity" (120). He writes that "hybridity is not simply divorced from material social structures such as wealth and poverty; rather, it is a product of such structures and rendered impotent as a political movement by its unwillingness to recognize the fact" (117). Indeed, throughout the novel, Sinai, the major advocate of hybridity, fails to admit that he is a member of the Westernized upper middle class that is detached from the slums and shantytowns where Amina Sinai encounters inequality in the shape of naked girls, beggars, disabled people, and untouchables (Rushdie, *Midnight's Children* 81). For instance, Sinai's clueless involvement in the confrontation between the Samuyukta Maharashtra Samiti and the Maha Guajarat Parishad—where he causes violence and bloodshed ("fifteen killed, over three hundred wounded" [189]) by uttering a meaningless rhyming couplet that the demonstrators then use as a chant—accentuates his aloofness as well as "the insularity of his class" (Pilapitiya 59). What is more, when the socialist Picture Singh confronts Sinai with "the unrelieved vileness of the rich," he shies away from the political consequences. Sinai defends his rich parents by further celebrating hybridity through the idea that "there is good and bad in all" (Rushdie, *Midnight's Children* 399). Although this narratorial statement might be true, it offers absolutely no ground for action. Tratner thus writes that "hybridity, seeking only to understand its opponents, . . . cannot ultimately create a new future: it really only acts mentally, not physically or materially" (121). I argue that Sinai partly fails because he is unaware of the fact that his vision of India is ultimately a function of his social status. Compared to Sinai, disadvantaged people like Shiva are, for obvious reasons, more interested in power.

Moreover, Sinai consistently foregrounds the characters' inherent pluralism and their potentialities for development. The narrator refers to himself as "all the Saleems" (Rushdie, *Midnight's Children* 332). His philosophy is that "a human being . . . is anything but a whole, anything but homogeneous; all kinds of everywhichthing are jumbled up inside him, and he is one person one minute and another the next" (230). Later on, Sinai points out that "each 'I,' every one . . . contains a similar multitude. I repeat for the last time: to understand me, you'll have to swallow the world" (370). The narrator rejects the Cartesian *cogito* and instead moves toward a poststructuralist conceptualization of human subjectivity (see also Flanagan 38).

The major problem with this approach is that the multifarious Sinai is influenced by all kinds of ideologies so that his actions lack a determinable purpose. To begin with, Sinai adopts the wealthy lifestyles of the Sinais and, despite his political ideals, he gets so used to it that he refuses to swap places with Shiva, the biological son of Ahmed and Amina Sinai. Second, as Chun-yen Chen has shown, Sinai's narration is haunted by the finger in the painting *The Boyhood of Raleigh* (1870) by Sir John Everett Millais, "a master signifier" (Chen 151) associated with British colonialism: he sees this finger practically everywhere. Third, his uncle Hanif's film *The Lovers of Kashmir* causes Sinai to assume that his mother is having an affair with Nadir Khan (Rushdie, *Midnight's Children* 212). Fourth, when Sinai becomes "a citizen of Pakistan" (340) following his amnesia, he is "wiped clean as a slate" (339) and easily internalizes the Pakistani propaganda to fight his own country. Although he consistently propagates a certain (pluralist and democratic) worldview, the narrator is incapable of sticking to his political ideas. Sinai is actually "falling apart" (38) because he lacks a center that would allow him to somehow navigate the different ideologies that surround him.

INTERTEXTUAL REFERENCES AND STYLISTIC DEVICES

Despite Sinai's political impotence in the story, the novel manages to implement his pluralist vision through its style, which explains the narrator's "overpowering desire for form" (307). He states that he cannot "abandon form" (424)—and this is because stylistic features closely correlate with the actualization of his political vision. *Midnight's Children* is a "polyphonic narrative form that emphasizes India's heteroglossic diversity" (Bennett 188). The novel contains a wide variety of intertextual references and it is not coincidental that it harks back to different media, factual and fictional narratives, Western and Eastern sources, as well as texts from diverse periods.[14]

---

14. Julia Kristeva writes that intertextuality is "a mosaic of quotations; any text is the absorption and transformation of another. The notion of intertextuality replaces that of intersubjectivity, and poetic language is read as at least double" (37).

Among other references, Rushdie resorts to the *Ramayana* and the *Mahabharata* (the two great Hindu epics of India), *The Arabian Nights*, Laurence Sterne's *Tristram Shandy* (1759–67), the painting *The Boyhood of Raleigh* (1870) by Sir John Everett Millais, the film *The Wizard of Oz* (1939), *Die Blechtrommel* (1959) by Günter Grass, *Cien años de soledad* (1967) by Gabriel García Márquez, Stanley Wolpert's historiography *A New History of India* (1977), and "Bombay talkie[s]" (Rushdie, *Midnight's Children* 339).[15] Like the frequent use of Hindi and Urdu words, this potpourri of different intertextual sources contributes to the heterogeneity of Sinai's style. Also, the source texts relate to various moments in literary and cultural history, thus counteracting the idea of the single or pure origin.[16] In addition, Rushdie treats these references in multiple ways that do not add up to a coherent system: in some cases, he follows the original almost to the core; in other cases, the source text is altered in some respects; and in yet other cases, he makes significant changes to the original. One might see these ways of dealing with intertextual sources as yet another instance of heterogeneity, but they also allude to Sinai's inability to order external influences in a coherent manner.

Two of the most obvious intertextual sources are *Tristram Shandy* and *The Arabian Nights*. Both *Midnight's Children* and Sterne's eighteenth-century novel lack standard chronology and they also share an interest in absurd digressions, the alleged significance of large noses, and humorous characters. At the same time, Rushdie's novel also transcends *Tristram Shandy*. While Tristram Shandy is "only" accidentally circumcised by a window sash, Saleem Sinai is intentionally sterilized by political agents of Indira Gandhi's regime. Furthermore, both novels start with chapters that lead up to the narrator's birth, but *Midnight's Children* goes one step further because in contrast to

---

15. Two sources that are less frequently mentioned are Shakespeare's *A Midsummer Night's Dream* (1595) and Beckett's *L'Innomable* (1953). In a sense, Sinai is an Indian changeling boy like the one Oberon and Titania quarrel over in Shakespeare's *Dream*. Also, the orgies in the Sundarbans mangrove forest in *Midnight's Children* (355) are reminiscent of what happens to Hermia, Lysander, Helena, and Demetrius in the Athenian woods (including "the time-shifting sorcery of the forest" [356]). Furthermore, in both *Midnight's Children* and Shakespeare's *Dream*, humans and supernatural creatures exist side by side. At one point, the first-person narrator of *L'Innomable* arbitrarily decides to no longer use the personal pronoun "I" because "it's too farcical" (Beckett 355). However, he later does so, because such use is still possible for him (368). The same is true of *Midnight's Children*: during his amnesia, Sinai refers to himself in the third person or by calling himself "the buddha" (300ff.), who lives in the present moment without thinking about the past or the future, but he later switches back to the first-person singular. What is more, Sinai fails—like the narrator of Beckett's novel.

16. I therefore disagree with the argument that "*Midnight's Children* begins, in every sense of the word, with *Tristram Shandy*" as well as the claim that one should view "the novel's formal and thematic engagement with *Tristram Shandy*" as being singular (Hawes 149, 163).

the narrator of Sterne's novel, Sinai is actually telepathic (see also Buchholz). *Tristram Shandy* is an extremely playful novel that ridicules the certainties implied by linear stories and other thought systems. It mocks every worldview so that the only one that can seriously be advocated is that of the satirist joker who takes nothing seriously at all. Rushdie's novel differs in this respect: *Midnight's Children* presents its readers with a serious political context, and it also contains a vision of India the narrator actually believes in (even though it is never implemented).

The Arabian Nights is another important intertextual source. For example, we learn that on August 15, 1947, "one thousand and one children" of midnight are born, and Sinai states that "the resonances of the number are strangely literary" (192). The narrator also speaks of "Lila's thousand and one infidelities" (129); the "one thousand and one firm proposals of marriage" Jamila receives every week (304); the one "thousand and one different gatherings" (394) Shiva is invited to; and so forth. Both *Midnight's Children* and *The Arabian Nights* thematize infidelity and the quintessentially unreliable nature of human relationships, and they both contain sexual humor and elements of crime fiction. Also, they share the communicative framework of a narrator and a narratee: in the first case Sinai talks to Padma, his wife-to-be, while in the second case Scheherazade talks to King Shahrayar. Whereas Scheherazade manages to tell King Shahrayar captivating stories to prevent him from killing her, Sinai does not always please his listener: Sinai can never be sure "whether she is listening or not" (117); she "covers her ears" (309) whenever she can no longer stand his story, and she even decides to leave him for a while (164).

The major difference between the two narratives concerns the addressee's motivation for marriage. The egocentric King Shahrayar marries Scheherazade because he benefits from her. She is not only an outstanding storyteller and master of the cliffhanger; she is also fertile and gives birth to three children. Padma, on the other hand, marries Sinai (428) *although* he is a terrible storyteller (at least from the perspective of her "what-happened-nextism" [39] and her dislike for self-conscious narration [65]), and of no use to her "as a lover" (424) (see also Batty 63). She ultimately does it for him; Sinai states that "Padma is a generous woman, because she stays by me . . . although I can't do much for her" (39).

Midnight's Children also realizes Sinai's vision of plurality by juxtaposing a number of styles and vocabularies. These various discourses constitute a "loose federation of equals, all points of view given free expression" (215). Sinai is a narrator who wants to "get it right." At times, he is so meticulous in his descriptions that he wonders whether he is not infected by what he calls the "Indian . . . urge to encapsulate the whole of reality" (75). He repeatedly states that he "confine[s] himself to fact" (144) and seeks to "provide absolute proof of [his] claims" (196). At other times, however, we witness him in the process of actively making things up. For instance, he occasionally inserts the phrase "yes, why not" (85, 110) into his narrative; he wonders whether it is his imagination that makes him believe that a baby blushes "in a sky-blue crib" (134); and he also states that "to save time," he places the members of his family "in the same row at the Metro cinema" (178–79). In such cases, Sinai is not reporting something that happened; rather, "the exotic flowers of the imagination blossom" (165). Florian Stadtler describes the oscillation between these two poles as follows: "Saleem locates his story between the tensions of realism and fantasy, myth and reality, in which he sees his life and India caught up" (132).

Sinai also uses a cinematic kind of narration, highlighting that "nobody from Bombay should be without a basic film vocabulary" (Rushdie, *Midnight's Children* 33). At one point, he cuts from a "close-up of [his] grandfather's right hand . . . to a long-shot" (33) of the whole person. Later on, he cuts from a "shot" of Amina Sinai and Nadir Khan to an "extreme close-up of nicotine" (212), and, at the end of one chapter, he zooms out slowly into a "long-shot" which is then followed by a "fade-out" (231). At a different point, he "permit[s] [himself] to insert a Bombay-talkie-style close-up" (336) of flying calendar pages, and he also superimposes "long-shots of street riots" and "medium shots of burning buses" (336). At first glance, the use of this film vocabulary follows the idea of "getting it right" by narrating with the mechanical precision of a camera. Upon closer inspection, however, we realize that his knowledge of film at times misleads Sinai: for instance, since he renders the meeting between Amina Sinai and Nadir Khan in terms of his uncle Hanif's film *The Lovers of Kashmir,* he mistakenly assumes that he is witnessing a "love scene" (212), that is, the unfaithfulness of his mother. His cinematic narration is also caught up in the narrative's oscillation between fact and fabulation.

Moreover, Sinai's narrative teems with omissions. The narrator tells us that "the trick is to fill in the gaps, guided by the few clues one is given" (412). Sinai might use these frequent ellipses to openly acknowledge gaps in his knowledge; he seems to convey the idea that things cannot be grasped in their entirety so that we are invited to let go and be less obsessive than the power-driven followers of Shiva. But one might also argue that the older Sinai, the narrating I at the extradiegetic level, is still functioning like a radio at the time of narration, sending messages to us as readers. From this perspective, the ellipses represent the brief interruptions of the broadcasting of the "All India Radio" so that we as readers (who serve as Sinai's second audience next to Padma) are implicated in the narrator's political vision.[17] John J. Su argues that *Midnight's Children* suggests Sinai's "ideals can endure *only* as ideals." For him the novel is about "the irresolvable political tensions between utopian ideals for the nation and efforts to bring them to fruition" (549). Indeed, the novel seems to favor Sinai's vision even though it is never implemented.

THE SENSE OF AN ENDING

The ending of *Midnight's Children* is extremely ambivalent. Sinai predicts that he will be reduced "to specks of voiceless dust" and "sucked into the annihilating whirlpool of the multitudes" (446), but we do not really know what this means. Of course, Sinai has got a "son," Aadam Sinai (who is the biological son of Shiva and Parvati-the-witch), but it remains unclear what he will do in the future. At the end, we wonder "what was beginning, what was ending, . . . and what would be born with [his] child" (401).

The novel leaves us without any suggestion concerning the question of how to reconcile the two extremes of Shiva and Sinai. Some of the novel's narrative techniques are infused with Sinai's vision, while others suggest that tyrants like Shiva will always prevail. Sinai and others who believe in hybridity might feel that Aadam Sinai will fuse Shiva's lust to power and Sinai's democratic principles. He is Shiva's biological son, but he is brought up and educated by Sinai. Aadam Sinai might thus come to embody a politically more effective type of hybridity. Others who do not believe in hybridity might argue that Sinai simply continues to dream his ineffective dream of a new and better India—to no avail.

What about the postcolonialism of *Midnight's Children*? Rushdie's novel is of course postcolonial simply because it deals with the period after the end of British colonialism. Bill Ashcroft et al. use the term "postcolonial" to "cover all the culture affected by the imperial process from the moment of colonization to the present day" (2). However, Patrick Williams points out that one does not necessarily have to see the lexeme "postcolonial" as a historical denominator that refers to the period after the dissolution of the European empires. Instead, the term can also denote a specific way of thinking, that is, a mind-set

---

17. A different way of filling the novel's gaps would be to follow Patrick Colm Hogan, who points out that the most important absent figure is Mahatma Gandhi. The implication of Sinai's statement that "in my India, Gandhi will continue to die at the wrong time" (Rushdie, *Midnight's Children* 164) is clearly that he died at the wrong time in real India as well. Hogan reads *Midnight's Children* as a quintessentially "Gandhian novel. . . . He [Rushdie] had to leave Gandhi out of the novel in order to allow the narrative to incorporate Gandhism" (Hogan 522).

that seeks to get "past colonialism's own narratives and ideologies" (451). *Midnight's Children* is postcolonial in this sense because it conveys Sinai's pluralist vision of postindependence India. At the same time, the novel demonstrates the tenacious presence of colonialist binaries despite the official end of British domination. However, I do not think that these elements necessarily make the novel "complicit" with oppression. *Midnight's Children* illustrates how difficult it is to move beyond the colonialist heritage even after the formal end of colonialism.[18]

WORKS CITED

Ahmad, Aijaz. "Jameson's Rhetoric of Otherness and the 'National Allegory.'" *Social Text* 17 (1987): 3–25.

Alber, Jan. "Towards Resilience and Playfulness: The Negotiation of Indigenous Australian Identities in Twentieth-Century Aboriginal Prose." *European Journal of English Studies* 20.3 (2016): 292–309.

Althusser, Louis. "Ideology and Ideological State Apparatuses." 1970. *The Norton Anthology of Theory and Criticism*. Ed. Vincent B. Leitch. New York: Norton, 2001. 1483–1509.

Ashcroft, Bill, Gareth Griffiths, and Helen Tiffin. *The Empire Writes Back: Theory and Practice in Post-Colonial Literatures*. London: Routledge, 1989.

Batty, Nancy E. "The Art of Suspense: Rushdie's 1001 (Mid-)Nights." *Ariel* 18.3 (1987): 49–65.

Beckett, Samuel. *The Unnamable*. 1953. New York: Grove Press, 1958.

Bennett, Robert. "National Allegory or Carnivalesque Heteroglossia? *Midnight's Children*'s Narration of Indian National Identity." *Bucknell Review* 43.2 (2000): 177–94.

Bhabha, Homi K. *The Location of Culture*. London and New York: Routledge, 1994.

Birk, Hanne, and Birgit Neumann. "Go-between: Postkoloniale Erzähltheorie." *Neue Ansätze in der Erzähltheorie*. Ed. Ansgar Nünning and Vera Nünning. Trier: WVT, 2002. 115–52.

Buchholz, Laura. "Unnatural Narrative in Postcolonial Contexts: Re-reading Salman Rushdie's *Midnight's Children*." *Journal of Narrative Theory* 42.3 (2013): 332–51.

Chen, Chun-yen. "Betrayal of Form: The 'Teeming' Narrative and the Allegorical Impulse in Rushdie's *Midnight's Children*." *Journal of Commonwealth Literature* 44.3 (2009): 143–61.

Conner, Marc C. "*Midnight's Children* and the Apocalypse of Form." *Critique* 38.4 (1997): 289–99.

Eagleton, Terry. *Ideology: An Introduction*. London: Verso, 1991.

Erney, Hans-Georg. "Indien und Pakistan aus der Sicht des Helden in *Midnight's Children*." *Anglia* 120.1 (2002): 86–92.

Flanagan, Kathleen. "The Fragmented Self in Salman Rushdie's *Midnight's Children*." *Commonwealth Novel in English* 5.1 (1992): 38–45.

---

18. I would like to thank Divya Dwivedi and the external reader for their extremely helpful comments on earlier versions of this essay.

Fludernik, Monika. "The Narrative Forms of Postcolonial Fiction." *The Cambridge History of Postcolonial Literature*. Ed. Ato Quayson. Cambridge University Press, 2012. 903–37.

———. "Histories of Narrative Theory (II): From Structuralism to the Present." *A Companion to Narrative Theory*. Ed. James Phelan and Peter J. Rabinowitz. Malden, MA: Blackwell, 2005. 36–59.

Galler, Matthias. "Historiographic Indian English Fiction: Indira Gandhi's Emergency Rule in *Midnight's Children*, *The Great Indian Novel*, and *A Fine Balance*." *Postcolonial Studies across the Disciplines*. Ed. Jana Gohrisch and Ellen Grünkemeier. Amsterdam: Rodopi, 2013. 285–303.

Genette, Gérard. *Narrative Discourse: An Essay in Method*. 1972. Trans. Jane E. Lewin. Ithaca, NY: Cornell University Press, 1980.

Gibbs, Raymond W. "Intentionality." *Routledge Encyclopedia of Narrative Theory*. Ed. David Herman, Manfred Jahn, and Marie-Laure Ryan. London: Routledge, 2005. 247–49.

Hall, Stuart. "Signification, Representation, Ideology: Althusser and the Post-Structuralist Debates." *Critical Studies in Mass Communication* 2.2 (1985): 91–114.

Hawes, Clement. "Leading History by the Nose: The Turn to the Eighteenth Century in *Midnight's Children*." *Modern Fiction Studies* 39.1 (1993): 148–68.

Hogan, Patrick Colm. "*Midnight's Children*: Kashmir and the Politics of Identity." *Twentieth-Century Literature* 47.4 (2001): 510–44.

Jameson, Fredric. "Third-World Literature in the Era of Multinational Capitalism." *Social Text* 15 (1986): 65–88.

Kristeva, Julia. "Word, Dialogue and the Novel." 1966. *The Kristeva Reader*. Ed. Toril Moi. New York: Columbia University Press, 1986. 36–37.

Mikics, David. *A New Handbook of Literary Terms*. New Haven: Yale University Press, 2007.

Narayan, Gaura Shankar. "Lost Beginnings in Rushdie's *Midnight's Children*." *Narrative Beginnings: Theories and Practices*. Ed. Brian Richardson. Lincoln: University of Nebraska Press, 2008. 137–48.

Nielsen, Henrik Skov. "Unnatural Narratology, Impersonal Voices, Real Authors, and Non-Communicative Narration." *Unnatural Narratives, Unnatural Narratology*. Ed. Jan Alber and Rüdiger Heinze. Berlin: De Gruyter, 2011. 71–88.

Pilapitiya, Kishani. "Resisting Power in Language: Linguistic Strategies in Salman Rushdie's *Midnight's Children*." *Journal of the Australasian Universities Language and Literature Association* 109 (2008): 47–68.

Prince, Gerald. "On a Postcolonial Narratology." *A Companion to Narrative Theory*. Ed. James Phelan and Peter J. Rabinowitz. Malden: Blackwell, 2005. 372–81.

Rushdie, Salman. *Midnight's Children*. London: Jonathan Cape, 1981.

———. "*Midnight's Children* and *Shame*." *Kunapipi* 7.1 (1985): 1–19.

Seltzer, Mark. *Henry James and the Art of Power*. Ithaca: Cornell University Press, 1984.

Sommer, Roy. "'Contextualism' Revisited: A Survey (and Defence) of Postcolonial and Intercultural Narratologies." *Journal of Literary Theory* 1.1 (2007): 61–79.

Stadtler, Florian. "'Nobody from Bombay should be without a basic film vocabulary': *Midnight's Children* and the Visual Culture of Indian Popular Cinema." *Salman Rushdie and Visual Culture: Celebrating Impurity, Disrupting Borders*. Ed. Ana Cristina Mendes. London: Routledge, 2012. 123–38.

Su, John J. "Epic of Failure: Disappointment as Utopian Fantasy in *Midnight's Children*." *Twentieth Century Literature* 47.4 (2001): 545–68.

Tratner, Michael. "What's Wrong with Hybridity: The Impotence of Postmodern Political Ideals in *Ulysses* and *Midnight's Children*." 2003. *Joyce, Imperialism, and Postcolonialism*. Ed. Leonard Orr. Syracuse: Syracuse University Press, 2008. 112–26.

Williams, Patrick. "Post-Colonialism and Narrative." *Routledge Encyclopedia of Narrative Theory*. Ed. David Herman, Manfred Jahn, and Marie-Laure Ryan. London: Routledge, 2005. 451–56.

PART III
VOICE AND NARRATOR

CHAPTER 7

"We are the people of the Apokalis"

Narrative Voice and the Negotiation of Power Structures in Indra Sinha's Animal's People

MARION GYMNICH

NARRATING DISASTERS AND THEIR AFTERMATH

In his article "Postcolonial Remains" (2012), Robert Young describes the postcolonial as an approach whose "objectives have always involved a wide-ranging political project—to reconstruct Western knowledge formations, reorient ethical norms, turn the power structures of the world upside down, refashion the world from below" (20). Postcolonial literary criticism constitutes an integral part of this project, which becomes apparent in attempts to link political and aesthetic readings. Along these lines, postcolonial critics have for instance stressed the necessity of making non-hegemonic, marginalized voices heard—in political and historical discourses as well as in (readings of) literary texts. Given this premise, narratological approaches, which have developed a range of categories for describing different types of narrators and narratees and their functions, promise to be a particularly useful ally for exploring in depth the ways in which narrative voices relate to and seek to challenge prevailing power structures. The narrative voice in Indra Sinha's novel *Animal's People* (2007), which will be discussed below, exemplifies the complex manner in which fictional narrators may invite readers to ponder political and ethical issues that are pertinent to postcolonial readings.

Animal's People is set in the aftermath of a catastrophe that struck the city of Bhopal in the night from the 2nd to the 3rd of December 1984. In that night, what is still considered to be the world's worst industrial disaster killed thousands of people in the capital of the Indian state of Madhya Pradesh. An accident in a pesticide plant run by the American Union Carbide Corporation led to "the release of 30–40 tons of a toxic gas, methyl isocyanate (MIC) spreading over approximately 30 square miles" (Mishra et al. 193). As a consequence, thousands of people in the city died, and more than 200,000 people were debilitated (cf. Mishra et al. 193). The autodiegetic narrative voice[1] in Sinha's novel is that of a survivor of this disaster who has been permanently debilitated. In order to do justice to the political and ethical implications of the way in which this voice is constructed, it is necessary to be aware of the scope of the catastrophe and to situate Sinha's *Animal's People* in the context of other narratives addressing the disaster in Bhopal.

There is still no exact information on the number of people who lost their lives in the hours, days, and weeks after the accident in Bhopal. The fatalities mentioned in accounts of the event vary significantly, ranging from 2,500 to 20,000 (cf., e.g., Mishra et al.; Muralidharan). The lack of exact and reliable information on the death toll is partially due to the fact that the corpses of the victims were removed from the streets, where many had died, as quickly as possible: "in the rush to dispose of bodies immediately after the explosion, no comprehensive count of the dead or of casualties took place." (Schultheis Moore 237) Most of the victims lived in the slum districts that were right next to the factory. While the gas that escaped from the Union Carbide factory was at first deemed nonlethal by the local medical authorities (cf. Muralidharan 5196), the disastrous consequences of exposure to MIC became obvious within a couple of hours. The toxic substance affected in particular the respiratory system, the eyes, and the gastrointestinal organs. It also has been shown to have a major impact on the neurological and the immunological levels. Pablo Mukherjee vividly describes the effect exposure to MIC has on the human body as follows:

> At first, the air smells of burned chilies. If you do not get away as fast as possible, soon you find yourself in a thick white mist. Your eyes, throat, and lungs begin to burn and fill up with oozing fluid and melting tissues. Then you lose control of your nervous system, vomit uncontrollably, and seize up

---

1. An autodiegetic narrator is the type of narrator who is identical to the protagonist, that is, who tells his or her own story, thus appearing both on the story/character level and on the discourse level/level of narrative transmission. With this type of narrator, it is important to distinguish systematically between the "I as character" and the "I as narrator," since they may differ very much in terms of their experience and judgments, given the fact that autodiegetic narrators typically tell their own story in retrospect.

with cramps. If you are lucky, you lose consciousness and die. If not, your death is a long, drawn out, agonizing affair. If you survive, your lungs and eyes will never work properly again. Muscle pains and ulcers will prevent you from working or leading a normal life. You will give birth to unimaginably deformed, dead babies. (217)

Thirty years later, many people who were exposed to the toxic gas in 1984 are still suffering from chronic illnesses, especially from permanent damage inflicted on the respiratory system. Beyond that, genetic defects (i.e., an increased number of chromosomal abnormalities) continue to endanger the health of future generations (cf. Mishra et al. 195). One cannot even begin to gauge the psychological impact the disaster has had on the people living in the city.[2]

The disaster led to prolonged legal disputes concerning the responsibility for the accident and the related issue of financial compensation. It is in particular negligence on the part of Union Carbide and their refusal to accept responsibility that has led critics to categorize the disaster as an "eco-crime": "The term 'eco-crime' seems appropriate given the transnational interdependencies between human actions and social and environmental effects at work in Bhopal, raising the possibility of reforms that criminalize globalized environmental violence" (Carrigan 160). The disaster and its aftermath continue to raise far-reaching ethical questions about the potential consequences of neocolonial economic power structures in a globalized world.

How can a complex event such as the disaster in Bhopal be remembered, examined, and interpreted in a narrative? Scientific papers have tried to deliver matter-of-fact accounts of the disaster, listing symptoms and providing data. Journalists sometimes seek to combine factual reports with an appeal to the readers' emotions and their conscience by drawing upon the experiences of individuals, thus trying to render the impact of the massive disaster more tangible. Accounts provided by a number of victims of the Bhopal disaster have been recorded and published, for instance in *The Bhopal Reader*, edited by Bridget Hanna, Ward Morehouse, and Satinath Sarangi in 2005. Generally, such survivors' reports tend to be short narratives, often focusing on the immediate consequences of the catastrophe. The majority of the literary texts that have addressed the disaster in Bhopal so far are written in Hindi, thus being primarily accessible to a more local readership. Indra Sinha's novel *Animal's People* is one of the first fictional texts about the disaster in Bhopal in English. Thus it was also among the first fictionalized accounts of the catas-

---

2. For an account of attempts to explore the psychological consequences, see in particular the article by Basu and Murthy.

trophe that was likely to reach a global readership.[3] The fact that Sinha's novel was shortlisted for the prestigious Man Booker Prize in 2007 increased the likelihood of the text being widely read.

Fictionalized accounts of disasters may have a significant impact on people's awareness of the events that are portrayed in them. Even more than texts by journalists, novels may invite readers to empathize with the victims and "to imagine what it is like to live the life of another person who might, given changes in circumstance, be oneself" (Nussbaum 5). From the point of view of postcolonial criticism, the empathy that may be evoked by novels arguably has to be seen in a somewhat ambivalent light. While empathy tends to be regarded as a prerequisite for intercultural understanding, one ultimately has to wonder to what extent empathy, let alone "identification" (Nussbaum 6), is actually possible. Can we really even begin to imagine what living in the aftermath of the Bhopal disaster could have felt like? Still, narratives evoking empathy presumably at least take us a step closer to grasping ways of experiencing the world that are radically different from the ones we are used to. Faced with fictionalized depictions of events like these, one may have to accept a cognitive gap on the part of the readers that can at best be bridged partially. At any rate, fictionalized accounts of disasters have the potential to confront readers with viable questions pertaining to the ethical and ideological dimension of the disaster; after all, literature is apt to be "disturbing in a way that history and social science writing frequently are not. Because it [literature] summons powerful emotions, it disconcerts and puzzles" (Nussbaum 5).

The question of *how* a disaster like the one in Bhopal can be narrated in an adequate manner is closely linked with another ethical question: *who* has the right to tell the victims' stories? Given the fact that the victims of the accident at the Union Carbide pesticide plant were primarily people living in the slums adjacent to the factory, one might conclude that the consequences ought to be presented from the perspective of the subaltern, who has traditionally been deprived of both a history and a voice (cf. Spivak).[4] Indra Sinha merely imagines a subaltern voice—a strategy that is very common in postcolonial literature. The fact that Sinha has spent most of his life in Europe

---

3. There are also several movies about Bhopal seeking to address an international audience, most recently *Bhopal: A Prayer for Rain*, which was released on 7 November 2014, thirty years after the disaster (Kumar).

4. On the concept of the subaltern, see also Young: "The preoccupation with the subaltern can be interpreted more generally to suggest the extent to which the postcolonial has always been concerned with a politics of invisibility: it makes the invisible visible. This is entirely paradoxical to the extent that its object was never, in fact, invisible, but rather the 'invisible visible': it was not seen by those in power who determine the fault lines between the visible and the invisible" (23).

(cf. Carrigan 161) appears to increase his distance from the events that are depicted in the novel. Yet Sinha has been involved in the British Bhopal Medical Appeal, which has funded hospitals in Bhopal, ever since it was founded in 1994, and has met with survivors of the disaster. According to Heather Snell, it was especially the fate of one particular victim—Sunil Kumar—that served as a source of inspiration for *Animal's People* (3). Kumar, to whom the novel is dedicated, was a Bhopal activist who committed suicide in 2006. It should be pointed out in this context that the consequences of exposure to MIC that Kumar suffered from are different from those ascribed to the protagonist of Sinha's novel. Thus, *Animal's People* should not be read as a straightforward biographical account. Even if a text does not seek to portray the life of a specific individual, the act of imagining what the victim of a disaster like the one in Bhopal might have experienced, thought, and felt invariably has ideological and ethical implications. The following analysis will seek to show that it is in particular the structure of Sinha's narrative, and specifically its narrative transmission, that invites readers to engage in these ideological and ethical issues.

THE UNRULY NARRATIVE VOICE IN *ANIMAL'S PEOPLE*

Sinha's *Animal's People* features one of the most memorable narrators in recent Anglophone literature. The novel's autodiegetic narrator, who consistently refers to himself as "Animal" throughout the text, is a victim of the Bhopal disaster, a nineteen-year-old man who has spent his entire life in the slums of Khaufpur (i.e., the fictional equivalent of Bhopal).[5] Strictly speaking, Animal cannot deliver a testimony of the night in which the accident happened, since he was too young at the time to remember anything, as the narrator points out when he looks back on his life: "My story has to start with that night. I don't remember anything about it, though I was there, nevertheless it's where my story has to start" (Sinha 14). As far as the aftermath of the disaster is concerned, however, Animal in many respects appears to be an ideal witness. In addition to suffering from the consequences of the accident himself, he knows many people who have been affected by the disaster as well, having lost family members or having been seriously injured. In the night when the accident happened, Animal lost his family. Moreover, the poison has apparently damaged the protagonist's muscles and neurological system, rendering him unable to walk or even stand upright. He thus has had to move on all fours ever since, spending much of his life on the streets, more often than not being forced to

---

5. According to Schultheis Moore, "Khaufpur" is a telling name, meaning "place of fear" or "terror town" (232).

scavenge food from the garbage. It is his inability to walk or stand upright that has earned him the cruel nickname "Animal." This name serves as a marker of his social position as an outsider, as Bartosch points out: "In an act of bold reappropriation, Animal takes on the name that the neighbouring children mocked him with and decides that by taking on the name 'Animal,' he can put aside humanity as well" (14). As Animal's appropriation of the pejorative nickname may perhaps already suggest, the narrator delivers an aggressive, defiant, at times even bawdy account of his life, refusing to conform to the patterns of those "sentimental narratives of pity" (Carrigan 161) that one might perhaps expect to find in the account of a victim's life. Throughout the text, the narrator repeatedly insists on his right to tell his story in his own, unruly fashion: "If you want my story, you'll have to put up with how I tell it" (Sinha 2). *Animal's People* is not just a narrative about the impact the accident in the pesticide plant has had on people's health in Bhopal; it is also a story about the long and frustrating legal fight for justice. Being a coming-of-age story, Sinha's novel simultaneously presents a vivid account of the protagonist's emotional as well as sexual needs and desires. Especially due to the narrator's position as a social outsider and the at times bawdy nature of his life narrative, Rob Nixon argues that "Animal joins a long line of picaros: canny, scheming social outliers governed by unruly appetites, scatologically obsessed, who, drawn from polite society's vast impoverished margins, survive by parasitism and by their wits" (451).

Accounts of a disaster such as the one that occurred in Bhopal, which is intimately linked with global as well as local economic and political power structures, inevitably vary depending on whose voice one chooses to listen to. In order to examine the potential impact of the specific fictional voice created in Sinha's novel, it turns out to be useful to analyze the narrator of *Animal's People* in terms of the narrative authority that can be ascribed to him. The concept of narrative authority derives from a basic principle of narratology, that is, the assumption that narratives are by definition structured hierarchically, consisting of a story/character level and a (superior) discourse level/level of narrative transmission. According to Susan Lanser, narrators per se have a higher degree of narrative authority than characters due to "the privileged status of narrators vis-à-vis narrated characters: because the narrator's acts literally bring the story into existence, his or her word carries greater authority than the word of a character" ("Sexing Narratology" 171). In other words, readers by default tend to be inclined to accept the narrator's depiction of the fictional world as trustworthy, which may at times discredit the characters' views of the fictional world. Yet narrative voices still vary considerably with respect to the *relative* degree of narrative authority ascribed to them by readers. In her influential study *Fictions of Authority* (1992), Lanser distinguishes between three basic types of narrative voices, which differ in terms of their relative degree of narrative authority. Narrative authority thus can be defined as the outcome of the way in which the relation of the narrative voice(s) to the narrated world is constructed within a narrative. Lanser's typology, which encompasses the authorial voice,[6] the communal voice, and the personal voice, has proved to be extremely useful in the context of feminist narratology as well as postcolonial narratology. It departs from structuralist typologies of narrators due to its emphasis on the potential *functions* of the different types of narrative voices. Structuralist narratology, which emerged in the 1970s, has traditionally been interested exclusively in the formal features of narratives, while some more recent, context-sensitive approaches within the field of narrative theory (including feminist and postcolonial narratologies) seek to *relate* structure and content in a systematic fashion, thus paying particular attention to the potential meanings and functions of the structural features of narrative texts. The categories introduced by Lanser, for instance, make it possible to explore the ideologically relevant negotiations of power structures on the discourse level that may result from the selection of specific narrative voices.

Drawing upon the typology of narrative voices developed in *Fictions of Authority*, one recognizes that Animal's narrative voice bears a lot of similarities with the type of narrator Lanser refers to as communal voice. Lanser uses the term "communal voice" to subsume "a spectrum of practices that articulate either a collective voice or a collective of voices that share narrative authority" (*Fictions of Authority* 21). In structural terms, a communal voice may appear in the guise of an "inclusive we," but it may likewise be evoked by an oscillation of different narrators within the same text or by the "voice of a single individual who is manifestly authorized by a community" (Lanser, *Fictions of Authority* 21). What the different manifestations of a communal voice have in common is that they serve to articulate collective experience and shared attitudes. Given the fact that the communal voice represents a collective (uniting the voices of many individuals), it can claim a comparatively high degree of narrative authority. Thus, the construction of a communal voice is one of the narrative strategies for empowering voices that have been marginalized or ignored in dominant discourses.

There are several factors that seem to suggest that an interpretation of the narrator in Sinha's novel as a communal voice representing the victims of the

---

6. The authorial voice defined by Lanser basically corresponds to the category of the overt heterodiegetic narrator as it is defined in structuralist narratology, that is, a narrator who does not double as a character and is made overt by his or her explicit comments and judgments. The other two types of narrative voice will be explained in more detail below.

Bhopal disaster is indeed tenable. Even the title of Sinha's novel—*Animal's People*—seems to allude to the fact that the narrator Animal can be interpreted as a communal voice, as a representative of a particular community (i.e., his "people"), who derives narrative authority from his role as a spokesperson. Moreover, the narrator repeatedly uses what may be seen as an "inclusive we," rhetorically highlighting the cognitive gap between "us Khaufpuris" (Sinha 292) and visitors to Khaufpur/Bhopal, who cannot even begin to fathom what living in this city in the aftermath of the disaster might mean. The emphasis on the opposition between "us" (= the victims) and "them" (= visitors) entails an explicit criticism of people feigning pity without being able to grasp what the inhabitants of the city have been going through: "What really disgusts me is that we people seem so wretched to you outsiders that you look at us with that so-soft expression, speak to us with that so-pious tone in your voice" (Sinha 184). On the basis of utterances like the ones just quoted, one may gain the impression that the narrator can indeed be regarded as a representative of several (partially overlapping) groups: the victims of the disaster, the subaltern inhabitants of the slum districts, and the people who are fighting for justice in the courts. In the final sentences of the novel, the narrator's allegiance with these groups and his function as a spokesperson is emphasized once more when he says: "We are the people of the Apokalis. Tomorrow there will be more of us" (366). A number of articles read Sinha's novel in a way that implicitly supports the interpretation of the narrator as a communal voice, even if the concept itself is not drawn upon. Alexandra Schultheis Moore, for instance, states: "*Animal's People* [. . .] gives voice to the subaltern residents of Khaufpur's poorest neighborhoods surrounding the pesticide plant" (239). Anthony Carrigan argues along similar lines when he claims that Sinha's novel provides the victims of the disaster with "imaginative agency" (168).

While there are certainly a number of factors that seem to invite a reading of the narrative voice in Sinha's novel in terms of what Lanser describes as a communal voice, this reading ultimately does not do full justice to the very complex way in which the narrative voice has been constructed in *Animal's People*, however. The narrator repeatedly insists on the unique nature of his experience, thus defying attempts to reduce him to the function of a mere representative of a community. The novel's haunting opening lines already serve to stress that the narrator regards his situation as exceptional, as an experience that is *not* shared by other victims: "I used to be human once. So I'm told. I don't remember it myself, but people who knew me when I was small say I walked on two feet just like a human being" (1). Time and again, the narrator claims that he is not even human anymore, thus presenting himself as a social outsider whose life can certainly not be seen as paradigmatic: "'My name is

Animal,' I say. 'I'm not a fucking human being, I've no wish to be one.' This was my mantra, what I told everyone" (23). By identifying entirely with his position as social outsider, the narrator rebels against being reduced to the role of a spokesperson of a group. Rebellion thus is a concept that should not be restricted to the analysis of literary characters; it can also be applied to narrators, as the example of *Animal's People* illustrates. The act of reading narrators as potentially rebellious voices resonates with the overall significance of the notion of the "voice" within postcolonial studies.

In *Animal's People*, the narrator's insistence on being a social outsider is also highlighted by the fact that he regards Khā-in-a-Jar, a "two-headed fetus spontaneously aborted the night of the explosion" (Schultheis Moore 238), as his alter ego. As Mukherjee puts it, "Animal and Kha mirror each other in that they have both been placed beyond the pale of normative humanity by the Kampani's poison gas" (227). Instead of striving to conform to physical and behavioral norms, Animal at times seems to revel in foregrounding those features of his body that others perceive as grotesque. In addition, he emphasizes his corporeality by not being shy about admitting his sexual needs. The distinctive character of the narrator's voice in Sinha's novel is further enhanced by linguistic features including the recurrent use of neologisms and expletives. Moreover, exclamations, elliptical sentences, and colloquial expressions contribute to a style Carrigan refers to as "everyday orality" (162). The way the narrator presents himself and his position within society renders it impossible to categorize him as "the generic subaltern" or even "the paradigmatic victim." Instead, the extremely vivid narrative voice serves to evoke an individual whose experience bears certain similarities to those of other victims but is nevertheless unique in many ways. According to Lanser's typology of narrative voices, one would thus have to classify Animal as a personal voice, which is highly individualized but may claim substantially less narrative authority than the communal voice. Drawing upon the distinction between a communal voice and a personal voice introduced by Lanser thus makes it easier to trace the shifting subject positions and the conflicting impulses that are articulated in the narrative voice in Sinha's *Animal's People*.

Due to the fact that Animal at times undoubtedly appears as a spokesperson of a social group, but at others as a unique social outsider, one could conclude that Animal's voice in fact oscillates between being constructed as a personal and as a communal voice, thus providing "a highly individual yet collectively responsive perspective on the disaster's effects" (Carrigan 161). In this way the narrator makes use of the narrative authority and the empowerment that is typically associated with the communal voice without compromising his need to be perceived as an exceptional individual, that is, as a personal voice. By oscillating between the stance of a communal voice and that of a personal voice, the narrator in *Animal's People* also serves to complicate the subject position of the subaltern, specifically the perception of the subaltern as a unified group. The oscillation between a communal voice and a personal voice pays tribute to the political power a collective may hope to claim, while stressing that subalternity needs to be seen "as a heterogenous social field populated by subaltern subjects differently subjected to interrelated power hierarchies" (Coronil 43). As Susie O'Brien puts it, "Animal's People illuminates the demand for 'something more' in the particularities of Animal's story, which confound the generalisations on which the institutions of both law and care operate" (26).

CREATING UNEASE: THE IDEOLOGICAL IMPLICATIONS OF THE CONSTRUCTION OF THE NARRATEE

While the portrayal of the narrator certainly turns *Animal's People* into a highly memorable narrative, the construction of the narratee—that is, the counterpart of the narrator on the discourse level/level of narrative transmission[7]—is equally remarkable. One may even argue that it is in particular the way the narratee is constructed throughout the text that invites the reader to ponder ethical and ideological questions. The narrator explains that he is recording the account of his life on tapes because he has been told to do so by an Australian journalist. In this way the text alludes to the long-standing tradition of the collaborative autobiography (cf. Couser), which has often been employed to make the voices of the colonized and marginalized heard through an intermediary, most famously perhaps in the genres of the slave narrative and the "as-told-to autobiographies" by means of which anthropologists, journalists, and poets sought to capture the supposedly vanishing traditional way of life led by the indigenous population of North America. It is a well-documented fact that collaborative autobiographies more often than not involved an extensive "editing" of the life narratives on the part of the (socially superior) collaborator(s). This type of interference is referred to obliquely in *Animal's People* in the (fictitious) "editor's note" that precedes the text. While the "editor's note" claims that "apart from translating to English, nothing has been

---

7. The narratee should not be confused with the actual readers of a text; the narratee is located on the discourse level/level of narrative transmission and is constructed in more or less detail by the specific ways in which the narrator refers to an addressee of the story he or she is telling.

changed," even the very act of translating of course already changes the text.[8] In the reading process, the chapter headings—"Tape One" to "Tape Twenty Three"—serve as a constant reminder of the narrative illusion that the account of the disaster is a collaborative autobiography. At the same time, the generic framework of the collaborative autobiography serves to suggest that the journalist functions as primary narratee in *Animal's People*.

Right from the start, the role of the journalist as primary narratee and editor is presented in a very critical light. The way the narrator remembers his first encounter with the journalist, during which the latter asked Animal to talk about his life, is already apt to raise ethical questions. Animal vividly recalls the journalist being barely able to hide his greed for a "good story," that is, one that will impress his readers:

> Such a look on your face . . . as you pushed aside the plastic sheet, bent your back through the gap in the wall. With what greed you looked about this place. I could feel your hunger. You'd devour everything. . . . When you saw me, your eyes lit up. Of course, you tried to hide it. Instantly you became all solemn. Your namasté had that tone I've come to know, a hushed respect as if you were speaking a prayer, like you were in the presence of the lord of death. (4)

The journalist is introduced as a hypocrite, as someone who pretends to have ethical reasons for his inquiry, while presumably all the while pondering the positive impact a gripping story of human misery may have on his career. The stance attributed to the narratee is reminiscent of Susan Sontag's critical assessment of strategies routinely employed in news coverage of disasters:

> Information about what is happening elsewhere, called "news," features conflict and violence—"If it bleeds, it leads" runs the venerable guideline of tabloids and twenty-four-hour headline news shows—to which the response is compassion, or indignation, or titillation, or approval, as each misery heaves into view. (18)

When the journalist is confronted with Animal, his reaction to the latter's situation appears to be thinly veiled voyeuristic pleasure, which is revealed in particular by the way the journalist's gaze invades Animal's space. The misery of the victim becomes a spectacle for the journalist and, by extension, for a

---

8. For similar interpretations of the "editor's note," see Carrigan (169–70) and Snell (2).

foreign/global public who will read the "sensational" story in the end.[9] The narrative thus explores the power structures informing the production of what Andrew Mahlstedt and others have referred to as "poverty porn."[10]

The fact that the journalist wants to publish Animal's story, thus presenting it to a potentially global public, serves to complicate the construction of the narratee. The journalist's promise that the report will make the narrator famous horrifies him, triggering the image of a virtually endless number of potential anonymous narratees: "'He says thousands of other people are looking through his eyes.' . . . I think of this awful idea. Your eyes full of eyes. Thousands staring at me through the holes in your head. Their curiosity feels like acid on my skin" (7). The image of multiple future readers looking at Animal that is first evoked by the journalist's words leads to the narrator consistently referring to the narratee as "Eyes." The specific way in which the narratee is constructed here is bound to make the actual reader aware of the potentially voyeuristic overtones implied in reading a narrative about the aftermath of a disaster or even about personal misery in general.[11] The fact that Animal is someone who, due to his disability, knows better than most what it means to be stared at with a mixture of curiosity, pity, horror, and disgust adds to the poignancy of the recurring references to a voyeuristic stance on the part of the narratee. Being painfully aware of the gaze of others is an experience that also plays a prominent role on the story level, as the protagonist is frequently stared at because of his disability. The anger felt by the narrator when he is confronted with the voyeuristic interest in his life is also addressed on the story level, for instance when Animal tells an American doctor: "People like you are fascinated by places like this. It's written all over you, all you folk from Amrika and Vilayat, jarnaliss, filmwallas, photographass, anthrapologiss" (184).

---

9. Cf. "You were like all the others, come to suck our stories from us, so strangers in far off countries can marvel there's so much pain in the world. Like vultures are you jarnaliss. Somewhere a bad thing happens, tears like rain in the wind, and look, here you come, drawn by the smell of blood" (Sinha 5).

10. On the term "poverty porn," cf. Mahlstedt: "Popularized by *London Times* columnist Alice Miles's critique of the 2009 film *Slumdog Millionaire*, 'poverty porn' suggests that media representations of the poor can be exploitative, using the oppression, destitution, or violence of poverty to elicit an emotional response—possibly even arousal—on the part of the viewer" (69).

11. Cf. Luc Boltanski's critical assessment of the effect the fictional depiction of suffering may have on readers: "Actually we know that one of the main motivations of fiction is the staging of suffering and that the spectacle of suffering has been seen as a cause of the spectator's pleasure, something which generally has been held to be paradoxical or enigmatic" (21).

The journalist originally tried to persuade the narrator to give a truthful account of his experience by projecting a narratee who will appreciate the account and who is bound to display empathy. In a letter he told the narrator:

> Animal, you must imagine that you are talking to just one person. Slowly that person will come to seem real to you. Imagine them to be a friend. You must trust them and open your heart to them, that person will not judge you badly whatever you say. (13)

The image that is sketched here of a supposedly ideal narratee, who will make the process of telling the story of one's life easier, is clearly meant to elicit a report of horror witnessed as well as experienced that holds nothing back. After some hesitation, the narrator accepts this challenge, saying: "You are reading my words, you are that person. I've no name for you so I will call you Eyes. My job is to talk, yours is to listen. So now listen" (13–14). While Animal's communication with the journalist as primary narratee is reminiscent of what Lanser refers to as a "private voice (narration directed toward a narratee who is a fictional character)," addressing the narratee as "Eyes" creates a "public voice (narration directed toward a narratee 'outside' the fiction who is analogous to the historical reader)" (*Fictions of Authority* 15). By adopting the stance of a public voice, Animal thus keeps the actual reader aware of the fact that he or she is being addressed. Thus, the reader cannot but feel implicated in the accusation of experiencing a voyeuristic pleasure when reading the narrative about suffering. The stance of the public voice seems apt to evoke unease on the part of the reader, giving rise to ethical questions that need to be discussed with respect to "poverty porn." In particular on the basis of its specific construction of the narratee, *Animal's People* manages to commemorate the Bhopal disaster, while simultaneously drawing attention to the by now customary violation of the subaltern's rights in representations of victims and socially marginalized individuals.

As the discussion above has shown, a narratological analysis of Indra Sinha's novel *Animal's People* serves to highlight ideological and ethical questions that are negotiated within the text and that are pertinent to postcolonial criticism in general. The novel tackles the multiple dilemmas associated with the acts of voicing, witnessing, and watching in the context of postcolonial disaster narratives by presenting a (fictitious) victim who is marginalized in several ways, yet struggles to claim agency by telling his own story in a highly idiosyncratic, irreverent, and provocative fashion. With its shifts between a personal voice and a communal voice, the account of the Bhopal disaster in

Sinha's novel emphasizes that the representation of victims in fictional and nonfictional texts may all too easily lead to generalizations and to a disregard for the need to acknowledge individuality and diversity. Moreover, the specific construction of the narratee as a public voice that is likely to evoke a certain feeling of unease on the part of the actual reader addresses ethical questions with respect to the representation and perception of suffering, which appears to be omnipresent in the news media as well as in fictional texts.

WORKS CITED

Bartosch, Roman. "The Postcolonial Picaro in Indra Sinha's *Animal's People*: Becoming Posthuman through Animal's Eyes." *Ecozon* 3.1 (2012): 10–19.

Basu, Amit Ranjan, and R. Srinivasa Murthy. "Disaster and Mental Health: Revisiting Bhopal." *Economic and Political Weekly* 38.11 (2003): 1074–82.

Boltanski, Luc. *Distant Suffering: Morality, Media and Politics*. Trans. Graham Burchell. Cambridge: Cambridge University Press, 1999.

Carrigan, Anthony. "'Justice is on our side'? *Animal's People*, Generic Hybridity, and Eco Crime." *The Journal of Commonwealth Literature* 47.2 (2012): 159–74.

Coronil, Fernando. "Listening to the Subaltern: Postcolonial Studies and the Neocolonial Poetics of Subaltern States." *Postcolonial Theory and Criticism*. Ed. Laura Chrisman and Benita Parry. Cambridge: D. S. Brewer, 2000. 37–55.

Couser, G. Thomas. "Collaborative Autobiography." *Encyclopedia of Life Writing: Autobiographical and Biographical Forms. Volume I: A-K*. Ed. Margaretta Jolly. London: Fitzroy Dearborn Publishers, 2001. 222–23.

Hanna, Bridget, Ward Morehouse, and Satinath Sarangi, eds. *The Bhopal Reader: Twenty Years of the World's Worst Industrial Disaster*. New York: The Apex Press / Mapusa, Goa: The Other India Press, 2005.

Kumar, Ravi, dir. *Bhopal: A Prayer for Rain*. Starring Mischa Barton, Martin Sheen, Kal Penn, Rajpal Yadav. UK, India, 2014.

Lanser, Susan S. *Fictions of Authority: Women Writers and Narrative Voice*. Ithaca: Cornell University Press, 1992.

———. "Sexing Narratology, Toward a Gendered Poetics of Narrative Voice." *Grenzüberschreitungen. Narratologie im Kontext/Transcending Boundaries. Narratology in Context*. Ed. Walter Grünzweig and Andreas Solbach. Tübingen: Narr, 1999. 167–83.

Mahlstedt, Andrew. "Animal's Eyes: Spectacular Invisibility and the Terms of Recognition in Indra Sinha's *Animal's People*." *Mosaic* 46.3 (2013): 59–74.

Mishra, Pradyumna, Ravindra M. Samarth, Neelam Pathak, Subodh K. Jain, Smita Banerjee, and Kewal K. Maudar. "Bhopal Gas Tragedy: Review of Clinical and Experimental Findings after 25 Years." *International Journal of Occupational Medicine and Environmental Health* 22.3 (2009): 193–202.

Mukherjee, Pablo. "'Tomorrow There Will Be More of Us': Toxic Postcoloniality in *Animal's People*." *Postcolonial Ecologies: Literatures of the Environment*. Ed. Elizabeth Deloughrey and George Handley. Oxford: Oxford University Press, 2011. 216–31.

Muralidharan, Sukumar. "Bhopal: Continuing Institutional Crisis." *Economic and Political Weekly* 39.49 (2004): 5196–98.

Nixon, Rob. "Neoliberalism, Slow Violence, and the Environmental Picaresque." *Modern Fiction Studies* 55.3 (2009): 443–67.

Nussbaum, Martha C. *Poetic Justice. The Literary Imagination and Public Life*. Boston: Beacon Press, 1995.

O'Brien, Susie. "Resilient Virtue and the Virtues of Resilience: Post-Bhopal Ecology in *Animal's People*." *Kunapipi* 34.2 (2012): 23–31.

Schultheis Moore, Alexandra. "'Disaster Capitalism' and Human Rights: Embodiment and Subalternity in Indra Sinha's *Animal's People*." *Theoretical Perspectives on Human Rights and Literature*. Ed. Elizabeth Swanson and Alexandra Schultheis Moore. New York: Routledge, 2012. 231–46.

Sinha, Indra. *Animal's People*. London: Simon & Schuster, 2008.

Snell, Heather. "Assessing the Limitations of Laughter in Indra Sinha's *Animal's People*." *Postcolonial Text* 4.4 (2008): 1–15.

Sontag, Susan. *Regarding the Pain of Others*. New York: Picador, 2003.

Spivak, Gayatri Chakravorty. "Can the Subaltern Speak?" *Marxism and the Interpretation of Culture*. Ed. Cary Nelson and Laurence Grossberg. Basingstoke: Macmillan, 1988. 271–313.

Young, Robert J. C. "Postcolonial Remains." *New Literary History* 43 (2012): 19–42.

CHAPTER 8

Questioning the Ideology of Reliability in Mohsin Hamid's *The Reluctant Fundamentalist*

Towards a Critical, Culturalist Narratology

GRETA OLSON

THIS ESSAY demonstrates how narrator unreliability can be employed as a strategy of ideological critique.[1] It does not speak from a position within the two dominant schools of research on unreliability, the cognitivist and the rhetorical—as in James Phelan's fine essay that follows here. Some narratologically minded readers will fault it, then, for lacking narrative nuance and for its (metaleptical) leaping between historical texts and a critical examination of premises that underlie models of unreliability. However, my intention is to uncover assumptions about human nature endemic to models of unreliable narration by observing attributions of unreliability that occurred in colonial contexts. This includes a critique of my own earlier work on unreliable narrators. Seen as a political tool, unreliable narration can no longer be viewed as an indication of a personalized narrator's defective qualities and of her putative moral, perceptual, or communicative deficiencies. This perspective coheres with postcolonial analysis, for instance, of Rushdie's unreliable narrators as storytellers that represent marginalized positions. Specifically, the unreliability of the narrator in Mohsin Hamid's *The Reluctant Fundamentalist* (2007) functions to destabilize dominant Western and U.S. American representations of the attacks of 11 September 2001 and their aftermath. Yet

---

1. My great thanks go to Natalya Behkta, Daniel Hartley, Jan Alber, Mirjam Horn-Schott, the editors, and peer reviewers for insights on earlier iterations of this essay.

the analysis of Hamid's novel gestures towards a larger project. This involves examining prevailing narratological models in terms of their possible perpetuation of hierarchies of privilege and power.

The standard model for detecting unreliable narration takes for granted a tacit communion between a preferred reader and the implied author (or the values suggested by the text). Not only is this communion constructed as normative but it can only prevail if the hypothesized author figure and her reader are presupposed to share equally privileged positions in terms of class, gender, and bio- and geopolitics. Historical examples demonstrate that unreliability has regularly been attributed to groups that had been rendered violently subordinate and, accordingly, adjudged communicatively inferior. Out of resistance, these same groups may well wish not to be maximally relevant, reliable, and transparent in their communications with those who yield power. The rhetorical function of an unreliable narrator may thus be, as in *The Reluctant Fundamentalist,* to point out underlying forms of neo-imperial oppression by mimicking one-sided Western representations of Muslims. Mine is an attempt to resolve discrepancies between classical narratological analysis, which assumes the universality and historical independence of narrative forms, and examinations of narrative texts in terms of their political commitments, as in postcolonial criticism.

The unreliability that marks the voice of Changez, the protagonist and homodiegetic first-person narrator of Pakistani author Mohsin Hamid's second novel, *The Reluctant Fundamentalist,* can be explained as a strategy for undermining the dominant representational strategies of a majority of "9/11" texts.[2] Typically, such texts highlight the complete unexpectedness of the attacks, with timelines beginning at 7:49 in the morning, when two of the hijackers boarded the plane that flew into the north tower of the World Trade Center (WTC), and make no mention of preceding American foreign interventions; they feature mimetically rendered first-person narratives of personal loss and stress the inexpressible suffering of Americans after the attacks (Butler; Hartnell 345). In them, "9/11" is treated as a series of events so horrific as to be virtually unspeakable and as a caesura in history, comparable only to the Holocaust (Olson, "Reading"). Such accounts worked to legitimize the jingoism that followed the attacks, including the curtailing of civil rights through the Patriot Act and incursions on human rights through extralegal rendition and torture. Dominant representational strategies also

---

2. I write "9/11" using quotation marks so as to signal that this nomenclature is in itself part of dominant representations of the events of 11 September 2001. The expression elides other 9/11s in history, including the U.S.-backed overthrow of democratically elected Chilean president Salvador Allende in 1973.

served a re-gendering function by reassigning middle-class American "soccer moms" as "security moms" and by figuring "helpless" Muslim and Arab women as needing protection by hyper-masculine U.S. American soldiers (Faludi; Olson, "Recovering"). Hamid's novel offers a counter-narrative of the same set of historical events. The novel's form undermines universalist assumptions about the existence of reliable and unreliable narrators, which are based on an assumed commonality between the reader and the author or her text, by showing them to rest on situated presumptions about appropriate communicative mores.

Given that readers' assessments of a narrator's reliability rest in part on the given narrative's paratextual framing, it bears mentioning that the visual packaging as well as the title of the novel encourage prospective readers to believe that it deals with a Pakistani man who has reluctantly become an Islamist fundamentalist, and hence—the equivalent in many readers' minds—a Jihadist terrorist. The Houghton Mifflin hardcover edition features a photograph of an olive-skinned, slightly bearded young man's face, the lower left half of which is overlaid by a green field featuring a number of crescent moons and stars familiar from the Pakistani flag. One of the man's eyes is covered by a stylized image of the stripes from the American flag. On the basis of the man's serious, if not hostile, expression and the other visual suggestions of his fragmented identity, one is invited to expect the story to be about an immigrant to the United States who regretfully embraces religious fundamentalism. In the "zone between text and off-text" (Genette 2), these paratextual signals concur with other ideologically normative representations of "terrorists." Whether the product of "authorial intention" (3) or the results of publishers' marketing strategy, these signals provide foils for the novel's rhetorical strategy of undermining dominant Western perceptions.

The novel consistently subverts reader expectations. The fundamentalism of the title refers, in fact, not to the narrator's remorseful embrace of fundamentalist Islam but rather to the mantra of the extremely successful economic assessment firm for which he works. Underwood Sampson's motto, "as they do their pitiless bit for globalization" (Olsson), is to *"Focus on the Fundamentals"* (Hamid 98; emphasis in original)—the fundamentals being a business's worth, the evaluation of which then determines whether it will be sold or dismantled. Like the other best minds and bodies of his country, Changez has been invited into the United States to be acculturated into the economic warrior class.

As readers, we, like the nameless American listener to whom Changez addresses his monologue in a café in Lahore, discover that his story is one of disenchantment with the American Dream. At what is arguably the moment of his most successful assimilation to financial warriorhood, when "his Pakistaniness was invisible" (71) during a business trip to Manila, he witnesses the destruction of the World Trade Towers on television. Believing that he is watching an action movie, Changez is surprised when he realizes that this is news and that he is "remarkably pleased" (72). On arriving back in JFK, Changez is met with the routine harassment to which many olive-skinned men are subject in the postattack era. Subsequently, he faces a number of hostile reactions to his person and even a potential attack by a man who calls him a "fucking Arab" (117).

The discrepancy between Changez's descriptions of his altering sentiments towards the United States and his contradictory characterizations of his behaviors, in other words his unreliability, extends to the instability of the plot. Conceived of as a thriller, the novel's monologic confession and occlusion of the American's voice creates a sense of claustrophobia, which is heightened by Changez's remarks: "You seem worried" (5), he tells him; "Do not look so suspicious" (11), and "Come, relinquish your foreigner's sense of being watched" (31–32). Yet he also remarks that in the area in which they are walking, "one can imagine being dragged against one's will, forever to disappear" (171), thus foreshadowing what will be Changez's extralegal rendition as a terrorist suspect or the American's possible abduction. The novel's ending leaves the reader uncertain as to whether or not the American is in fact a CIA operative who has been sent to assassinate him.

The exclusion of other voices from Changez's dramatic monologue forces the reader to adjudge the narrative solely on the basis of the narrator's utterances. Signals of unreliability are reflected in remarks such as "I am not in the habit of inventing untruths! And moreover, even if I were, there is no reason why this incident would be more likely to be false than any of the others I have related to you" (152; cf. also 183). The reader may think that the narrator doth protest too much when he "so frequently states that he does not intend to poison his auditor" (Scanlan 274), or when he casts doubt on the verity of his recited life story altogether:

> But how odd! I cannot now recall many of the details of the events I have been relating to you. But surely it is the gist that matters; I am, after all, telling you a history, and in history, as I suspect you—an American—will agree, it is the thrust of one's narrative that counts, not the accuracy of one's details. (118)

At once an attestation of fallibility, this statement also critiques American narrative histories, including postattack ones, with their emphasis on the nation's innocence and continued exceptionalism. This includes the standard "9/11" narrative that the United States represented a "beacon" of democracy that had been attacked without warrant by evil and envious enemies of freedom.

Signs of unreliability are amplified by the opacity created deictically through the impersonal use of "you" to address the American listener. The unnamed man's reactions are expressed as "your" words and actions in a manner that unnervingly decreases the distance between him and the implied reader. The reader is interpellated in a manner that aligns her with the listener's imputed perceptions. Thus while Changez addresses a clearly identifiable White American man on the intradiegetic level, slippage occurs because this "you" sounds as though it could refer to the reader. In this manner, the novel reproduces a quality of epistemological uncertainty that Monika Fludernik has ascribed to "second-person fiction [which] owes its charm, but also its uncanniness, to the transgressive quality of its address pronoun, which seems to be directed to the real reader rather than remaining safely confined within the realms of fiction" (117; cf. also Richardson 312).

Albert Camus's *The Fall* (*La Chute*, 1965) provides the most important template for *The Reluctant Fundamentalist*, whose intertextual references also include "The Legend of Sleepy Hollow" (1820) and *Heart of Darkness* (1899/1902). *The Fall*'s narrator, Jean-Baptiste, implicates his unheard listener in a compulsively related monologue. His name also anticipates Hamid's character Juan Bautista. Resembling both Scheherazade of *One Thousand and One Nights* and Coleridge's Ancient Mariner, Jean-Baptiste refuses to end his monologue and suggests that his listener needs to be just as penitent and aware of crimes of negligence as is he. By appropriating Camus's novel and its motive of falling, *The Reluctant Fundamentalist* brackets conventional representations of the September attacks on a topological level. The collapse of the WTC towers and the frequently censored and hence all the more powerful photographs of the men and women who jumped from the towers have dominated "9/11" iconography generally (Olson, "Reading"). The fall of and from the towers is signaled by Changez's account of watching the WTC collapse on television. As in Camus's novella, it represents a historical fall from grace, in this case for the United States as it reacted to the attacks by retreating into isolationist politics, unilateral acts of foreign aggression, and anti-Muslim racism.

These reactions are recreated in the somewhat overdetermined elements of Changez's ambivalent love story with his erstwhile girlfriend Erica and the United States. This includes his disenchantment with the methods of the United States and its stand-in Underwood Sampson. Further, (Am)Erica's gradual retreat from her relationship with Changez into an idealization of her deceased lover Chris—an echo of Christopher Columbus—is not unlike that "powerful *nostalgia*" (113; emphasis in original) that marked the postattack climate with its prelapsarian desire for security and resuscitation of a myth of an untouched, innocent North American continent.

Changez's version of the truth mirrors Western media bias. Ian Ward has identified this bias as the ubiquitous assumption of "hyperterrorism" (249) that includes envisioning the world in "binary terms—good versus evil, us versus them" (Westwell 816). This is Hamid's contention when he states: "The dramatic monologue form that I finally decided on allowed me to capture the way in which the world sees itself today, in a sense of mutual suspicion. It almost mimics the global media where so often you hear one side of the story. My novel is written in a form that takes the reverse side of the media" (Khan 3). Changez reflects on the one-sided reporting of postattack events by telling his American listener: "I had been avoiding the evening news, preferring not to watch the partisan and sports-event-like coverage given to the mismatch between the American bombers with their twenty-first century weaponry and the ill-equipped and ill-fed Afghan Tribesmen below" (99). The prejudiced reporting that Changez's one-sided narration mimics contributed to the manner in which those who looked Muslim were treated after the attacks.

Further, Changez's vision of his listener confirms a number of subcontinental prejudices about how Americans—and thus many imputed readers—look, act, and expect Pakistanis to be, rendering the narrative an exercise in dramatizing Occidentalist projections. Rather insultingly, Changez suggests that the American's suit looks as though it could have been bought in Des Moines (2)—in other words, it fits poorly and is unfashionable. The man's razor hair cut and muscular body suggest that he has had military training or subscribes to military-inspired disciplinary practices. Changez's assessment of his interlocutor (and the implied reader) has been called an exercise in "reverse ethnic profiling" (Solomon). The listener appears so convinced of his viewpoint that he adjudges Changez to be a threat that must be eliminated—a view that likely contradicts the reader's growing conviction that Changez's so-called anti-American activities are motivated by his hope that Erica will recognize him on television.

The listener is, in turn, quite stereotypically surprised that, despite his beard, Changez and other Pakistanis enjoy drinking alcohol and that attractive young women sport jeans and T-shirts in Lahore. Changez may also parody his interlocutor's expectations of Pakistani English. He varies his address between excessive and flowery politeness, as in his initial "Excuse me, sir, but may I be of assistance?" (1), and more direct speech patterns. By constantly anticipating and commenting on his listener's appearance and reactions, Changez exercises a narrative authority over him that resembles neo-imperialist practices of framing subjects in accord with prevailing ideological needs.

The narration represents a "talking back" to power. The American literally never gets a word in, and his paranoid reaction to this situation—as signaled by his nervous glances and probable reaching for his gun (184)—becomes apparent. Muneeza Shamsie describes this reversal of the "traditional colonial narrative" as follows: "Changez vocalizes, the American does not; the American remains nameless; he is interpreted through Changez's monologue and thus appropriated" (20). The direct address in the "you" pronoun reveals not only the American listener's but also the implied reader's complicity in the United States' War on Terror. The novel's detailed references to the Northeast of the United States and its play on postattack fears suggest that it is intended for a primarily American readership (Mukherjee 286).

According to the majority of narratological models, Changez's attestations of being a "liar" or "sociopath" suggest his obvious unreliability and literary kinship with, for instance, Dostoevsky's Underground Man or Ralph Ellison's invisible man (see A. Nünning for what is still the most complete list of text signals of unreliability), or the narrator of the "Tell-Tale Heart" (1843), to whom Changez may refer when he states that the American's nervous glances resemble "a steady tick-tick-tick . . . seeming to beat in your head" (31). Yet rather than as a sign of a lack of mental stability or truthfulness on Changez's part, these utterances signal instead the unreliability of the American narratee. Instead of doubting Changez's account, the reader questions the American's mind-set. Thus while referencing now canonical instances of narrator unreliability, Changez's remarks actually mimic dominant media images of Muslims as untrustworthy, unbalanced, dangerous, and beyond the law, stereotypes that are reiterated in words such as "liar" and "sociopath." These remarks are illustrative of the novel's larger rhetorical strategy of having Changez appropriate the paranoid mind-set of his American narratee and the West. As he pointedly states: "It seems an obvious thing to say, but you should not imagine that we Pakistanis are all potential terrorists" (183). In the nature of what Michel Foucault termed "biopolitics," modern forms of governance comprise the cultivation and protection of some forms of human life and labor at the expense of others (*History of Sexuality, Society*). Changez explains his awareness of these biopolitical valuations as follows:

> A common strand appeared to unite these conflicts and that was the advancement of a small coterie's concept of American interests in the guise of the fight against terrorism, which was defined to refer only to the organized and

politically motivated killing of civilians by killers not wearing the uniforms of soldiers. . . . [T]he lives of those of us who lived in lands in which such killers also lived had no meaning except as collateral damage. (178)

This devaluation of certain non-American lives is not dissimilar to Underwood Sampson's employees' assessment of firms and assiduous disregard for the personal consequences.

The reading of *The Reluctant Fundamentalist* developed here—as a semi-parodic mirror of American bias—does justice to the cultural critique that *The Reluctant Fundamentalist* demonstrably performs. However, identifying the novel's strategic employment of narrator unreliability reveals something larger about the cultural premises upon which the underlying narratological concept rests. According to the original Boothian model, unreliability is detected through the reader's sense of the ironic discrepancy between the narrator's account of events and experiences and that of the implied author; in models that eschew the concept of the implied author, the gap is located between the narrator's account and the values implied by the totality of textual signals (Olson, "Reconsidering"). Variously described as reading against the grain, filling narrative gaps, or resolving narrational inconsistencies, detecting unreliability is, according to most accounts, based on an awareness of discordances in the narrator's account either in relation to itself or to other information supplied by the text. This generally involves the reader's realization of the narrator's fallibility and increasing sense that she must read with care and not take what is narrated at face value. (See Phelan's rhetorical account of character narration in *Living to Tell about It*, 38–53, and in this volume.)

According to Dan Shen's overview, accounts of unreliability can be divided into those based on rhetorical approaches and those relying on cognitive models. Rhetorical approaches define narrator unreliability on the basis of discrepancies of perception or reporting between the implied author and the narrator or between the totality of text signals and the narrator. By contrast, "Constructivist/Cognitivist" (Shen) approaches depend on individual readers developing strategies for interpreting the text. Yet, as Shen points out in relation to Tamar Yacobi's and Ansgar Nünning's work, constructivist approaches also resort to describing inconsistencies between the person of the narrator and implied authorial norms.

Detecting unreliable narration depends on the reader's making an analogy between the mores of human communication and the illusion of a communicative situation as constructed in the fictional text. As Booth wrote in *The Rhetoric of Fiction*: "We react to all narrators as persons" (273). Or, as Theresa Heyd stated more recently:

> Humans are not only very able to, but in fact strive to identify anthropomorphic figures wherever they may present themselves. . . . It is therefore not at all surprising that readers involuntarily construe a narrator persona for fictional pieces of narrative, and this is in line with their experience of real-world narratives. (9)

Models of reliability rely on the perception that a narrator violates one or more interpersonal communicative norms. To the degree that the model is explicitly pragmatic, it includes reference to Grice's conversational maxims of quality, relation, and quantity (Zipfel 117–20). According to Booth's original account, the detection of unreliability is based on the insightful reader's and the implied author's shared, ironic recognition of the narrator's failings: "The author and reader are secretly in collusion, behind the speaker's back, agreeing upon the standard by which he is found wanting" (*Rhetoric of Irony* 304). Subsequent accounts tend, like Booth's, to personalize narrators and make attributions about their behaviors that do not differ in kind from those made about people in communicative situations more generally. They are also apt to assume a commonality of perception between the postulated reader and the imputed person behind the text. Thus as the present author wrote in an earlier essay on unreliable narration: "As with third parties who witness an ironical comment's being made and its not being understood by the addressee, the reader 'feel[s] drawn into a conspiracy with the speaker' (Sperber and Wilson 313), here the implied author or those text signals that give the impression of there being a person behind the narrator of a text" (Olson, "Reconsidering" 105).

If Shen is correct, even cognitivist accounts ultimately rest on analogies between the attribution of unreliability to a communicative partner and the assignment of similar traits to narrators. This speaks, one might argue, for the general applicability of this approach. I would contend, however, that these models presuppose an equality between communicative partners that has its implicit basis in a Kantian-inspired deontological ethics, that is an ethics that is based on intrinsic "ought(s)" and "should(s)" regarding behavior rather than a Utilitarian ethics that bases rational decisions on considerations of what would produce the best outcome for the majority. Deontological ethics assumes an absolute equality between participants in interpersonal interactions. The reliance on Kant's epistemology is explicit in pragmatic accounts of unreliability, with their debts to Grice's theory of conversational implicature. Grice cites Kant as having inspired the four categories and maxims that make up the Cooperative Principle of conversation: "Echoing Kant, I call these categories Quantity, Quality, Relation, and Manner" (45).

Another Kantian concept underlies pragmatic models of human interaction, including those based more widely on relevance, which assumes interlocutors' similar communicative goals; such models implicitly postulate an equality between autonomous, self-determining rational subjects in interpersonal interactions. On the basis of this assumed equality, Kant can argue in *The Groundwork of the Metaphysics of Morals* (1775) that there is an ultimate rational basis for all moral actions: subjects need only follow the imperatives of, one, asking whether their actions are performed not in accordance with the contingencies of a given, specific situation but in relation to a universally applicable model of behavior; and, two, of not treating persons or situations as a means to an end but as ends in themselves.

Booth's *Rhetoric of Fiction* anticipates Grice's work by applying a communicative model to readers' interactions with narrative fiction; for him, communication transpires between the implied author and the "postulated reader" at the possible expense of the unreliable narrator (Olson, "Reconsidering" 94). Booth's ultimate call to authors to make their readers into their best possible selves (*Rhetoric of Fiction* 397) and subsequent claims that fictional narratives create more ethical persons similarly assume that communicative participants share sociocultural privilege. Only if this is the case can we assume as readers that it behooves narrators to communicate succinctly, truthfully, relevantly, and clearly to establish a sense of trust and similarity.

I want to move now from Booth's original conceptualization of unreliability, also as it was further explicated in his *A Rhetoric of Irony* (1974), while acknowledging the many subsequent challenges to this model that have been made in cognitivist and pragmatic accounts of unreliable narration and in Phelan's refinement of the rhetorical model. I want to ask the reader to consider the premises about how communication works underlying Booth's model and ones like it that assume an ironic shared sensibility between the reader and the implied author—or, as in cognitivist accounts, between the reader and the ethos suggested by the text. The assumption of communicative equality that underlies notions of implicature and relevance proves historically problematic when it concerns communicators in radically unequal power relations. As philosophers such as Christine Battersby have shown, Kant does not regard all persons as equal; rather, women, for instance, are treated in his texts as "neither fully rational ('persons'), nor fully instinctual ('animals')" (66); hence they cannot logically be treated "as autonomous, self-directed agents who could appropriately be held responsible for their actions" (64). Personhood for Kant can only be achieved through attaining autonomous rationality, a criterion that also renders the status of slaves, servants, and non-Whites problematic (Harvey).

Kant's historically comprehensible if highly unattractive hesitation to assign rational and autonomous personhood to women and non-Whites highlights a larger pattern of assigning inherent fallibility to those in socially subservient positions, one that postcolonial critique has readily pointed out. Historically, those in subordinate positions have been accused of intrinsic unreliability by those attempting to control them. The attestation of unreliability is, for example, a regular feature of colonial discourse, one that justifies the disempowerment of the colonized due to their inability to uphold the value on reliability. As Homi Bhabha writes: "The incalculable colonized subject—half acquiescent, half oppositional, always untrustworthy—produces an unresolvable problem of cultural difference for the very address of colonial cultural authority" (33).

Albeit in an abbreviated and under-contextualized form, I offer two examples of the attribution of unreliability to subjects in colonial discourse. These examples point to what I see as the implausibility of a model of unreliable narration that rests on the assumption of a personal likeness between the reader and the implied author, by demonstrating that ascriptions of unreliability are historically contingent and rest on assumptions about normative communicative behaviors. The authors of both of the following passages assume a commonality of perception between themselves and their implied addressees at the expense of those they pejoratively describe. The argument proceeds in stages quite similar to those commonly described in the discovery of a narrator's unreliability. The object of the negative description is found to be deficient in terms of the assumed standards of the preferred reader and the author. In the first example, the Dutch cartographer and naturalist Bernhard Romans justifies the state of slavery in 1775 by writing that African slaves are categorized by "treachery, theft, stubbornness, and idleness" and that these qualities result from their "life at home [in Africa thus] put[ing] it out of all doubt that these qualities are natural to them and not originated in their state of slavery" (105; qtd. in Cantor 460). Here, the attestation of "treachery" to an entire group functions as a synonym for personal unreliability to express the deficiencies of those described.

The second attribution of unreliability occurred within the context of the violent U.S. American subordination of the southern Philippines after the Spanish-American War (1899–1902). The first military governor of the Moro Provinces, General Leonard Wood, argued that the use of harsh disciplinary methods was the only option to establish order and security in the region:

> The Moros . . . are as a class a treacherous unreliable lot of slave hunters and land pirates. . . . Firmness and the prompt application of disciplinary mea-

sures will maintain order, prevent loss of life and property and permit good government and prosperity among these people. Dilatory tactics, indecision and lack of firmness will result in a carnival of crime and an absolute contempt for all authority in this region. (Hagedorn 45)

Wood's attestation of the Moros' unreliability serves as a justification for their continued subordination in the name of an allegedly much-needed domesticizing control.

In historical terms, unreliability has been attributed to groups that for ideological reasons were deemed intrinsically inferior; reliability, by contrast, could and can only be ascribed to those who are socioculturally similar. Moving along the spectrum from nonfictional to fictional narrative discourse, we find that in older and newer literary texts, attributions of unreliability are made to those who are dominated over. These include, for instance, the innumerable "leaky" and untrustworthy women in early modern English plays, and the "shifty" persons of color in racist U.S. American fictional narratives up until this day. These are just two examples of how assumptions about intrinsic personal deficiencies are translated into fictional renderings, and thus also into normative judgments about textual figures' reliability. The impetus to create and diagnose unreliable narrators is a regular practice in modern fiction. My earliest example of an unreliable narrator to date is Moll Flanders (Olson, "Reconsidering"), although there may well be earlier ones. Understanding the detection of unreliable narration in terms of evidence of the superior perspicacity of the implied author and the preferred reader rests on the assumption of normatively posited qualities of communicative clarity, relevance, and the ability to detect irony, all of which can only be assumed to be present between equally empowered persons. In accounts of unreliable narration that eschew the role of the author/implied author, it is the reader's cultural habitus that allows her to detect the inferiorly situated narrator's communicative or perceptual failures. Thus Booth's assumption of a universal concept of unreliability was oblivious to its historical contingency. This is a point that Fredric Jameson makes not only about Booth's postulation of the universality of implied and reliable narrators but also about the ahistoricism of literary criticism (and narratology) more generally: "The fact that the implied or reliable narrator described by Booth is possible only in a situation of relative class homogeneity, and indeed reflects a basic community of values shared by a fairly restricted class of readers: and such a situation is not brought back into the world by fiat" (357).

Specific narrative fictions provide forums for uncovering the historical contingency of concepts such as that of the unreliable narrator. Individual postcolonial readings of novels such as *Wide Sargasso Sea* (1966) and *Midnight's Children* (1980) reveal their narrators' unreliability to be politicized strategies for thwarting mores of narrating that presuppose reliability as a norm. In the context of describing unequal power arrangements based on racism as they are reflected on fictionally, Henry Louis Gates Jr. draws on Bahktin's notion of double-voicedness to indicate the "re-semanticization of the familiar meaning to have a 'decolonized'" significance (51). By exploiting and subverting the hierarchically dependent communicative value of reliability, decolonizing fictions revise implicitly authoritarian narrative mores. This includes a resistance to the correlation between reliable narration and the ownership of reality and equality between persons that this correlation presupposes.

I do not wish to suggest that all decolonializing narrations programmatically feature unreliable narrators, an assumption that might be taken to suggest that reliable communication is the exclusive prerogative of colonizers. Rather, it is to say that unreliability needs to be understood as a rhetorical strategy that can be used to uncover and trouble the position of sociocultural and representational privilege from which the reader may begin her engagement with a fictional narrative. Postcolonial, feminist/queer, and critical race scholarship has repeatedly demonstrated the intrinsically political relationship between textual form and semantic content. It remains, then, for more definitional and theoretical narratological research to incorporate these politically engaged assessments into an analysis of the power arrangements that underlie narratologial models purporting to be universal.

Fictional renderings can destabilize the position from which attributions of unreliability have traditionally been made. The unreliable narration of *The Fall* evinces "the impossibility of simplistic and naïve perception of the readers as automatically and unequivocally superior to the unreliable narrator" (Marcus 325). *The Reluctant Fundamentalist* functions similarly. By interpellating its reader so that she aligns with the position of Changez's "ugly" and "terror"-fied American listener, and, as in the paratextual signals, by playing into Western-centric assumptions about the inherent untrustworthiness of "terrorists," the novel enacts a critique of the position from which the attribution of unreliability is made when based on an implicit assumption of sameness between the values of the reader and a putative person "behind" the text. Simultaneously, it suggests that dominant U.S. biases concerning men like Changez are more inconsistent than Changez's uneven storytelling. As an instance of "transcultural narrative unreliability" (Helff 140), the novel demonstrates that narrator reliability, understood as an ethical value, can potentially only be achieved through the exclusion of counter positions, including those of cultural others.

Read against the sociocultural coordinates of Booth's original postulation, the novel enacts a subversive critique of the process by which a narrator's unreliability is diagnosed when it is understood as a personal communicative, perceptual, or moral failing. It demonstrates this process to be culturally bound and ideologically determined. Reifying the author's and reader's common position of privilege, judgments of unreliability, including the reliability found to be deficiently lacking in the narrator, assume the validity of prescriptive values and norms. An analysis of *The Reluctant Fundamentalist*'s resistance to what I am calling the ideology of reliability creates an awareness that the attribution of unreliability perpetuates processes in which the determination of supposedly intrinsic weakness has been used to reify representational privilege. Attentiveness to the historical examples of assigning unreliability then renders the accepted process of attributing unreliability to narrators problematic, unless this attribution is made with a sensibility to the narrator's or focalizer's social and material conditions.

Vera Nünning has pointed out the necessity of accounting for historically bound normative expectations of personhood in analyses of unreliability. In her reading of *The Vicar of Wakefield* (1766), she argues that late eighteenth-century readers adjudged the novel's narrator-protagonist to be a highly sympathetic portrait of ideal manhood, whereas Primrose's emotionality now appears excessive and his narration unreliable. Her contention illustrates a larger potential fault in classical and postclassical narratological work. In aiming to be applicable to any number of individual narrative realizations, narratological accounts of forms and attendant functions attempt to be universal. Yet, as in the majority of accounts of narrator unreliability, this leads to a lack of attention to materially inscribed hierarchies that regulate communicative behaviors and the narratological concepts that are derived from them.

This is not to deny the usefulness of conceptualizations of unreliable narration. Rather, it is to suggest that the model of detecting unreliability that rests on the assumption of likeness on the part of the reader and the implied author or the values suggested by that author's text needs to be modified. As I have argued elsewhere, unreliability is not exclusive to tellers, or speakers in Genettian terms; it may also characterize focalized narration, where a focalizer's recorded lexis and mental impressions can be evaluated independently of any presumed narrating figure (Olson, "Like a Dog"). When recognized as such, unreliable narration—whether by a narrator in the conventional sense or by a focalizer—signals the need to read with greater acuity to resolve textual discrepancies. The recognition of unreliability interrupts the fluid narrativization process and urges the reader to imagine alternative stories. Further, the recognition of textual instability that unreliable narration triggers depends on readers' familiarity with the textual gesture of implying multiple tellings and reading strategies.

The analysis of narrator unreliability in Mohsin Hamid's "9/11" novel demonstrates how the subversion of a communicative norm articulates political criticism, in this case of the "rightness" of dominant American perceptions of terrorism and terrorists. To recognize *The Reluctant Fundamentalist*'s ideological critique, the reader must attend to the political context to which the text responds. On the one hand, unreliable narration in *The Reluctant Fundamentalist* interpellates the reader into occupying the position of the suspicious American. On the other hand, it mimics dominant, myopic American forms of narrating 11 September 2001. As Changez insists: "In history, as I suspect you—an American—will agree, it is the thrust of one's narrative that counts, not the accuracy of one's details."

A critical narratology such as the one I have endeavored to employ here to problematize Boothian and post-Boothian models of unreliable narration functions to review narratological categories in terms of their historical situatedness. This can be achieved through a development of models sensitive to the hierarchies of power implicit in narrational mores once assumed to be ahistorically valid. The politics of form I am calling for incorporates insights from feminist, queer, and postcolonial and critical race theory to review existent narratological concepts and models (see Olson and Copland). It asks how differing linguistic and intellectual trajectories of narratological analysis create ruptures, discontinuities, and the non-translatability of concepts rather than an absolutist framework for interpreting narration (Martínez). Accordingly, narrative models are refined to the extent that they challenge rather than reify existing hierarchical disparities based on violently defended forms of difference.

WORKS CITED

Battersby, Christine. *The Phenomenal Woman: Feminist Metaphysics and the Patterns of Identity*. Cambridge: Polity Press, 1998.

Bhabha, Homi. *The Location of Culture*. London: Routledge, 1994.

Booth, Wayne. *The Company We Keep: An Ethics of Fiction*. Oakland: University of California Press, 1989.

———. *Rhetoric of Fiction*. Chicago: Chicago University Press, 1961.

———. *A Rhetoric of Irony*. Chicago: Chicago University Press, 1974.

Butler, Judith. *Precarious Life: The Powers of Mourning and Violence*. London: Verso, 2004.

Camus, Albert. *The Fall*. New York: Vintage Books, 1991.

Cantor, Milton. "The Image of the Negro in Colonial Literature." *The New England Quarterly* 36.4 (1963): 452–77.

Faludi, Susan. *The Terror Dream: Fear and Fantasy in Post-9/11 America*. New York: Metropolitan Books, 2007.

Fludernik, Monika. "The Category of 'Person' in Fiction: You and We. Narrative Multiplicity and Indeterminacy of Reference." *Current Trends in Narratology*. Ed. Greta Olson. Berlin: De Gruyter, 2011. 101–41.

Foucault, Michel. *The History of Sexuality: An Introduction*. Harmondsworth: Penguin Books, 1987.

———. *Society Must Be Defended*. New York: Picador, 2003.

Gates, Henry Louis Jr. *The Signifying Monkey: A Theory of African-American Literary Criticism*. New York: Oxford University Press, 1988.

Genette, Gerard. *Paratexts: Thresholds of Interpretation*. 1987. Cambridge: Cambridge University Press, 1997.

Grice, Paul H. "Logic and Conversation." 1967. *Syntax and Semantics 3: Speech Acts*. Ed. Peter Cole and Jerry L. Morgan. New York: Academic Press, 1975. 41–58.

Hagedorn, Herman. *Leonard Wood: A Biography*. Vol. 2. New York: Harper & Brothers, 1931.

Hamid, Mohsin. *The Reluctant Fundamentalist*. London: Hamish Hamilton, 2007.

Hartnell, Anna. "Moving through America: Race, Place, and Resistance in Mohsin Hamid's *The Reluctant Fundamentalist*." *Journal of Postcolonial Writing* 46.2–3 (July/September 2010): 336–48.

Harvey, David. "Cosmopolitanism and the Banality of Geographical Evil." *Public Culture* 12.2 (2000): 529–64.

Helff, Sissy. "Multicultural Australia and Transcultural Unreliable Narration in Indo-Australian Writing." *Bernard Hickley, A Roving Cultural Ambassador: Essays in His Memory*. Ed. Maria Renata Dolce and Antonella Riem. Udine: Forum Edizioni, 2009. 135–47.

Heyd, Theresa. "Unreliability: The Pragmatic Perspective Revisited." *Journal of Literary Theory* 5.1 (2011): 3–17.

Jameson, Fredric. *Marxism and Form: Twentieth-Century Dialectical Theories of Literature*. Princeton: Princeton University Press, 1974.

Khan, Anna H. R. "Mohsin Hamid: Author of *The Reluctant Fundamentalist* Speaks about Novel and Personal Experiences." *Stanford Daily* 23 Apr. 2007: 3.

Marcus, Amit. "Camus's *The Fall*: The Dynamics of Narrative Unreliability." *Style* 40.4 (2006): 314–33.

Martínez, Matías. "Dos Passos Instead of Goethe! Some Observations on How the History of Narratology Is and Ought to Be Conceptualized." *Diegesis* 1.1 (2012): 134–41.

Mukherjee, Ankhi. "'Yes, sir, I was the one who got away': Postcolonial Emergence and the Questions of Global English." *Études Anglaises* 62–63 (2009): 280–91.

Nünning, Ansgar. "Unreliable Narration zur Einführung: Grundzüge einer kognitiv-narratologischen Theorie und Analyse unglaubwürdigen Erzählens." *Unreliable Narration: Studien zur Theorie und Praxis unglaubwürdigen Erzählens in der englischsprachigen Erzählliteratur*. Ed. Ansgar Nünning. Trier: WVT, 1998. 3–40.

Nünning, Vera. "Die Historische Variabilität von Werten und Normen: *The Vicar of Wakefield* als Testfall für eine kulturgeschichtliche Erzählforschung." *Unreliable Narration: Studien zur*

Theorie und Praxis unglaubwürdigen Erzählens in der englischsprachigen Erzählliteratur. Ed. Ansgar Nünning. Trier: WVT, 1998. 257–85.

Olson, Greta. "'Like a Dog': Rituals of Animal Degradation in J. M. Coetzee's *Disgrace* and Abu Ghraib Prison." *Journal of Narrative Theory* 44.1 (2014): 116–56.

———. "Reading 9/11 Texts through the Lens of Critical Media Studies." *New Theories, Models and Methods in Literary and Cultural Studies: Theory into Practice.* Ed. Greta Olson and Ansgar Nünning. Trier: WVT, 2013. 161–85.

———. "Reconsidering Unreliability: Fallible and Untrustworthy Narrators." *Narrative* 11.1 (2003): 93–109.

———. "Recovering from the Men We Loved to Hate: Barack Obama as a Representative of Post-Post September 11 White House Masculinity." *Beyond 9/11: Transdisciplinary Perspectives on Twenty-First Century U.S. American Culture.* Ed. Christian Klöckner, Simone Knewitz, and Sabine Sielke. Transcription 6. Frankfurt: Lang, 2013. 93–119.

Olson, Greta, and Sarah Copland. "Towards a Politics of Form." *European Journal of English Studies* 20.3 (2016): 207–21.

Olsson, Karen. "I Pledge Allegiance." *New York Times.* 22 Apr. 2007. Web. 30 Jan. 2015.

Phelan, James. *Living to Tell about It: A Rhetoric and Ethics of Character Narration.* Ithaca: Cornell University Press, 2005.

Richardson, Brian. "The Poetics and Politics of Second Person Narrative." *Genre* 24 (1991): 309–30.

Scanlan, Margaret. "Migrating from Terror: The Postcolonial Novel after September 11." *Journal of Postcolonial Writing* 46.3–4 (2010): 266–78.

Shamsie, Muneeza. "Covert Operations in Pakistani Fiction." *Commonwealth Essays and Studies* 31.2 (2009): 15–25.

Shen, Dan. "Unreliability." *The Living Handbook of Narratology.* 27 June 2011. Web. 30 Jan. 2015.

Solomon, Deborah. "Questions for Mohsin Hamid: The Stranger." *New York Times.* 15 Apr. 2007. Web. 30 Jan. 2015.

Sperber, Dan, and Deirdre Wilson. "Irony and the Use-Mention Distinction." *Radical Pragmatics.* Ed. Peter Cole. New York: Academic Press, 1981. 257–317.

Ward, Ian. "Towards a Poetics of Terror." *Law, Culture and the Humanities* 4 (2008): 248–79.

Westwell, Guy. "Regarding the Pain of Others: Scenarios of Obligation in Post-9/11 Cinema." *Journal of American Studies* 4 (2011): 815–34.

Zipfel, Frank. "Unreliable Narration and Fictional Truth." *Journal of Literary Theory* 5.1 (2011): 109–30.

CHAPTER 9

The Immigrant Experience in Jhumpa Lahiri's "The Third and Final Continent"

Postcolonial and Rhetorical Perspectives

JAMES PHELAN

JHUMPA LAHIRI'S "The Third and Final Continent," the final story in her 1999 Pulitzer Prize–winning collection *Interpreter of Maladies*, is a moving tale about immigration: the Bengali character narrator tells the story of his relocation from Calcutta to London in 1964 and then from London to Cambridge, Massachusetts, in 1969. Lahiri constructs the progression of the story by intertwining two sets of instabilities: those involving the character narrator's adjustment to Cambridge and those involving his—and his wife Mala's—adjustment to their arranged marriage, which took place in Calcutta shortly before the character narrator departed for the United States. Before Mala joins him in Cambridge, he lives for six weeks in a room he rents from a 103-year-old woman, Mrs. Croft. She initiates him into U.S. culture with what I will call the Splendid Ritual: she exclaims, "There is an American flag on the moon!" (182) and requires him to respond by shouting, "Splendid." Mrs. Croft also becomes what Judith Caesar calls the catalyst in the resolution of the intertwined instabilities, as she and the character narrator gradually come to respect each other across their differences, and they both extend that respect to Mala in a scene that functions as the turning point in the story.

Critics have used the lenses of postcolonial and cosmopolitan theory to illuminate the story's fresh take on the political dimensions of immigration and naturalization.[1] These critics contend that Lahiri complicates standard

---

1. Other issues have also been explored: see Caesar on space, Garg and Khushu-Lahiri on food, and Brada-Williams on the story's placement in the final position in the collection.

postcolonial ideas about how large-scale power relations—between native-immigrant, first world–third world, white-brown, center-margin—operate in the immigrant experience. As Elizabeth Jackson puts it, Lahiri "deconstruct[s] simplistic binaries of power based on geographical origin, geographical location, and cultural identity" (113). Jackson identifies the turning point scene, where Mrs. Croft's and Mala's warm connection across their cultural differences leads to a new warmth between the character narrator and Mala as a telling case in point.

In an insightful analysis, Susan Koshy argues that the stories in *Interpreter of Maladies* "reveal not only the growing relevance of relationships to those who are less than kin and more than stranger but also . . . the dislocation and consequent unreliability of the very categories through which we demarcate the familiar and the unfamiliar" (598). In addition, the collection explores what Koshy calls "minority cosmopolitanism" through its concern with "diasporic citizenship" and the process of naturalization. In Lahiri's stories, Koshy argues,

> the diasporic citizen inhabits an indeterminate space of belonging that aggregates the discrepant identifications and trajectories associated with contiguous words like *resident alien, immigrant, exile,* and *minority subject*. But it is the process of naturalization as much as a specific identity like immigrant or refugee that is the subject of Lahiri's fiction. Lahiri's stories explore naturalization not just as a formal process by which citizenship is acquired but also as a social process that extends beyond the conferral of formal citizenship and follows multiple, unpredictable pathways. (598–99)

Applying this framework to "The Third and Final Continent," Koshy makes three related points. (1) Lahiri uses the arranged marriage (rather than the more common choice of romantic love) as a metaphor for immigration and naturalization, thereby highlighting the difficulties of each. (2) Lahiri uses the turning point scene as an allegory for naturalization. The character narrator and Mrs. Croft develop mutual respect within an awareness of difference, and when they both extend that respect to Mala, they make possible the acceptance necessary for the successful marriage; a similar respect within the recognition of difference is necessary for naturalization. (3) Lahiri uses small events and "ordinary affects" as ways to mediate between individual subjectivity and larger social structures. Classifying "The Third and Final Continent" as an epic short story, in which the unnamed character narrator stands in for a whole generation of male Indian immigrants, Koshy notes that Lahiri nevertheless focuses on "quirky encounters and thick quotidian details to create the eventfulness of this journey" (604). As a result, the story "brings into view the dislocations produced by migration and globalization, but from a perspective far removed from macrostructural causes" (605).

As a rhetorical theorist interested in the purposes of narratives, I find that Jackson and Koshy impressively elucidate key aspects of Lahiri's exploration of immigration and naturalization. I also note that their analyses proceed in the now time-honored fashion of politically oriented criticism: they use relevant concepts from cultural and political theory to thematize the characters and events of the story. While this method has amply proven its utility, it also leaves room for me to ask two other questions. How do additional core components of narrative contribute to Lahiri's exploration of the immigrant experience? How might Lahiri's practice feed back into our theoretical understanding of one or more elements of narrative? The first question is especially pertinent in light of Koshy's point that Lahiri provides "a perspective [on the dislocations of immigration] far removed from macrostructural causes." What better way to get further inside Lahiri's perspective than by analyzing how it develops through her careful crafting of the multiple narrative elements of "Final Continent"? And such an analysis leads naturally to a consideration of the second question. For these reasons, I shall home in on Lahiri's handling of two elements that have been relatively undertheorized: reliable narration and character-character dialogue.[2] My goals are to show that rhetorical theory can productively build on the conclusions of the postcolonial and cosmopolitan critics and that Lahiri's practice can illuminate a rhetorical understanding of these two techniques.

A RHETORICAL APPROACH TO NARRATIVE COMMUNICATION

Rhetorical theory defines narrative as somebody telling somebody else on some occasion and for some purpose(s) that something happened (see Phelan, *Living*). I do not claim that this definition is superior to all others since different definitions can undergird different valuable critical projects. I do claim, however, that conceiving of narrative rhetorically is a better approach to the project of understanding narrative communication than conceiving of nar-

---

2. Other elements are also worthy of further investigation, especially progression and temporality, but I have elected to stay with how Lahiri's perspective emerges through her handling of other perspectives. Wayne C. Booth's *The Rhetoric of Fiction* is the locus classicus for an account of the uses of reliable commentary (especially by noncharacter narrators). For some good recent work on dialogue, see Thomas.

rative as a textual structure that synthesizes a what (story) and a how (discourse). That common conception underlies the still dominant narrative communication model proposed by Seymour Chatman in *Story and Discourse* (1978), one that depicts a linear sequence of transmission among agents of the telling (with those agents in brackets located within the text):

From a rhetorical perspective, characters are conspicuous by their absence from this model. From a story/discourse perspective, characters are absent because they are part of story, not discourse, and the model would account for character-character dialogue as part of what the narrator transmits to the narratee. From a rhetorical perspective, that account is workable for cases in which a reliable narrator clearly frames and comments on the dialogue, but it is inadequate for all those cases in which such commentary is unreliable or in which the narrator only identifies which character speaks. In those cases, the main transmission via dialogue goes from author through character(s) to audiences. Rhetorical theory has no problem in recognizing character-character dialogue as an element of both story and discourse, an event and narration by another means.

Even more important, the rhetorical perspective allows us to see synergies among narrative elements that are not visible in Chatman's model. Consider, for example, this passage from Faulkner's *The Sound and the Fury*:

> Through the fence, between the curling flower spaces, I could see them hitting. They were coming toward where the flag was and I went along the fence. Luster was hunting in the grass by the flower tree. They took the flag out, and they were hitting. Then they put the flag back and they went to the table, and he hit and the other hit. Then they went on, and I went along the fence. Luster came away from the flower tree and he went along the fence and they stopped and we stopped and I looked through the fence while Luster was hunting in the grass.
>
> "Here, caddie." He hit. They went away across the pasture. I held to the fence and watched them going away.
>
> "Listen at you now." Luster said. "Aint you something, thirty three years old, going on that way. After I done went all the way to town to buy you that cake. Hush up that moaning." (3)

Among other things, Faulkner communicates to his audience that the trigger for Benjy's moaning is the word "caddie." (I bracket the issue that this communication is clearer on a second reading of the novel.) If we try to explain that communication according to Chatman's model—or even according to a revision of it that included characters—we're at a loss because the communication does not follow the linear transmission he sketches. Instead, Faulkner delivers that information by constructing a synergy among Benjy's narration, the golfer's call to the caddie, and Luster's address to Benjy. None of the individual agents has any idea of what Faulkner communicates through the synergy of their distinct utterances.

In sum, shifting from a story/discourse perspective on narrative communication to a rhetorical one means shifting from a view of narrative as a binary structure of textual components to a view of it as a rhetorical action in which an author (or, if you prefer, as I do, an implied author) seeks to influence an audience in some ways rather than others by drawing on the components as flexible resources that can be combined (or not) in a multitude of ways.

A RHETORICAL APPROACH TO RELIABLE CHARACTER NARRATION

As I argue in *Living to Tell About It,* character narration is an art of indirection: the implied author uses a single text to address at least two different audiences (her own and the character narrator's narratee) to accomplish at least two different purposes (her own and the character narrator's). Skillful implied authors can communicate to their audiences whether the two purposes of the narration converge, diverge, or do some of each. Narrative theorists—including the implied author of *Living to Tell*—have focused primarily on situations in which those purposes diverge, that is, on unreliable narration. I want to begin to redress the balance, after briefly reviewing some conclusions about unreliability.

Noting that the three common functions of narration are to report, to interpret, and to evaluate, I identify two ways that each function can be inadequate—either by distorting or not going far enough—and thus offer a taxonomy of six types of unreliability: misreporting and underreporting, misinterpreting and underinterpreting, and misevaluating and underevaluating. In all cases, the judgment of unreliability is not made against some ideal of "objective narration" but rather against inferences about what the implied author would posit as adequate reporting, interpreting, or evaluating.

Rhetorical theory is ultimately more interested in the effects of unreliable narration on the narrator-audience relationship than it is in the taxonomy. Effects, both affective and ethical, can vary along a spectrum from estranging to bonding (see Phelan, "Estranging Unreliability"). For example, Faulkner begins Jason's section of *The Sound and the Fury* with estranging unreliability: "Once a bitch always a bitch, what I say" (180). Jason expects his audience to agree and to acknowledge his superior insight, while Faulkner implicitly guides his audience to disagree vehemently. In contrast, Mark Twain uses Huck Finn's unreliable interpreting and evaluating of his decision to tear up the letter to Miss Watson informing her where to find the runaway Jim—"All right, then, I'll *go* to hell," he famously declares (201)—to strengthen the bond between Huck and his audience.

The essence of reliable narration is the implied author's communicating matters that she endorses through the filter of an ontologically distinct character. Authors adopt such filters because anchoring the narration in the perspective and experiences of an actor and teller in the storyworld can increase the thematic, affective, and ethical force and significance of the whole narrative. As with unreliability, it is helpful to distinguish among subtypes. I propose a spectrum of reliable narration, corresponding to the range of implied author—character narrator—audience relationships, and I identify three salient subtypes at different points along that spectrum.[3]

At one end (let's make it the left) is *restricted narration*. In restricted narration, the implied author limits the character narrator's function to reliable reporting and uses both the reliability and the restriction to convey interpretations or evaluations that the character narrator remains unaware of. In restricted narration, the narrating-filter often becomes thin, as the implied author directs primary attention to other characters or foregrounds the activity of the experiencing-I. Consider, for example, this passage from *Huckleberry Finn*: "Just then Sherburn steps out on to the roof of his little front porch, with a double-barrel gun in his hand, and takes his stand, perfectly ca'm and deliberate, not saying a word. The racket stopped, and the wave sucked back" (146). Twain uses Huck's reliable reporting to convey implicit interpretations and evaluations of Sherburn's imperious authority that Huck remains oblivious to. In addition, the narrating-Huck's filter becomes very thin: since Twain's primary purpose is to set the stage for the encounter between Sherburn and the mob from Bricksville, he does not want to call attention to idiosyncrasies of Huck's perspective.

---

3. In *Living to Tell About It*, I identify both restricted narration and mask narration, but I do not place them along the spectrum I propose here.

In the middle of the spectrum is *convergent narration*. In convergent narration, the implied author's, the character narrator's, and the authorial audience's views of the reporting, interpreting, and evaluating coincide even as the narrating-filter is thick and the experiencing-I is likely to be in the foreground. Consider, for example, Jane Eyre's description of her marriage to Rochester: "I have now been married ten years. I know what it is to live entirely for and with what I love best on earth. I hold myself supremely blest—blest beyond what language can express; because I am my husband's life as fully as he is mine" (500). The passage presents the narrating-Jane's report, interpretation, and evaluation of the marriage of experiencing-Jane, and it constitutes an affectively and ethically powerful summary precisely because the sentiments and judgments of the implied Brontë, Jane, and the authorial audience converge here.

At the right end of the spectrum is *mask narration*. In mask narration, the character narrator's reporting function recedes and the interpreting and evaluating functions move to the foreground as the implied author uses the character narrator to thematize one or more aspects of the narrative. While the filter remains in place, it is thinner than in convergent narration, and the implied author's voice is at most only slightly refracted through the mask. Consider, for example, Nick Carraway's famous interpretive and evaluative meditations at the end of *The Great Gatsby*, meditations that end with "So we beat on, boats against the current, borne back ceaselessly into the past" (189). Nick's thematizing of the narrative is also the implied Fitzgerald's thematizing of it, one that gains power because it is rooted in Nick's prior experiences, observations, and reflections, all of which Fitzgerald's audience has shared.

A RHETORICAL APPROACH TO CHARACTER-CHARACTER DIALOGUE

Once we approach character-character dialogue as not just an event but also narration by another means, we can see that it is an even more complex art of indirection than character narration. It entails additional speakers with different purposes (implied author and at least two characters), and the implied author must simultaneously motivate each character's speech within its mimetic context and within that of her own communicative purpose. Just as character narration occurs along two tracks, that between the narrator and the narratee, and that between the implied author and the audience, so too does dialogue. The character-character track (and of course sometimes more than two characters are involved) is the location for *conversational disclosures*: the reporting, interpreting, and evaluating offered by the characters to each other. The implied author-audience track is the location for what I call *authorial disclosures*: the reporting, interpreting, and evaluating the implied author offers to her audience by means of the conversational disclosures (see Phelan, "Conversational"). The two tracks may overlap completely (as when one character supplies information to another that the implied author needs the audience to know) or partially (as when the implied author uses the conversational disclosure to communicate matters that the characters are not aware of).[4] Conversational disclosures can be as reliable or unreliable as character narration, and all the subtypes of reliability and unreliability and their effects can be found in dialogue.

To round off what could be a much longer discussion, I highlight two additional points. (1) Whereas narration to a narratee typically presupposes a global act of storytelling by an individual or collective agent (even if the "global" act turns out to be only a segment of a larger narrative), dialogue is typically intermittent, locally determined, and embedded within one of those acts of global storytelling. Consequently, the gaps between conversational disclosure and authorial disclosure often increase as a narrative progresses. As characters remain bound to their local, intermittent exchanges, implied authors use the sequence of *authorial disclosure across conversations* to guide their audiences to piece together aspects of those local exchanges into larger authorial communications. (2) Implied authors often create synergistic effects through the juxtaposition of dialogue and character narration by taking advantage of the multiple voices at play in those juxtapositions. By orchestrating those voices, authors once again often communicate more than the participants in the dialogue and the character narrator (whether a participant or not) are themselves aware of.

LAHIRI'S SYNERGIES

I shall focus on the sequence of three scenes involving the Splendid Ritual because they are crucial to Lahiri's exploration of the politics of immigration and illustrative of her handling of reliable narration, dialogue, and their synergies. Lahiri introduces the Ritual during the character narrator's first meeting with Mrs. Croft, when she assesses his suitability as a lodger. In the following passage she juxtaposes restricted narration and dialogue.

---

4. The two tracks will never completely diverge because the authorial disclosure will always contain the conversational disclosure.

> "There is an American flag on the moon!"
>
> "Yes, madame." Until then I had not thought very much about the moon shot. It was in the newspaper, of course, article upon article. The astronauts had landed on the shores of the Sea of Tranquillity, I had read, travelling farther than anyone in the history of civilization. For a few hours they explored the moon's surface. They gathered rocks in their pockets, described their surroundings (a magnificent desolation, according to one astronaut), spoke by phone to the president, and planted a flag in lunar soil. The voyage was hailed as man's most awesome achievement. . . .
>
> The woman bellowed, "A flag on the moon, boy! I heard it on the radio! Isn't that splendid?"
>
> "Yes, madame."
>
> But she was not satisfied with my reply. Instead she commanded, "Say 'splendid'!" (179)

Lahiri uses the synergy between the restricted narration and the dialogue to communicate much more than the character narrator is aware of, in large part because the character narrator does not pick up on salient aspects of the authorial disclosure. First, by putting the focus of Mrs. Croft's exclamation on the planting of the American flag rather than, say, the "giant leap for mankind" that Neil Armstrong described, Lahiri constructs Mrs. Croft's exclamation as celebrating the extension of the imperial power of the United States from the earth to the moon. Second, Mrs. Croft's commanding the non-American character narrator who wants her approval to join in her salute is its own small-scale exercise of American power. In this way, Lahiri dramatizes the macrostructural relations between the United States and India that underlie the personal relations between host and immigrant.

But, as Jackson and Koshy point out, Lahiri also wants to explore how such power relations break down or otherwise get complicated. Here she uses Mrs. Croft's dialogue to indicate that Mrs. Croft has a genuine, almost childlike ability to marvel at the moon landing and that she wants to share her pleasure in it with her new boarder. The authorial disclosure, in other words, is that her marveling at the moon landing is also a way to connect with this stranger whose age, sex, race, and nationality are so different from hers. (This inference also invites reflection on how the implied Lahiri enacts her connection with the character narrator across differences of gender and age.) Third, Lahiri uses the character narrator's restricted reporting of what he had read about the landing to convey her own sense of the mixed quality of the event: on the one hand, the astronauts had traveled "farther than anyone in the history of civilization," but on the other, they had found only rocks and a "magnificent desolation." By using the passive voice in the last sentence of the restricted narration, she distances both the character narrator and herself from the assessment that the voyage was "man's most awesome achievement."

Together these communications have multiple effects that give a significant texture to the politics of the scene. Lahiri guides her audience to view Mrs. Croft as a kind of benevolent, even endearing, dictator to whom the character narrator must pay tribute. She invites her audience to smile at the incongruities of the scene, even as it remains very serious for the character narrator. As the scene continues, Lahiri shifts from restricted narration to narration that is simultaneously reliable and unreliable.

> I was both baffled and somewhat insulted by the request. It reminded me of the way I was taught multiplication tables as a child, repeating after the master, sitting cross-legged . . . on the floor of my one-room Tollygunge school. It also reminded me of my wedding, when I had repeated endless Sanskrit verses after the priest, verses I barely understood, which joined me to my wife. I said nothing.
>
> "Say 'splendid'!" the woman bellowed once again.
>
> "Splendid," I murmured. I had to repeat the word a second time at the top of my lungs, so she could hear. (179–80)

The narration is reliable because the character narrator at some level registers the first layer of Mrs. Croft's command and evaluates it appropriately: as in the other situations, she is imposing her view of things on him, regardless of his own (lack of) connection to them. But the narration is unreliable because the character narrator misses the second layer of Mrs. Croft's communication. This misinterpretation has bonding rather than estranging effects because the occasion of the dialogue and all the differences between Mrs. Croft and himself position Lahiri's audience to be extremely sympathetic. Lahiri calls attention to how far apart Mrs. Croft and the character narrator are at this early point in their relationship even as he registers the similarity between her command and those other situations in which he has submitted to another's authority. Finally, Lahiri uses the comparison with the character narrator's marriage vows to provide a link between his distance from Mrs. Croft and his distance from Mala.

Once the character narrator rents the room, the Splendid Ritual becomes a daily occurrence. At the end of his first week, however, something changes:

> When I approached the bench she peered up at me and demanded:
> "What is your business?"

"The rent, madame."

"On the ledge above the piano keys!"

"I have it here." I extended the envelope toward her, but her fingers, folded together in her lap, did not budge. I bowed slightly and lowered the envelope, so that it hovered just above her hands. After a moment she accepted, and nodded her head.

That night when I came home, she did not slap the bench, but out of habit I sat beside her as usual. She asked me if I had checked the lock, but she mentioned nothing about the flag on the moon. Instead she said:

"It was very kind of you!"

"I beg your pardon, madame?"

"Very kind of you!"

She was still holding the envelope in her hands. (184)

The restricted narration thins the filter of the narrating-I, putting the emphasis of the scene on the character-character interaction itself. Lahiri then uses the synergy between the restricted narration and the dialogue, including the authorial disclosure across this conversation and the first one, to guide her audience's interpretations and evaluations of that interaction. Early in the scene Mrs. Croft is again demanding and commanding, but this time the character narrator does not acquiesce. Instead he does what he thinks is right, countering her command ("On the ledge . . . !") with his assertion ("I have it here") and following through by making it easy for her to take the money. When she does, Lahiri guides her audience to infer that a shift in their power dynamic has occurred. Later in the passage, Lahiri highlights one consequence of that shift. First, she briefly departs from the restricted narration to have the character narrator call attention to the fact that Mrs. Croft "mentioned nothing about the flag on the moon." Then Lahiri again relies on the authorial disclosure across conversations to signal the significance of the difference in this night's exchange. It is not just that "It was very kind of you!" replaces "Splendid!," but also that Mrs. Croft pays the compliment twice, presumably because it was so unexpected the first time the character narrator did not quite understand what "it" refers to. The larger communication, never directly expressed by the character narrator,[5] is that he and Mrs. Croft have

---

5. Some close readers might ask whether we should attribute the larger effects of this passage not just to Lahiri but also to the character narrator's deliberate design. While I would not argue strongly against such a reading, I don't see enough other signs of the character narrator's self-consciousness and aesthetic control to make me find it more persuasive than my hypothesis that Lahiri moves him from one kind of narration to another according to the effects she seeks at any given point.

now established a personal connection across their many differences, a connection rooted in each's admirable ethical response to the other. Although the power hierarchy has not disappeared, it has softened. The benevolent dictator has become a grateful host, and the subaltern lodger has become a man worthy of a compliment. Furthermore, these changes loom larger precisely because they arise out of the deviation from the ritual repetition of "Splendid!" and its implicit politics of interpellation. In other words, his acting on his sense of what is right rather than acquiescing to Mrs. Croft's instructions has led her to see him in a different light, and that vision, in turn, gives a new dimension to their relationship.

After the character narrator and Mala have been living together in their own apartment in Cambridge for a week, they are "still strangers" (192) to one another. He suggests they take a walk, and "without thinking" (193) he leads her to Mrs. Croft's, where they find her lying on the floor.

> "I broke my hip!" Mrs. Croft announced, as if no time had passed.
> "Oh dear, madame."
> "I fell off the bench!"
> "I am so sorry, madame."
> "It was the middle of the night! Do you know what I did, boy?"
> I shook my head.
> "I called the police!"
> She stared up at the ceiling and grinned sedately, exposing a crowded row of long gray teeth. Not one was missing. "What do you say to that, boy?"
> As stunned as I was, I knew what I had to say. With no hesitation at all, I cried out, "Splendid!"
> Mala laughed then. Her voice was full of kindness, her eyes bright with amusement. I had never heard her laugh before. (194–95)

Lahiri begins with dialogue, mixes restricted narration with reliable interpretive commentary, and then moves to convergent narration. Once again the synergy leads to multiple communications, many of which the character narrator is not aware of. Here are the salient features of Lahiri's communication up to the character narrator's utterance of "Splendid!" (1) Mrs. Croft and the character narrator, despite all their differences and his having moved out of her house, converse as old friends. Her use of "boy" in this dialogue has a different tone and force than it did when she first said, "There's an American flag on the moon, boy!" He has moved from stranger to something closer to a surrogate son. (2) Mrs. Croft gives the character narrator more credit than during the previous enactments of the Splendid Ritual: earlier she had prompted him by asking, "Isn't it splendid?"; here she asks, "What do you say to that, boy?" (3) His ability to answer shows how well he knows her (at least in one way), a demonstration that in turn highlights the gap between him and Mala.

At the end of the passage, Lahiri shifts to convergent narration, as the character narrator reports, interprets, and evaluates Mala's response to his performance in a way that both Lahiri and her audience warmly endorse. Just as he has never heard her laugh before, he has also never expressed this affective and ethical appreciation for her before. That expression deepens the audience's affective and ethical bond with him.

As the scene continues, Lahiri continues to build on the bonding effects of the convergent narration, making it the most affectively and ethically powerful scene in the story. Finally noticing Mala, Mrs. Croft commands her to stand.

> Mala rose to her feet, adjusting the end of her sari over her head and holding it to her chest, and, for the first time since her arrival, I felt sympathy. I remembered my first days in London, learning how to take the Tube to Russell Square, riding an escalator for the first time, being unable to understand that when the man cried "piper" it meant "paper," being unable to decipher, for a whole year, that the conductor said "mind the gap" as the train pulled away from each station. Like me, Mala had traveled far from home, not knowing where she was going, or what she would find, for no reason other than to be my wife. As strange as it seemed, I knew in my heart that one day her death would affect me, and stranger still, that mine would affect her. I wanted somehow to explain this to Mrs. Croft, who was still scrutinizing Mala from top to toe with what seemed to be placid disdain. . . . At last Mrs. Croft declared, with the equal measures of disbelief and delight I knew well:
> "She is a perfect lady!"
> Now it was I who laughed. I did so quietly, and Mrs. Croft did not hear me. But Mala had heard, and, for the first time, we looked at each other and smiled. (195–96)

Lahiri continues the convergent narration with special emphasis on the character narrator's interpretations and evaluations. More specifically, the character narrator's reliable interpreting and evaluating is rooted in his empathetic response to Mala, one based less on his having previously undergone the scrutiny of Mrs. Croft than on his experience of adjusting to his second continent. It is an ethically admirable imaginative leap—and one that converts the opening section of the story in which the character narrator briefly summarizes his time in London from interesting backstory to events with ongoing relevance.[6] In addition, Lahiri invites her audience to make the link between Mala's travel and that of the astronauts: "far from home, not knowing where she was going or what she would find." Finally, the character narrator's empathetic drawing on his past to interpret Mala's present situation leads him to project a future in which each cares for the other.

As noted above, Mrs. Croft serves as the catalyst for the connection between the married couple. Her imperiousness evokes the character narrator's sympathy for Mala, and her clear approbation evokes the shared smile. But Lahiri builds another, subtler progression into the narration. After the character narrator thinks about his future with Mala, he comments, "I wanted somehow to explain all this to Mrs. Croft," a sign of how much he wants to continue to connect with her across their differences.[7] Yet after Mrs. Croft passes judgment on Mala, he laughs just loudly enough for Mala but not Mrs. Croft to hear, a signal from Lahiri that his main desire to connect now appropriately gets transferred to his wife.

Before I leave this crucial scene, I want to note another kind of synergy that operates within it, one that becomes visible when we ask how Lahiri makes Mala's laugh mimetically plausible. Surely it is more plausible for Mala to be simply perplexed by the exchange between her husband and Mrs. Croft. After all, Mala doesn't know Mrs. Croft and she barely knows her husband, let alone why he would answer Mrs. Croft's question with "Splendid!" But in reading and teaching the story, I find that my students and I readily accept Mala's laughter. We do so, I suggest, primarily because we laugh (or at least smile) at this variation in the Splendid Ritual. I conclude, then, that Lahiri uses the authorial disclosure across conversations to construct a synergy that I call *crossover narration* (Phelan, "Implausibilities"). Crossover narration occurs when an author links the telling of two independent sets of events by *transferring the effects* of the telling of one to the telling of the other. In this case, the laughter generated in the audience by the narration of this variation in the Splendid Ritual crosses over from the interaction between Mrs. Croft and the character narrator (the first set of events) to Mala's response to that

---

6. A full-scale rhetorical analysis would have much more to say about the role of the second continent in the narrative progression.

7. Lahiri's communication about the character narrator's relation to his mother, who became mentally unbalanced after her husband died, is worthy of more commentary. Suffice it to say that Mrs. Croft becomes a quasi-mother figure to him (at one point he has to remind himself that "I was not her son"), and that his mother's response to her husband's death adds another layer to the character narrator's thoughts about how Mala's death would affect him and how his would affect her. See Caesar's good discussion of this issue.

interaction (the second set of events). Because readers laugh, they are likely to think, "Of course Mala laughs; anyone would."

MASK NARRATION

After the turning point, Lahiri has the character narrator cover, first, the "honeymoon of sorts" he and Mala enjoyed, and second, the next thirty years of his life, years that included their becoming parents to a son. Lahiri ends the story with a passage that morphs from the character narrator's thoughts about his son to mask narration, with the pivot occurring with his reference to the astronauts.

> In my son's eyes I see the ambition that had first hurled me across the world. In a few years he will graduate and pave his way, alone and unprotected. But I remind myself that he has a father who is still living, a mother who is happy and strong. Whenever he is discouraged, I tell him that if I can survive on three continents, then there is no obstacle he cannot conquer. While the astronauts, heroes forever, spent mere hours on the moon, I have remained in this new world for nearly thirty years. I know that my achievement is quite ordinary. I am not the only man to seek his fortune far from home, and certainly I am not the first. Still, there are times I am bewildered by each mile I have traveled, each meal I have eaten, each person I have known, each room in which I have slept. As ordinary as it all appears, there are times when it is beyond my imagination. (197–98)

This mask narration is somewhat different from Nick Carraway's at the end of *The Great Gatsby* because it remains anchored in the "I," giving it slightly more refraction through the mask. The character narrator's thematizing is in line with Koshy's description of "Final Continent" as an "epic short story" in which the character narrator stands in for a whole generation of Indian men ("I am not the only man"). But what is especially effective here is Lahiri's reference to the astronauts. First, the character narrator's comparison sets up his double-sided interpretation of his experience, his assessment of it as both "ordinary" (unlike theirs) and "beyond [his] imagination" (like theirs). The comparison also points to the extraordinary temporal dimension of his immigration and naturalization, one that makes so much difference to his son. Second, the comparison also implicitly brings Mrs. Croft into the passage because she is so closely associated with the astronauts. Mrs. Croft is also present through the references to "each meal I have eaten, each person I have known, each room in which I have slept." In addition, the character narrator's attitude of wonder at his experience on three continents is similar to Mrs. Croft's wonder at the flag on the moon. Indeed, I would argue that the passage's implicit references to Mrs. Croft are the source of its persuasiveness. Above all the mask narration effectively completes Lahiri's exploration of the complexities, idiosyncrasies, and wonders of immigration and naturalization.

CONCLUSION

If this analysis has been even somewhat persuasive, then it supports the larger claim that rhetorical theory and postcolonial theory can be productive partners in coming to terms with Lahiri's story. Postcolonial theory provides both key concepts and attention to politics that illuminate Lahiri's thematic purposes. Rhetorical theory provides a thicker description of the means by which Lahiri accomplishes those purposes, even as it adds to our understanding of the affective and ethical layers of Lahiri's story. Finally, Lahiri's practice feeds back into a rhetorical understanding not only of reliable narration, character-character dialogue, and the synergies between them but also of narrative communication itself.

WORKS CITED

Booth, Wayne C. *The Rhetoric of Fiction*. 1961. Chicago: University of Chicago Press, 1983.

Brada-Williams, Noelle. "Reading Jhumpa Lahiri's *Interpreter of Maladies* as a Short Story Cycle." *MELUS* 29.3-4 (2004): 451–64.

Brontë, Charlotte. *Jane Eyre*. 1874. New York: Penguin, 1996.

Caesar, Judith. "American Spaces in the Fiction of Jhumpa Lahiri." *English Studies in Canada* 31 (2005): 50–68.

Chatman, Seymour. *Story and Discourse: Narrative Structure in Fiction and Film*. Ithaca: Cornell University Press, 1978.

Faulkner, William. *The Sound and the Fury*. 1929. New York: Vintage, 1990.

Fitzgerald, F. Scott. *The Great Gatsby*. 1925. New York: Scribner's, 1992.

Garg, Shweta, and Rajyashree Khushu-Lahiri. "Interpreting a Culinary Montage: Food in Jhumpa Lahiri's *Interpreter of Maladies*." *Asiatic* 6.1 (2012): 73–83.

Jackson, Elizabeth. "Transcending the Politics of 'Where You're From': Postcolonial Nationality and Cosmopolitanism in Jhumpa Lahiri's *Interpreter of Maladies*." *ARIEL* 43.1 (2012): 109–25.

Koshy, Susan. "Minority Cosmopolitanism." *PMLA* 126.3 (2011): 592–609.

Lahiri, Jhumpa. "The Third and Final Continent." *Interpreter of Maladies*. Boston: Houghton Mifflin, 1999. 173–98.

Phelan, James. "Conversational and Authorial Disclosure in the Dialogue Novel: The Case of *The Friends of Eddie Coyle*." *Narrative, Interrupted: The Plotless, the Disturbing and the Trivial in Literature*. Ed. Markku Lehtimäki, Laura Karttunen, and Maria Mäkelä. Boston: De Gruyter, 2012. 3–23.

———. "Estranging Unreliability, Bonding Unreliability, and the Ethics of *Lolita*." *Narrative* 15.2 (2007): 222–38.

———. "Implausibilities, Crossovers, and Impossibilities." *A Poetics of Unnatural Narrative*. Ed. Jan Alber, Henrik Skov Nielsen, and Brian Richardson. Columbus: The Ohio State University Press, 2013. 167–84.

———. *Living to Tell about It: A Rhetoric and Ethics of Character Narration*. Ithaca: Cornell University Press, 2005.

Thomas, Bronwen. *Fictional Dialogue: Speech and Conversation in the Modern and Postmodern Novel*. Lincoln: University of Nebraska Press, 2012.

Twain, Mark. *Adventures of Huckleberry Finn: A Case Study in Critical Controversy*. Ed. Gerald Graff and James Phelan. Boston: Bedford-St. Martin's, 2004.

PART IV

STRATEGIES, NARRATIVE AND POSTCOLONIAL

CHAPTER 10

Ideology, Dissidence, Subversion

A Narratological Perspective

MONIKA FLUDERNIK

I N *Faultlines: Cultural Materialism and the Politics of Dissident Reading* (1992), Alan Sinfield characterizes his manner of analysis as follows:

> It is designed to epitomize a way of *apprehending the strategic organization of texts*—both the modes by which they produce plausible stories and construct subjectivities, and the *faultlines and breaking points* through which they *enable dissident reading*. (9; my emphasis)

This definition of the cultural materialist project combines two major procedures—the critical analysis of the "strategic organization" of a text, for which read: its formal engagements assessed from a critical perspective; and the search for chinks in the ideological mail of the story that the text is trying to convey. In the quoted passage, the ideology of the text is first linked to the telling of a plausible story designed to persuade the addressee as a cover-up for the ulterior motives of the originators or representatives of a particular ideology. The lifting of the ideological mask from the text is then, secondly, figured in the image of the faultline, a metaphor taken from geology. I read this metaphor to suggest that where the plausible story wears thin or shows holes, the seething volcanic mass of social unrest and intellectual dissidence has a chance to erupt. However, in Sinfield's book such potential lava outbreaks remain off limits; what he is interested in, rather, are geological soundings of the crust that forms on the surface of the volcanic fault line and which allow the scientist to probe the layers of submerged dissidence or ideological contradiction.

Sinfield's locus of dissidence in the metaphor of the faultline therefore sees ideology as a tale that has a seemingly perfect shape but in fact constructs its glossy surface on a layer of contradictions and inconsistencies that put the covering narrative under subliminal tension. The task of the cultural materialist critic is to diagnose the "cultural work" (Tomkins) that the story is performing while at the same time lancing the sore pustules on the skin to detect the pus beneath them and to provide a vent for the underlying tensions to emerge, though not in an actual earthquake but in the analytical prose of the geologist-critic alerting us to the illusionist nature of the suave language of the textual surface with its dissimulation of ideological closure.

For the narratologist, Sinfield's formula and metaphor open a way of reconsidering the form versus function debate but also to question the rather static framework of narratology, which—due to its descriptive focus—has had comparatively few models with a processual emphasis. To start with, I would like to review in what manner narratology has traditionally dealt with ideology (section 1). I will then base my illustration of South Asian texts on conceptualizations of the process of reading or, more generally, on a dynamic (rather than merely typological) model (section 2), trying to combine Sinfield's insights with narratological parameters. My example texts will be Nayantara Sahgal's *A Time to Be Happy* (1957) and Mohsin Hamid's *How to Get Filthy Rich in Rising Asia* (2013).

Before moving on to section 1, however, it may be necessary to explain more fully what I refer to as *narratology*. This is important since classical narratological typologies like those by Gérard Genette and Franz Karl Stanzel had little use for ideology and tried to define narrative on purely formal grounds, focusing on the close reading of texts. The ideology of the story for them would figure as part of the meaning or interpretation of the story but not of its formal construction. For the Russian Formalists, on the other hand, the question of ideology was clearly a central issue, and with the advent of feminist narratology and postcolonial theory within narrative studies, it has come to be perceived as of crucial importance. Since the link between classical narratology and ideology criticism is almost nonexistent, this essay will necessarily position itself within "postclassical" narratological persuasions (see Herman; Alber and Fludernik) and will try to extend functional parameters that are already in evidence in recent narratological work.

IDEOLOGY IN THE HISTORY OF NARRATOLOGY: A SURVEY

One of the key areas in which narratology has paid extensive attention to ideological issues is that of speech and thought representation. The two critics who immediately come to mind are Boris Uspensky and Mikhail Bakhtin. Uspensky (originally in 1970) introduced the category of "point of view on the ideological plane" (chapter 1, 8–17), which he ranged alongside that of the "phraseological plane" (chapter 2), the spatial and temporal plane (chapter 3), and the psychological plane (chapter 4). Putting the ideological first, he clearly marked its prominent position. Uspensky distinguishes between texts in which there exists "a single, dominating point of view" (8) and those in which there are "multiple evaluative views" (9). These multiple views can be coordinated, as in Lermontov's *A Hero of Our Time* (1840), in which the protagonist Pechorin is represented from his own point of view in his diary, from that of the narrator Maxim Maximovich (subsuming Pechorin's), and from that of another character, Doctor Werner, again subsumed under the narrator's evaluative system. Finally, if all points of view are placed one beside the other with no attempt to coordinate them, a "polyphonic narration" emerges (10), for which Bakhtin is cited as the terminological source.

Uspensky next goes on to illustrate that *characters* can either be "objects" (or perhaps targets) of ideological evaluation, or they can be "vehicle[s]," that is, they themselves do the evaluating (11–12). Uspensky proceeds to cite a few examples of the choice of lexemes (epithets, adjectives) that signal an ideological viewpoint, as when the pagan ruler in a Christian epic is referred to as "the pagan dog Tsarkalin" (14) or the Old Believers' religious service is modified by the epithet "pseudo-ecclesiastical" (14). Analogous examples can be found in the history of English literature, with incriminating epithets deployed to refer to persecuting tyrants in Middle English saints' legends and reprobatory language used to talk about the dealings of denominational antagonists in the controversialist literature of the sixteenth century.[1]

Lexical choice thus signals evaluative stance. Uspensky notes this connection between the lexical and ideological planes but emphasizes that they cannot be reduced to one another. Linguistic features can be used to "characterize" a point of view; they serve as markers or symptoms of evaluation. When the "phraseological features" (15) are employed by the author to signal

---

1. For the first, see the *South English Legendary*: "þe luþer man" (1967, 296, l. 147), "þe ssrewe" (274, l. 273, l. 279) or "þis wicche" and "þis luþer womman" (55, ll. 29, 25). For the second, see the examples cited in Lederer.

that the narration is conducted from a particular point of view, "for example, [by] the use of quasi-direct speech [i.e., FID—free indirect discourse] (in the authorial text)," this "may indicate quite definitely the author's use of the point of view of a certain character" (15). Uspensky acknowledges that lexical aspects may help to position a character socially and regionally, but they may additionally link him or her to a specific "world view" or "ideological position." Uspensky's example is Alexander Pushkin's *Eugene Onegin* in the analysis of Yuri Lotman.[2] Mikhail Bulgakov's *Heart of a Dog* (original 1925), to use my own example, likewise contrasts the language of Filipp Filippovic—urbane and educated—with those of the socialist lodgers in the house and of the dog-become-man, with clear ideological contrast signaled in the process.

Uspensky's insights have been deployed with advantage by Manfred Pfister in his *Theory of Drama* (*Das Drama* 90–103; *Theory and Analysis of Drama* 57–68) to evolve his concept of *Perspektivenstruktur* (*perspective structure*). Polyphony corresponds to Pfister's open perspective, whereas a closed perspective manipulates the different viewpoints on stage in one particular direction intended to win the audience's assent. Illogically, Pfister calls a play in which the different characters are only the author's mouthpieces an *aperspectival structure* (*Theory of Drama* 66), presumably echoing Genette's *non-focalization* for authorial narrative, though this apparent inconsistency disappears once one hears that aperspectivism is *monoperspectival,* whereas open and closed perspectival structures come under *polyperspectivity* (68). Nünning and Nünning apply Pfister's perspective structure to the issue of multiperspectivism in fiction. However, they do not focus on ideological contradictions; at least the question of ideology is not treated as a separate issue in any of the essays in the volume.

We owe the most prominent contribution to the study of ideology in narrative to Mikhail Bakhtin. He locates ideology both performatively in the staging of carnival and phraseologically (to use Uspensky's terminology) in the interbraiding of voices in Dostoevsky's novels. Although he focuses on stylistic clashes, as does Uspensky, Bakhtin's emphasis rests on the utopian vision of a chorus of voices that compete with one another to create a polyphonic symphony of ideological diversity and exuberant nonconformity. In chapter 1 of *Problems of Dostoevsky's Poetics* (5–46), Bakhtin characterizes Dostoevsky's achievement in terms evocative of present-day narrative ethics with their concern to preserve the alterity of the other:

---

2. The text by Lotman he cites is an early essay ("O probleme"; see Uspensky 9, fn. 3), but the same argument can be found in Lotman, *Structure of the Artistic Text.*

The uniqueness of Dostoevsky lies not in the fact that he monologically proclaimed the value of personality (others had done that before him); it lies in the fact that he was able, in an objective and artistic way, to visualize and portray personality as another, as someone else's personality, without making it lyrical or merging it with his own voice—and at the same time without reducing it to a materialized psychic reality. (12–13)

Discussing *The Brothers Karamazov*, Bakhtin underlines the "freedom and independence" (13) that characters are allowed to achieve. He counters the criticism that Dostoevsky's prose is "*multi-styled* or styleless" by calling it "*multi-accented* and contradictory" (15; original emphasis) and explains the distinctiveness of Dostoevsky's oeuvre in its combination of the "unification of highly heterogeneous and incompatible material . . . with the plurality of consciousness-centers not reduced to a single ideology" (17). Dostoevsky's "*polyphonic novel*," Bakhtin proposes, "*is dialogic through and through*" (40; original emphasis).

In "Discourse in the Novel," Bakhtin extends the polyphonic model to include ironic clashes of style in the hybridization of authorial and figural language. His example is Dickens's *Little Dorrit*, in which he discovers numerous instances of "*pseudo-objective motivation*" (305; original emphasis). In the novel, "'two languages,' two semantic and axiological belief systems" (304) are blended in "a typical double-accented, double-styled *hybrid construction*" (304; original emphasis), namely that of free indirect discourse and stylistic borrowing from characters' language. He comments on the following passage:

> It followed that Mrs. Merdle, as a woman of fashion and good breeding *who had been sacrificed to the wiles of a vulgar barbarian* (for Mr. Merdle was found out from the crown of his head to the sole of his foot, the moment he was found out in his pocket), must be actively championed by her order for her order's sake. (*Little Dorrit*, book 2, ch. 33; qtd. in Bakhtin, "Discourse" 307; original emphasis)

This ironic representation of *communis opinio* about Mrs. Merdle's situation after her husband's bankruptcy and suicide points up "the hypocrisy and greed of common opinion" (307). Bakhtin proceeds to note that Dickens's "entire text is, in fact, everywhere dotted with quotation marks that serve to separate out little islands of direct speech and purely authorial speech, washed by heteroglot waves from all sides" (307). He also notes that in Dickens, "one and the same word often figures both as the speech of the author and as the speech of another—and at the same time" (308). From the libertarian embracing of a multiplicity of voices Bakhtin here moves to the comic vision of Dickens and his ironic or satirical use of dialogic discourse.

In the remainder of the essay, Bakhtin also considers *skaz* (e.g., Gogol's "The Overcoat"), where the "speech of such narrators is always *another's speech*" (313; original emphasis),[3] as well as dialogue and a variety of free indirect discourse and stylistic borrowing (317–19) as further examples of *heteroglossia*, the combination of different voices, in narrative. Thus, he even treats the use of dialogue as a strategy of heteroglossia ("In Turgenev, social heteroglossia enters the novel primarily in the direct speeches of his characters, in dialogues" [316]). Rather than providing a free mixture, these instances of heteroglossia are now discussed as quite deliberate meaning effects in which the author's intentions are "refracted" in the characters' language:

> Heteroglossia, once incorporated into the novel (whatever the forms for its incorporation), is *another's speech in another's language*, serving to express authorial intentions but in a refracted way. Such speech constitutes a special type of *double-voiced discourse*. It serves two speakers at the same time and expresses simultaneously two different intentions: the direct intention of the character who is speaking, and the refracted intention of the author. (324; original emphasis)

What Bakhtin means to indicate is, however, not the full control of author over represented characters and their speech (for which read: ideology), but the inevitable "dialogizing" of characters' language owing to its framing within authorial discourse:

> The following must be kept in mind: that the speech of another, once enclosed in a context, is—no matter how accurately transmitted—always subject to certain semantic changes. The context embracing another's word is responsible for its dialogizing background, whose influence can be very great. Given the appropriate methods for framing, one may bring about fundamental changes even in another's utterance accurately quoted. Any sly and ill-disposed polemicist knows very well which dialogizing backdrop he should bring to bear on the accurately quoted words of his opponent, in order to distort their sense.... [T]hus it is, for instance, very easy to make even the most serious utterance comical. (340)

This is a crucial passage not only for its immediate meaning, but also because it articulates ideas that resurface in later ideological studies and particularly

---

3. On *skaz* see Cornwell; Schmid.

in postcolonial theory. What Bakhtin is saying in this paragraph complements his earlier remarks on dialogism or heteroglossia by adding the crucial insight that not only does stylistic clash introduce important ideological effect, but that the *framing* of another's language is already bound to undermine the status of the speaker's words. I see this as putting an emphasis on the deliberate ideological manipulation of others' discourse and hence as a move away from the heteroglossic utopia presented earlier in the article. In fact, what Bakhtin correctly notes is the compromising of quoted language by quotational strategy, and this manipulation can occur in fiction as well as rhetoric. The postcolonial rewriting of colonial and orientalist discourse, analogously, may employ the same words but frame them ironically and convert their meaning into the opposite of their originally intended meaning. By relating language as style to consciousness, Bakhtin inevitably links style to ideology; yet his concept of ideology uneasily vacillates between a critical use of heteroglossia and its utopian openness in Dostoevsky. Postcolonial theory, by contrast, since it is primarily focused on the ideological level and only marginally interested in speech representation, has been struggling with the dichotomy between the exercise of ideological positions in discourse, on the one hand, and subjects' unconscious ideological commitments or complicity, which criticism has to uncover, on the other. Their model is therefore more agonistic and less language-oriented.

Besides Bakhtin, important forays into the territory of ideology have come not so much from narratologists but from Marxist and postcolonial critics using narratological analysis to demonstrate the imbrication of stories with ideology. Besides György Lukács (1885–1971), the two most important contributors to a Marxist discussion of narrative ideology are Fredric Jameson (esp. "Third World Literature") and Pierre Macherey (esp. *A Theory of Literary Production*), though the work of Edward Said (esp. *Culture and Imperialism*) and Chidi Amuta (*The Theory of African Literature*) as well as Aijaz Ahmad (*In Theory*) also needs to be noted. While the more properly narratological contributions by Bakhtin and Uspensky focus on ideology as conveyed by linguistic means, especially through speech and thought representation and the lexical choices indicative of perspective (which can be ideological and social as well as merely psychological), the Marxist critics named above instead concentrate on narrative as a reflection and/or resolution of social and particularly class-related contradictions under the capitalist and colonial systems. In addition, Bakhtin (in his work on the carnivalesque—*Rabelais*) and Macherey as well as Ahmad underline the importance of narrative for the expression of resistance and the strategic deployment of subversion (Williams, "Marxist Approaches"; see also Said, *Culture and Imperialism, Politics of Dispossession*). As a result, they are more interested in plot than in focalization and speech and thought representation, and much of their criticism focuses on cultural analysis. Postcolonial theorists (see Said, *Politics of Dispossession*) have moreover emphasized that colonialism destroyed the creation of cultural and national identity for the colonized by preventing their own narrative self-representations. Postcolonial literature, therefore, is much more than a retaliative "writing back to the center"; it more basically allows the formerly oppressed to find their own voice and history in the act of narration.[4] As Patrick Williams ("Post-Colonialism" 453) mentions, the production of liberationist narratives by traditional storytellers in the Algerian War of Independence often led to their arrest. (Williams's source is Fanon.)

Since the 1990s, with the popularization of postcolonial theory and postcolonial studies in general, narratological analyses of postcolonial literature have become fairly widespread. The specificities of postcolonial texts (often in contrast to colonial narratives and anticolonial literature or literature of subversive intent) have been studied by several narratologists (Fludernik, "When the Self Is an Other," "The Hybridity of Discourses," "Narrative Forms"; Gymnich, "Linguistics and Narratology," "Writing Back"; Prince; Richardson, *Unnatural Voices*, "U.S. Ethnic and Postcolonial Fiction"). These critics have utilized the whole list of narrative features familiar from classical narratology to trace the peculiarities of postcolonial writing, especially showing how certain techniques are adopted or manipulated for the purpose of "writing back" or for the subversive undermining of colonial ideology. This list includes, first and foremost, the basic decision on a choice of language: should one use one's native tongue to proclaim one's ability to write a novel in Gikuyu, Tamil, or Xhosa? Or write in English and show the colonizers one can do it better than them? (Only think of the lexical and stylistic brilliance of the South Asian novel.) Besides language choice, other key features that lend themselves to be "turned against" the colonizer are the following:

- genre (adopting and transforming the novel as a European format; using native genres to infiltrate the novel model thematically, formally, and intertextually);
- narratorial ductus (using colloquial and creolized forms of English as narrator's language; assuming narrative authority for the colonial subject);

---

4. Williams ("Post-Colonialism" 453) cites the rewriting of London history from the eighteenth century to the present from a "black" perspective in Sukhdev Sandhu's *London Calling* (2003).

- plot (maneuvering native protagonists from marginal to central position; defeating Western power or presenting a hope for liberation at the end of the text; revising Western (hi)stories of the indigenous nation);
- time management (manipulating "Western" abstract time to include mythic and fantastic temporal frameworks; combining and condensing several time levels[5]);
- person (experiments with *we*-narrative and collective agency—see Ahmad 199–200; using a colonized subject as narrator);
- focalization (narrating from the perspective of the native subject; experimenting with juxtaposition and supernatural "voices");
- generic revision and rewriting of classic Western texts (reinterpretation of Western genres and subversively reshaping key works such as *The Tempest* or *Jane Eyre*—see Gymnich, "Writing Back");
- language, voice (standardizing, say, Indian English in contrast to the colonial ridiculing of natives who cannot speak "properly"; creolizing English as in Rushdie's work); and
- use of satire, irony, parody to upstage critique and resistance humorously.

As Williams ("Post-Colonialism" 454) notes, much postcolonial literature is actively experimental, as if to signal that breaking out of the colonial straitjacket is possible only by bending and transforming the models of Western writing. (Yet, it has to be noted that this trend is a recent one since the bulk of early texts, including immigration novels, were resolutely realist and low modernist in tone.) The analysis of postcolonial literature in itself is of course an ideological minefield, as Williams's references to Arif Dirlik's controversial work indicates; nor will everybody agree that postcolonial authors should be separated into "good" refuseniks writing against colonialism and "bad" novelists who are "complicit" with the West, like Naipaul (implying they have been brainwashed by colonial ideology), as Mishra and Hodge seem to imply, and Williams apparently seconds ("Post-Colonialism" 455).

What postcolonial critics and narratologists have so far failed to look at is to what extent *native* narrative traditions differ from European patterns of narration and whether this difference would in fact require a modification of narratology in the same way in which the study of oral narrative or medieval narrative or second-person fiction may have necessitated a revision of the

---

5. Williams ("Post-Colonialism" 454) mentions time slips in Caryl Phillips's *Crossing the River* (1993) and *The Nature of Blood* (1997); note also Ayi Kwei Armah's *Two Thousand Seasons* (1973)—a contraction of African history into one story.

standard typologies and an extension of concepts and categories.[6] However, since our topic in this volume is ideology, this question need not be followed up at this point.

More important to our present purposes is the question of how the noted features of narrative relate to their ideological content. I have myself argued elsewhere (Fludernik, "Narrative Forms") that in most cases the various aspects of narrative that lend themselves to a critical or subversive interpretation in postcolonial texts are not *inherently* critical techniques but can be found in equal measure in colonial and conservative narratives. Their subversive quality, that is, accrues to them from their specific context and their semantic and thematic quality in individual texts. Just as free indirect discourse can be encountered as a narrative strategy both in a modernist novel with a strong anticolonial slant *and* in literature from the American South that blindly echoes "racist" attitudes (I am here thinking of a whole swath of short stories and novels written between the 1830s and 1960s), most of the techniques listed above allow themselves to be used for almost any conceivable ideological purpose. It is only when, for instance, the free indirect discourse gives us a sympathetic portrayal of the plight of the colonial subject, as in Mulk Raj Anand's *Untouchable* (1935), and there is no comparable insight into the mind of the colonizers, that the critical nature of the technique may emerge. Statistics seem to provide some promise of pointing up which techniques are most often employed in a postcolonial context. As both Margolin and Richardson ("U.S. Ethnic and Postcolonial Fiction") have been able to demonstrate, among *we*-narratives postcolonial texts are particularly foregrounded; almost half of the currently known *we*-narratives concern themselves with postcolonial settings and protagonists. However, the subversive thrust of such texts is, in my view, rather limited, consisting in the emphasis on community as against an implied contrast with a "Western" preference for individuality. Moreover, many non-postcolonial *we*-texts are focused on rural communities, conveying a conservative ideology. Political statements in *we*-texts are rare: Raja Rao's *Kanthapura* (1938), the epic of a village's fight for independence, is a famous exception.

Having provided a summary of existing approaches to ideology in narrative/narratology, with special emphasis on postcolonial literature, I would now like to turn to two example texts and to the methodological question of how exactly ideology emerges in them.

---

6. For oral narratives, see Lucius-Hoene and Deppermann. For medieval texts, see Fludernik, "Through a Glass Darkly" or von Contzen. For second-person narratives, see Fludernik, "Introduction: Second-Person Narrative," "Second-Person Narrative as a Test Case"; or Richardson, *Concepts of Narrative*.

IDEOLOGIES IN THE SOUTH ASIAN NOVEL: THE IRONIES AND INDIRECTIONS OF POSTCOLONIALISM

In its formalist inclinations, narratology has—as we have seen—been concentrating on an application of narratological parameters and concepts to postcolonial texts. The emphasis has above all been on determining whether postcolonial fiction utilizes specific techniques exclusively (answer: none) or predominantly (more likely) in order to enact its politics of subversion and resistance. This way of putting the question incorrectly aligns the ideological content with the strategies employed in the texts, whereas—as I just argued—the narrative features themselves are easily found in texts with entirely opposite political persuasions. Moreover, it is important to remember Meir Sternberg's "Proteus Principle" with its observation that a particular technique or formal element does not link to one and only one function, but that most formally distinguishable features tend to have a variety of functions, just as any function can be served by a whole number of different devices. Likewise, in the realm of ideology there are, I would contend, no package deals that will ensure the delivery of a particular outlook or worldview. As Bakhtin has already demonstrated, a writer's radical political persuasions are no guarantee that his narrative technique will be innovative (his example is Tolstoy). Similarly, narrative experimentalism does not guarantee an anticolonial stance. In fact, many political activists have been keenly aware of the fact that in order to get a radical message across, one needs to package it in harmless and inoffensive sops that betray their bitter pill only on consumption. The other conundrum, particularly for postcolonial texts, is the question of what would be the norm against which contemporary writers from Africa and Asia are positioning themselves. Given that the old colonial novel is dead and gone and that Western fiction has been adopting postmodernist and postcolonial models, a distinction between "Western" and "non-Western" literature is turning into an increasingly spurious enterprise.

The major question as I see it is therefore not to find a list of parameters that will "signal" ideological positions, but to try to understand how textual ideologies arise in the process of reading. I would like to illustrate this on the basis of two very different novels, a 1957 classic of Indian literature about Independence, Nayantara Sahgal's *A Time to Be Happy*, and a recent much-noted novel decrying the effects of globalization, Mohsin Hamid's *How to Get Filthy Rich in Rising Asia* (2013).

How does Nayantara Sahgal's *A Time to Be Happy* convey ideologies? The main technique consists in ironizing the colonial mind and those imitating it. Most of this irony is thematic and contextualist: Sir Mathur acquiring white girlfriends in London while being considered too dark for social intercourse in India; Indian politeness versus Mr. Weatherby's blustering and curses. The narrator, in many ways a mouthpiece for the author, moreover comments on these contradictions. Much of the irony is, however, muted by the sympathetic focus on Sanad, the unnamed first-person narrator's friend and son of his patron Govind Narayan, and on his suffering and disorientation. While the narrator has found a home in India, Sanad—an exemplar of hybridity—feels culturally homeless, and this state of unrootedness, described in a series of metaphors, serves as another strategy of critique, this time a critique of the British tradition of education in India (see Viswanathan) in the wake of Macaulay and the Anglicists. The most important strategy endorsing an Indian point of view comes from the plot level—the narrator and major protagonists are all Indians, the British characters merely marginal figures. The problems caused by British rule and their institutions are underlined by the extensive use of dialogue in the novel, which produces an almost philosophical debate between opposing points of view. Finally, authorial pronouncements and purple passages of praise for India round off the list of ideologically inflected devices in the text. One could moreover argue that the very masked time structure of the novel is perhaps meant to emphasize the disappearance of Western temporalities, replacing supposedly "Western" activity and efficiency with the near-stasis or *longue durée* of Indian impassivity and sempiternity.

Born during the heyday of the Independence movement and written in the aftermath of its achievement, *A Time to Be Happy*—composed, after all, by a member of the Indian English-educated elite—registers the ideological rifts that have opened up to expose a faultline of cultural contradictions that Independence is utopically meant to heal. On the one hand, the narrator nostalgically dwells on traditionally Indian artistic sophistication and manners, which are contrasted lexically and in the juxtapositions of plot and dialogue with the formerly victorious British colonizers and the postindependence nouveaux-riches who lack culture and ape colonial mores rather than helping Indian traditions to be resuscitated. These ironic reversals manifest themselves in stylistic clashes. On the other hand, the first-person narrator also shows some sympathy for those he is implicitly ridiculing and demonstrates his own hybrid inconclusiveness by veering between his admiration for the *zamindar* past and a half-hearted adoption of Gandhian village utopianism. The text thus ironizes or at least questions all ideologies represented in the text and itself betrays an ideological stance, which is one of noncommitment and the refusal to decide for any of the options. Like Sanad, the narrator practices an ideology of sitting on the fence, feeling unhappy and torn between various interpellations and leaning toward each of them in turn. Yet this is indeed the situation of the class to which Sahgal herself belonged. The careful balancing of pro- and anticolonial viewpoints, of utopian and dystopian evaluations of Indian independence represents a canny analysis of the state of India's intelligentsia in the 1950s.

Let me now turn to Mohsin Hamid's second-person novel *How to Get Filthy Rich in Rising Asia* (2013). Here formal matters are foregrounded, since this is a text written in the style of a self-help book, though it ironically undermines the ostensible usefulness of the model. The novel goes beyond the frames of other second-person texts such as Lorrie Moore's *Self-Help* (1985) or Pam Houston's "How to Talk to a Hunter" (1990) with a prominent addressee function and a guidebook format. Whereas in these stories the emphasis is on the consciousness of the (female) protagonist referred to by the pronoun "you," eliciting the (female) reader's near-identification, here the (male) *you*-protagonist is also addressed by the narratorial voice. In fact—as in the opening of Italo Calvino's *If on a Winter's Night a Traveller* (originally 1979)—the *you*-protagonist competes with the text-external reader at whom the "you" initially seems to be directed via the model of the self-help manual for the position of addressee. From the beginning, the narratorial voice engages in meta-narrative reflections: "Look, unless you're writing one, a self-help book is an oxymoron. You read a self-help book so someone who isn't yourself can help you, that someone being the author" (Hamid 3). This is the opening of the novel. Much later in the novel, we get the following chapter opening:

> Distasteful though it may be, it was inevitable, in a self-help book such as this, that we would eventually find ourselves broaching the topic of violence. Becoming filthy rich requires a degree of unsqueamishness, whether in rising Asia or anywhere else. For wealth comes from capital, and capital comes from labor, and labor comes from equilibrium, from calories in chasing calories out, an inherent, in-built leanness, the leanness of biological machines that must be bent to your will with some force if you are to loosen your own financial belt and, sighingly, expand. (119)

In both passages the narratee at first appears to be the actual reader; it only emerges later that the narratee is actually (also?) the protagonist (who will remain nameless):

> This book is a self-help book. Its objective, as it says on the cover, is to show you how to get filthy rich in rising Asia. And to do that it has to *find you, huddled, shivering,* on the packed earth under your mother's cot *one cold, dewy morning.* Your anguish is the anguish of *a boy* whose chocolate has

> been thrown away, whose remote controls are out of batteries, whose scooter is busted, whose new sneakers have been stolen. This is all the more remarkable since *you've never in your life seen any of these things.*
>
> . . .
>
> *Your mother* has encountered this condition many times, or conditions like it anyway. . . . [W]hen a mother like yours sees in *a third-born child like you* the pain that makes you whimper under her cot the way you do, maybe she feels your death push forward a few decades . . . into this, *the single mud-walled room* she shares with all of her surviving offspring. (4–5; my emphasis)

Note how the narratee in this passage gets transformed into "a boy" and acquires a mother and siblings as well as a father and a specific location of residence. The child's universal anguish, exemplified by the loss of toys, is immediately undermined by the note that this specific "you" lacks any such objects. Later the narrator intervenes to predict the narratee-protagonist's eventual success:

> As you lie motionless afterwards, a young jaundiced village boy, radish juice dripping from the corner of your lips and forming a small patch of mud on the ground, it must seem that getting filthy rich is beyond your reach. But have faith. You are not as powerless as you appear. Your moment is about to come. Yes, this book is going to offer you a choice. (10–11)

The irony of the book lies not only in the plot but in the stylistic clash between the narrator's economese of globalization and the language of needs and emotions associated with a child trying to survive in unfavorable circumstances. There is, hence, in the manner of using the address function in this novel an ideological clash between the "Western" capitalist regime and a discourse of humanism and sympathy, which has a history of Western patronizing of the native working-class poor.

The format of the *Bildungsroman*—a common template for postcolonial literature (adopting a Western genre for the achievement of cultural identity)—is being subversively undermined by the details of the lessons the protagonist imbibes. The boy—who remains nameless throughout—is shown to struggle to the top by dint of hard work, but more importantly by ruthless enterprise and corrupt practices, building an empire of water bottling. He falls in love with the "pretty girl" (who likewise remains nameless). Both give up love for wealth, becoming very rich and then losing it all. In old age they finally meet again, move in together, and have a very harmonious and fulfilled life until first she and then he dies. The message of this plot is, clearly, that neither of the two need have struggled to become filthy rich or glamorous in order to have found contentment in their lives. They lost the best part of their existence to ambition.

The incongruity between the capitalist message articulated by the narrator and the implied meaning of the stories of the two protagonists is underlined by the recurrent stylistic clash between the language of economics and the language of human concerns. It serves not merely the ends of irony but helps to avoid too much identification or empathy between the reader and the *you*-protagonist. Normally, second-person fiction is quite strongly empathy-inducing—especially in a *Bildungsroman* format. Here, however, the many comments of the unreliable narrator figure tend to serve as a wedge inserted between the text and the fictional world:

> You have done so [cutting costs] admirably well. At the two-star hotel that is your residence, you have negotiated a long-term, month-by-month room rental for less than half the standard rate, taking full advantage of both your willingness to pay cash and the fact that you once gave a job to the hotel manager's late father, who described you with undying, referring of course to the sentiment, not the man, veneration. You also eat sparingly, your metabolism having slowed enough for you to make do with a single meal a day. (201–2)

In passages such as these, the protagonist becomes a doll manipulated by the narratorial discourse, illustrating the theses that he wants to convey, although as soon as the narrative concentrates on the protagonist from his own perspective, a more sympathetic ductus emerges. In chapter 9, the narrator conveys the most empathy-enhancing episode from the protagonist's life, the funeral of his father, in the *third* person, claiming ignorance of whose funeral it is. There is a "luxury automobile" (174) near the graveyard, and "a pair of male figures in suit" (174–75) are in mourning and "must be closely related to the fellow who has died" (175). The "elder," that is, the "man in his sixties," sobs convulsively; since we know that the man is the former *you*-protagonist, the teenage boy must be his grandson (we assume the son has decided to stay abroad). The scene is told from a "drone" perspective, surveying the town from above.

As a novel debunking the new economy, this text conveys a clear ideology, but, textually speaking, it performs this critique by means of indirection, by a pretense of endorsement and its invidious undermining. From a postcolonial perspective, the novel is also interesting since it demonstrates that South Asia's economic plight may lead disadvantaged individuals to an overenthusiastic adoption of behavioral patterns that reiterate those of colonial venture and early capitalist unconcern for the masses. In addition to this, the protagonist's acquisition of filthy riches turns out to be a disappointment not only because of his renunciation of true love while he is in the grip of ambition; his craving for economic power *à l'occidental* and his very success result in his son's adoption of the West as his real home. Thus, he loses his son, who, thanks to the father's money, can afford to start a life abroad, escaping the father's heritage of exploitation and corruption, but at the same time severing all links to his native identity. In terms of the postcolonial framework, therefore, the father is punished for adopting precisely those Western modes of enterprise recommended by the guidebook narrator, as a result failing in the one aim that had motivated his struggles to get filthy rich—to hand on his patrimony to his next of kin.

CONCLUSION

The two novels illustrate two entirely different ways of handling ideology, even though they both utilize irony as their basic strategy. The difference can be seen especially if one looks at the process of reading and how ideology is conveyed processually in time.

Whereas Sahgal's novel weaves a fine tissue of very sympathetic figures who each serve as counterfoils to the others, Hamid's text lives from the confrontation of the intrusive narrator figure with the unnamed *you*-protagonist and has a much more linear plotline. Sahgal's novel presents to the reader many different viewpoints. Like the character Sanad, who is traumatized by his hybridity, the reader traces the pros and cons of India's relationship to British colonialism and—with the narrator persona—comes to a final optimistic though perhaps rather illusory conclusion. That seeming resolution of conflicts and contradictions emerges in connection with a reassertion of Indian national identity (implied through the vicarious figure of a Gandhian hero), but it is muted by an acknowledgment of continued British influence and a concession of Indian folly in over-imitating the British model. The whole text therefore takes the reader through a series of views that are partially endorsed and partially ironized and deposits him or her in a final neutralization of opposites, though also underlining the fraught condition of inevitable hybridity to which the protagonists of all types are subjected.

By contrast, Hamid's text—like Sahgal's a novel written for both a South Asian and a Western audience—adopts a very decided ideology and, in the figure of the narrator, takes this viewpoint to its absurd self-destructive end. It achieves the narrator's debunking by means of the story of the *you*-protagonist, which demonstrates the failure of new economic tenets on a practical human level. The novel therefore performs a clear deconstruction of a theoretical position, inflecting the message satirically. As a consequence, the processuality of our reception is dominated by linearity, with the ostensible new economy message undermined first by the unlikely candidate (a poor slum child), then by the corrupt practices of the *you*-protagonist—in contradistinction to the business ethos usually adopted by the new economy and in self-help texts—and finally by the failures of narratorial discourse and the protagonist's business ventures. Despite this practical debunking, the metafictional reflections of the narratorial voice indicate that the publication of the book is an economically relevant enterprise; they explicitly articulate the profit motive for the writer of self-help literature (and authors in general) and predict the possible uselessness of this literature for the reader. The narrator's self-help advice mirrors the ruthless business practices he is advocating—like the protagonist, who is supplying tainted water to make a profit, he is selling bad advice in attractively packaged prose. Ultimately, the text cannot be utilized by the reader to acquire riches, whether filthy or not, but—thanks to its blatant ideological contradictions—it might serve the ethically benign function of alerting him or her to the pitfalls of globalized capitalism. What it certainly demonstrates is a playful and subversive use of second-person narrative that is here utilized quite like new economic business practices to achieve effects not originally intended by their inventors. Rather than empathetically drawing the reader into the life of a second-person protagonist, the *you*-narrative of Hamid's novel produces disaffection and resistance in the reader, achieving ethical and affective dissonance. The protagonist's business tactics also slyly mimic Western rapacity during the colonial period, which now reemerges as a neocolonial imitation of Western exploitative economic ideology and practice. Unlike Sahgal's portraits of Indians that help the Western reader to understand and sympathize, Hamid's text makes one feel excluded, keeps one at arm's length, and thus interpellates us to acknowledge our difference, a difference born from economic status as much as cultural alterity.

WORKS CITED

Ahmad, Aijaz. *In Theory: Nations, Classes, Literatures*. 1992. London: Verso, 1994.

Alber, Jan, and Monika Fludernik, eds. *Postclassical Narratology: Approaches and Analyses*. Columbus: Ohio State University Press, 2010.

Amuta, Chidi. *The Theory of African Literature: Implications for Practical Criticism*. London: Zed Books, 1989.

Anand, Mulk Raj. *Untouchable*. 1935. London: Penguin Books, 1986.

Armah, Ayi Kwei. *Two Thousand Seasons*. 1973. London: Heinemann, 1979.

Bakhtin, Mikhail M. "Discourse in the Novel." 1975. *The Dialogic Imagination: Four Essays by M. M. Bakhtin*. Ed. Michael Holquist. Trans. Caryl Emerson and Michael Holquist. Austin: University of Texas Press, 1990. 257–422.

———. *Problems of Dostoevsky's Poetics*. 1929, 1963. Ed. and trans. Caryl Emerson. Minneapolis: University of Minnesota Press, 1984.

———. *Rabelais and His World*. 1965. Trans. Hélène Iswolsky. Bloomington: Indiana University Press, 1984.

Cornwell, Neil. "Skaz Narrative." *The Literary Encyclopedia*. 2005. <http://www.litencyc.com/php/stopics.php?rec=true&UID=1561>.

Dirlik, Arif. "The Post-Colonial Aura: Third World Criticism in the Age of Global Capitalism." *Critical Inquiry* 20 (1994): 328–56.

Fludernik, Monika. "1050–1500: Through a Glass Darkly; or, The Emergence of Mind in Medieval Narrative." *The Emergence of Mind: Representations of Consciousness in Narrative Discourse in English*. Ed. David Herman. Lincoln: University of Nebraska Press, 2011. 69–100.

———. "The Hybridity of Discourses about Hybridity: Kipling's 'Naboth' as an Allegory of Postcolonial Discourse." *Crossover: Cultural Hybridity in Ethnicity, Gender, Ethics*. Ed. Therese Steffen. Tübingen: Stauffenburg, 2000. 151–68.

———. "Introduction: Second-Person Narrative and Related Issues." *Style* 28.3 (1994): 281–311.

———. "The Narrative Forms of Postcolonial Fiction." *The Cambridge History of Postcolonial Literature*. Ed. Ato Quayson. Cambridge: Cambridge University Press, 2012. 903–37.

———. "Second-Person Narrative as a Test Case for Narratology: The Limits of Realism." *Style* 28.3 (1994): 445–79.

———. "When the Self Is an Other: Vergleichende erzähltheoretische und postkoloniale Überlegungen zur Identitäts(de)konstruktion in der (exil)indischen Gegenwartsliteratur." *Anglia* 117.1 (1999): 71–96.

Gymnich, Marion. "Linguistics and Narratology: The Relevance of Linguistic Criteria to Postcolonial Narratology." *Literature and Linguistics: Approaches, Models, and Applications. Studies in Honour of Jon Erickson*. Ed. Marion Gymnich, Ansgar Nünning, and Vera Nünning. Trier: WVT, 2002. 61–76.

———. "'Writing Back' als Paradigma der postkolonialen Literatur." In *Kulturelles Wissen und Intertextualität: Theoriekonzeptionen und Fallstudien zur Kontextualisierung von Literatur*. Ed. Marion Gymnich, Birgit Neumann, and Ansgar Nünning. Trier: WVT, 2006. 71–86.

Hamid, Mohsin. *How to Get Filthy Rich in Rising Asia*. London: Hamish Hamilton, 2013.

Herman, David, ed. *Narratologies: New Perspectives on Narrative Analysis*. Columbus: Ohio State University Press, 1999.

Houston, Pam. "How to Talk to a Hunter." 1990. *Cowboys Are My Weakness*. New York: Washington Square Press, 1992. 13–20.

Jameson, Fredric. "Third World Literature in the Era of Multinational Capitalism." *Social Text* 15 (1982): 65–88.

Lederer, Thomas. *Sacred Demonization: Saints' Legends in the English Renaissance*. Vienna: Braumüller, 2007.

Lotman, Yuri. "O probleme znachenii vo vtorichnykh modeliruiushchikh sistemakh" ["Concerning the problem of meaning in the secondary modeling systems"]. *Trudy po znakovym sistemam*, II (Uch. Zap. TGU, vyp. 181). Tartu: Tartu University Press, 1965. 31–32.

―――. *The Structure of the Artistic Text.* Trans. Gail Lenhoff and Ronald Vroon. Michigan Slavic Contributions 7. Ann Arbor: University of Michigan, 1977.

Lucius-Hoene, Gabriele, and Arnulf Deppermann. *Rekonstruktion narrativer Identität: Ein Arbeitsbuch zur Analyse narrativer Interviews.* 2nd ed. Wiesbaden: Verlag für Sozialwissenschaften, 2004.

Macherey, Pierre. *A Theory of Literary Production.* Trans. Geoffrey Wall. London: Routledge & Kegan Paul, 1978.

Margolin, Uri. "Telling Our Story: On 'We' Literary Narratives." *Language and Literature* 5 (1996): 115–33.

Mishra, Vijay, and Bob Hodge. "What is Post(-)colonialism?" *Colonial Discourse and Postcolonial Theory.* Ed. Patrick Williams and Laura Chrisman. Hemel Hempstead: Harvester Wheatsheaf, 1993. 276–90.

Moore, Lorrie. *Self-Help: Stories.* New York: Alfred A. Knopf, 1985.

Nünning, Vera, and Ansgar Nünning, eds. *Multiperspektivisches Erzählen: Zur Theorie und Geschichte der Perspektiven-Struktur im englischen Roman des 18. bis 20. Jahrhunderts.* Trier: Wissenschaftlicher Verlag Trier, 2000.

Pfister, Manfred. *Das Drama: Theorie und Analyse.* Munich: Fink, 1977.

―――. *The Theory and Analysis of Drama.* Trans. John Halliday. Cambridge: Cambridge University Press, 1991.

Prince, Gerald. "On a Postcolonial Narratology." *A Companion to Narrative Theory.* Ed. James Phelan and Peter J. Rabinowitz. Malden: Blackwell, 2005. 372–81.

Rao, Raja. *Kanthapura.* 1938. Oxford: Oxford University Press, 1994.

Richardson, Brian, ed. *Style.* Special issue of *Concepts of Narrative* 34.2 (2000).

―――. *Unnatural Voices: Extreme Narration in Contemporary and Modern Fiction.* Columbus: Ohio State University Press, 2006.

―――. "U.S. Ethnic and Postcolonial Fiction: Toward a Poetics of Collective Narratives." *Analyzing World Fiction. New Horizons in Narrative Theory.* Ed. Frederick Luis Aldama. Austin: University of Texas Press, 2011. 3–16.

Sahgal, Nayantara. *A Time to Be Happy.* 1957. New York: Alfred A. Knopf, 1958.

Said, Edward. *Culture and Imperialism.* London: Chatto, 1993.

―――. *The Politics of Dispossession.* London: Vintage, 1994.

Sandhu, Sukhdev. *London Calling: How Black and Asian Writers Imagined a City.* London: HarperCollins, 2003.

Schmid, Wolf. "Skaz." *The Living Handbook of Narratology.* <http://wikis.sub.uni-hamburg.de/lhn/index.php/Skaz, 2013>.

Sinfield, Alan. *Faultlines: Cultural Materialism and the Politics of Dissident Reading.* Los Angeles: University of California Press, 1992.

The South English Legendary: Corpus Christi College Cambridge MS 145 and British Museum MS Harley 2277, etc. Ed. Charlotte d'Evelyn and Anna J. Mill. Volume I. EEETS OS 235. Oxford: Oxford University Press, 1967.

Sternberg, Meir. "Proteus in Quotation-Land: Mimesis and the Forms of Reported Discourse." *Poetics Today* 3.2 (1982): 107–56.

Tomkins, Jane. *Sensational Designs: The Cultural Work of American Fiction, 1790–1860*. New York: Oxford University Press, 1985.

Uspensky, Boris. *A Poetics of Composition*. Trans. Valentina Zavarin and Susan Wittig. Berkeley: University of California Press, 1983.

Viswanathan, Gauri. *Masks of Conquest: Literary Studies and British Rule in India*. London: Faber & Faber, 1990.

von Contzen, Eva. *Reading for the Discourse: Hagiographic Narration in the Scottish Legendary*. Manchester University Press, 2016.

Williams, Patrick. "Marxist Approaches to Narrative." *Routledge Encyclopedia of Narrative Theory*. Ed. David Herman, Manfred Jahn, and Marie-Laure Ryan. London: Routledge, 2005. 282–87.

———. "Post-Colonialism and Narrative." *Routledge Encyclopedia of Narrative Theory*. Ed. David Herman, Manfred Jahn, and Marie-Laure Ryan. London: Routledge, 2005. 451–56.

CHAPTER 11

The Apocalypse That Will Never Be

Decolonization, Proleptic History, and Satire in India, c. 1946–51

BAIDIK BHATTACHARYA

AWAY FROM both the apologists and the detractors of globalization, and also from contentious debates on the "death" of the postcolony in globalization, this essay uses the rhetoric of death as a point of departure to interrogate the naturalized relationship between the postcolony and its nationalist appropriation, and to rethink the implications of decolonization within postcolonial history.[1] Is it possible to conceptualize the postcolony away from the political moorings of the nation-state? What are the resources to imagine the postcolony when it is delinked from the national narratives? In the following pages I engage with these questions as I read a set of satires written around the time of the decolonization of India in 1947 by the noted Bengali satirist Paraśurām (Rajshekhar Basu, 1880–1960). These satires reformulate decolonization as a projected apocalyptic event,[2] and locate an ambiguity at the heart of the postcolony as a social territory that is *not* always-already claimed by nationalist politics. The disjuncture between two territorial

---

 1. An earlier version of this essay was presented at the Centre for Studies in Social Sciences, Calcutta. I would like to thank Sibaji Bandyopadhyay, Gautam Bhadra, Partha Chatterjee, Rajarshi Dasgupta, and Bodhisattva Kar for their generous comments. I would also like to thank Divya Dwivedi, Rajeswari Sunder Rajan, and Mallarika Sinha Roy for their comments. All translations from Bengali are mine.
 2. Apocalypse, in the secular idiom, suggests revealing or unveiling; even the etymology (derived from Greek *apokaluptein*) suggests uncovering. Apocalypse in these satires primarily suggests this sense of enabling gaze.

principles (the postcolony and the nation, which are not interchangeable) and the discontinuity between two temporalities (postcolonial and national times, which are, again, not identical) are occasioned in these texts by the violence of apocalyptic events, and they are available in the moment of laughter that is designed through the satirical structure of these texts. I have argued elsewhere that the satires of Paraśurām mark a distinct phase in the literary modernity of India (Bhattacharya), and here extend that frame of modernity to envelop postcolonial history.

STORIES OR ALMOST STORIES

This essay, then, is about the incredible and unrealized apocalypses in Paraśurām's satires published in the collection *Galpakalpa* (1952)[3] and the way they enable a different account of decolonization and an alternative vision of postcolonial history. These stories, written between 1946 and 1951, evidently rely on a plurality of genres; the ambiguity of *kalpa* seems deliberate. Taken as a derivational suffix, *kalpa* means "resembling," and the collection thus becomes not exactly of stories (*galpa*), but of narratives resembling stories. The point becomes persuasive as we realize how Paraśurām emphasizes the storyness of his other stories collected in similar volumes around the same time.[4] My suggestion here is to think of these stories as exceeding conventional protocols of storytelling or even to cross expected structures of such narrative practices to enter into an unspecified zone of generic anonymity—where they may resemble recognizable literary conventions but may not be defined as such. It is the twilight zone where the edges of a given literary form blur and break down, and through the broken remnants one catches the glimpses of other, dissimilar narrative *dispositifs*; it is the zone of plurality where different genres coalesce in mutual empowerment and tension but collectively refuse a governing proper name. These "stories" embody and employ such textual ambiguity.

However, the second meaning of *kalpa* is radically different in nature. When taken as a noun—and this turns *galpakalpa* into a compound word—it may refer to Hindu scriptures (*Kalpasūtra*), a ritual rule or holy time (*kalpārambha*), or the mythical day of the Hindu god Brahmā (*kalpa*) after

---

3. All the stories discussed in this essay are from this collection, with the only exception of "Gagan Chaṭi" ["The Heavenly Slipper"]; it is included here because of its thematic similarity. References to stories from *Galpakalpa* are abbreviated in the text as Paraśurām followed by page number, and references to "The Heavenly Slipper" are noted separately.

4. For example, *Krishakali ityādi galpa* [*Krishnakali and Other Stories*] (1953), *Ānandībaī ityādi galpa* [*Anandibai and Other Stories*] (1957).

which universal annihilation or apocalypse ensues. In this new sense, the title does not indicate formal ambiguity, but rather describes the concern of the collection that finds its representation in apocalyptic events. In either case, the collection marks a distinct phase in Paraśurām's oeuvre in terms of both its formal innovation and overtly political concern. Indeed, the turbulent world one encounters in *Galpakalpa* is a far cry from the delightful and languid *āddā*s of his early stories,[5] or even from the urbane everyday life one encounters in his oeuvre more generally. And as such, I suggest, the stories (or almost stories) in the collection need to be read as condensed political history contained in ingenuous rhetorical devices. Through a series of projected—and as we will see shortly, deferred—apocalypses, these stories figuratively represent the birth of the postcolony as *kalpārambha,* or as an epochal break in sequential history. They thematize the postcolony in two distinct ways: First, they relate the territorial imagination to contemporary history of volatile and violent experiences like world wars, partition, religious riots, and famine to structurally situate the postcolony within a larger web of catastrophic events. The postcolony is related to these events and is indeed a further stage for the unfolding of their aftermath. Even when related to contemporary history, however, the postcolony remains "untimely" in these stories[6]—there is a repeated suggestion running through these texts that it embodies and extends the legacies of preceding events, but its own existence is not reducible to them. The territorial imagination of the postcolony, while asserting difference from earlier spatial ensembles, establishes the territory as a proleptic one because there is no fit and competent community to inhabit the land, and the land thus remains open to a coming community.[7] This is partly why these texts invoke catastrophic events, but subsequently postpone them indefinitely to allow the postcolony to consolidate in the interim.

The other thematization begins with the same series of apocalypses that define a mode of belonging to the postcolony. Here we must distinguish

---

5. For a social account of *āddā* and its representation in Paraśurām's stories, see Chakrabarty.

6. The notion of "untimely" is borrowed from Nietzsche's *Ecce Homo*, where he discusses the "untimely" nature of his own writing for which there is no competent audience yet, and as a result, the writing must await an uncertain future readership. The suggestion of being "untimely" is of course of being ahead of time, but as such also of being an excess or even counterpoint to the contemporary frame of history.

7. Gérard Genette defines narratological prolepsis as "any narrative maneuver that consists of narrating or evoking in advance an event that will take place later." He further distinguishes between "external" and "internal" prolepsis and between "completing" and "repeating" prolepsis, depending on how a narrated event affects the "first narrative" (40, 71). The texts I discuss in this essay, however, use prolepsis not simply as a narrative strategy, or not as one strategic choice out of many others, but posit prolepsis as the very condition of being.

between the theological sense of apocalypse available in Judeo-Christian traditions and the secularized version of it that has been an integral part of modernist or even postmodernist aesthetics and imagination.[8] Though in both cases, the apocalyptic event occasions a temporal and spatial rupture, in the previous instance it performs a preordained role and in the latter case opens up the prospect of continued and repeatable critique. The apocalypses, or rather their promise, which one confronts in Paraśurām's text, certainly belong to the second order as they open the postcolony for critical exploration. The series begins with the first story in the collection—"Gāmānuṣ Jātir Kathā" or "The Tale of the Gamman Tribe"—that is built around projected nuclear holocausts and was written a few months after the catastrophic events of Hiroshima and Nagasaki. This central template is extended creatively to think about other apocalyptic events that shape the membership to the postcolony within a distinctly ethical environment. These texts invoke and negate apocalyptic events or use the violence of such events to suggest a caesura between the postcolony as a territory and its political qualification that is not necessarily national. I argue below that the ethics of belonging is the mediator between the two orders of territorial participation, but such an ethical project is completed within the deframed futurity that the postcolony as a proleptic territory promises. Indeed, the codes of belonging, or the contours of citizenship, to this futurity suggest an immanent ethical project that allows us to chart a different postcolonial history.

It is important to note at this stage that apocalypses, as Jacques Derrida argues, have a markedly textual mode of existence because until they happen one can only write or talk about them.[9] This is more so with deferred apocalypses since they do not share one's frame of history or existence, and are always part of a captivating order of futurity that occupies some distant location and time. Yet they are available before themselves, before their *proper* occurrences, through texts—within textual traditions and references—and as a textual/political horizon for one's present practices. Apocalyptic literature is interesting specifically for this reason—it names and describes a possibility that cannot be named and described, and that must remain beyond the purview of representation or indeed must mark the end of, among other things, representation itself. The texts I will discuss below struggle against similar representational crises, but negotiate them through a common pattern; they develop in three stages—projected apocalyptic crisis, unusual resolution

---

8. For a recent survey of both traditions, see Fiddes.

9. In "No Apocalypse, Not Now (full speed ahead, seven missiles, seven missives)." This is aptly illustrated by Derrida's example—nuclear war—that has given birth to innumerable textual accounts without ever occurring so far.

of that crisis, and the emergence of a different order of things as an aftermath of the crisis. It is through this pattern, and by critically investigating apocalypses as (post)colonial events, that they secure their representational certainty.

APOCALYPSES AND "UNTIMELY" HISTORY

Satire as a genre—and Paraśurām's texts are no exceptions—is structurally ahistorical. Narrative emplotment of satire represents history in displacement—it is never an exercise in historical realism or in history "as it really was," if we remember Ranke's famous dictum, but is a representation of history as it never was or, conversely, as it would never be. Satire even represents historical events as they *could have been*, by exploring their surrogate sequencing, and suggests a speculative mode of existence for such events that is routinely denied in official history. This structural displacement, however, must not be taken as creating a blank space from which satire operates or from which its narrative commences. Rather, this displaced narrative is an attempt to avoid the authority of history—its monopolized power over the "institution of the real" (de Certeau 186 and *passim*)—as a way to open historical events within the dominion of alterity. Decolonization and its aftermath, the central theme of Paraśurām's texts, for instance, is conceived within similar narrative protocols and historical possibilities. The account of decolonization one encounters in these stories is not simply the textbook version of "independence from foreign rulers" or its various nationalist adaptations. It is not even a pallid narrative of skepticism and negation, to retrieve the other major narrative strand surrounding decolonization, in its depiction of decolonized India. These stories open decolonization as an event the unfolding of which is still incomplete, implications obscure, and contours not yet fully recognized. Decolonization, in short, is a naked event in these stories and its meaning is the putative object of knowledge.

To put it differently, there is a distinct shift from usual historiographical practices to what I call *satirical practices* in these texts. The standard procedure of historiography establishes the authority of past events as/within a complex edifice of narratological relations, or consists of a passage from archives to narratives within a wider context of institutions, disciplines, and professional etiquettes. The authority of such historiographical procedures functions within the moment of narration, within its *here* and *now*, but the narrative thus created also responds to the event itself or its embeddedness in a lost historical time. This dual function of the narrative in history—its authority and genealogy, its authorization and authenticity—is structurally reversed in these satires. Paraśurām's stories represent decolonization not only as a historical event rooted in the past but as an event that inaugurates a discrete order of narrative futurity for the emergent nation. This narrative order does not refer back to any authority emerging from the past, does not claim a constitutional continuity between the event and its narration, and does not even construct its referent as a natural outcome of colonial history. It is, rather, a *history of the future*. Thus the account of apocalypse in Paraśurām's texts—whether in the form of a projected economic doom, an impending collision with an asteroid, or a nuclear holocaust—is conceived within an explicative narrative that constructs the future as an object of knowing. And by foregrounding the apocalyptic possibility, the narrative strives to be a means through which this history of the future becomes thinkable.

Such a history is not available outside the event and its representation, or outside the testimony of the text that authorizes displaced history beyond the "institution of the real." And this relationship uniquely constructs the temporal schema of these texts. Paraśurām's stories employ, I suggest, three different temporal frames to represent postcolonial history. The first temporal frame, which I call the *mundane order of history*, is the initial phase when the cultural space of the nation is rearranged as a precondition for the central event. This order of history in the text is often coterminous with that of its production. The second frame, the *incredible order of history*, encloses the central event the text communicates and as such is the primary reference through which the discourse of postcoloniality is to be constructed. It inaugurates the peculiar sense of futurity in these texts by separating the object of discourse from the regulatory order of discourse, by establishing a caesura between postcolonial history and the future of the postcolony accessible only in the fullness of a violent revelation. The text is designed to support this sudden and violent turn of history—or a certain deterritorialization of it (hence the reliance on satire/satirical practices)—beyond any historical precedence, seriality, and sequencing. The third and final frame, the *magical order of history*, is the most transient of the three as it repeatedly slips out of the space of narration. This final order of history is an immanent one, and these texts can only gesture toward this emerging form of history but cannot fully represent it within their linguistic domain.

In "Gagan Chaṭi" or "The Heavenly Slipper," for example, the projected collision with an asteroid provides the central event for the narrative. The possibility is a real one and it is represented in the text through diverse reactions to this impending catastrophe. The disgruntled head-pundit Kunjabihari Talapatra argues that it is a sign of the nineteenth-century educationist Vidyasagar's wrath over the evident mismanagement and vagary of the secondary school board; because of the distinct shape of the asteroid (like a slipper, and hence the name), he takes it to be the slipper of the eminent educationist who hurls it from the heaven as a desperate censure of the board. However, the opposition spokesman Birupaksha Mandal retains the slipper theory, but, on the evidence of a longer snout, proposes that in point of fact it comes from the well-known medical practitioner from the nineteenth century Mahendralal Sarkar as a condemnation of a range of scandals in different medical colleges and hospitals. Hemanta Chattaraj, a versifier with a devotional inclination, proclaims that this is an expression of divine anger against unprecedented "rise in various vices like theft, bribery, adultery, hypocrisy, transgression, dishonesty etc., [against] the incompetence of the state government, the squandering of the riches, [and] the cinema-craze of younger generations." The only recourse against such divine scourge, Chattaraj believes, is a return to the proper ways of *dharma* ("Gagan Chaṭi" 136–37).

It soon transpires, however, that this heavenly body is an asteroid that has deviated from its original path in the asteroid belt, between the orbits of Mars and Jupiter, and is now heading toward the earth because of the latter's gravitational pull. It is also possible, different reports suggest, that this huge asteroid is formed through a collision of smaller asteroids, and as a consequence it now emits heat and light, and follows this erratic path. With the dwindling distance between the two heavenly bodies and with the fear of mass extinction unfolds the *incredible order of history,* the second temporal frame of the text. The asteroid—an ahistorical body despite these scientific speculations—violently separates the second order from the first to release history into a terrain for which there is no narrative precedence and for which, perforce, the text has to invent its own narrative strategies. The occasion for this new narrative order is partly constructed within the text through deliberate citing of scientific jargons and discourses, as if to situate the unthinkable within the abstraction of theoretical astronomy, but the text also makes it clear that no amount of scientific speculation can prepare one for the terrible future. It is a different realm of events and hence must formulate its own representational protocols.

Initial responses to this impending disaster are distinctly religious. Leaders of various religious communities—Hindu, Christian, Jewish, Muslim, Buddhist—urge their devotees to prepare for the Armageddon by confessing their vices and sins and by praying for forgiveness. The 1008 Shree Byomshankar Maharaj, a descendant of the medieval Hindu monk Adi Shankaracharya's nephew, for example, publishes and distributes five million copies of a testimony in which he lists all his misdeeds and sins—acts like killing bugs, tasting forbidden meat, deliberate lying, and "casting evil eye" on female disciples.

He encourages fellow Hindus to follow his suit since, he argues, just like the body must be cleansed before a medical surgery, the individual soul must go through a spiritual catharsis before meeting its end. This sets the tone for further testimonies and confessions:

> Men and women gathered in front of the Monument [in Kolkata] and in all available parks of the city to confess their sins loudly. A procession with musical band started from Barrabazar and went round the city through Netaji Subhash Road. Many respectable and important citizens joined the procession, and beating their chests cried out their respective sins in piteous voice; because of the musical band, however, their words remained somewhat indistinct.
>
> British radio ceaselessly broadcast "Nearer my God to Thee." Delhi radio continuously blared "Raghupati Raghab" [a devotional chant] and Lucknow and Patna radios "Ramnam sach hai" [a devotional chant in Hindi]. "Samukhe santiparabar" [a devotional song composed by Rabindranath Tagore] was played in Kolkata. Only Moscow radio remained silent, because communists do not share an amicable relationship with god. ("Gagan Chaṭi" 139)

Soon the trend acquires a global dimension. The Oxford Group of Britain leads an initiative of mass confession and the practice soon spreads to other countries. The four most influential nations—the USA, the USSR, Britain, and France—jointly publish a "White Book" detailing their wrongdoings in the last fifty years and announce a principle of universal fraternity. Pakistan also joins this ethos of global camaraderie but concurrently reiterates its claim over Kashmir ("Gagan Chaṭi" 139).

Such satirical practices violently suppress within the text the signs of available history to release an order of narrative that constructs its own system of representation. The available signs are suppressed but not erased; they are transported to a new representational regime. This synchronized operation of denial and resurrection—where history is simultaneously suppressed and cited—perform two crucial functions in the text: First, it sets a boundary between and separates what is known and what might be surprising, or between the mundane and the incredible. This separation also secures a place for the text within history where it functions as a hinge between two narrative orders—historical and revelatory. And second, it constitutes the reader of the text as participating in the transition from the first to the second order of narration and thus becoming a witness to the peculiar futurity the text represents. Acts of public confession in the text, for example, are embodiments of such dual function. Every confession carefully builds and crosses the boundary between the known and the incredible, between what is common knowledge and what might constitute a shock. The underbelly of modern and independent India is not in itself a surprising piece of information; but it is the ritual of public confession that accentuates its extent, and allows the text to explore available history and its itinerant future. Within the space of the text one encounters the possibility and designation of history's other, the yet-to-come postcoloniality, that crucially determines the narrative structure. Quite crucially, this encounter also constitutes the possible reader as a witness, as a postcolonial participant in this incredible act of alterity—a position that enables the project of decolonization to be that of ethical responsibility.

This act of witnessing is designed within the text as a narrative *dispositif* through a series of confessions. Indeed, the text is construed as a series of citations of these confessional acts that are loosely held together by the central apocalyptic possibility, and the experience of reading is carefully planned to emulate the practice of sifting through an historical archive. I argue that this is an attempt to construct an archive of the future, a representational act that does not yet have an extra-archival referent or object. The postcolony does not exist outside this act of representation and the archival authority the text vouches for, but it is nonetheless a tangible and immanent political horizon. In "Paraś Pāthar" or "The Philosopher's Stone," the sequence is repeated with great effect. The chance discovery of a philosopher's stone by the middle-class, middle-aged lawyer Pareshbabu leads to an economic calamity. As he starts producing gold out of junk, and that too in large quantities, the world economy plunges into an unprecedented crisis—gold becomes incredibly cheaper by the day; the gold standard goes to the dogs; inflation and related economic disorders engulf every nation; Britain begins to repay America's dollar loan in cheap gold; economists urge to introduce a radium or uranium standard instead of gold; some of them even propose the ancient barter system as the only antidote. Let us look at a typical section that represents this apocalyptic scenario through a series of citations:

> It isn't easy to restrain Churchill these days; he has become insane and has said: We shall not allow the Commonwealth to be destroyed, and we shall not waste time in complaining to the UNO. Let British rule be extended to India once again, and let our army arrest and detain that scoundrel Paresh in the Isle of Wight. There he can produce as much gold as he wishes, but that gold will be empire-gold, treasure of the United Kingdom, and we will distribute it.

Bernard Shaw has said: Gold is a worthless metal as it cannot be used to make plough, sickle, axe, boiler or engine. Pareshbabu has done a great service in destroying the false reputation of gold. He should now try to make it as strong as steel. I am ready to shave my beard with a golden razor.

A spokesperson of Russia has written to Pareshbabu: Dear Sir, we cordially invite you to take residence in our country—it is an excellent place. We don't have racial discrimination here, and we shall treat you with great devotion and care. Destiny has bestowed you with incredible power, but, if you excuse us, not with enough intelligence. You know how to make gold, but not how to make good use of it. We shall teach you. You will be elected to the presidency of the Soviet Union if you happen to harbor political ambition. We shall provide a gorgeous palace for you on a vast strip of land of hundred acres in Moscow. If you prefer privacy, we shall give you a whole city in Siberia—it is an amazing place, known as *Uttarkuru* in your scriptures. (Paraśurām 85)

The text functions on this economy of citation—it cites history in displacement or as historical metafiction to produce its internal coherence. This consistency evacuates formal history of its content but cites the same history to authorize this new representational order. Bernard Shaw and Winston Churchill, like the bunch of "respectable citizens" in "The Heavenly Slipper," are vital signs of history and it is in their presence and in their name that the narrative of these incredible events originates. But such citations do not officiate beyond the designation of authority, or do not function in the life of the new narrative order after the moment of its inception. In their limited responsibility they produce a narrative repertoire—what I call the archive of the future—by exploiting the generic flux of these texts. But these citations play a more significant role, again through their restricted disposition, in facilitating the emergence of a future that comes to inhabit the evacuated historical signs. Narrative future occupies and emerges through these emptied historical signs, but, significantly enough, it is not in itself an empty space, not a *tabula rasa* ready to be inscribed upon, but a contested political site. Individual entrepreneurship of Pareshbabu provides the immediate context of this future that grows through recognizable but empty signs of history—but its apocalyptic possibilities can only be grasped in its asymmetrical relationship with the present, in the comparative framework of how the familiar signs function in this new representational order. Churchill's concern with the gold standard, Shaw's wit, and the Soviet leader's eagerness to relocate Pareshbabu in Siberia are important markers that stake out different claims on this emergent site, but they do not impose a new order on available history but cite it in displacement. The alterity of history or one's encounter with it, the text seems to suggest, is possible only through history.

THE KINGDOM TO COME

The fact that these apocalypses are not realized events within the space of the text—and are always put on hold—allows one to read the territorial politics of the postcolony. However, this deferral must not be taken as negation; it constitutes a political horizon, an unrealized but immanent element of postcolonial history against which or under the shadow of which the postcolony as a territorial unit unfolds. The open textual world one encounters in lieu of a definite apocalyptic closure closely mirrors, as it were, the open-ended possibility of the postcolony as a *desired territory*. It is possible to argue that these permeable textual boundaries broadly represent the fluid geography of a freshly partitioned colony and a tentatively bordered nation-state, and the delimited textual world depicts the imaginary promises of decolonization that cannot as yet be restricted. It is also possible to see such overlapping boundaries—textual and territorial—or rather the lack of their finality, as insinuating a land of political complexity that repeatedly thwarts any suggestion of tidy and standardized frontiers. While these are valid and tempting readings, I pursue a somewhat different course in arguing that deferred apocalypses and porous borders enable these texts to explore the postcolony as a political space that emerges through the immanent violence of such apocalypses and becomes a *functional territory* only under a continued possibility of their repetition. There are two immediate implications of this reading: First, it postulates the postcolony as an immanent territory, and not a natural and ready-made outcome of colonial history, that conditionally develops into a cohesive whole. And second, such immanent and threatened territory demands a relationship of responsibility from its inhabitants as a condition of belonging. In other words, citizenship of this territory is not a portable identity but is embedded in a set of cultural and ethical practices that delineate a specific notion of postcolonial belonging.

"Rāmrājya" or "The Kingdom of Ram," for example, uses a double-narrative frame to stage such practices. The story narrates a séance session in which the retired district judge Subodh Ray and his friends try to communicate with the mythic Hindu king Ram. The group—though seemingly a motley one, but fairly representative of contemporary political interests—is thoroughly disenchanted with independent India and initially plans to invoke Gandhi to explore his idea of Rāmrājya (the kingdom of Ram; figuratively, the ideal realm). On a second thought, however, they decide to invite Ram for a "first-hand account" (Paraśurām 90). During the ritual of establishing contact, it transpires that the medium is possessed not by Ram but by his companion the monkey-god Hanuman. The initial exchange between the group and Hanuman (Mahabir in the following excerpt) sets the mood:

> SUBODH: Listen Mahabirji, we do have our independence now, but nothing else . . .
> KABIRATNA [PROFESSOR]: We don't have food, clothing, shelter, dharma, truth, sacrifice, modesty, austerity . . .
> ABADHBIHARI [PATRIOT WITH COMMERCIAL INTEREST]: All of them are incorrigible thieves, robbers, black-marketers, pickpockets . . .
> BHUJANGA [YOUNG PATRIOT]: Capitalist tyranny, cry of the proletarian, oppression, fascism, hoaxing, verbal trickery, nepotism-involving-nephews-brothers-in-law-sisters-in-law-cousins . . .
> KANAI [ELDERLY PATRIOT]: Treachery instigated by foreign gurus, renunciation of Indian tradition, circulating propaganda to achieve sectarian interests, indoctrinating workers and peasants, spoiling impressionable youths, pistol, bomb . . .
> MAHABIR: Stop it, stop it! Tell me what you want. (Paraśurām 91)

Hanuman, however, does not offer a concrete solution initially. Instead he tells the group a story of an ancient country called Gonarda where the king Gobardhan had a million cows. Because of some deadly sin, the king attracted the wrath of the mendicant Agastya and perished with his family and subjects. The herd of cows, as a result, became orphaned, confused, and disorderly. Their attempt to find a protected life ended in finding a king, a lion from the nearby forest, who agreed to rule and defend them but demanded a cow every day in return as tax. This arrangement soon became too onerous as the lion's demand increased manifold and the cows became wary of his whims. To find an alternative, the cows met an elderly and sagacious ox for counsel and received a new mantra: "*Gohitāya govirgabāṅ śāsanam*," or the rule of the cows by the cows and for the betterment of cows. The irony is not lost in the text as one of the listeners duly comments, "Amazing! Almost like *government of the people, by the people, for the people*" (Paraśurām 92). Hanuman, however, continues with his allegorical story and describes how with this newfound mantra the cows of Gonarda were able to kill the lion and establish a political system of their own. The rulers in this new system were cows, but soon they developed physical features like their previous king lion and demanded the same tax. These new rulers were also killed by the herd and were replaced by yet another set of new leaders. And this new group soon followed the same trend of developing lionlike features and becoming equally tyrannical—this circle was repeated again and again, and at the end, because of contentious rivalry and infighting, Gonarda became a huge wasteland littered with dead cows. The story prompts the next set of exchanges:

> KANAI: What is the moral of your story? Do you mean to say democracy is a dreadful system?
> MAHABIR: A country is ruled by its people and not by any system. Whether democracy or something else, these are only words and people interpret them according to their whim and interest.
> SUBODH: You are absolutely right. Britain, America, Russia, they all brag about their respective political systems saying theirs is the only genuine democracy.
> MAHABIR: Whatever the name of the system, common people do not rule directly; they either elect their representatives, or naively submit to one or few leaders because of their cunning. Common people live a comfortable and happy life if these representatives are wise, honest, selfless, disciplined, and competent. But they suffer miserably if these representatives are foolish, dishonest, self-centered, undisciplined, and incompetent—no system is of any help then. (Paraśurām 93)

The story of Gonarda and Hanuman's gloss propose a practice of belonging that is at once political and ethical. This practice problematizes the postcolonial transition from subjecthood to citizenship—a widely commented phenomenon in political theory—in at least two distinct ways. Centrality of such practice implies that the subject-citizen transition is not a natural or given one, that it simply does not happen on its own but has to be earned. Even though the formal transition may seem structurally determined by historical events, the content of the new identity is not as readily available. Such transition demands conscious political action to entrench the formal transition within a set of ethical responsibilities and practices—"wise, honest, selfless, disciplined, and competent"—that would produce the ideal *dēmos* for the postcolonial democracy. Conditional identity of the ideal and the ethical practice, forming a code of belonging to the postcolony, is the first vital implication for the postcolonial territory. This precondition of belonging separates the postcolony from the preceding spatial ensemble. The second implication follows from this spatial difference as it inaugurates a new style of territorial imagination. The parable of Gonarda as a virtual dystopia alerts one to the structure of this imagination—that it can only develop in conjunction with its threatening alterity—as a set of two, as utopia-dystopia—and not as an independent spatial category, at least not yet. It is this proximity of these possibilities—the postcolony as the *model place* and the *wasteland* like Gonarda (the difference between the two relying on ethical citizenship)—that distinctly characterizes the territorial imagination in Paraśurām's stories. And it is this proximity again that conscripts postcolonial citizenship within an irreducible duality of the ideal self and its sinister reverse.

The text strongly suggests a discourse of modular citizenship that would turn the postcolony into an ideal lived space. Exchanges between Hanuman and the group, especially when they discuss the mythic Rāmrājya as an instance of historically realized kingdom, skillfully capture this sense of modularity and advocate the consequent vision of conscripting the ideal postcolonial citizen. Rāmrājya, according to Subodh, is a "one party saintocracy [*rṣitantra*]" (Paraśurām 94) where the saints dictate the code of conduct for every citizen, including the king. Hanuman, however, tries to see continuity between such ancient systems of governance and modern democracies by emphasizing the role of *lōkmat,* or public opinion, in both. Even the saints, he maintains, merely express popular *lōkmat* in their prescriptions for ideal and ethical conducts (Paraśurām 94). It is the possibility of a Gonarda behind every Rāmrājya, however, that provides the peculiar inflection of *lōkmat* in the text. *Lōk* has a peculiar semantic plurality, or polysemy, here—it may mean an individual person, an association of such persons to form the public, or even a world or sphere. This polysemic range can indeed be taken as forming one of the sequences of belonging in the text—individual, social, territorial—that does not simply add on cumulatively but adds up to the postcolonial lived space. It is clearly the privileged sequence in the text and also the structure of modular citizenship since it is the successful transition from one stage to the other in this sequence that leads to the ideal *lōk* of Rāmrājya; but the success of this sequencing, perhaps much more importantly, depends on preventing or at least holding back the reverse and sinister version of the *lōk* one encounters in Gonarda. The production of this ideal *lōk*—both individual citizen and collective public—functions in the text as what I have suggested to be a mode of conscription. There is only one model of such production, and only one set of practice. The postcolony, in other words, is conceived within the vigorous juxtaposition of two territorial possibilities—one desired and the other abnegated, but both are real enough as territorial options and it is the production of the ideal *lōk* that ensures the triumph of the first over the second.

The real possibility of a dystopia is maintained within the text as a shadow of deferred apocalypses. Devastation of Gonarda in Hanuman's parable functions as a virtual reminder of such postponed events. But his juxtaposition of two different territorial models to map the postcolony also indicates a different spatial ensemble that can unfold only under the shadow of apocalypses. Indeed, the text appeals to two different territorial traditions to visualize the future of the postcolony—examples offered by received wisdom (Rāmrājya, Gonardā, etc.) and instances of contemporary nation-states (Britain, United States, Russia, etc.). The futurity that I have identified above as a peculiar mode of almost all the stories in *Galpakalpa* here finds a distinct form of representation—heterogeneity of traditions, both textual and spatial. The futurity of the text emerges through the complex negotiation of these traditions as the text progressively dissolves the boundaries between them and offers this amalgam as a way of mapping the new territorial order. Projection of the future territory through available textual and territorial traditions finds an intriguing piquancy in "Gāmānuṣ Jātir Kathā" or "The Tale of the Gamman Tribe." The story unfolds thirty years after a nuclear holocaust that has wiped out the human race. The opening lines evoke a peculiar sense of futurity and narration:

> The period I am talking about unfolds almost after thirty years of human extinction. It is possible to ask if all of us are dead, who is the author of this story, or who even is the reader. But there is no need to be worried about this. Both authors and readers exist beyond time and space, they are omnipresent and omniscient. (Paraśurām 65)

It is this mode of narration that allows heterogeneous traditions to exist within the space of the text, but increasingly eliminates the traces of their sources to forge its own narrative *dispositifs*.

The text, likewise, presents a world inhabited by Gamman (Gamma-man)—mice that went through genetic mutation as a result of nuclear radiation, and now look and behave like human beings. Indeed, the text takes great care to emphasize their genesis through gamma-ray radiation, and indeed argues that there is so much similarity between these mutated mice and earlier human beings that it would be wrong to call them mice anymore—hence the new name, Gamma-man or Gamman. After establishing their genealogy, the story depicts a session of the world peace conference convened by these Gammen and uses a similar narrative style of citing speeches to construct its narrative. It is, however, the reformulated history and tradition of territorial imagination in the new world that arrests our attention—Count Notenough represents a not-so-rich nation that threatens world peace by its imperial ambition, Lord Grabearth is the spokesman for the largest existing empire and elaborates on his imperialist ideals, General Keepoff is from a new nation that advocates revolutionary principles, and Abaldasji is the voice of the colonized world and vigorously opposes Lord Grabearth's imperialist mission. The text builds on received territorial vocabulary of empire and colony but progressively obscures their genealogy to release its new world order. It is not simply a model of territorial repetition with minor difference, but a textual means to evoke the order of future territoriality.

Apocalyptic events form the condition for such textual *dispositifs* since it is in the shadow of such imminent events that this territory becomes operative. The increasing omission of sources (we no longer meet Churchill or Shaw of "The Heavenly Slipper" but see more generalized and almost type characters) is a textual way of characterizing the territorial imagination as a threatened one, and also of suggesting that if one removes the threat the ensemble may revert back to the older one. The territorial progress, in other words, is not defined by historical signs alone, not by signs that may become meaningful within given territorial relations, but by the text's ability to weave these signs into a newer territorial matrix through which these signs would map new domains of power and authority. Moreover, it is the reworking of these signs that would secure the future order, and in their present significatory chain they can simply gesture toward this future but cannot represent it. The territorial imagination becomes operational as a proleptic one under this continued threat.

WORKS CITED

Bhattacharya, Baidik. "Jokes Apart: Orientalism, (Post)colonial Parody, and the Moment of Laughter." *Interventions: International Journal of Postcolonial Studies* 8.2 (2006): 276–94.

Chakrabarty, Dipesh. "*Adda*: A History of Sociality." *Provincializing Europe: Postcolonial Thought and Historical Difference*. Princeton: Princeton University Press, 2000. 180–213.

de Certeau, Michel. *The Practice of Everyday Life*. Trans. Steven Rendall. Berkeley: University of California Press, 1984.

Derrida, Jacques. "No Apocalypse, Not Now (full speed ahead, seven missiles, seven missives)." Trans. Catherine Porter and Philip Lewis. *Diacritics* 14.2 (1984): 20–31.

Fiddes, Paul S. *The Promised End: Eschatology in Theology and Literature*. Oxford: Blackwell, 2000.

Genette, Gérard. *Narrative Discourse: An Essay in Method*. Ithaca: Cornell University Press, 1980.

Nietzsche, Friedrich. *Ecce Homo: How One Becomes What One Is*. Trans. R. J. Hollingdale. London: Penguin, 1992.

Paraśurām. *Paraśurām Granhābalī* [Collected Works of *Paraśurām*]. Vol. 1. Calcutta: M. C. Sarkar, 1969.

———. "Gagan Chaṭi." *Paraśurām Granhābalī* [Collected Works of *Paraśurām*]. Vol. 2. Calcutta: M. C. Sarkar, 1969.

PART V

NARRATIVE, THEORY, IDEOLOGY

CHAPTER 12

In the Absence of Post-

MIEKE BAL

CRYSTALS OF TIME

A postcolonial narratology must not only explore the predicaments of the question of relevance of one body of theory for the understanding of another body of narrative texts. Also it must demonstrate a surplus value, insights not otherwise gained, for the intercultural encounter. This relevance must be demonstrable for both popular narratives and the kind of complicated ones we tend to consider "literary" or "artistic." So, I begin with a novel recommended to me by the bookseller whose judgment I tend to consider apt for the average taste of readers in my neighborhood. I often buy what he recommends. The popularly acclaimed Bengali writer Jhumpa Lahiri recently republished her earlier novel *The Namesake* (2003). It is part of the growing number of novels of migration, recounting the difficulties of characters that are, either by their own volition or through their parents' earlier decisions, thrown into a world that is culturally foreign to them. The intercultural situation of migration has been a central topic in much of my film and curatorial work. This has sensitized me even more to the importance of focalization: the representation of all forms of the perception of narrative content, regardless of who does the narrating. In this essay, I will privilege a mode of focalization that is particularly relevant for anything called "post-": memory.[1]

---

1. On cultural consequences of migration, see Bal and Hernández Navarro, 2*MOVE*, *Art and Visibility*. For my films on migration, see http://www.miekebal.org/artworks/films/.

The main character of *The Namesake*, called Gogol for reasons he understands only much later, hates his name and changes it in adulthood to Nikhil. This name has the double advantage of sounding more "Indian" and of being easily Americanized to "Nick." More clarity, then, on both sides. However, when he is already fully "Nikhiled" the narrator keeps calling him Gogol, including when the voice phrases the man's focalization. This puzzled me. It enticed me to read against the grain. Paying attention to focalization has always been my primary tool for such reading.[2]

Every single time I read the name in these passages, I felt slightly bothered. Had the author been sensitive to the importance of focalization, I thought, she would either have matched the character's decision and used the chosen name, or somehow differentiated between the two in ways readers could work with to make sense of the confusion of his identity that is obviously at the root of this name game. Until on page 241 the two names cross swords. At a party, the following exchange occurs:

"Hey there," Gogol says. "Need any help?"
"Nikhil. Welcome." Donald hands over the parsley. "Be my guest."

The common English phrase "be my guest," meaning "do as you like," suddenly gets a slightly ironic inflection in which the notion of "guest" is taken literally for just a moment. Gogol does not belong. Not at the party, given by friends of his wife, nor in its very American Yuppy culture. The passage has no character that focalizes. It is narrated in an objectifying tone. From then on, it dawned on me that the persistence of the name Gogol, in all its Russianness, stands for the persistently "Indian" misdirected longing of the character. Born in the United States, he is unable to put down roots in either place, that of his parents and his own. So, due to that rootlessness, the Russian name turns out appropriate after all.

I am more interested in the treatment of the main character's mother, Ashima, however. She is the one who is married off from India to an Indian-born man working in the United States. Two key moments in her life set her in an intercultural, interlingual plight. The first is giving birth to her son (later to be called Gogol). When the doctor tells her the delivery is going to take a lot more time, she doesn't understand the key word and asks: "What does it mean, dilated?" (3) It may require a stretch of the imagination that a woman who experienced her entire pregnancy in New Jersey would not have

---

2. On focalization and the other narratological terms used in this essay, see Bal, *Narratology*.

had any prior interaction about it with others; she would surely have come across the concept of dilation, but clearly, the point is that we see that word anew as strange, somewhat threatening, and in need of explanation. The text then describes the gestures the doctor uses to communicate, and all we get is Ashima's vision-based understanding: "explaining the unimaginable thing her body must do in order for the baby to pass." (3) This is a clear-cut instance of character focalization. Ashima sees the gesture the doctor makes, and she interprets it as "unimaginable."

Much later, when Gogol is an adult—hence, at least after twenty years of living and working in the United States—Ashima is being told that her husband "has expired." Again, she doesn't get it, but this time, the lack of understanding is thickened:

> Expired. A word used for library cards, for magazine subscriptions. A word which, for several seconds, has no effect whatsoever on Ashima. "No, no, it must be a mistake," Ashima says calmly, shaking her head, a small laugh escaping from her throat. "My husband is not there for an emergency. Only for a stomachache." (168–69)

While the first lack of understanding might still be due to her relatively recent arrival, the second one retrospectively "explains" the first. In both cases, a form of denial is added to surprise, and to the awkwardness of talking about such intimately bodily things to a man (for the birth) and through a telephone (for the death). Embarrassment, connected to cultural and sexual difference together, is at issue, not linguistic ignorance. The two come together when Ashima ponders: "For being a foreigner, Ashima is beginning to realize, is a sort of life-long pregnancy—a perpetual wait, a constant burden, a continuous feeling out of sorts." (49) The metaphor is doing the telling, more than the very American phrase "feeling out of sorts." It is in the equation foreigners = pregnancy that Ashima's focalization is expressed. She contributes time, specifically duration, to our understanding of the experience.

This, it turns out, is elaborated throughout the novel, especially in the form of memories. These are "multitemporal" as well as "multidirectional" memories. Juxtaposing memories of the past, future memories, and acts of memory in the present, the narrator crosses the fine line between memory and the imagination (62–63), all this negotiated through memories of wishes that remain unfulfilled (127). The key memory is of a trip Gogol made with his father, to the end of a stretch of coast. The sentence that ends the chapter is an injunction by the father, who tells his son:

"Try to remember it always"... "Remember that you and I made this journey, that we went together to a place where there was nowhere left to go." (187)

Now that we have understood the way focalization functions to cross the bridge and overcome the gaps migration has dug, including between father and son, the entire novel, it seems, unfolds to heed the injunction.[3]

Keeping the attention on memory as a specific form of focalization, through systematic attention to focalization we can grasp how multitemporality and multidirectionality join forces in complicating the sense of history as a series of events. The string of events we call history now becomes a constellation from which rays go out in all directions. Futurality itself, then, is multidirectional, encompassing the past as well as the times of others. If subjectivity is porous, however, then memory and history are inseparable. This is why one of the most insightful descriptions of historical time is a perfectly adequate description of memory. In "Theses on the Philosophy of History," Benjamin imaginatively speculates on the *arrest* of thought. This arrest constitutes a break with linearity, with "homogeneous, empty time," a kind of de-automatization and "filling" or embodiment of time. This arrest puts the present forward, making that present both subjective and political. Moreover, it results in a great force, causing a "shock" that, in turn, leads to a crystallization of time into a constellation (262).

Like crystals of snow, crystals of time offer a model for thought that eludes the straitjacket of linearity that leaves both historical contradiction and subjective experience by the wayside. Instead, the Benjaminian idea of shock, or *choc en retour*, of arrested thought allows us "to grasp time as dense with overlapping possibilities and dangers—an understanding of the present as ... the site of multidirectional memory" (Rothberg 80).[4]

In such a conception of memory, time and direction merge, or freeze, in the merging of focalization and the image; hence the relevance of the concept for visual analysis. Deleuze puts it thus, in a classical passage that gives density to Gogol's memory of his father's injunction to remember:

> What constitutes the crystal-image is the most fundamental operation of time: since the past is constituted not after the present that it was but at the same time, time has split itself in two at each moment as present and past, which differ from each other in nature, or ... it has to split the present in two

---

3. I use the phrase "act of memory" to foreground the active nature and present tense of memory. See Bal, Crewe, and Spitzer.

4. On multidirectional memory, see Rothberg.

heterogeneous directions, one of which is launched towards the future while the other falls into the past. Time has to split at the same time as it sets itself out or unrolls itself: it splits in two dissymmetrical jets, one of which makes all the present pass on, while the other preserves all the past. Time consists of this split, and it is this, it is time, that we *see in the crystal*. (82)

The "emanation of past reality" that Barthes marveled at in photography (88) is compounded by an emanation of another's (past or present) reality. In Lahiri's novel, the father and the son are as "other" to each other as possible. Memory mediates to turn this very readable, popular novel into a document of "migratory aesthetics," an encounter not based on alterity—a vexed concept that implies an unmentioned superior "self"—but one groping toward affective understanding, against all odds of circumstance and history. The miracle of such an encounter will only happen if you allow the other to be, whether you see what she sees or not.

My brief reading of Lahiri's novel brings me to a further consideration of the complexities of focalization. Keep in mind this concept of a permeable, de-individualized but strongly sensorial subject in time as a (multidirectional) crystallized constellation. Here lies the relevance of focalization for postcolonial narratology. But to fully make that case, I need to call on some complicating ideas. For, such relevance depends not only on narrative structure but also and in fact, primarily, on ethical and political effects. And it is there that the vexed preposition "post-" as used in the term "postcolonial" must be challenged. And who better to call on, then, but Gayatri Chakravorty Spivak—as a scholar and a writer?

FOCALIZATION AS ABSENCE

In a brief but illuminating analysis in her recent book, *An Aesthetic Education*, of some passages from Coetzee's much-discussed 1999 novel *Disgrace*, Spivak demonstrates her bold way of making literary analysis, *as such*, relevant for ethics and politics (322–27). Her method: to imagine "absent things." She notices that in Coetzee's novel, the narration keeps the focalization systematically away from the main character's daughter, the rape survivor Lucy. This is a significant absence because focalization gives access to characters' perceptions and feelings. This is why it is a key term in any narrative analysis.

When present, a character's focalization facilitates empathy; when absent, it precludes such emotional involvement. Hence, the distribution of affect across the novel depends on it. "What if," asks Spivak, we imagine the absent focalization of Lucy? This "what if?" question enables her to come up with an interpretation that does justice to the feminist necessity to bring the woman character to convincing life, as well as "explains" how she can take the position she does in relation to the postapartheid situation—with a certain hesitation to use the prefix coming from an awareness of the problematic meaning of the prefix "post-"—in which her rape happened.[5]

The logic of this move is entirely convincing in that absent focalization, as I have argued many times (most explicitly in *Death and Dissymmetry*), is just as much a feature of a narrative text as its presence; "who cannot focalize?" as important a question as "who focalizes?" Deciding to invent Lucy's focalization turns a reader into an interactive one. What she calls "the nestling of logic and rhetoric" (317) brings the ethical, the epistemological, and the political together, in a tense but firm entanglement. The knot works through a readerly act of tracing intertextuality, "working both ways" (319). The reader is in charge both of restoring reference "in order that intertextuality may function; and to *create* intertextuality as well" (318; emphasis added). This quotation comes from a discussion of Tagore and Mozart, but prepares us for the Coetzee analysis to come.

Is the creation of Lucy's focalization not a breach of the textual grounding of interpretation, so indispensable to keep personal projection at bay, and to guarantee teachability? No, Spivak claims, since the literary text "gives rhetorical signals to the reader, which lead to activating the readerly imagination" (323) so that no reader has to be submissive and be "content with acting out the failure of reading" (323). In fact, the text provokes such disobedience by means of its rhetoric that restricts focalization too emphatically to the character of Professor Lurie, who is under ethical scrutiny. Spivak calls this readerly response to the text's provocation *counterfocalization*. And as with all opposition, such acts are bound to the text they counter. She claims the text provokes it: "This provocation into counterfocalization is the 'political' in political fiction—the transformation of a tendency into a crisis" (324). The *literary* act of interactive reading is the site where the political can happen.

Spivak makes this specific when she writes:

> It is precisely this limited validity of the liberal white ex-colonizer's understanding that *Disgrace* questions through the invitation to focalize the enigma of Lucy. (326)

---

5. To keep this discussion succinct, I refer to the more extensive discussion of "what if?" questions in my recent book *Thinking in Film*. This paragraph and a few following ones are spin-offs of my article on Spivak's book in *PMLA*, "Masterly Maxims."

What is the textual basis for this invitation? It can only be the incongruent absence of Lucy's focalization, which is so striking that it alone works as an invite. The discrepancy between Lucy's presence as a character, her importance in the sad adventure of her father, and the absence of her focalization make for what, in theories of reception, used to be called a "gap": something the absence of which is so noticeable that readers tend to feel challenged to fill it in.

The importance of this invitation goes far beyond the feminist aspect (to make the focalization of the woman character and her typical woman's plight visible). Spivak brings the different political elements together: "If we, like Lurie, [the male main protagonist and Lucy's father] ignore the enigma of Lucy, the novel, being fully focalized precisely by Lurie, can be made to say every racist thing" (326). This suggests that focalization, including and perhaps especially in its negativity, is key to a postcolonial (with the same qualms about "post-") narratology. And indeed, as we know, many are the colonial novels where "natives" are merely elements of the décor, of the bottom of the power structure, and of the narrative need to fill the diegetic universe.[6]

Although this example works toward an understanding of the special relevance of focalization for postcolonial narratology, a detour is necessary to frame such an assertion. Spivak's work is so apt to discuss the issue to which this volume is devoted because, while she is doubtlessly one of the most reputed postcolonial critics, she is not specifically a narratologist; rather, she is intimately knowledgeable about philosophy. Her deep knowledge of Kant, Marx, and Gramsci is a red thread through her books. And, given her interest in what we call less and less happily "postcolonial" theory, it comes as no surprise that the discussions of such canonical and inexhaustible philosophical texts never lose sight of the social-political implications of the ideas gleaned from the encounter. Thus, a philosophical tradition is brought to bear on contemporary social issues of a keen actuality. Meandering through her work runs the philosophical underpinning of her analyses of (narrative) literature. This distinguishes her work from formalist deployments of structuralist ideas.

This solid philosophical background does not make her texts always easy to read for literary and other cultural scholars eager to get ideas—preferably quickly—about "how to do" postcolonial literary studies. That may be all for the good; quick fixes can only lead to clichés, condescending nods of the kind that used to be called, disparagingly, "politically correct," and projection of Western preoccupations on what we think we have understood but still keep

---

6. Spivak refers here to two essays on Coetzee's novel of the many that wonder about this aspect, precisely because they don't dare make that bold Spivakian move (McDonald; Attwell).

"othering." Hence, Spivak's immersive work with philosophy, precluding such fast understandings, is also what makes her work useful for our current exploration of a postcolonial narratology.

The key Spivakian concept, and the one that builds the bridge between classical analysis of (present) focalization and the absent one coming to visibility through the "what if?" question, is "critical intimacy." This concept evokes the migratory nature of knowledge, but in it inheres the need for criticality; yet with intimacy, condescension is avoided and empathy facilitated. The concept stipulates that a particular kind of focalization—with intimacy and critique bound together—is the best way to get access to interculturality. It is worth the effort of meeting the challenge of Spivak's writing because the meandering tour through Western philosophy and (not only) Western literature with what she has termed "critical intimacy" is enriching, on all levels, and more so because it is so unorthodox in style and consistently feminist in argument. She broaches many important subjects pertaining to the cultural issues raised by the social world today; not only its literature, but taking literature as a serious participant. Spivak's work moves so naturally between the political, ethical, and aesthetic domains that her ultimate promotion of the *epistemological* as the key to an aesthetic education almost passes unnoticed. And yet, how do we know, and how do we know we know: this is why "education" matters, is difficult, and is possible. Education, I think, is the central kind of narrative, or staging, where critical intimacy is necessary as a mode of focalizing.[7]

In an earlier response to Spivak's book *A Critique of Postcolonial Reason: Towards a History of the Vanishing Present*, I proposed that Spivak's prose is best read as oral discourse, specifically the talk of a teacher who, committed to her students' education, is attentive to seeing eyes waver, hands moving to write down a note, ears pricked up, and other signs of difficulty that requires some side-stepping. In narratological terms, we can say that her writing stages the "second person" to whom the teaching is addressed; in terms of this essay, the "focalisee." In other words, my interpretation of Spivak's writing style narrativizes it.

Once seen as the mode of a teacher, every deviation from the straight-and-narrow of exposing a logical argument can be considered generous, interactive, and indispensable. The possibility to immediately attend to individual students' needs is the primary reason why live teaching is still needed. I was inspired by Spivak's writing, and felt justified in this figurative, personifying mode of reading her by her own use of figures, such as the "native informant,"

---

7. "Critical Intimacy" has become the title of the final chapter of my book *Travelling Concepts in the Humanities*, a chapter in which Spivak's 1999 book was my case.

to make intellectual points. She deploys that figure, for example, as a figure of methodology to articulate and qualify her "critically intimate" encounter with Kant. This is why "critical intimacy" is another of her figurations of her intellectual position.

To understand what probing the absent focalizer—Spivak's proposal—entails, I propose that the 2012 book, equally voluminous, challenging, and demanding, is rather not, in my view, best read through the figure of the teacher. The primary and paradoxical reason I find this no longer the most productive approach is that here the author stages herself with insistence and frequency explicitly as a teacher. She initially defines her work in a phrase, "of the classroom situation," and throughout the book that situation is extensively described. Her adventures in different teaching situations may have an interest of their own, but the figure has lost its figurativity; it no longer triggers the reader's imagination: the "what if?" question. This leads to my assertion that explicit focalization may be less illuminating than its absence as a trigger of the imagination.

An additional paradox ensues, which has its bearing on the field of postcolonial studies: staging herself as a teacher across national and linguistic borders—identifying with the image of her that circulates so widely—with many anecdotes about teaching in India and Bangladesh, she deploys a memorial mode that has become increasingly popular in the United States. In the wake of feminism, postcolonialism, and other new movements that have had such a decisive and defining impact on the academic modes of thinking—and don't take me wrong, that impact was and is fabulous—this *personalizing* account now passes as almost standard. In my view, however, this probing of personal memories in academic work has one drawback: when not carefully measured and monitored but sliding toward particularity, it tends to cultivate an individualism poorly suitable for the teaching situation, which may get in the way of the arguments, and which is especially unsuitable for the intercultural situation. Only when this personal mode really contributes theoretically and analytically to the academic content, it works. Otherwise, individualism takes over. To put the paradox strongly to create a frame for my discussion: the more "Indian" the figure of the teacher on the level of anecdote, the more "American" her intellectual style becomes, to the detriment of the "postcolonial" aspect of the writing. It takes an analysis through the concept of focalization—inflected as "critical intimacy"—to see this.

From this difference between these two books and my intuitive bracketing of the "teacherly" mode of reading for the most recent one, I learned that explicitness does not stimulate the imagination, while, as Spivak rightly insists, the latter is key to the aesthetic. In other words, even a scholarly book has an aesthetic, and even a specifically narrative side to it, which is instrumental in the pleasure of reading it. And that pleasure is the royal road to readability. It so happens that the imagination is Spivak's major weapon against the hopelessness she keeps mentioning in her book. She provisionally defines it as "'thinking absent things,' hardly distinguishable from thinking" (16). Note the importance of the share the imagination has in thinking as such.

In view of this, I contend that the focalization and subsequent self-figuration of the teacher in *An Aesthetic Education* is not "absent" *enough*. In this book, then, I have been looking for another mode to what she calls "instrumentalize" her text, a mode in accordance with her arguments, and making true on the author's request to get "interactive readers" (3). This mode is based on what I'd like to propose as maxim spotting. For this, a mode of focalization that is indeed interactive—it compels the reader to "spot" the maxims—is more suitable than critical intimacy here. A maxim is a short utterance given as a statement, a thesis; something like an internal, partial summary, or an aphorism. I like to think of Adorno's *Minima Moralia* from 1951 as a prime example of the genre. Maxims are so relevant for my argument because they are subjective but not psychological. The subjective nature of the maxim allows adherence, empathy, agreement, rejection; but some response is almost inevitable. They solicit activity on the part of the reader, an activity that does not separate intellectual and sense-based responses. Subjective but not psychological: here we have a definition of focalization.

An example of a maxim. In the discussion of the translation of Kant's definition of maxims, we read: "a general assumption of continuous translatability is waylaid by the diachronic heterogeneity of our globe" (14). Food for thought: about translation—discussed throughout and the focus of chapter 12—about globalization, discussed in many of the essays, albeit mostly sideways; about heterogeneity and the vexed parasynonym "alterity," discussed with a lot of skepticism, and about time, the diachronic in the contemporary, and all the issues surrounding that term. And about the subjectivity of the one whose vision is expressed here. That's a lot of thinking that this utterance solicits. These subjects brought together in one short sentence join forces in making up the nonlinear coherence of a book that is itself heterogeneous. Only when we treat this as a maxim can this complex of multiple meanings come to visibility. This is the beauty of the concept of focalization: through the interactivity solicited in this writing, and the maxim spotting that the reader performs, it allows us to *see*, and even sensually experience, such insights as no convoluted argumentation can convey so clearly.[8]

---

8. For more extensive discussion of Spivak's 2012 book, see the April 2014 issue of *PMLA*.

SEEING IT

So far I have treated focalization in fiction, an absent focalizer, in academic writing that invites critical intimacy, and in a writing, also academic yet almost opposite, that invites maxim spotting, that foregrounds itself as a maxim. These examples all raised issues of focalization, of further differentiating it so as to adapt itself to intercultural situations. And I could add more examples, from film, painting, and as I have done before, anthropology. Neither narrative nor its backbone focalization is bound to literature, or textuality, for that matter. Moreover, the absence or negative of narrative functions is as telling as their presence or explicit invocation. There is an elective affinity, although not an identification, between focalization and seeing. Reading focalization and practicing counterfocalization where needed is an activity with political relevance.

To avoid an impression of overgeneralization (diluting the concept), this calls for some unpacking. I will do that through a close look at a cluster of neighboring concepts that all touch visuality, both as sense perception and as insight. These concepts are the "gaze," "focalization," and "iconicity." They are different but affiliated. They are often conflated, with disastrous results, or, alternatively, kept separate, with impoverishing results. They are all three "traveling concepts"—concepts taken from one domain to another, with changes in use, meaning, and analytic value along the way. The following consideration describes the travels through which they have gone. I will give my view of what happened with these concepts in the cultural field, and move back and forth between that general development and my own intellectual itinerary.[9]

In order to see the relevance of such concept probing for a postcolonial narratology, I briefly invoke work by Indian artist Nalini Malani, whose shadow plays stage acts of memory that I would qualify, with Max Silverman, as palimpsestic. Malani has been working with the diffuse, repressed, or otherwise distorted memories of religious-political violence in the wake of partition (1947), superimposed by the violence of Hindus committed against Muslims (1992–93) and the violence in Gujarat in 2002. Note that these three waves of violence seem acts of repeating, and thus constitute together also a palimpsest of a different kind.[10]

The "gaze" is a key concept in visual studies, one I find important enough to fuss about if fuzziness is to be avoided. It is widely used in fields whose

---

9. The following paragraphs are a revision of some segments from *Travelling Concepts*.
10. The factual violence on three historical moments is not the issue here; the memory of it, or its forgetting, is the impulse Malani brings to making her shadow plays.

FIGURE 1. Nalini Malani, *In Search of Vanished Blood,* 2012 (overview). Six channel video play with five reverse painted Mylar cylinders. dOCUMENTA (13), Kassel. Used with permission from the artist.

members participate in cultural studies, both as a common word and as a concept. Norman Bryson's analysis of the life of this concept, first in art history, then in feminist and gender studies, amply demonstrates why it is worth reflecting on. He rightly insists that feminism has had a decisive impact on visual studies; film studies would be nowhere near where it is today without it. In turn, film studies, especially in its extended form, which includes television and the new media, are a key area in cultural studies. The itinerary Bryson sketches is largely informed by the centrality of the concept of the gaze in all the participating disciplines. One of these is literature. If we realize that film studies, at least in the United States, grew out of English departments, the time-and-space map becomes decidedly interesting.[11]

The concept of the gaze has a variety of backgrounds. It is sometimes used as an equivalent of the look, indicating the position of the subject doing the looking. As such, it points to a subject position, real or represented. It is also used in distinction from the look, as a fixed and fixating, colonizing, mode of looking—a look that objectifies, appropriates, disempowers, and even, pos-

---

11. See Bryson's introduction to *Looking In: The Art of Viewing.* This text, in fact, was one of the reasons that I became more acutely aware of the importance of concepts. Silverman offers an excellent, indeed, indispensable, discussion of the gaze in Lacanian theory.

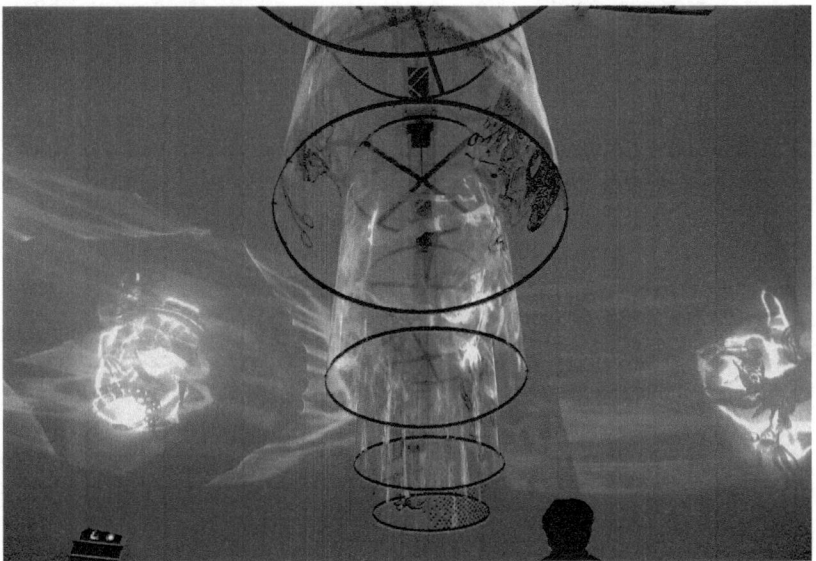

FIGURE 2. Nalini Malani, *In Search of Vanished Blood*, 2012 (detail a). Six channel video play with five reverse painted Mylar cylinders. dOCUMENTA (13), Kassel. Used with permission from the artist.

sibly, violates. This makes it an important concept for a critique of colonialism—and of the remnants of it, or renewed forms, in so-called postcolonial literature and art. It increases the difficulty of looking at Malani's 2012 installation *In Search of Vanished Blood*. As its title indicates, this work, like Spivak's maxims, solicits an interactive viewer willing to *search* for what is *vanished*, the trauma of violence.[12]

In its Lacanian sense, the gaze is very different from—if not opposed to—its more common usage as the equivalent of the look or a specific version of it (Silverman). The Lacanian gaze is, most succinctly, the visual order (equivalent to the symbolic order, or the visual part of that order) in which the subject is caught. In this sense, it is an indispensable concept through which to understand all cultural domains, including text-based ones. The gaze is the world looking (back) at the subject. Nothing makes this clearer than a shadow play based on slowly turning cylindrical shapes that cast on the surrounding walls evocations of figures from Indian epic and mythology, popular painting, Greek mythology, and recent literary texts—artifacts that all have in common

---

12. See Bryson for a distinction between the "gaze" and the "glance" as two versions of the look. On Malani's shadow plays, see Huyssen, and Bal, *In Medias Res*. The title of her 2012 work, shown at Documenta that year, resonates with the subtitle of Spivak's 1999 book.

that they represent, evoke, or resist violence in and for the present. This is how, in this work, the world and its history look back at us. Significantly, the viewer is trapped between the cylinders and the shadows on the walls, and cannot help being "in" the shadows.[13]

In its more common use—perhaps between ordinary word and analytical concept—the gaze is the look that the subject casts on other people, and other things. Feminism initiated the scrutiny of the gaze's objectifying thrust, especially in film studies, where the specific Lacanian sense remains important (Silverman). Cultural critics, including anthropologists, have been interested in the use of photography in historical and ethnographic research. More broadly, the meaning-producing effects of images, including textual-rhetorical ones, have been recognized. In this type of analysis, the gaze is also obviously central. Using the shadows of cultural memories as her medium, Malani makes an appropriating gaze impossible. The figures are fugitive, moving, ungraspable, whereas the viewer is caught between the subject and object position.[14]

The objectification and the disempowering exoticization of others further flesh out the issues of power inequity that the concept helps to lay bare. This is its relevance for postcolonial theory. Indeed, the affiliated concepts of the other and alterity have been scrutinized for their own collusion with the imperialist forces that hold the gaze in this photographic and cinematic material. Merging in her work the mythologies of India as well as Greece, Malani makes any distinction between self and other, already precluded by the form and medium of the work, also impossible on the level of content.

Enabling the analysis of noncanonical objects, such as snapshots, the concept is also helpful in allowing the boundaries between elite and larger culture to be overcome. Between all these usages, an examination of the concept itself is appropriate. Not to police it, or to prescribe a purified use for it, but to gauge its possibilities, and to either delimit or link the objects on which it has been brought to bear. Only with such examination can it prove its usefulness for postcolonial narratology.

So far, in its development in the cultural community, the concept of the gaze has demonstrated its flexibility and inclination to social critique. But, for the issue of postcolonial methodology, it also has a more hands-on kind of relevance. For it has an affiliation with—although is not identical to—the concept of focalization in narrative theory. This is where my own involvement came in. In my early work, I struggled to adjust that concept. In fact, in

---

13. Ernst van Alphen's analysis of Charlotte Delbo's writings is suggestively titled "Caught by Images" (in *Art in Mind*).

14. See, for example, Hirsch (1997; 1999).

narrative theory, the concept of focalization, although clearly visual in background, has been deployed to overcome visual strictures and the subsequent metaphorical floundering of concepts such as perspective and point of view.

It is precisely because the concept of focalization is *not* identical to that of the gaze or the look (although it has some unclear yet persistent affiliation with both of these concepts of visuality) that it can help to clarify a vexed issue in the relationship between looking and language, between art history and literary studies, but also, between mainstream and postcolonial narratology. The common question for all three of these concepts is what the look of a represented (narrated or depicted) figure does to the imagination of the reader or the look of the viewer. This is why Spivak's imaginative leap to her "what if?" question that enabled her to sketch in the absent focalizor Lucy is decisively important to develop a specifically postcolonial use of the concept of focalization.

Focalization was the object of my first academic passion when, in the seventies, I became a narratologist. Retrospectively, my interest in developing a more workable concept to replace what literary scholars call perspective or point of view was rooted in a sense of the cultural importance of vision, even in the most language-based of the arts. My long-term argument with the master of narrative theory, Gérard Genette, for example, turned out entirely based on cultural-political disagreement. Hence, vision must not be understood exclusively in the technical-visual sense. In the slightly metaphorical but indispensable sense of imaginary—akin but not identical to imagination—vision tends to involve both actual looking and interpreting, including in literary reading. And, while this is a reason to recommend the verb "reading" for the analysis of visual images, it is also a reason *not* to cast the visual out of the concept of focalization. The danger of dilution here must be carefully balanced against the impoverishment caused by the excess of conceptual essentialism that goes by the proud name of "rigor."[15]

The term "focalization" also helped overcome the limitations of the linguistically inspired tools inherited from structuralism. These were based on the structure of the sentence and failed to help account for what happens between characters in narrative, figures in image, and the readers of both. The great emphasis on conveyable and generalizable content in structuralist semantics hampered attempts to understand *how* such contents were con-

---

15. I have been greatly—indeed, decisively—inspired by Genette's three volumes of *Figures*, especially the third volume, translated into English as *Narrative Discourse: An Essay in Method*. When his response to criticism appeared (*Narrative Discourse Revisited*), I understood how deep the cleft was between our conceptions of literature.

veyed—to what effects and ends—through what can be termed "subjectivity networks."[16]

The hypothesis that readers *envision*, that is, create, images from textual stimuli, cuts right through semantic theory, grammar, and rhetoric, to foreground the presence and crucial importance of *images* in reading. The fact that Malani makes her viewers come to terms with being caught in images that evoke past violence—especially against women—in the present demonstrates that the importance of images lies in their rigorous present tense. At one point, when I managed to solve a long-standing problem of biblical philology "simply" by envisioning, instead of deciphering, the text, seeing, in the present, the violence done to young girls millennia ago, I savored the great pleasure and excitement that come with discovery. Let me call the provisional result of this first phase of the dynamic of the concept-in-use, the gaze-as-focalizor.[17]

The second phase goes in the opposite direction. Take "Rembrandt," for example. The name stands for a *text*—"Rembrandt" as the cultural ensemble of images, dis- and reattributed according to an expansive or purifying cultural mood—and for the discourses about the real and imaginary figure indicated by the name. The images called "Rembrandt" are notoriously uninterested in linear perspective and also highly narrative. Moreover, many of these images are replete with issues relevant for a gender perspective—such as the nude, scenes related to rape, and myth-based history paintings in which women are being framed. For these reasons combined, focalization imposes itself as an operative concept. In contrast, "perspective" can only spell disaster. But, while narrativity may be medium-independent, the transfer of a specific concept from narrative theory—in this case, focalization, which is mostly deployed in the analysis of verbal narratives—to visual texts requires the probing of its realm, its productivity, and its potential for propagation versus the risk of dilution.[18]

This probing is all the more important because of the double ambiguity that threatens here. Firstly, focalization is a narrative inflection of imagining, interpreting, and perception that *can*, but need not, be visual imaging. This would allow disparaging presentations of "others" through actions, for

---

16. For an elaboration of subjectivity networks, I must refer to my book *Death and Dissymmetry*.

17. This happened several times in my work on the Book of Judges (*Death and Dissymmetry*). A key text remains W. J. T. Mitchell's opening chapter, "What Is an Image?," in *Iconology*. The word "envision" yields a tentative concept in Schwenger.

18. In chapter 1 of *Travelling Concepts*, I have discussed these two possible results of interdisciplinarity, following Stengers.

FIGURE 3. Nalini Malani, *In Search of Vanished Blood*, 2012 (detail b). Six channel video play with five reverse painted Mylar cylinders. dOCUMENTA (13), Kassel. Used with permission from the artist.

example, to pass unnoticed. To conflate focalization with the gaze would be to return to square one, thus undoing the work of differentiation between two different modes of semiotic expression, while erasing the critical potential of a subtler narrative analysis. Secondly, and conversely, the projection of narrativity on visual images is an analytic move that has great potential but is also highly specific. To put it simply: not all images are narrative, any more than all narrative acts of focalization are visual. Yet narratives and images have *envisioning* as their common form of reception. This is why Spivak's bold envisioning of the absent focalizing acts of Lucy is so crucial to a postcolonial, that is, critical narratology. The differences and the common elements between the two concepts are equally important. This is also why Malani's shadowy images move, turn, appear, and disappear. This is how they hold us: as Huyssen has it, by their "visual lure and aesthetic fascination" that keep the present tense active beyond a mere, because powerless, lament about gendered violence (52).

In my own work, the examination of the concept of focalization for use in the analysis of visual images was all the more urgent because the new area of visual imagery appears to carry traces of the same word by which the concept is known. This was a moment of truth: is focalization in narratology "only a metaphor" borrowed from the visual domain? If so, does its deployment in visual analysis fall back on its literal meaning?

Instead, and supported by Malani's images, I claim the concept of focalization helps to articulate the look precisely through its movement. After traveling, first from the visual domain to narratology, then to the more specific analysis of visual images, focalization has received a meaning in visual analysis that overlaps neither with the old visual one, focusing with a lens, nor simply with the new narratological one—the cluster of perception and interpretation that guides the attention through the narrative. Or, as in Malani's work, the multiple narratives brought in to facilitate "acts of memory." It now indicates neither a *location* of the gaze on the picture plane, nor a *subject* of it, such as either the figure or the viewer. What becomes visible is the *movement* of the look—a movement Malani makes so inevitable on all levels that nothing can offer a more convincing, because experiential, argument than this artwork.[19]

In that movement, the look encounters the limitations imposed by the gaze, the visual order. For the gaze dictates the limits of the figures' respective positions as holder of the objectifying and colonizing look, and the disempowered object of that look. The tension between the focalizor's movement and these limitations is the true object of analysis. For it is here that structural, formal aspects of the object become meaningful, dynamic, and culturally operative: through the time-bound, changing effect of the culture that frames them. Thanks to its narratological background, the concept of focalization imported mobility into the visual domain that usefully and productively complemented the potential to structure envisioning that had been carried over from visual to narrative in the first phase. We do not even have to fall back on such notoriously fuzzy and deceptive concepts as *implied viewer*, by analogy to an implied author that is tenaciously problematic.

For all these reasons combined, I privilege focalization as the most important concept in postcolonial narratology. Its potential to not only facilitate precise and hence teachable interpretations but also to entice interactive reading with empathy, to facilitate experiential participation in the movement inherent in representation, especially in the memories of colonial but also postcolonial violence, and exposed to the hilt in Malani's shadow play that makes all of us participants in that violence in the present tense, is key for a deployment of narratology in contexts where readers lack specific knowledge and might therefore be tempted to judge prematurely, to cast aside a book, or to look down on an action. A consistent attention to focalization, both present and

---

19. Inspired by the philosophy of images as embodied and moving by Henri Bergson, I have developed the idea that images move by definition. An extensive argument in *Thinking in Film*; a very short version in "Art Moves."

absent, instead promotes an exciting discovery of new visions, imaginative and enriching. If we want our students to be politically aware and ethically sensitive, this is the best breeding ground for such attitudes.

WORKS CITED

Adorno, T. W. *Minima Moralia: Reflections from Damaged Life*. 1951. Trans. E. F. N. Jephcott. London: Verso, 2006.

Attwell, David. "Race in Disgrace." *Interventions* 4.3 (2002): 331–41.

Bal, Mieke. "Art Moves." *Migration: Contemporary Art from India*. Arken Bulletin (2013): 25–29.

———. *Death and Dissymmetry: The Politics of Coherence in the Book of Judges*. Chicago: University of Chicago Press, 1988.

———. *In Medias Res: Inside Nalini Malani's Shadow Plays*. Ostfildern: Hatje Cantz, 2016.

———. "Masterly Maxims." Response to *An Aesthetic Education*, by Gayatri Chakravorty Spivak. *PMLA* 129.3 (May 2014): 491–97.

———. *Narratology: Introduction to the Theory of Narrative*. Toronto: University of Toronto Press, 2017.

———. *Thinking in Film: The Politics of Video Installation According to Eija-Liisa Ahtila*. London: Bloomsbury, 2013.

———. *Travelling Concepts in the Humanities: A Rough Guide*. Toronto: University of Toronto Press, 2002.

Bal, Mieke, Jonathan Crewe, and Leo Spitzer, eds. *Acts of Memory: Cultural Recall in the Present*. Hanover: University Press of New England, 1999.

Bal, Mieke, and Miguel Hernández Navarro. *2MOVE: Video, Art, Migration*. Murcia: Cendeac, 2008.

———, eds. *Art and Visibility in Migratory Culture*. Thamyris /Intersecting: Place, Sex and Race (Book 23). Amsterdam: Rodopi, 2011.

Barthes, Roland. *Camera Lucida: Reflections on Photography*. Trans. Richard Howard. New York: Hill and Wang, 1981.

Benjamin, Walter. "Theses on the Philosophy of History." 1940. *Illuminations: Essays and Reflections*. Ed. Hannah Arendt. Trans. Harry Zohn. New York: Schocken, 1968. 253–64.

Bryson, Norman. *Vision and Painting: The Logic of the Gaze*. London: Macmillan, 1983.

Deleuze, Gilles. *Cinema 2: The Time-Image*. Trans. Hugh Tomlinson and Robert Galeta. Minneapolis: University of Minnesota Press, 1989.

Genette, Gérard. *Narrative Discourse: An Essay in Method*. Trans. Jane E. Lewin. Foreword by Jonathan Culler. Ithaca: Cornell University Press, 1983.

———. *Narrative Discourse Revisited*. Trans. Jane E. Lewin. Ithaca: Cornell University Press, 1988.

Hirsch, Marianne, ed. *The Familial Gaze*. Hanover: University Press of New England, 1999.

Hirsch, Marianne. *Family Frames: Photography, Narrative, and Postmemory*. Cambridge: Harvard University Press, 1997.

Huyssen, Andreas. *William Kentridge, Nalini Malani: The Shadow Play as Medium of Memory*. Milan: Charta, 2013.

Lahiri, Jhumpa. *The Namesake*. 2003. London: Fourth Estate, 2012.

McDonald, Peter D. "Disgrace Effects." *Interventions* 4.3 (2002): 321–30.

Mitchell, W. J. T. *Iconology: Image, Text, Ideology*. Chicago: University of Chicago Press, 1986.

Rothberg, Michael. *Multidirectional Memory: Remembering the Holocaust in the Age of Decolonization*. Stanford: Stanford University Press, 2009.

Schwenger, Peter. *Fantasm and Fiction: On Textual Envisioning*. Stanford: Stanford University Press, 1999.

Silverman, Kaja. *The Threshold of the Visible World*. New York: Routledge, 1996.

Spivak, Gayatri Chakravorty. *An Aesthetic Education in the Eera of Globalization*. Cambridge MA: Harvard University Press 2012.

———. *A Critique of Postcolonial Reason: Towards a History of the Vanishing Present*. Cambridge MA: Harvard University Press 1999.

Stengers, Isabelle, ed. *D'une science à l'autre: des concepts nomades*. Paris: Editions du Seuil, 1987.

van Alphen, Ernst. *Art in Mind: How Images Shape Contemporary Thought*. Chicago: University of Chicago Press, 2005.

CHAPTER 13

The Addressee Function, or the Uses of Narratological Laity

Lessons of Khasak

DIVYA DWIVEDI

READING, and more generally audienceship, play a constitutive role in narrativity: if narrative (diegesis) is telling, it implies the one who is told (dative) as much as the one who tells. Just like narratives, narratologies too, as indeed literary theories in general, have their addressees. If narratives have both actual readers and the implied reader or authorial audience, then narratology too has both readers and implied addressees: those who read/ follow/study narratology on the one hand, and on the other that theoretical entity who is the subject of the act of reading as theorized correspondingly and into whose shoes the reader of that narratology would have to step in order to follow its line of reasoning. Hence, *Paideia* is implicit in one way or another in both narratology and in narrative, and is embedded in the concept of reading and in the theoretical question: *What is reading, the phenomenon of which the reader is the subject?* Is it a single and continuous temporal phenomenon for a single subject? Is it a qualitatively distinct act extended over a single discrete reading of a literary text, of which there can be two kinds, the qualitatively lay reading and the qualitatively expert one? Or can a single act be said to comprise rereadings by the same subject of the same text or—why not—of what Roland Barthes calls "intertext"? The narratological concept of *reader* implicitly comprehends the reader of narrative in his or her simultaneous capacity as the implied pupil of narratology, even if a particular narrative theory does not treat the former as the latter, and even if an actual reader of literature, often termed "lay,"[1] may or may not engage in reflections on a text's features as narrative.

The relationship between narratology, the reader of narrative, and the narratological addressee can be studied under the title "addressee function," which shall be proposed in what follows as a counterpart of what Foucault called the "author function," that is, a relation to the figure of the author as a discursive property of certain discourses that is the ideological product of specific discursive operations. It is ideological insofar as it limits the possibilities of meaning, in this case narrative and literary meaning, by assigning the origin of discourse, the author, as the source of meaning. However, in addition to the author function, we must identify another discursive property, the addressee function, which certain discourses possess and which limits the possibilities of meaning. Narratology had been held to be a descriptive and scientific discourse for a long time, but it is not ideologically neutral, as becomes clear precisely in the ideological salience of the addressee function and its specifically pedagogical dimension in narratology. Different narrative theories posit the figure of the addressee in terms of a certain kind of reader or readers who are more or less privileged in relation to narrative meaning, and are discursive constructs that have a pedagogical and an ideological function. The ideological function of education is central to postcolonial literary theory as a critique of the epistemic enterprise of colonialism, of which literary education formed a core.[2] The locus of the postcolonial literary analysis is the play of voices and the generation of subjectivities in the text, for which draw on narratological concepts of narrator, character, and implied author and implied reader, concepts that pertain to both the author function and the addressee function. A comparison of interventions in rhetorical narratology and natural narratology (as a part of cognitivist approaches) with those in postcolonialist literary theory, which are all pursuits within "narrative inquiry,"[3] reveals the specific operations through which these constructs are obtained as well as their respective pedagogical and ideological valence. The comparison shows not so much the superiority of one theoretical approach over the other two as the ideological operation of an addressee function in each. Close analysis of voice and narration in O. V. Vijayan's novel *The Legends of Khasak* reveals a resistance to this ideological control over narrative meaning that takes the form of a special kind of focalization, which will be called *dispersive focalization*.

---

1. Other terms used to relativize the lay reader are the "professional reader" or the "competent reader."

2. See Vishwanathan; Trivedi.

3. See Huber et al. for an overview of the rise of narrative-based interdisciplinary approach to pedagogy as such, as a thinking with narratives.

THE ADDRESSEE FUNCTION

Every narratological model can be analyzed for the way it positions *its* addressee on the one hand, and the concept of "reader" it has on the other. It may assign two different reader profiles to each, as is the case with the distinction between lay and theoretical levels of engagement with narratives. The addressee of such a model is either a narratologist or an apprentice of narratology, be it an undergraduate or graduate student, while the concept of reader comprehends lay propensities. Another model may conceptualize the reader as the locus traced by an educational journey that arrives at the level of understanding to be possessed by the addressee implicit in the abstraction and sophistication of that model, and the actual reader of such a narratological treatise might, in fact, happen to be someone who makes that journey. Two different pedagogical possibilities correspond to these contrasting narratological models.

Now, to say that narratology confirms/dispels the reader's laity is to attribute a kind of authorial agency to this type of discourse that is read alongside narratives. Yet doubtless, the narratologist is not an author like Marcel Proust.[4] Pointing out in "What Is an Author?" that some discourses such as letters, contracts, or anonymous texts posted publicly may have a signer, a guarantor, or an editor, respectively, but not an *author,* Foucault defines the "author function" as a "characteristic of the mode of existence, circulation and functioning of *certain* discourses within a society," though not all (211; emphasis added). Further, the author function is not the same across all these latter discourses, and different kinds of authorship are assigned to literary works (for example, Shakespeare), scientific theories and knowledge (physics, structural linguistics), historiography (Pliny), and even a scientific discourse (Freud, Marx) (Foucault, "Author" 216–19).

> There exist properties or relationships peculiar to discourse (not reducible to the rules of grammar and logic) and one must use these to distinguish the major categories of discourse. The relationship (or nonrelationship) with an author, and the different forms this relationship takes, constitute—in quite a visible manner—one of these discursive properties. (220)

Narratology, having its origins in structuralism, might be categorized as a scientific discursivity, but the theoretical subjectivation of the lay reader suggests that its pedagogical and hence ideological dimension cannot be confined

---

4. Unless of course he or she is Jorge Luis Borges, or Roland Barthes writing on Roland Barthes.

to an analysis of the internal consistency of its concepts and arguments. To study the pedagogical and ideological dimensions, it is necessary to investigate another discursive property or relationship that belongs to discourse alongside the author function, which, for Foucault, results from "a series of specific and complex operations" and "is an ideological product" (216, 221).

It is conceivable that certain discourses are also endowed with something like an *addressee function*: another characteristic of the mode of existence, circulation, and functioning of certain discourses within a society, namely the discursive property or relationship with what Jakobson would call the receiver (66–67). To keep the parallel with the author function, the addressee functions of narratology and of narratives would, at first glance, be different—as are those of fictional and nonfictional narratives, individual and community narratives, and what are called grand narratives. However, we will see that they overlap and get entangled in some respects since narratology, in identifying and conceptualizing different categories of authors and addressees, concerns itself with precisely the addressee function of narratives: author, implied author, narrator, character-narrator, narratee, implied reader, authorial audience, real reader, competent, and of course lay reader.[5] In accordance with their respective conceptions of narration, different narrative theories propose different sets of addressees, and it is in the dynamics between the elements of each set that the different operations that obtain their respective addressee function shall be discerned. Somewhat in the way that Jakobson's "conative function" (however it may be implemented) is the "*Einstellung*," that is, the disposition, "set,"[6] or "orientation" of the message "toward" the receiver and not the receiver him- or herself, and hence is a function in the message, so should the proposed addressee function of narratives as well as of narrative theories be understood as their *Einstellung* towards the reader and the student of narrative (Jakobson 66). The difference that the Foucauldian emphasis makes is that this function need not be "set" (*eingestellt*) through inscription in discourse, that is, through textual signs such as indexicals, imperatives, or the vocative case. There are other operations of narratological discourse that are of equal ideological and political significance. The figure of the reader has been given a context-bound political valence, as for instance by Gayatri Chakravorty Spivak, whose program for an aesthetic education to supplement cultural politics draws upon (a crippled version of) the concept of implied reader in order to say that the "death of (the authority of) the author . . . is the

---

5. For an overview of these distinctions, see Nünning; Prince.
6. Not in the set-theoretical sense used in the previous sentence, but in the sense of setting something, fitting it together to make it function in specific ways.

birth of the reader" (12). The birth of the reader is also the birth of a new discursive property. How is the reader *subjectivated* in narratological education?

THE AUTHORIAL AUDIENCE

The authorial audience is a concept in rhetorical narratology that invokes both author and audience in a text-based operation that is avowedly pedagogical: the book teaches the reader. The basic definition of narrative according to recent versions of rhetorical narratology is "somebody telling somebody on some occasion and for some purpose that something has happened" (Phelan and Rabinowitz 323). The concept of narrative voice is engaged at two ends: not only "who speaks" but also who hears (Phelan, "Voice" 137). Insofar as the effect of the text as a whole (to its reader) is to espouse certain beliefs, values, and "norms and choices," the imputed source of these values and this effect is an author-image constructed in the reading, which Wayne Booth first called the implied author (1983 [1961]).[7] At the same time, the narrative comprises various voices generated through selection and crafting of diverse narrational techniques in the text, any of which, or a combination of which, an actual reader may identify or sympathize with. These voices could be the speech of narrator(s), character(s), and the idiomaticity and register deployed in what F. K. Stanzel calls the figural narrative situation (where an overt narrator is absent),[8] but also the distances, divergences, and dissonances between sets of these entities. Values are read, not simply as corresponding to each entity (representing his or her standpoint, as it were) but, more interestingly, in this active distancing of one voice or position from another, and the erection thereby of hierarchies. The distances privilege certain positions and undermine others: they are evaluative. Thus, actual readers may have different readings, yet rhetorical narratology trains its addressee to read more and more carefully to isolate other voices of a given narrative and then attend to the distance between them and other voices, and between the values each bespeaks (Phelan, "Voice" 140). As a result, a rich array of unreliabilities confronts the reader in the course of arriving at the implied author: misreporting, misinterpreting, misregarding, misevaluating (145). Each of these is a mutually affecting assessment of the distance between pairs of narrative agents, and a demand is placed on the reader to actively measure the distance (the *mis-*), in other words, unreliability, in order to arrive—the place of arrival is the "authorial audience" that hears

---

7. See also Shen for an overview of "implied author" and the diverse definitions of and debates on the term.

8. See Stanzel 141.

the double voicing (141). This is the "hypothetical audience" that the author, as the intelligence (and intention) responsible for the textual design, bears in mind (though of course, by author is meant here implied author and its ideal reader) (Rabinowitz 126). The ideal or "implied reader" upon which the operation of unreliability depends is, as Wolf Schmid points out, "ultimately one of the attributes of the concrete reader's reconstructed implied author" (51–52).

This minimalist sketch of rhetorical narratology nevertheless shows that the gaps generated by such double-voiced narrative discourses and conceptualized as "unreliability" serve to trace the twisted path laid out by the text and its devices, leading the reader on a learning curve toward authorial audienceship. The path is not a reliable one, but rather a more difficult education whose pedagogical tool is unreliability. Who teaches?—that which Phelan calls narrative progression:

> I define narrative progression as the synthesis of a textual dynamics governing the movement of a narrative from beginning through middle to end and a readerly dynamics consisting of the authorial audience's trajectory of responses to that movement. ("Cognitive Narratology" 310)

Instead of a platonic maieutics wherein the soul undergoes an assisted anamnesis, the reader in rhetorical narrative theory of "unreliability" navigates a web of narrative distances that is potential and must be actualized by a reader who thereby actualizes him- or herself *qua* reader. Since the narrative distances between voices are also ideological, ethical, and political, according to Phelan, the narrative strategies entail a pedagogy of reading ideology itself, which would remain invisible if the distance did not emerge as distances. The reading of distances clearly introduces distances within the reader him- or herself, prompting a journey from values hitherto held to their defamiliarization. Since the rhetorical theory of unreliability provides general concepts (such as implied author, authorial audience, narrative audience, narrator, character, misreporting, misinterpreting, misevaluating, etc.) to designate the nature of narrative as communicative act, it educates its addressee formally to attune him- or herself to specific narratives: "we move from narrative to theory and then back to narrative in a continuous loop" ("Voice" 137). In this conceptual system, the reader of literary narratives is theorized as a dynamic and active element in a communicative act that can thus be seen as a pedagogical act.

The addressee function here can be described, following Foucault, as the set of operations of which "reading" is not the source but the result. No one segment of the readerly dynamics or the narrative progression is a reading in itself. Rather, integrated conceptually, it yields the idea of a journey made by the actual reader toward becoming the authorial audience. This is not simply an actual journey but a discursive construct that puts specifically *defined* entities in a relationship: implied author, which is the author function of narrative fiction; the story and narration (see Shen); and the actual reader's context- and identity-dependent construal of textual cues.

THE LAY READER

A different addressee function obtains in natural narratology, which is part of the cognitive approach to narrative. Monika Fludernik distinguishes between the reader's level and the theoretical level on the basis of the approach that each has to the narratorial person. The narrator is seen as an element strictly of natural narratives, that is, oral, spontaneous, conversational storytelling, so that any notion of the narrator of a written text, that too a fictional one, is an extrapolation from natural narratives to more complex ones like novels. Readers perform such "interpretative moves" even in texts without "linguistic markers signalling the presence of a speaker (*I*, deictic elements, expressive markers, stylistic foregrounding)" ("New Wines in Old Bottles" 622). This extension of the real-world schema of (oral) telling to such a (written) text by the reader is

> an unwarranted application of the communicational mode to narrative *texts,* to *writing*. . . . This weakness of the communicational model, however, relates to the *theoretical* level of analysis exclusively. In terms of readers' reactions to individual texts, the tendency to attribute stylistic features to a hypothetical narrator persona and/or a character *is a simple fact.* However, this fact (that readers are led by the illusionism of the narrative to impose a communicational framework on the text) does not necessitate the stipulation of a narrator persona on the theoretical level at all. After all, narratologists are then repeating readers' interpretative moves on a theoretical level, without due consideration of the illusionism involved. (622; emphasis added)

That is, this extrapolation is a fact: the natural tendency of the readers to entertain the illusion of there being a narrator even when there is none, a tendency that owes to the human cognitive faculty of narrativization. In contrast to Phelan's loop, an altogether different kind of gap emerges here between the reading and the theory. The reader can never realize what the theory recognizes, given that Fludernik prohibits the theorist from stepping in the reader's shoes; by implication, the reader who steps in the shoes of the theorist would cease to "read," and hence, to remain the reader is to be a lay reader. This gap between the lay reader and the theorist is posited on the basis of a concept of reading as narrativizing, and is "closed" in the *theory of reading*, not in the reading activity:

> I have myself proposed to close this gap between theory and practice by introducing the term narrativization. When readers read narrative texts, they project real-life parameters into the reading process and . . . treat the text as a real-life instance of narrating. It then turns out to be a useful strategy to hypostasize the existence of a narrator figure who is telling us the story and whose presence and existence seem to be vouchsafed for by the stylistic features of authorial diction. (633)

The narratologist's theoretical work is to posit this illusionism as obtaining in fact for the reader but not for herself. The illusion is then not the kind that gets dispelled by the theory that would explain its generation. Rather, the theory here *generates* the illusion from the reality itself, by positing it as the reality of reading, namely, our narrativizing faculty. The gap is closed in the sense that it is confirmed. Even when experimental narratives defy the conventional schemas (of telling and viewing), it is only by new schemas, which are actually new mixtures of old ones, that narratologists can explain them. Thus, while the communicational model of narrator is limited and illusionist, no alternative theory of the narrator or narration need be pursued since the illusionism continues to explain the reader.

> It does not really *matter* to a reader who is speaking . . . who sees or who speaks because the entire point of the narrative is to give us a portrait of each character's motivations and thoughts. The concern is to get the optimum of information by whatever means. (Fludernik 636)

Narratology need not bring the reader to a different theoretical awareness of narrator or narrative function.[9] The reader is the subject of the illusion or of

---

9. Manfred Jahn demonstrates the illogicality of treating the narrators as an illusion in the case of omniscient narration while treating the figural narrative situation (focalized by a character) as an illusion of immediate access to the character's mind. If the former involves a theoretically nonexistent narrator, the latter would involve the opposite, and the same theory based on natural narratives would not be able to accommodate both illusions. Jahn suggests that "the truly unwarranted move is to hypostatize a corrective level of narratological abstraction that is somehow superior to what the reader sees a text as being, doing, and meaning" (697). However, for Fludernik the theoretical level is only correct and not "corrective" since

the subjective apparatus that makes illusions alone possible, even though these illusions are taken as the *stuff* of the sense of reality and of ordinary experiences that lay readers, and people in general, make.

In a related and cognitively inspired narratological proposal, David Herman and Lisa Zunshine emphasize that readings of narratives are embedded in people's mind-reading propensities and the habit (indeed, the cognitive architecture) of entertaining theories of the intentions behind others' actions and behavior that they carry forward in their reading of narratives.

Similar to narrativization in Fludernik, a reader's theory of mind, or ToM, is an operation that is effortless in the sense that we "'intuitively' connect people's behavior to their mental states," and it "enables most of us to constrain the range of possible interpretations" of characters, narrators, and other narrative segments (Zunshine 277, 271). Implied as well as real authors are unavoidable given our propensities to posit what Daniel Dennett calls *intentional stances*. Analogous to the gap between lay and theoretical levels in Fludernik is the difference between lay and professional concerns: "a flagrantly 'wrong' . . . interpretation" by a lay reader "is still 'effortless' from the point of view of cognitive psychologists" since we do correlate conduct with ToM (Zunshine 276). Further, the interpretations are limited to a range by the operation of "processing" levels of intentionality embedded recursively ("I believe that you think that she believes that he thinks that X") and mostly cannot exceed four levels due to cognitive overload (278–79). The effortlessness posited here is a name for the operations that define the addressee function in this cognitivist narratological paradigm. Condemned to illusionism, the reader in such theories is then a thorough subject, thoroughly subject to his condition. The theoretical work of the addressee function in this narratological discourse (underpinned by a loan from that of cognitive science) prohibits the reader from escaping his illusionist level/dwelling to enter the theoretical level.

IDEOLOGY AND THE ADDRESSEE FUNCTION

The addressee function or the subject of reading can be approached qua function in the same way as the author function. Foucault asks us "to grasp the subject's points of insertion, modes of functioning, and system of dependencies" and to see the author function as "an ideological product, since we present him as the opposite of his historically real function . . . the ideological figure by

---

readers develop illusions based on their cognitive propensities and not on "direct access to any real facts, either of the world at large, or of a text," which might be pointed out as a corrective (Jahn 697).

which one marks the manner in which we fear the proliferation of meaning" ("Author" 221–22). This is particularly evident in the idea of the implied author as an author-image to which the design of the text is ascribed. Its counterpart in the addressee functions of the implied reader or authorial audience, and of the lay or folk reader too, has to be recognized. The theoretical positing of the reader is the (other) source of signification (besides the author) precisely; this manner (the operations) in which one "limits, excludes and chooses" and practices "thrift" (221) with meaning has to be examined in the cases of both the author and the reader, whence the need to treat them as *functions*.

Fludernik treats the lay projection of narrative voice as issuing from the common sense of real-life parameters (623). This restriction to common sense secures the reader, and to that extent literature, ideologically since it secures them to the realm of the familiar, the conventional, and the repeating, even if expanding, script or frame. It is the lack of freedom to make a different kind of sense than the one prevailing (especially in one's own cognitive architecture). The addressee function of "reader" here refers to the one thus subjected ideologically in being defined by a restricted conception of nature and reality. Our literary and narrative illusions are the fond offspring of our reality or our realism. It is all in the family. On the other hand, Phelan treats "voice as learnable synesthesia" ("Voice" 138). However, this education is circumscribed by the "authorial audience" and "implied author," which readers may or may not reach. Luc Herman and Bart Vervaeck survey the various readerly uses of implied author as "really all about . . . authorizing your own reading. . . . The idealized ego of a real reader . . . [is] an enhanced projection of one's own reading habits—in cognitive terms: one's frames and scripts" (13–14). Even, or precisely, when this subject position accommodates persons from different sociohistorical contexts (that is, actual readers), it remains priorly determined by their identity, their context, no matter how contingent or historical. This contextualism of the narratological category of "reader" does not change the fact that this representational concept of "reader" is a specific regimentation of reading as a movement. Is the alternative, then, to study real readers and acts of reading empirically, freeing them from the idealizations proposed by narratologists as professional readers? Marissa Bortolussi and Peter Dixon propose to do this by positing textual features found by "trained observers" (professional readers? narratologists?) and empirically studying "reader constructions" relative to these features (28). To do this, they further posit the "statistical reader," which is "aggregate measures of groups of individuals . . . to provide insights into the general characteristics of populations of readers" obtained by drawing on "standard data analysis procedures" (34, 44). Here is yet another kind of installation of a difference between trained and general reading obtained through operations combining professional determination of a text and statistical determination of reading.

Narratology might not contribute to the containment of the proliferation of meaning in narratives in the case of any reader other than a professional reader or, of course, an apprentice. However, this does not imply that simply blocking out the theoretical level would make the nonprofessional readers safe from the ideological operations of the addressee or author functions. Blocking theory in a literature classroom would be difficult; additionally, education in narratives (and even in reflecting on their narrative structure) is not the preserve of professional domains, but is set into motion in the non-simple event of reading itself, even outside the classroom. Reading has been studied at macro levels (discourse-level processes: narrative features, epistemic background, construction of meanings and situational models) and micro levels (lower-level processes: grammatical parsing, word choice, syntax) of text comprehension and as a multilayered combination of the two. The subjectivation of reading through those addressee functions should not, however, be seen as a failure or a falsity in comparison with the true conception of the movement of reading in engagement with narratives. The functions as discursive properties or relationships are to be identified by Foucault as parts of what makes a discourse work and produce knowledge and regular "effects of power" (*Power/Knowledge* 131). We do read in the ways theorized above and we do make sense of narrative and of literature in these ways, but not exclusively or permanently. Instead of a rectification, the successful working of a discursive regime (of narratology), which does generate kinds of power/knowledge in relation to narratives, should be studied for the points where they cease (rather than fail) to function and where other potential movements begin to leak away.

VOICES OF KHASAK AND DISPERSIVE FOCALIZATION

O. V. Vijayan's 1969 novel *Khasakinte Itihasam* occasions such a point of leakage. In 1997 he translated it into English as *The Legends of Khasak*. First published serially in *Mathrubhumi Weekly* from 1968, "this novel literally revolutionized Malayalam fiction. [It] created a new readership with a novel sensibility and transformed the Malayali imagination forever," as the poet and critic K. Satchidanandan recalled in his obituary for Vijayan in 2005 (para. 3). The protagonist Ravi is a young college dropout driven by an unnamed restlessness to suspend the ordinary goals of educated middle-class families. He foregoes a doctoral position at Princeton to seek a "sarai," literally an inn, a halting station in a remote village called Khasak in the northern Kerala district of Palakkad, where he becomes the *maash* (master) at the new one-teacher District Board school. Ravi immerses himself in the ways of the villagers—the legends of places and local traditions, the stories of people's pasts, and their current conflicts—while the villagers react to the novelty of his figure as well as of the school in different ways that, in the course of the narrative, adumbrate what a school inspector during the annual visit to Ravi's school calls "the lost village" (Vijayan 79). The stagnant village is, in fact, rent through with clashing paradigms of education. The mullah's madrassa and the astrologer Gopalu Panikker's Sanskrit school are rivaled by the untouchable Kelan's upper-primary school for English and math. The District Board school and its new *maash* are promoted initially by Khasak's feudal chief, Sivaraman Nair, who tries to consolidate the Hindus against the Muslims but begins to find an obstacle in Ravi. Then there are the lessons that Ravi submits to: "there are far too many classes in my school for any teacher to handle" (155).

The narrative would appear to be dominated by Ravi's time in Khasak, but it strays too often to focalize the residents and even outsiders who might come there at times, such as the inspector, the wandering mendicants called *Pandarams*, and, of course, Ravi himself. Several narrated events completely exclude Ravi, making it untenable to consider *Khasak* as essentially Ravi's quest. If the experiences and stories revealed through this dispersed focalization can be taken together as "the legends of Khasak," then it can be said that the narrative is focalized through Khasak itself, which therefore cannot be considered merely as the space of the narrative, the storyworld or the setting, but perhaps as a kind of character, the protagonist even, albeit not a "social mind," that is, "joint, group, shared, or collective, as opposed to intramental, or individual or private thought . . . also known as socially distributed . . . cognition" (Palmer 41).[10] The relationship of the narration to the educational paradigms and the restlessness that reigns over the lost traveler and the lost village is illuminating for considerations of the addressee functions in narrative theory.

Nizam Ali, a resident of Khasak whose origins are unknown and whose many transformations leading him in and out of the village suggest a restlessness nearly equaling Ravi's, occupies several chapters of the novel where the transpirations never intersect Ravi's story. He appears out of nowhere to the old mullah of the mosque and the shrine of Sayed Mian Sheikh, to whose legend Khasak traces its origins (and which embraces Arabic influences as well as local lower-caste and outcaste cults that are rejected by increasingly

---

10. In Vijayan's novel, however, the idea of Khasak goes beyond that of a social unit by focalizing the very landscape that witnesses the constant breaking away of characters from what might be the social mind by means of dispersive focalization, as will be seen ahead.

sanskritizing Hinduism and reformist Islam[11])—a teenage vagabond snake-catcher whom the mullah adopts as his successor following the legend and custom. There is an unnamed rebelliousness about him that is suggested at first in a passage focalized on the mullah: Ali's "hair [is] more voluptuous than" that of the mullah's own wife or his daughter Maimoona. Maimoona too is bewitched by Ali's curls, and Ali himself gazes at their reflection in the mirror, forgetting to call the prayers as instructed by the mullah. The hair, which the mullah feels "reaching out to him in vile temptation," is also a metonymy for the growing attraction between Ali and Maimoona, and of the mullah's growing jealousy for his own daughter (20). It is on them that the mullah turns his ire, but refusing to shave his locks like a good Muslim, Ali becomes a beedi roller in Attar's factory in the neighboring town of Koomankavu, and rises to start a rival beedi factory. When the mullah forces Maimoona's marriage to an old widower, Ali returns in cold rage to work for Attar and then becomes the leader of its miniscule workers' union, which the budding local communist party office tries to hijack as the "new proletariat" (29). When "a dozen men marched in procession, the first procession Koomankavu had seen," a strike followed by a worker getting beaten by the factory owner results in the arrest of the owner as well as Nizam Ali, the union leader (29).

> Nizam Ali lay beaten black and blue inside a police cell. He rose with the dawn winds in a slow resurrection. The charges against him were grievous—collusion with a foreign power [the USSR], war against the state, incitement to murder.... Through the rhythms of pain and blankness, this question nagged him—what were the police doing in his war with the mullah? (29)

He asks for audience with the inspector of the tiny rural station:

> "Yajaman," Nizam Ali said, "I quit all this."
> The Inspector eyed the prisoner with curiosity.
> "Wisdom dawns late," he said, "isn't that so?"
> "Yes, Yajaman. Such is maya."

---

11. For an overview of specific ways in which these practices related to sacred groves (*kavu*, as in the town Kooman-kavu) from pre-brahmanical times became caste-marked and have undergone postcolonial transformations shaped by reformist discourses, see J. R. Freeman; R. Freeman; Osella and Osella, *Social Mobility*. For an overview of transformations in the case of Muslim communities with their caste distinctions, see Osella and Osella, "Islamism." The autochthonous deities of Kerala and their temples are being converted apace to the mainstream Hindu gods and goddesses conformant with north India, parallel to the growth of the Hindu nationalist and fundamentalist organization RSS in Kerala.

This was surely a political detenu with a difference. The Inspector smiled, "Maya?"

"Yes, Yajaman. The unreal aspect of things. But the maya has ended. The Old One visited me in the cell last night."

"The Old One? In the cell?"

"Yes, Yajaman, Sayed Mian Sheikh."

The Inspector turned to the constable.

"What is this I hear? Someone in the cell, without permission . . ."

The constable was puzzled. Nizam Ali hastened to intervene, "Yajaman, it is a djinn, a ghost . . ."

The Inspector sighed in relief, leaned back in his chair and spoke to the constable in admonition, "You men will never learn! Must you beat them on the head?" Turning to Nizam Ali who stood in a trance, the Inspector said, "Sit down on the chair. Now will you make us lock you up again?"

"Insha Allah, there will be no more trouble on my part. Mian Sheikh will guide me wisely."

"Who? The ghost?"

"Yes, Yajaman."

"Now listen, Ali, I shall read out this statement to you. Will you sign it?"

"Yes, Yajaman."

The Inspector took out a frayed yellow sheet from a pile of government stationery, and wrote out a document for the renegade: I, Nizam Ali, do hereby pledge to eschew violence and to work for a change of government only through constitutional means, and . . . [. . .]

When the thumb impression was made, Nizam Ali said hesitantly,

"A request . . . [. . .] Below my name and thumb impression [. . .] Add the word Khazi."

"Certainly, but what does that mean?"

"The Old One ordained me last night, I am his Khazi from now on."

The Inspector felt expansive as one does when dealing with the gently insane.

"As you wish, Ali," [. . .] And he turned to the constable, "Get him some herbal oil and bathe him in plenty of cold water."

Nizam Ali cast his dusky eyes on the Inspector and chanted a benign spell, "*Al Hamdo Lillahe Rabbil Aalemeen. Ar Rahmanir Rahim. Malike Yaumiddin.*" (30–31)

In the turn of events and this subsequent exchange, various discrepant voices and discourses talk past each other and nevertheless all seems to end well for each concerned party.

To isolate some layers of this narrative segment: (1) The materialist communist party members quote "the spectre" to the receptive unionists whose reverence for the spirits of the *kavus* accommodates all ghosts and gods of all religions (29). (2) One of the latter, (the erstwhile subaltern) Nizam Ali, cites the ghost of Khasak's patron saint, Sayed Mian Sheikh, to the patronizing town inspector, who represents the postcolonial state's juridical and penal function, and is mainly concerned with whether Nizam Ali is "gently insane" or actionable. (3) The inspector recites the release document—which establishes Nizam Ali as the subject of the law and the Indian constitution—to the receptive "detenu," who, though he wonders about the police's role "in his war with the mullah," *assumes* the practices of the state's institutional system (namely, prison torture and the thumb impression above the new title "Khazi" on government stationery) to become a very different subject ordained by another authority: Khasak's first *qazi*[12] and tamer of local spirits. No character *reads* (in the ToM sense) the other's mind accurately, and indeed does not so much misread as locate the other(s) as a subject in a discourse in which he already occupies a specific subject position. The receptivity in each stratum nestling within this single exchange has less to do with intelligibility than with what Foucault called a "system of acceptability" ("What Is Critique?" 53).[13] Only, the strata here are fragments, overlapping and clashing but not consolidating.

The narration selectively focalizes each character as well as collective agents like the communist party, the workers, and onlookers of the nipped revolution, and the idioms and registers of their speech and of the focalizing passages in the narration overlap, preventing the extrapolation of a narratorial voice from the narrative voice. Rather, the focalization is *dispersive*. For instance, focalization presents Nizam Ali's experience in the cell and his bewilderment amidst his anguish, but his exchange with the inspector is externally focalized, that is, described from the outside, focusing on his speech and behavior, without any indication of his intention, plan, and real feelings. Does he really believe the Old One visited him or is it a tactical pretense that puts him in the category of the incredulous, like the inspector and the communist party? And if it is a tactic in "his war against the mullah"—the most definite statement of Nizam Ali's inner action in this moment and thus

---

12. A judge ruling over all legal matters of Muslims in accordance with the Sharia; but Nizam actually begins practicing rites of *mantravādam*, that is, "essentially contingent and private rites of controlling, marshalling, or exorcising various gods and demons" (R. Freeman 322).

13. According to Foucault, "Each society has its régime of truth, its general politics of truth: that is, the types of discourse it accepts and makes function as true" (*Power/Knowledge* 131).

an interpretation of the telos of his repeated insurrections and resurrections provided by the very focalization—does the focalization, nevertheless, not withhold that over which the war rages, and that which in each antagonist wars with the other? The preceding and following chapters of the novel contain indications that the answer is not, at least not exclusively, his love for Maimoona. Suggestions of his relationship with a "lower-caste" woman, Neeli (66–67), his sorcery and austerities (61, 149), his reconciling with the mullah later on and yet becoming "agonized, ecstatic" at the mullah's death from cancer (152), and most enigmatically his "gazing into Maimoona's cracked mirror . . . carefully tending the incipient curls" (20) that defy institutional Islam: what upheavals quiver in this deceptively revelatory thought of "his war against the mullah"? The focalization is dispersive because this phrase, which apparently presents his inner action, in fact suspends the focalization on him. It mentions the war but does not interpret it or spell its intentionality. It simultaneously absents both the character's inner action and the possibility of narratorial knowledge.

The inspector, again, is focalized in the response: "This was surely a political detenu with a difference. The Inspector smiled, 'Maya?.'" The operative words are "this" and "surely" and the phrase "a political detenu with a difference." The elevated diction of the phrase lends it a satirical quality in keeping with the inspector's self-congratulatory and patronizing indulgence, but such diction recurs in the external focalization of the inspector as he "wrote out a document for the *renegade*." Here, "renegade," like "detenu," could be the inspector's gloss but also carries over from the earlier narration of Nizam Ali's waking up in the cell: "He rose with the *dawn* winds in a slow *resurrection*" (where the focalization is uncertain between internal and external) or "cast his *dusky* eyes on the Inspector and chanted a *benign* spell" (external focalization), and the earlier description of Ali through the metonymy of his "*incipient* curls" (focalization external).[14] Throughout the novel, the elevated diction is distributed over the two kinds of focalization and with valuations ranging from satirical distance from to metaphysical commentary on a character or event. In the dispersing focalizations, characters cannot be read stably, so that the implied author and the authorial audience cannot be ascertained. Dispersive focalization can be defined as the narrative technique whereby the same verbal segment of a narrative executes multiple focalizations (internal, external, uncertain) that can, moreover, focalize different characters and positions. It stands in contrast to Spivak's proposal of "counterfocalization," namely, that readers should use their imagination to compensate for the absent focalization of certain characters in a

---

14. All emphases in the quoted passages are added.

narrative, for instance of Lucy in Coetzee's *Disgrace,* to reconstruct a politically acceptable implied author of that text (see Bal in this volume; Spivak 323–24). However, this is no more than Zunshine's ToM-based model of reading narratives, since Spivak treats absent focalization as "the failure of reading" and thus equates focalization with reading a character (323).

NARRATIVE EDUCATION, NARRATOLOGICAL EDUCATION

Dispersive focalization is at the heart of *The Legends of Khasak,* which remains an untimely interjection in an unnatural voice in what Vijayan's 1997 afterword called the "post decolonization diglossia" (175). Such untimely interjections initiate a leakage at the subject's—here the addressee function's—point of insertion and circulation in the discourses of both narrative studies and postcolonial studies, since, according to Spivak, the "production of the colonial subject" has "a relationship with the implied reader of British literature" (42). Spivak's theorization of this relationship posits an addressee function whose ideological production needs to be examined as much as do those posited in cognitive and rhetorical narratologies, especially as it derives in certain ways from the latter and also supports her proposal for an aesthetic education that would prepare us "at all cost to enter into another's text" (6). The addressee function of Spivak's postcolonial theory of reading (for the era of globalization) is defined as a double bind, that is, living with contradictory instructions: the colonial as well as postcolonial reader is implicated in the double bind of saying "yes" to (the implied author of) the colonial text that purports to liberate the reader from his or her own cultural politics of class and gender into the metropolitan one of global capital through a literary education, and of also saying "no" to the violence, exploitation, and cultural silencing that the colonial/capitalist intervention perpetrates upon the natives. Spivak sees this as the double bind of an "enabling violation," both poison and cure, and asks for "learning the double bind—not just learning about it" or "learn[ing] to resolve double binds" (41, 1). The addressee function of the pedagogy of the double bind must learn what it already is—a double bind. Whence Spivak speaks of performing the double bind or epistemological performance, that is, "transforming the way in which objects of knowledge are constructed. . . . It is always through such . . . transformations that we begin to approximate the implied reader" (41).

In defining the implied reader, Spivak posits that a narrative text constructs a subject "laid out in the pages of the story," particularly the central character or hero, by figuring forth "a value system" that the successful reader must "identify with" and "relate to" (42, 38, 36). Such a reader assumed in advance by the text is "the implied reader [who] is imagined, even in the most simple reading, according to rudimentary or sophisticated hypotheses about persons, places and times" (37). She might have called it the authorial audience, but the contrast with Phelan and Rabinowitz suggests that it is just as well she does not. For Spivak the reader too assumes this "latent destiny of the text[s]" since "you cannot make sense of anything written or spoken without at least implicitly assuming that it was destined for you" (37). The successful reader approximates the implied reader and hence "literature buys your assent in the most clandestine way" in the service of epistemic or "ideological transformation"; when reading another's text, the implied reader becomes "culturally alien and hegemonic," and the actual reader's assent is alienating while the "identity-in-difference" is exciting and pleasurable (38, 42). The task of literary pedagogy is to "negotiate and make visible what is merely clandestine" in this "alienating cultural indoctrination" of colonial and postcolonial readers of imperialist texts that buy the assent of the colonized to their own colonization (37). Thus, Spivak posits *both* a successful reader who assents to the implied reader in general *and* a "necessarily limited and divided assent to implied readership," which produces "the successful colonial subject," with the latter premised on the former (45). Indeed, her aesthetic-educational project of teaching imperialist and vernacular literature together in order to visibilize clandestine assent and the contradiction of implied readership is premised on a subject position that is the locus of successful identification with the implied reader, an identification she also calls "naïve" (36).

Why assume as fact a weak and "naïve" model of implied readership in the first place, one which is nowhere to be found in narratology? Because Spivak is "in search of a model for the colonial subject as implied reader" (48). This subject could be the classroom student or the naïve lay reader of narratives who, first, identifies with the text, nay, with the here, and second, is confronted with the gaps between the epistemic system of the mother tongue and that of the colonial/global tongue (English):

> The development of readership thrives in the difference and deferment staged between hero and reader. (45)

> Scratching at the epistemic fracture by awkwardly assuming a language to be an "epistemic system." . . . The authority of felicitous implied readership is questioned in such teaching and learning. (52)

The addressee function of Spivak's narrative pedagogy[15] comprises operations that preclude a narratological pedagogy like Phelan's that would reject a naive definition of the implied reader or authorial audience. This is perhaps her own principle of thrift, somewhat similar to Fludernik's, which controls reading in the name of a naïve reader. The addressee of the Spivakian text would have to assent to a naïve concept of implied reader in order to assent to the Spivakian double bind. This oscillation between a naïve and a divided/fractured reading produced by inter-literary study might resemble Phelan's loop of readerly dynamics that brings the actual reader to authorial audienceship, but only superficially. In rhetorical narratology, authorial audience is far from the naïve identification of the initial reader; it is an abstraction set up through a complex reading process that identifies many more voices and values than the hero's, listens to the gaps between them, and also constructs, rather than identifies with, the narrator (a concept absent from Spivak's discussion here). There is a further step not mentioned in the earlier account of the addressee function in Phelan: "authorial audience [is a] role that actual readers can choose to take on. We have the interpretive freedom not to take on these roles" ("Voice" 141). Once actual readers have arrived at the lineaments of the authorial audience after careful consideration of gaps and unreliabilities, they can evaluate this figure and either assent to it or remain distant from it. The freedom to do so is not an attribute that individual readers are priorly armed with but something they may acquire as a result of their increasing attunement to narrative distances, and is hence "interpretive" in a precise sense.

There can be no disagreement with Spivak's claim at the end of her essay that "any number of 'correct' readings can be scrupulously taught here, with some degree of assurance that the reader's space of the mother tongue will secure the quotation marks by way of repeated colonial and postcolonial encounters, among them the one in the [inter-literary] classroom" (52). But there is no conceptual preparation to support this conclusion other than that each contingent reader is circumscribed by his or her language and epistemic system and brings it mechanically into a collision with that of the texts. In order for an aesthetic education to prepare for politics, a narratological education would be needed. But then the aesthetic education might no longer follow Spivak's model of reading. "Access to subjectivity and access to the other's language" require more than the provocation of a multilingual literary classroom, although this is an important provocation (Spivak 53). They require

---

15. She characterizes its yoking of English and vernacular texts as "'inter-literary', not comparative" (52).

study in the arts of subjectivity-construction, which differ across discourses, much as the author and addressee functions differ across discourses. Narrative discourse is distinctively complex in the way it sets up subjectivities, subject positions, and speaker functions. "Multi" dissembles the histories by which modern Indian languages that Spivak calls vernaculars were installed as official languages of provincial administrations, with Hindi acquiring an oppressive national hegemony through state imposition and a Hindu identity through retrospective sanskritization: "Artificially sanskritized 'Hindi,'" which was, as Alok Rai demonstrates, "produced . . . in the exigencies of a *regional* politics [became] available—purified of locality, historical adulteration [by other local dialects, Persian and Arabic], regional colour—as a vehicle of 'national' aspirations of a regional elite. . . . [I]t could only be the 'mother tongue' of the 'nation' which *it* produced" (109–10). It received and continues to receive spirited resistance from the living classical southern Indian language Tamil, which has an unbroken literary speech community of 3,000 years and belongs to a family other than Sanskrit. The untimeliness of Vijayan's debut novel was also the singular language he crafted into Malayalam (itself derived from Tamil) of Palakkad in northern Kerala, where Khasak lies in the novel (for the shaping of modern Malayalam, see Kumar). It did not represent the speech of actual communities, just as the English in his translation by and large does not resemble colloquialisms of Indian or any other English. This makes the leap from language to subjectivity more tenuous.

Not all subjectivities, particularly literary and fictional, are constructed through techniques analogous to those of natural narratives. Not all require a speaking subject once focalization and the unspeakable sentences of free indirect discourse compose the narrative situation, nor does all focalization project an intentional stance. Such assumptions and incumbent operations obtain addressee functions that regulate the proliferation of reading even when they avow the calibrated proliferation of *readings*. Contention over these structures entails careful attention to the narratives and to the theoretical concepts of narrative structures—in other words, a narratological education. Counteracting the principle of thrift or austerity in the addressee functions of respective narratologies, as well as of other theories of literature and narrative, narratological education would lavish time, that of rereading, as well as an unaccountable cost, that of humanities education.[16] The reader is what never stays the same. The reader is the abstract phenomenon of the movement that can be called an education provided we reconceptualize this term. The concept of

---

16. See Brennan.

"reader" would then be the potentiality of the outside of ideology and a narratological category of reader would need to follow from a similar potentiality.

WORKS CITED

Bortolussi, Marissa, and Peter Dixon. *Psychonarratology: Foundations for the Empirical Study of Literary Responses*. Cambridge: Cambridge University Press, 2003.

Boothe, Wayne. *The Rhetoric of Fiction*. Chicago: Chicago University Press, 1983.

Brennan, Tim. "The Education Debate: A Postmortem." *American Literary History* 4.4 (1992): 629–48.

Denette, Daniel. *The Intentional Stance*. Cambridge: MIT Press, 1989.

Fludernik, Monika. "New Wine in Old Bottles? Voice, Focalization, and New Writing." *New Literary History* 32.3 (2001): 619–38.

Foucault, Michel. *Power/Knowledge: Selected Interviews and Other Writings 1972–1977*. Ed. Colin Gordon. Trans. Colin Gordon et al. New York: Pantheon, 1980.

———. "What Is an Author?" *Aesthetics, Method, and Epistemology. Essential Works of Foucault, 1954–1984*, Vol. 2. Ed. James D. Faubion. Trans. Robert Hurley et al. New York: The New Press, 1998. 205–22.

———. "What Is Critique?" *The Politics of Truth*. Ed. Sylvie Lotringer and Lysa Hochroth. New York: Semiotext(e), 1997. 41–83.

Freeman, J. R. "Gods, Groves and the Culture of Nature in Kerala." *Modern Asian Studies* 33.2 (1999): 257–302.

Freeman, Rich. "The *Teyyam* Tradition." *Blackwell Companion to Hinduism*. Ed. Gavin Flood. Oxford: Blackwell, 2003. 307–26.

Herman, David. "Narrative Theory and the Intentional Stance." *Partial Answers* 6.2 (2008): 233–60.

Herman, L., and Bart Vervaeck. "The Implied Author: A Secular Excommunication." *Style* 45.1 (2011): 11–28.

Huber, Janice, Vera Caine, Marilyn Huber, and Pam Steeves. "Narrative Inquiry as Pedagogy in Education: The Extraordinary Potential of Living, Telling, Retelling, and Reliving Stories of Experience." *Review of Research in Education* 37 (2013): 212–42.

Jahn, Manfred. "The Cognitive Status of Textual Voice." *New Literary History* 32.3 (2001): 695–97.

Jakobson, Roman. "Linguistics and Poetics." *Roman Jakobson: Language in Literature*. Ed. Krystyna Pomorska and Stephen Rudy. Cambridge: The Belknap Press of Harvard University Press, 1987. 62–94.

Kumar, Udaya. "Shaping a Literary Space: Early Literary Histories in Malayalam and Normative Uses of the Past." *Literature and Nationalist Ideology: Writing Histories of Modern Indian Languages*. Ed. Hans Harder. New Delhi: Social Science Press, 2010. 19–50.

Nünning, Ansgar. "Implied Author." *The Routledge Encyclopedia of Narrative Theory*. Ed. Herman, David, Manfred Jahn, and Marie Laure Ryan. London: Routledge, 2005.

Osella, Filipo, and Caroline Osella. "Islamism and Social Reform in Kerala, South India." *Modern Asian Studies* 42.2/3 (2008): 317–46.

———. *Social Mobility in Kerala: Modernity and Identity in Conflict*. London: Pluto Press, 2000.

Palmer, Alan. *Social Minds in the Novel.* Columbus: Ohio State University Press, 2010.

Phelan, James. "Cognitive Narratology, Rhetorical Narratology, and Interpretive Disagreement: A Response to Alan Palmer's Analysis of *Enduring Love.*" *Style* 43.3 (2009): 309–21.

———. "Voice; or Authors, Narrators, and Audiences." *Teaching Narrative Theory.* Ed. David Herman, Brian McHale, and James Phelan. New York: Modern Language Association Publications, 2010. 137–50.

Phelan, James, and Peter J. Rabinowitz. "Narrative Judgments and the Rhetorical Theory of Narrative: Ian McEwan's *Atonement.*" *A Companion to Narrative Theory.* Ed. J. Phelan and P. J. Rabinowitz. Malden: Blackwell, 2005. 322–36.

Prince, Gerald. "Reader." *The Living Handbook of Narratology.* Ed. Peter Hühn, John Pier, Wolf Schmid, and Jörg Schönert. Hamburg: Hamburg University Press, 2013. <http://www.lhn.unihamburg.de/article/reader>.

Rabinowitz, Peter J. "Truth in Fiction: A Re-examination of Audiences." *Critical Inquiry* 4 (1976): 121–41.

Rai, Alok. *Hindi Nationalism.* Delhi: Orient Longman, 2001.

Satchidanandan, K. "A Sage and an Iconoclast. O. V. Vijayan, 1930–2005." *Frontline* 22.8 (March 12–25, 2005): n. pag. Web. 31 May 2015. <http://www.frontline.in/static/html/fl2208/stories/20050422003113200.htm>.

Schmid, Wolf. *Narratology: An Introduction.* Berlin: de Gruyter, 2010.

Shen, Dan. "Implied Author, Authorial Audience, and Context: Form and History in Neo-Aristotelian Rhetorical Theory." *Narrative* 21.2 (2013): 140–58.

Spivak, Gayatri C. *An Aesthetic Education in the Era of Globalization.* Cambridge: Harvard University Press, 2012.

Stanzel, Franz K. A. *Theory of Narrative.* Trans. Charlotte Goedsche. Cambridge: University of Cambridge, 1986.

Trivedi, Harish. *Colonial Transactions: Colonial Rule in India.* Manchester: Manchester University Press, 1993.

Vijayan, O. V. *The Legends of Khasak. Selected Fiction.* Penguin: Delhi, 1998. 1–176.

Vishwanathan, Gauri. *Masks of Conquest: Literary Study and British Rule in India.* New York: Columbia University Press, 1989.

Zunshine, Lisa. "Theory of Mind and Experimental Representations of Fictional Consciousness." *Narrative* 11.3 (2003): 270–91.

CONTRIBUTORS

JAN ALBER is professor of English literature and cognition at RWTH Aachen University, Germany. Publications include *Narrating the Prison* (Cambria Press, 2007) and *Unnatural Narrative: Impossible Worlds in Fiction and Drama* (University of Nebraska Press, 2016). He is currently working on several research projects that concern empirical literary studies.

MIEKE BAL is an independent cultural theorist, critic, video artist, and occasional curator. She works on gender, migratory culture, psychoanalysis, and the critique of capitalism. Her work comes together in *A Mieke Bal Reader* (2006). *In Medias Res: Inside Nalini Malani's Shadow Plays* appeared in 2016 (Hatje Cantz). Her video project *Madame B*, with Michelle Williams Gamaker, is widely exhibited. Her most recent film is *Reasonable Doubt,* on René Descartes and Queen Kristina (2016).

BAIDIK BHATTACHARYA is assistant professor of English at the University of Delhi. Publications include *Postcolonial Writing in the Era of World Literature: Texts, Territories, Globalizations* (Routledge, 2018); "Reading Rancière: Literature at the Limit of World Literature," *New Literary History* 48.3 (2017); and "On Comparatism in the Colony: Archives, Methods, and the Project of *Weltliteratur,*" *Critical Inquiry* 42.3 (2016). He is currently working on a monograph tentatively titled *Literature at the Limit of World Literature: Colonial Histories and Critical Methods.*

SARAH COPLAND is assistant professor of English at MacEwan University. She has published work on modernist narratives, prefaces, and poetry; the new modernist studies; rhetorical and cognitive approaches to narrative theory; and short stories and short story theory in *Narrative, Modernism/Modernity, Blending and the Study of Narrative* (de Gruyter, 2012), and *intervalla*. She coedited, with Greta Olson, a special issue on the politics of form for the *European Journal of English Studies* (2016), which was published through Routledge's special-issue-as-book program in 2017. Her current book project is entitled *Front Matters: The Rhetoric and Pedagogy of Modernist Prefaces.*

DIVYA DWIVEDI is assistant professor in the Department of Humanities and Social Sciences at the Indian Institute of Technology Delhi. Her publications include "The Paradox of Testimony and First-Person Plural Narration in Jensen's *We, the Drowned*" (coauthored with Henrik Skov Nielsen, *CLCWeb: Comparative Literature and Culture*, 2013); *The Public Sphere from Outside the West* (coedited with Sanil V., Bloomsbury Academic, 2015); and "Anti-mimetic Theory and Postcolonialism" in the *Edinburgh Companion to Contemporary Narrative Theories* (forthcoming). Currently she, together with Shaj Mohan, is completing the book project *Gandhi and Philosophy: On Theological Anti-Politics*, which is forthcoming with Bloomsbury Academic.

MONIKA FLUDERNIK is professor of English literature at the University of Freiburg, Germany. She is also the director of the graduate school Factual and Fictional Narration (GRK 1767). Her major fields of interest include narratology, postcolonial studies, "Law and Literature," and eighteenth-century aesthetics. She is the author of *The Fictions of Language and the Languages of Fiction* (1993) and the award-winning *Towards a "Natural" Narratology* (1996). Among her several edited volumes are *Hybridity and Postcolonialism: Twentieth-Century Indian Literature* (1998) and *Beyond Cognitive Metaphor Theory: Perspectives on Literary Metaphor* (2011). She is currently coediting the *Handbook of Narrative Factuality* with Marie-Laure Ryan.

MARION GYMNICH is full professor of English literature and culture at Bonn University, Germany. She has published several monographs as well as more than ninety articles in journals and edited volumes and has (co)edited thirteen edited volumes. Her main fields of research are narratology (in particular feminist narratology), genre theory, postcolonial studies, memory studies, and Anglophone literature from the nineteenth century to the present. Currently, she is coauthoring a study on orphans in Anglophone literature from the nineteenth century to the present.

PATRICK COLM HOGAN is Board of Trustees Distinguished Professor in the Department of English and the Program in Cognitive Science at the University of Connecticut. He is the author of over twenty books, most recently including *Imagining Kashmir: Emplotment and Colonialism* (University of Nebraska Press, 2016); *Sexual Identities: A Cognitive Literary Study* (Oxford University Press, 2018); and *Literature and Emotion* (Routledge, 2018). Current work includes continuing development of the collaborative *Literary Universals Project* (http://literary-universals.uconn.edu).

UDAYA KUMAR is professor at the Centre for English Studies, Jawaharlal Nehru University, New Delhi. His publications include *Writing the First Person: Literature, History, and Autobiography in Modern Kerala* (Permanent Black, 2016) and *The Joycean Labyrinth: Repetition, Time, and Tradition in "Ulysses"* (Clarendon, 1991). His current research interests include death and contemporary culture, cultural histories of the body, and forms of vernacular thought.

MARTIN LÖSCHNIGG is associate professor of English and chair of the section on the New English Literatures in the University of Graz, Austria. His publications include a study of fictional autobiography (Trier, 2006), a study of First World

War poetry (Heidelberg, 1994), and a short history of Canadian literature (Stuttgart, 2001, together with Maria Löschnigg), besides coedited volumes on Canadian and First World War literature and narratives of migration. He is currently engaged on a volume of essays on constructions of the "enemy" in contemporary film (with Marzena Sokolowska-Paryz) and a study of rewritings in the postcolonial literatures.

HENRIK SKOV NIELSEN is professor at Aarhus University, Denmark, and guest professor at Tampere University, Finland. He is the head of the Narrative Research Lab (http://www.nordisk.au.dk/forskningscentre/nrl) and the Centre for Fictionality Studies (http://fictionality.au.dk/). Publications include "Ten Theses about Fictionality" with James Phelan and Richard Walsh in *Narrative* 23.1 (2015) and "Natural Authors, Unnatural Narratives" in *Post-Classical Narratology: Approaches and Analyses* (Ohio State University Press, 2010).

GRETA OLSON is professor of English and American literary and cultural studies at the University of Giessen, general editor of the *European Journal of English Studies*, and cofounder of the European Network for Law and Literature Research. Publications include "Law's Pluralities: Arguments for Cultural Approaches to Law," *German Law Journal* 18.2 (2017); "The Politics of Form," with Sarah Copland, *European Journal of English Studies* 20.3 (2016); *Criminals as Animals from Shakespeare to Lombroso* (2013); and *Current Trends in Narratology* (2011). She works on cultural approaches to law, the politics of narrative, critical media and American studies, and feminism and sexuality studies.

JAMES PHELAN is Distinguished University Professor of English at Ohio State University. The editor of *Narrative,* he is also the author of numerous books on narrative theory, including *Experiencing Fiction* (Ohio State University Press, 2007); *Reading the American Novel* (Wiley-Blackwell, 2014); and *Somebody Telling Somebody Else* (2017). He is currently working on a rhetorical theory of fictionality.

GERALD PRINCE is professor of romance languages, associate faculty at the Annenberg School of Communication, and a member of the graduate groups in linguistics and in comparative literature at the University of Pennsylvania. The author of several books—including *Narratology: The Form and Functioning of Narrative* (Mouton, 1982); *A Dictionary of Narratology* (University of Nebraska Press, 1987, 2003); and *Narrative as Theme* (University of Nebraska Press, 1992)—Prince is currently writing a guide to the novel in French from 1951 to 2000.

RICHARD WALSH is a reader in English and related literature at the University of York, U.K. He is the author of *The Rhetoric of Fictionality: Narrative Theory and the Idea of Fiction* (Ohio State University Press, 2007) and the coeditor of *Narrating Complexity* (Springer, 2018). His work ranges over literary and cultural topics in narrative theory, including reflexiveness and ideology in fiction, fictionality within and beyond fiction, emergent and interactive narrative, and the relation between narrative and selfhood. More fundamentally, he is interested in the scope and (especially) the limits of narrative as a mode of cognition.

INDEX

"9/11" texts: dominant representation strategies of, 157–58, 157n2; *The Reluctant Fundamentalist* (Hamid) as counternarrative to, 156–63

Abelson, Robert P., 6
abstraction: definition of, 5; formalism and, 5–8
action, as cognitive frame, 57
act of memory, Bal on, 234n3
Acts of Meaning (Bruner), 58
Aczel, Richard, 16
addressee function: double bind in, 267; Dwivedi on, 29, 251–72; Foucault on, 256; ideological salience of, 252; ideology of, 259–61; of narratology vs. narrative, 254; in natural narratology, 257–58; Phelan on, 269; receiver concept and, 254; Spivak on, 267–71; Spivak's reading process and, 267
Adorno, T. W., 240
Aesthetic Education, An (Spivak), 235–40
Ahmad, Aijaz: on Jameson, 124n6; on Marxist approaches to narrative, 199
Ahmad, Nayeema, "I Am Still Alive," 49–50
Ahmed, Naseer, 41
Akbar, M. J., 46
Alber, Jan: narratological analysis of *Midnight's Children*, 26, 120–38; on postclassical narratology, 194; on postcolonial narratology, 121; usage of Althusser's concept of ideology, 120n1; usage of hypothetical intentionalism, 120n2
allegory: collection of objects vs., 85; Jameson on, 40, 40n4, 124; in *Midnight's Children* (Rushdie), 26, 123–26, 124nn4–5; in "The Third and Final Continent" (Lahiri), 174
allographic prefaces: colonizer-colonized dynamic in, 105; contextual rhetorical analysis of Forster's preface to Anand's *Untouchable*, 26, 102–19; "highjacking and interception" in, 105, 118; as paratext, 105; "protection and patronage" in, 105, 118; Singh's criticism of, 104–5
Althusser, Louis, 7, 19; concept of ideology, 120n1
Amuta, Chidi, 199
analepsis, 122
Anand, Mulk Raj: barriers to readership, 104; belief in social purpose of literature, 102n2; Forster's preface to *Untouchable*, 26, 102–19; genesis of narrative, 102–4; intended readership, 104; life experiences with untouchability, 116n12; need for critical edition of work, 116–17, 117n14; representations of untouchability in, 114–16; reviews and praise for, 103; struggle to publish, 103–4. See also *Untouchable* (Anand)
"Anguish" (Rehbar), 46–47
Anil's Ghost (Ondaatje), 64
Animal's People (Sinha): autodiegetic narrator in, 142, 142n1, 145; collaborative

autobiography in, 150–51; communal voice in, 147–50, 153–54; complexity of voice in, 148–49; construction of narratee in, 150–54; everyday orality in, 149; fictitious editor's note in, 150–51; inclusive "we" in, 148; linguistic features enhancing voice in, 149; narrative voice and negotiation of power in, 27, 141–55; opening lines of, 148; personal voice in, 149–50, 153–54; private voice in, 153; public voice in, 153–54; role of journalist in, 151–53, 152n9; significance of narrator's name in, 145–46, 145n5; subaltern voice in, 144–45, 149; unruly narrative voice in, 145–50; voyeuristic overtones in, 152, 152n11

anthropology, postcolonialism and, 11–12

aperspectival structure, 196

apocalypse: aftermath of crisis, 217; in "The Heavenly Slipper" (Paraśurām), 218–21; in "The Kingdom of Ram" (Paraśurām), 223–27; in Paraśurām's satires, 28, 213–28; in "The Philosopher's Stone" (Paraśurām), 221–23; projected crisis, 216–17; secular concept of, 213n2, 215–16; in "The Tale of the Gamman Tribe" (Paraśurām), 216, 227–28; textual mode of, 216–17, 216n9; theological concept of, 215–16; unusual resolution of crisis, 216–17

Appadurai, Arjun, 76n1

applied narratology, 3–4

Arabian Nights, The, as intertextual source: in *Midnight's Children* (Rushdie), 132, 133; in *The Reluctant Fundamentalist* (Hamid), 160

archival approach, in *Litanies of the Dutch Battery* (Madhavan), 87–88

Armah, Ayi Kwei, 201n5

Arnold, David, 82n6

Arunima, G., on objects as historical experience, 77

Ashcroft, Bill, 55, 98n6, 135

Athar, Abdul Gani Beg, "The Enemy," 48–49

Attwell, David, 237n6

author: communicative act in fiction, 20; fictive discourse and, 20–22; focalization and, 19–20; implied (*see* implied author); migrant literature vs. conventions of, 60–61, 63, 64–67, 70–71; Ondaatje's questioning of established notion of, 65; Ondaatje's undermining of conventional self-narration, 64–67, 70–71; rhetorical narratology and, 20–21, 26; Vassanji's subversion of conventional first-person discourse, 60–61, 63, 70–71

author function, 29, 252, 253–54, 259–60

authorial audience: definition of, 106; distinction of, 107n7; Dwivedi on, 251–52, 255–57; of *Huckleberry Finn* (Twain), 106; narrative voice and, 255–56; Phelan on, 255–57, 269; reliability and, 255–56; of *Untouchable* (Anand) and Forster's preface, 106–11, 107n8

authorial disclosures, 180, 180n4, 181, 186; in "The Third and Final Continent" (Lahiri), 181, 186

authorial voice, 147, 147n6

autobiographical pact, 20, 65n12

autodiegetic narrator: in *Animal's People* (Sinha), 142, 145; defining and distinguishing, 142n1

Azhar, Maūlana Muhammad, 39

Baer, Ben Conisbee, 104, 104n4

Bakhtin, Mikhail: on Dostoevsky's ideology, 196–97, 199; on double-voiced discourse, 16, 168, 198; on heteroglossia, 198–99; on ideology in narrative, 195, 196–99, 203; on *Little Dorrit* (Dickens), 197–98; on skaz, 198; on speech genres, 15–16

Bal, Mieke: on act of memory, 81n3, 234n3; on crystallization of time, 234–35; on cultural consequences of migration, 231, 231n1; on focalization and memory, 231–35; focalization as first academic passion of, 245; on focalization in postcolonial narratology, 28–29, 231–50; on gaze, 28–29, 241–48; Genette and, 245, 245n15; on ideological issues in narratology, 24; on maxim spotting, 240; on migratory aesthetics, 235; on *The Namesake* (Lahiri), 231–34; on point of narratology, 4; on "post-," 231, 235; on Spivak and absent focalization, 235–40, 245; on traveling concepts, 241; on "what if?" questions, 236–40, 236n5, 239, 245

Balzac, Honoré de, *The Wild Ass's Skin*, 78, 79

Banich, Marie, 42

Barthes, Roland: on cultural codes, 93n1; on emanation of past reality, 235; on intertext, 251; on object status in narratives, 74–75; on reality effect, 74–75; on transcultural ubiquity of narrative, 3

Bartosch, Roman, 146
Başoğlu, Metin, 42
Basu, Amit, 143n2
Battersby, Christine, on Kant and personhood, 165
Batty, Nancy E., 133
Baudrillard, Jean, *The System of Objects*, 75
Bauman, Zygmunt, 70
Beckett, Samuel, *L'Innomable*, 132n15
Bengali satires. *See* Paraśurām, satires of
Benjamin, Walter: on allegorist *vs.* collector, 85; on arrest of thought and time, 234
Bennett, Donna, on polybridity, 62, 62n7
Bennett, Robert, on *Midnight's Children* (Rushdie), 124–25, 131
Bergson, Henri, 248n19
Berman, Jessica, 104n4
Between Two Men (Clark), 103
Bhabha, Homi: on colonial discourse, 166; on concept of self, 56, 63; on counter-discourse, 10; on double temporality, 66; on nationhood, 11–12, 38; on paradigmatic concepts in South Asian texts, 23; on "Third Space," 129
Bhattacharya, Baidik: on apocalypse, decolonization, and postcolony in Bengali satires, 28, 213–28; on coming community (postcolony), 28, 223–28; on decoupling of postcolony and nation, 28, 213–14; on "The Heavenly Slipper" (Paraśurām), 214n3, 218–21; on "The Kingdom of Ram" (Paraśurām), 223–27; on narrative dispositifs, 214, 221, 227–28; on "The Philosopher's Stone" (Paraśurām), 221–23; on prolepsis, 215; rhetoric of death used by, 213; on satire's relationship to history, 217–18; on satirical practices, 217–23; on stories or almost stories, 214–17; on "The Tale of the Gamman Tribe" (Paraśurām), 216, 227–28
Bhopal: A Prayer for Rain (film), 144n3
Bhopal Gas tragedy: as eco-crime, 143; effects of toxic gas in, 142–43; history of, 141–43; interpretation in narrative, 143–45; movies about, 144n3; narrative voice in *Animal's People* (Sinha), 27, 141–55
Bildungsroman, 206–7
biopolitics: Foucault's concept of, 162; in *The Reluctant Fundamentalist* (Hamid), 162–63

Birk, Hanne: on *Midnight's Children* (Rushdie), 123; on postcolonial narratology, 121
Blackburn, Stuart, 82n6
Blaise, Clark, 58n3
Blechtommel, Die (Grass), 132
body, as narrative object, 87–88
Boltanski, Luc, on fictional depiction of suffering, 152n11
Bombay talkies, 132
Booth, Wayne: on implied author, 255; on reliability and unreliability, 163–65, 167, 170, 175n2
Bortolussi, Marisa, on statistical reader, 260–61
Bose, Sugata, 13, 23
"both . . . and" model, 4–5
bottom-up methodology, 3–4
Bouts de bois de Dieu. Banty mam Yall, Les (Sembène): attributive discourse in, 97; characters' relation to French language in, 98–99; character use and knowledge of languages in, 97–98; concern with own legibility, 95; glosses in footnotes *vs.* text, 96; metacultural signs in, 94; metalinguistic signs in, 94–99; metanarrative signs in, 26, 94–100; metanarrative signs in, character utterance of, 94; metanarrative signs in, narrator deployment of, 94; metanarrative signs in, number and distribution of, 94–95; metaproairetic signs in, 94; non-French terms in, 95–96, 95n3; original French *vs.* English translation, 94n2; railroad strike depicted in, 94; settings of, 99–100; social and cultural change in, 99; thematic complex of language-related matters in, 96–99
Boyhood of Raleigh, The (painting), 131, 132
"Boy Is Guilty, The" (Jehangir), 47–48
Brada-Williams, Noelle, 173n1
Brennan, Timothy, 9, 13, 270n16
Bristow, Robert, 83–84, 83n7
Brock, Richard, 9
Brontë, Charlotte, *Jane Eyre*, 179
Brothers Karamazov, The (Dostoevsky), 197
Bruner, Jerome, 58
Bryson, Norman, 242, 242n11, 243n12
Buchholz, Laura, 15, 133
Bulgakov, Mikhail, *Heart of a Dog*, 196

"Burnt-Out Sun, The" (Hamadani), 45, 45n7
Butler, Judith, 157

Caesar, Judith, 173, 173n1
Calvino, Italo, 205
Camus, Albert, *The Fall,* 160
Canada, migrant literature from: *A Place Within* (Vassanji), 56–63, 69–71; *Running in the Family* (Ondaatje), 56–58, 63–67, 69–71; *Tales from Firozsha Baag* (Mistry), 56–58, 67–71
Canli, Turhan, 42
Cantor, Milton, 166
Carrigan, Anthony, 143, 144–45, 146, 149
Caruth, Cathy, 42
Cat's Table, The (Ondaatje), 64
center vs. margin, in concept of self, 55–56, 62–63, 66–67, 70
Césaire, Aimé, *Notebook of a Return to My Native Land,* 105n5
Chakrabarty, Dipesh, 215n5
Chakravorty, Gayatri, 97n4
Chambers, Iain, on concept of self, 56, 70
character-character dialogue: Phelan on, 27, 175–87; in "The Third and Final Continent" (Lahiri), 175, 180–87
character: differentiation through objects, 76; metanarrative signs and, 94; as space of citation, 88; voice vs. narrator voice, 16
Chatman, Seymour: on contextualism, 5; narrative communication model of, 176
Chatterjee, Partha, 13
Chaturvedi, Vinayak, 13
Chaudhuri, Supriya, 76n1
Chen, Chun-yen, 131
Chicago School, 20
chronological parameters, of return journeys, 57
Cien años de soledad (Márquez), 132
Clark, F. Le Gros, *Between Two Men,* 103
co-determination, 15–16
Coetzee, J. M., absent focalization in *Disgrace,* 15, 235–37, 266–67
cognition, narrative as form of, 5–7
cognitive models: of nation, 40, 40n3; of unreliability, 156, 163–64
collaborative autobiography, 150–51

collection of objects, 84–88; allegory vs., 85; metonymies vs., 85
colonial discourse, 9–12, 27; unreliable narration in, 166–67
coming community, in Paraśurām's satires, 28, 223–28
commodity exchange, and status of objects in narratives, 75
communal voice: in *Animal's People* (Sinha), 147–50, 153–54; in Lanser's typology, 147
conative function, 254
Conner, Marc C., on *Midnight's Children* (Rushdie), 123
contextualist narratology: calls for, 2; formalism and ideology in, 2–8; framing as imperative vs. problem, 1–2; general and particular in, 5–8; limited results of, 2; Prince's restrictive definition of, 3–4
convergent narration, 179; in *Jane Eyre* (Brontë), 179; in "The Third and Final Continent" (Lahiri), 184–86
conversational disclosures, 179–80, 180n4
Cooper, Frederick, 9
Cooppan, Vilashini, 14
Copland, Sarah: contextual rhetorical analysis of Forster's preface to Anand's *Untouchable,* 102–19; on flesh-and-blood and authorial audiences, 26, 106–11; on politics of form, 170; on power dynamics in Dalit studies, 24, 26; on rhetorical narratology, 26
Cornwell, Neil, 198n3
Coronil, Fernando, 150
cosmopolitanism, minority, 174
cosmopolitan self, 55
counter-discourse, postcolonial, 12
counterfocalization, 29, 236, 266–67
Couser, G. Thomas, 150
Cowasjee, Saros, afterword to *Untouchable* (Anand), 116
criminal investigation prototype: disfigured, in Kashmiri fiction, 47–48; in non-Kashmiri portrayals of Kashmir, 40
critical intimacy, 238–40
Critique of Postcolonial Reason: Towards a History of the Vanishing Present (Spivak), 238
cross-cultural narratology, Hogan on, 2–3
Crossing the River (Phillips), 201n5
crossover narration, 186–87

INDEX

Culler, Jonathan, concept of naturalization, 57
cultural code: definition of, 93; metanarrative signs of, 93
cultural materialism, 193–94
cultural work, 194
Culture and Imperialism (Said), 199

Dalit studies, 11, 13–14, 17; Copland on power dynamics in, 24, 26
Dalmia, Vasudha, 13
Dasenbrock, Reed W., 97n4
Days and Nights in Calcutta (Blaise and Mukherjee), 58n3
Death and Dissymmetry (Bal), 236
de Certeau, Michel, 58, 217
decolonization: decoupling of nation and postcolony in, 28, 213–14; in Paraśurām's satires, 28, 213–28; as projected apocalyptic event, 213
deductive methodology, 3–4
Delbaere, Jeanne, 65n13
Delbo, Charlotte, 244n13
delectation of memory, 25
Deleuze, Gilles, 234
Dennett, Daniel, 259
Depperman, Arnulf, 202n6
Derrida, Jacques, on textual mode of apocalypse, 216–17, 216n9
Devi, Mahasweta, 97n4
"Diachronization of Narratology, The" (Fludernik), 4
diasporic citizenship, 174
Dickens, Charles, *Little Dorrit*, 197–98
Diengott, Nilli, 5
diglossia, post-decolonization, 267
Dirks, Nicholas, 12
Dirlik, Arif, 13, 201
disasters: impact of fictionalized accounts, 144; narrating, Gymnich on, 141–45; narrative voice in *Animal's People* (Sinha), 27, 141–55; "poverty porn," 152, 152n10; right to tell victims' stories, 144; voyeurism in narratives about, 152, 152n11
disclosures: authorial, 180, 180n4, 181, 186; conversational, 179–80, 180n4
discourse: colonial, 9–12, 27, 166–67; counter-, postcolonial, 12; double-voiced, 16, 168, 198, 255–56; fictive, 20–22; Foucault's regime of, 9
"Discourse in the Novel" (Bakhtin), 197–98
disfigured narrative: Hogan's definition of, 44; in Kashmiri fiction, 37, 41–52
Disgrace (Coetzee), Spivak's imagining of absence in, 15, 235–37, 266–67
dispersive focalization: counterfocalization vs., 266–67; definition of, 266; in *The Legends of Khasak* (Vijayan), 29, 252, 261–67
dispositifs, in Paraśurām's satires, 214, 221, 227–28
dissident reading, 193–94
Dixon, Peter, on statistical reader, 260–61
Doležel, Lubomír, 17
Dostoevsky, Fyodor, ideology in works of, 196–97, 199
double bind, in addressee function, 267
double-voiced discourse, 16, 168, 198, 255–56
dual temporality of narrative, 19, 66
Dubreuil, Laurent, 98n6
Dulai, Suijit, 102n2
During, Simon, 38
Dwivedi, Divya: on addressee function and narratological laity, 29, 251–72; on authorial audience, 251–52, 255–57; on dispersive focalization, 29, 252, 261–67; on ideological issues in narratology, 24; on lay reader, 257–59; on *The Legends of Khasak* (Vijayan), 29, 252, 261–67; on narrative/narratological education, 267–71

Eagleton, Terry, concept of ideology, 5–6, 120n1
Eakin, Paul John, 58
"East Isn't East" (Said), 69
Eaton, Richard M., 10
eco-crime, 143
education (pedagogy): Dwivedi on, 29, 251–72; Spivak on, 235–40, 267–71
Einstellung, 254
embodied space, 58
emotional memory: definition of, 42; functional, properties of, 43; impaired regulation of, 42; and Kashmiri fiction, 25, 41–45; preparatory function of, 43; Rushdie on, 43–44

Empire Writes Back, The (Ashcroft, Griffiths, and Tiffin), 55
emplotment, of nationalism: cognitive models of nation and, 40, 40n3; criminal investigation prototype and, 40; family separation and reunion prototype and, 38, 39; heroic prototype and, 38–39; Hogan on, 25, 37–52; Kashmir, by Kashmiris (disfigured), 37, 41–52; Kashmir, by non-Kashmiris, 37–41; plot prototypes in, 25, 38–41; revenge prototype and, 40; romantic prototype and, 38, 39, 41
"Enemy, The" (Athar), 48–49
epistemic violence, 23
Erney, Hans-George, on binary thinking, 128n13
estranging unreliability, 178
ethnography, postcolonialism and, 11
ethos, Forster's appeal to, 110, 111, 112
Eugene Onegin (Pushkin), 196
Eurocentrism: false universalism of, 2–3, 10; postcolonialism vs., 10–14
evaluation, unreliable, 177, 255
experiencing, as cognitive frame, 57
Experiencing Fiction (Phelan), 106
experientiality, in migrant literature, 56–57, 69–70

Fall, The (Camus), as intertextual source in *The Reluctant Fundamentalist* (Hamid), 160, 168
false universalism, 2–3, 10
Faludi, Susan, 158
family, nation as, 40
family separation and reunion prototype: disfigured, in Kashmiri fiction, 48–51; in non-Kashmiri portrayals of Kashmir, 38, 39
Fanon, Frantz, 9, 68, 200
Fat-hul-Jawwad (Azhar), 39
Faulkner, William, rhetorical analysis of *The Sound and the Fury*, 176–77, 178
Faultlines: Cultural Materialism and the Politics of Dissident Reading (Sinfield), 193–94
feminist narratology: Diengott's attack on, 5; Lanser's gender-based critique of voice, 3; Lanser's typology of voice in, 147; Prince's inductive approach in, 3; Warhol on criticism vs., 4

fiction: generality and particulars in, 6–7; narration and acts of narration in, 18–19; narrativity, 21; panfictionality doctrine and, 21–22
Fictions of Authority (Lanser), 147, 153
fictive discourse, 20–22
Fiddes, Paul S., 216n8
Figueira, Dorothy, 11, 14
figural narrative situation, 255, 258n9
Fitzgerald, F. Scott, *The Great Gatsby*, 179, 187
Flanagan, Kathleen, 131
Flaubert, Gustave: objects and realism of work, 75; "A Simple Heart," 75
Fleming, Ian, 74
flesh-and-blood reader: distinction of, 107n7; of *Untouchable* (Anand) and Forster's preface, 106–11
Fludernik, Monika: cognitive-narratological model of, 25, 57–58; definition of narratology, 194; "The Diachronization of Narratology," 4; on history of ideology in narratology, 195–202; on *How to Get Filthy Rich in Rising Asia* (Hamid), 194, 203, 205–9; "The Hybridity of Discourse," 121, 200, 202; on ideologies in South Asian texts, 194, 203–9; on ideology in narratology, 193–212; "Introduction: Second-Person Narrative," 202n6; on Marxist approaches, 199–200; "Narrative Forms," 200; on narrativization, 257–59, 260; on narratology and literary criticism, 15, 28; natural narratology model of, 57, 257–58; on neo-imperialism and globalization, 24; on postclassical narratology, 194; on postcolonial narratology, 121, 199–209; on process of reading, 194, 203–9, 257–59, 260; return journey analysis using work of, 57–58, 63, 66, 69, 70; "Second-Person Narrative as a Test Case," 202n6; on Sinfield's cultural materialism, 193–94; "Through a Glass Darkly," 202n6; on *A Time to Be Happy* (Sahgal), 194, 203–5, 208; on unreliability, 160; "When the Self Is an Other," 15, 200
focalization, 15, 19–20; as absence, 235–40, 245, 266–67; Bal on, 28–29, 231–50; counterfocalization, 29, 236, 266–67; crystallization of time in, 234–35; definition of, 231; dispersive, 29, 252, 261–67; gaze and, 244–48; in *Litanies of the Dutch Battery* (Madhavan), 81; maxim

spotting and, 240; memory as mode of, 231–35; as most important concept in postcolonial narratology, 248–49; in *The Namesake* (Lahiri), 231–34; narrative function of, 270; overcoming linguistic limitations through, 245–46; unreliable narration in, 169–70

foregrounding: focalization and, 19; metanarrative signs and, 94

formalism, 2–8, 203; abstraction and generality in, 5–8; engagement with ideology, 8; tension with ideology, 1–2

formalist poetics, 5–8

Forster, E. M., preface to Anand's *Untouchable*: appeal to ethos, 110, 111, 112; appeal to logos, 111–12; appeal to pathos, 111, 112; colonizer-colonized dynamic in, 105, 107–8; Copland's contextual rhetorical analysis of, 26, 102–19; disclosure of ending in, 105, 113; establishment of "us" group of readers in, 110–11, 111n10; flesh-and-blood reader and authorial audience, 106–11, 107n8; "highjacking and interception" in, 105, 118; modeling of rhetorical reading in, 113–14; Nasta on, 105n6, 108–9, 114, 116; opening anecdote of, 108–11; paratext of, 105, 107, 107n9; positioning of readers relative to *Passage to India*, 108–11, 113–14; as precondition for publication, 104, 108; "protection and patronage" in, 105, 118; responses to potential objections and criticisms in, 112; rhetorical appeals of, 107, 110, 111–12; Singh's textual analysis of, 104–5, 108; Sommerfield's comments on, 104

Foucault, Michel: on addressee function, 256; on author function, 29, 252, 253–54, 259–60; on effects of power, 261; on regime of discourse, 9; on subject positions, 56; on system of acceptability, 265, 265n13

fractured tales: Hogan's explanation of, 45–46; Kashmiri, 45–51

Freedgood, Elaine, on non-allegorical reading of objects, 85

Freeman, J. R., 263n11

Freeman, Rich, 263n11, 265n12

Friedman, Susan Stanford, 2–3

Frow, John, 7

functions, objects as, 74

Gajarawala, Toral, 11, 14

Galler, Matthias, 125

Galpakalpa (Paraśurām), 214–15, 214n3

Gandhi, Mahatma: absence in *Midnight's Children* (Rushdie), 135n17; and anticolonialism, 9; and genesis of *Untouchable* (Anand), 102–4

Garg, Shweta, 173n1

Gates, Henry Louis, Jr., 168

gaze: Bal's critique of, 28–29, 241–48; Bryson's concept of, 242, 242n11, 243n12; focalization and, 244–48; Lacanian concept of, 243–44

general: alignment with formalism, 7; in fictive and nonfictive rhetorics, 6–7; forms of generality, 6; relationship with particular, 5–8

Genette, Gérard: Bal and, 245, 245n15; classical narratology of, 194; focalization concept of, 19–20, 81n3; on homodiegetic narration with zero focalization, 126; on non-focalization, 196; paratext concept of, 20, 105, 158

genre, in postcolonial literature, 200

Gibbs, Raymond W., 120n2

Gikandi, Simon, 10, 13

Gitanjali (Tagore), 105n5

globalization, 24, 27

God's Bits of Wood. See *Bouts de bois de Dieu. Banty mam Yall, Les* (Sembène)

grand narratives, Lyotard on, 9

Grass, Günter, *Die Blechtommel*, 132

"Grave Robber, The" (Kamil), 48

Great Gatsby, The (Fitzgerald), mask narration in, 179, 187

Grice, Paul H., conversational maxims of, 164, 165

Griffiths, Gareth, 55, 98n6

Groundwork of the Metaphysics of Morals, The (Kant), 165

group identity: cognitive models of nation and, 40, 40n3; Kashmiri, non-Kashmiri portrayals and, 37–41; Kashmiri, trauma and disruption of, 37, 41–52

Guha, Ramachandra, introduction to *Untouchable* (Anand), 116

Gymnich, Marion: on construction of narratee, 150–54; "Linguistics and Narratology," 200; on narrating disasters and their aftermath, 141–45; on narrative authority, 146–48; on narrative voice in *Animal's People* (Sindha), 27, 141–55; on narratology and literary criticism, 15; on neo-imperialism and globalization, 24, 27; "Writing Back," 200, 201

Haas, Brian, 42
Habibullah, Wajahat, 42
Hagedorn, Herman, 166–67
Hall, Stuart: on concept of self, 56; on interpellation of narrator, 126n8
Hamadani, Anees, "The Burnt-Out Sun," 45, 45n7
Hamid, Mohsin: *How to Get Filthy Rich in Rising Asia*, 194, 203, 205–9; *The Reluctant Fundamentalist*, 27–28, 156–72 (see *Reluctant Fundamentalist, The*)
Hanna, Bridget, 143
Harrow, Kenneth W., 97n4
Hartnell, Anna, 157
Harvey, David, 165
Hawes, Clement, 132n16
Heart of a Dog (Bulgakov), 196
Heart of Darkness (Conrad), as intertextual source in *The Reluctant Fundamentalist* (Hamid), 160
"Heavenly Slipper, The" (Paraśurām), 214n3
Heble, Ajay, 65
Helff, Sissy, 168
Herman, David: definition of narrative, 103n3; on flesh-and-blood readers and authorial audience, 106, 110; on generality, 6; on norms and normative frameworks, 117; on postclassical narratology, 194; on reading, 259; on text and context, 71
Herman, Luc, 260
heroic prototype: as default for national identification, 38–39; invasion component of, 38; in narrative negotiation of Kashmiri nationhood, 25; in non-Kashmiri portrayals of Kashmir, 38–39; trauma and inconceivability of, 44, 46; usurpation component of, 38
Hero of Our Time, A (Lermontov), 195
heterodiegetic narration, 20
heteroglossia, 198–99
Heyd, Theresa, on narrators as persons, 163–64
Hinduization of India, 13–14

Hirsch, Marianne, 244n14
history of future, satire as, 218
history: postcolonialism and, 11–12; satire and, 217–18
Hodge, Bob, 9, 201
Hogan, Patrick Colm: on "Anguish" (Rehbar), 46–47; on "The Boy Is Guilty" (Nazir) 47–48; on "The Burnt-Out Sun" (Hamadani), 45, 45n7; on cross-cultural narratology, 2–3; on emotional memory and trauma, 25, 41–45; on emplotment of nationalism, 25, 37–52; on "The Enemy" (Athar), 48–49; on "The Grave Robber" (Amin), 48; on "I Am Still Alive" (Ahmad), 49–50; *Imagining Kashmir*, 41; on Kashmiri fiction, 25, 37, 41–52; on *Midnight's Children* (Rushdie), 127, 135n17; on non-Kashmiri portrayals of Kashmir, 37–41; on plot prototypes, 25, 38–41; on "The Second Meeting" (Mohi-ud-din), 46; *Understanding Nationalism*, 38, 41–42; on "The Voice" (Santosh), 50–51
homodiegetic narration, in *Midnight's Children* (Rushdie), 126
Houston, Pam, 205
How Our Lives Become Stories: Making Selves (Eakin), 58
How to Get Filthy Rich in Rising Asia (Hamid), 203, 205–9; Bildungsroman format of, 206–7; Fludernik on ideology of, 194; irony in, 205–8; narratee in, 205–6; narrative voice in, 205; self-help style of, 205; you-protagonist of, 205–9
"How to Talk to a Hunter" (Houston), 205
Huber, Janice, 252n3
Huckleberry Finn (Twain): authorial audience of, 106; restricted narration in, 178
Huggan, Graham, 66
Huyssen, Andreas, 243n12, 247
hybridity, 23, 24, 67; in *Midnight's Children* (Rushdie), 130
"Hybridity of Discourse, The" (Fludernik), 121, 200, 202
hypothetical audience, 256
hypothetical intentionalism, 120n2

I Am Still Alive" (Ahmad), 49–50
iconicity, 241

identitary parameters, of return journeys, 57–58

ideological thematics, 5–8

ideology, 2–8; Althusser's concept of, 120n1; ambivalence in *Midnight's Children* (Rushdie), 120–38; Bakhtin on, 195, 196–99, 203; Eagleton's concept of, 120n1; engagement with formalism, 8; Fludernik on, 193–212; in history of narratology, Fludernik on, 195–202; Marxist approaches in, 199–200; particulars in, 7; in South Asian texts, Fludernik on, 194, 203–9; systematic nature of, 5–6; tension with formalism, 1–2; Uspensky on, 195–96, 199

If on a Winter's Night a Traveller (Calvino), 205

Ilaiah, Kancha, 11

illusionism, of readers, 257–59, 258n9

Imagining Kashmir (Hogan), 41

imperative, contextualist narratology as, 1–2

implied author: Alber on, 120n2; authorial audience and, 255–57; authorial disclosures and, 180; Bal on, 248; character-character dialogue and, 179–80; Dwivedi on, 252; lay projection of narrative voice, 257–59, 261; limited concept of, 20; Phelan on, 177–80; reliability and, 157, 163–69, 177–79, 255–56

implied reader, 15; authorial audience and, 255–57; Dwivedi on, 251–52; reliability/unreliability and, 160–62; Spivak analyses of, 15, 267–71; Spivak's reading process and, 254–55; unreliability and, 256

incredible order of history, 218, 219

India: apocalypse, decolonization, and postcolony in Bengali satires, 28, 213–28; contextual rhetorical analysis of Forster's preface to *Untouchable*, 102–19; Dalit studies in, 11, 13–14, 17, 24; genesis of *Untouchable* (Anand), 102–4; Hinduization of, 13–14; ideological ambivalence in *Midnight's Children* (Rushdie), 120–38; narrative voice in *Animal's People* (Sinha), 27, 141–55; role of objects in *Litanies of the Dutch Battery* (Madhavan), 76, 80–88; Vassanji's return journeys to (*A Place Within*), 56–63

India, and Kashmir: depiction in "The Burnt-Out Sun" (Hamadani), 45; disfigured stories in Kashmiri fiction, 37, 41–52; emplotment of nationalism by non-Kashmiris, 37–41; heroic prototype and, 38; revenge prototype and, 40; sacrificial prototype and, 39

indices, objects as, 74

inductive methodology, 3–4

Indulekha (Menon), role of objects in, 76–77, 79–80

informants, objects as, 74–75

L'Innomable (Beckett), 132n15

In Search of Vanished Blood (video installation), 243–48

intentional stances, 259, 270

interpretation, unreliable, 177, 255

Interpreter of Maladies (Lahiri), 173. See also "Third and Final Continent, The" (Lahiri)

interpretive turn, in postcolonialism, 12

intertext, 251

intertextuality: definition of, 131n14; in *Midnight's Children* (Rushdie), 131–33, 132nn15–16; in *The Reluctant Fundamentalist*, (Hamid), 160, 162

In Theory (Ahmad), 199

intradiegetic narration, 25

"Introduction: Second-Person Narrative" (Fludernik), 202n6

Ireland, trauma and emplotment in, 42

Jackson, Elizabeth, on "The Third and Final Continent" (Lahiri), 174, 181

Jahn, Manfred, 258n9

Jakobson, Roman, 254

Jamal, Arif, 50

Jameel, Muhammad, 39

Jameson, Fredric: on allegories, 40, 40n4, 124; on Marxist approaches to narrative, 199; on reliability and unreliability, 167

Jane Eyre (Brontë), convergent narration in, 179

Jeevitanauka (film), 84–85

Jehangir, Nazir, "The Boy Is Guilty," 47–48

Jha, D. N., 13

Jones, James A., 97n4

Kabir, Ananya Jahanara, 45n7, 48n8

Kamboureli, Smaro, 64nn10–11, 66

Kamil, Amin, "The Grave Robber," 48
Kanaganayakam, Chelva, 66
Kanthapura (Rao), 202
Kantian philosophy: and critical intimacy, 239; and maxims, 240; and reliability, 164–66
Karunanayake, Dinithi, 104
Kashmir, non-Kashmiri portrayals of: criminal investigation prototype in, 40; emplotment of nationalism in, 25, 37–41; family separation and reunion prototype in, 38, 39; film portrayals, 38, 39; heroic prototype in, 38–39; plot prototypes in, 25, 38–41; revenge prototype in, 40; romantic prototype in, 38, 39; sacrificial prototype in, 38, 39
Kashmiri fiction: "Anguish" (Rehbar), 46–47; "The Boy Is Guilty" (Nazir), 47–48; "The Burnt-Out Sun" (Hamadani), 45, 45n7; criminal investigation prototype in, 47–48; emotional memory and trauma in, 25, 41–45; "The Enemy" (Athar), 48–49; family separation and reunion prototype in, 48–51; film portrayals, 51n9; "The Grave Robber" (Amin), 48; heroic prototype in, difficulty with, 41, 46; "I Am Still Alive" (Ahmad), 49–50; revenge prototype in, 41, 48; romantic prototype in, 41, 46–47; sacrificial prototype in, 41, 46, 48–51; "The Second Meeting" (Mohi-ud-din), 46; trauma and disfigured stories in, 25, 37, 41–52; "The Voice" (Santosh), 50–51
Kazi, Seema, 42, 44
Khan, Anna H. R., 161
Khushi-Lahiri, Rajyashree, 173n1
Kim, Sue J., on contextualism, 1
Kindt, Tom, 2
"Kingdom of Ram, The" (Paraśurām), 223–27
Kirby, E. D., 42
Koshy, Susan: on diasporic citizenship, 174; on minority cosmopolitanism, 174; on "The Third and Final Continent" (Lahiri), 174–75, 181, 187
Krishnaswamy, Revathi, 13
Kristeva, Julia, on intertextuality, 131n14
Kumar, Ravi, 144n3
Kumar, Sunil, 145
Kumar, Udaya: on archival principle, 87–88; on collector's attitude, 84–86; on delectation of memory, 25; on *Indulekha* (Menon), 76–77, 79–80; on *Lakshmikesavam* (Menon), 77, 79–80; on *Litanies of the Dutch Battery* (Madhavan), 76, 80–88; on objects, in postcolonial context, 75–76, 79–80; on objects (status in narrative), 25, 74–90; on objects and character differentiation, 76; on objects and modernity, 76–77, 79–80; on objects and remembrance, 81–82; on shaping of modern Malayalam, 270; on trauma and narration, 24; on *The Wild Ass's Skin* (Balzac), 78, 79

Lacanian gaze, 243–44
Lahiri, Jhumpa: *The Namesake*, 231–34; "The Third and Final Continent," 27–28, 173–89 (*see* "Third and Final Continent, The")
laity, narratological, 251–72
Lakoff, George, 44
Lakshmikesavam (Menon), role of objects in, 77, 79–80
languages: Bakhtin on, 196–99; in *Les Bouts de bois de Dieu. Banty mam Yall* (Sembène), 95–99; choice in postcolonial texts, 200; colonial persistence in, 10; postcolonial context of, 24, 25–26; Spivak on access to, 269–70; Uspensky on, 195–96
Lanser, Susan: on authorial voice, 147, 147n6; *Fictions of Authority*, 147, 153; gender-based critique of voice, 3; on narrative authority, 146–48; typology of narrative voice, 147–50
Lanthanbatheriyile Luthiniyakal. See *Litanies of the Dutch Battery*
Larsen, Neil, 9
Lawrence, D. H., 102
lay readers, 257–59; projection of narrative voice, 257–59, 260; subjectivation of, 253–55, 258–59, 261; terms to relativize, 252n1
Lazarus, Neil, 11
Lederer, Thomas, 195n1
LeDoux, Joseph, 42
"Legend of Sleepy Hollow" (Irving), as intertextual source for *The Reluctant Fundamentalist* (Hamid), 160
Legends of Khasak, The (Vijayan): dispersive focalization in, 252, 261–67; language in, 270; revolution in Malayalam fic-

tion, 261; social mind in, 262, 262n10; as untimely interjection, 267
Lejeune, Philippe, autobiographical pact concept of, 20
linguistic code, metanarrative signs of, 93
"Linguistics and Narratology" (Gymnich), 200
Litanies of the Dutch Battery (Madhavan): archival principle in, 87–88; characters as spaces of citation in, 88; collector's attitude in, 84–86; focalization in, 81; geological series in, 83–84; historical narrators in, 88; imagination and creativity in, 84; macrohistories in, 82; objects and narrative in, 25, 76, 80–88; remembrance and location in, 81–82, 88; sea and transoceanic connections in, 83; shops and poetry of things in, 80–81
Little Dorrit (Dickens), 197–98
lived space, 58
Living to Tell About It (Phelan), 177
L. O. C. (film), 38
logos, Forster's appeal to, 111–12
London Calling (Sandhu), 200n4
Long, Lynellyn, on return journeys, 57
Looking In: The Art of Viewing (Bryson), 242n11
Loomba, Ania, 9, 12, 62
Löschnigg, Martin: on migrancy and concept of self, 55–58, 69–71; on narratives of return journeys, 25, 55–73; on *A Place Within* (Vassanji), 56–63, 69–71; on *Running in the Family* (Ondaatje), 56–58, 63–67, 69–71; on *Tales From Firozsha Baag* (Mistry), 56–58, 67–71
Lotman, Yuri, 196, 196n2
Lucius-Hoene, Gabriele, 202n6
Lukács, György, 199
Lyons, F. S. L., 42
Lyotard, Jean-François, 9

Macherey, Pierre, on Marxist approaches to narrative, 199
Madhavan, N. S.: archival approach of, 87–88; collector's attitude of, 84–88; *Litanies of the Dutch Battery*, 25, 76, 80–88; poetry of things, 80–81
magical order of history, 218
Mahabharata (Hindu epic), 132

Mahlstedt, Andrew, on "poverty porn," 152, 152n10
Making Stories (Bruner), 58
Makonda, A., 97n4
Malani, Nalini, gaze and shadow plays of, 241–48
Malayalam: *The Legends of Khasak* (Vijayan), 252, 261–67; role of objects in *Indulekha* (Menon), 76–77, 79–80; role of objects in *Lakshmikesavam* (Menon), 77, 79–80; role of objects in *Litanies of the Dutch Battery* (Madhavan), 25, 76, 80–88
Mannathukkaren, Nissim, 11
Marcus, Amit, 168
margin, center *vs.*, 55–56, 62–63, 66–67, 70
Margolin, Uri, 202
Márquez, Gabriel García, 132
Martínez, Matías, 170
Marxist approaches: to narrative ideology, 199–200; to postcoloniality, 9
masking, focalization and, 19
mask narration, 179; in *The Great Gatsby* (Fitzgerald), 179, 187; in "The Third and Final Continent" (Lahiri), 187–88
Masks of Conquest (Vishwanathan), 9
Mattoo, Neerja, Kashmiri fiction edited and translated by, 42n5, 45–50
maxim spotting, 240
McDonald, Peter D., 237n6
memory: act of, Bal on, 234n3; delectation of, 25; emotional, in Kashmiri fiction, 25, 41–45; focalization and, 231–35; location and, Kumar on, 25; multidirectional, 233–34; multitemporal, 233–34; relationship between public and private, 24; witness literature and, 21
Menon, Dilip, on oceanic geographies, 83
Menon, O. Chandu, *Indulekha*, 76–77, 79–80
Menon, Padu, *Lakshmikesavam*, 77, 79–80
metacultural signs, 93; in *Les Bouts de bois de Dieu. Banty mam Yall* (Sembène), 94
metalepsis, 25, 68
metalinguistic signs, 93; in *Les Bouts de bois de Dieu. Banty mam Yall* (Sembène), 94–99
metamnemonic novel, Ondaatje's *Running in the Family* as, 65n12
metanarrative signs: affinity for multiculturalism, 93–94; in *Les Bouts de bois de*

Dieu. Banty mam Yall (Sembène), 26, 94–100; characterization with, 94; constituting and foregrounding ideology with, 94; of cultural code, 93; defining narrator and narratee with, 94; definition of, 93; functions of, 94; illustration of theme with, 94; of linguistic code, 93; as markers of difference, 100; narratological questions about, 99–100; Prince on, 24, 25–26, 93–101; of proairetic code, 93

metaphors, for nationhood, 40, 40n3

metaproairetic signs, 93; in *Les Bouts de bois de Dieu. Banty mam Yall* (Sembène), 94

metonymy, 17; collection *vs.*, 85

metropole, in postcolonialism, 9, 13, 29

Midnight's Children (Rushdie): Alber's narratological analysis of, 26, 120–38; allegorical structure of, 123–26, 124nn4–5; allegory of nationhood in, 26; Bennett (Robert) on, 124–25, 131; binary thinking in, 128, 128n13; Birk on, 123; character pluralism and potentialities in, 130–31; cinematic narration in, 134; Conner on, 123; crime of passion in, 128, 128n11; fictionalized versions of historical events in, 125; first-person and omniscient narration in, 126, 126n9; Hogan on, 127, 135n17; homodiegetic narration with zero focalization in, 126; hybridity critique in, 130; ideological ambivalence of, 120–21; ideological functions of narrative strategies in, 121–22; intertextual references in, 131–33, 132nn15–16; multifariousness of human subject in, 129–31; multiple narrative beginnings and digressions in, 122–23; narrative discourse *vs.* fabula of, 26; narrative omissions in, 134–35, 135n17; narrator interpellation in, 126n8; narrator's telepathy in, 126–29, 127n10; Neumann on, 123; as polyphonic narrative, 125, 131; postcolonial narratology in, 121, 135–36; representations of blood in, 125n7; sense of ending in, 135–36; styles and vocabularies in, 133–35; "Third Space" in, 121, 129–31; unreliable narration in, 167–68

Midsummer Night's Dream, A (Shakespeare), 132n15

migrant literature: analysis using Fludernik's cognitively based model, 57–58, 63, 66, 69, 70; concept of self in, 55–58, 69–71; conventions of authorship challenged in, 60–61, 63, 64–67, 70–71; cultural consequences in, 231, 231n1; experiential dimension of, 56–57, 69–70; immigrant experience in "The Third and Final Continent" (Lahiri), 173–89; narratives of return journeys, 55–73; *A Place Within* (Vassanji), 56–63, 69–71; *Running in the Family* (Ondaatje), 56–58, 63–67, 69–71; *Tales From Firozsha Baag* (Mistry), 56–58, 67–71; vision *vs.* narrative in, 69–70. *See also specific works*

migratory aesthetics, 235

Mikics, David, 124n4

Miles, Alice, 152n10

Millais, Sir John Everett, 131, 132

mimesis: Doležel on, 17; fiction and, 22; objectified voice and, 19; objects and, 81; Ricoeur's three-fold model of, 7

Mineka, Susan, 42

Minima Moralia (Adorno), 240

minority cosmopolitanism, 174

Mishra, Pradyumna, 142, 143

Mishra, Vijay, 9, 201

Mistry, Rohinton: background of, 67; construction of self, 69; hegemonic discourse of, 68; ideological implications of, 68–69; metalepsis in story, 68; "Swimming Lessons," 67–69; *Tales From Firozsha Baag*, 56–58, 67–71

Mitchell, W. J. T., 246n17

modernity, objects as talismans of, 76–77, 79–80

Mohi-ud-din, Akhtar, "The Second Meeting," 46

monoperspectivity, 196

Moore, Lorrie, 205

Moore-Gilbert, Bart, 60, 63

Morehouse, Ward, 143

Mufti, Aamir, 13, 14, 23

Mukherjee, Ankhi, 162

Mukherjee, Bharati, 58n3

Mukherjee, Pablo, 142–43, 149

Muliyil, Joseph, *Sukumari*, 83

Müller, Hans-Harald, 2

multidirectional memory, 233–34

multiperspectivity, 196

multitemporal memory, 233–34

mundane order of history, 218

Muralidharan, Sukumar, 142

Murthy, R. Srinivasa, 143n2

Nanda, Meera, 12, 13

Narayan, Gaura Shankar, 123

narratee: actual readers vs., 150n7; construction in *Animal's People* (Sinha), 150–54; in *How to Get Filthy Rich in Rising Asia* (Hamid), 205–6; interpellation of, 19; metanarrative signs defining, 94

narration: as art of indirection, 177; imposition of form on material, 18; myriad forms of, 18; process of, 18

narrative: as act of communication, 103n3; Anand's choice of, 102–4; definitions of, 103n3, 175–76, 255; emergence from context, 5; as form of cognition, 5–7; vs. not narrative, 103, 103n3; semantic or world-creating properties of, 103n3

Narrative as Rhetoric (Phelan), 106

narrative authority: in *Animal's People* (Sinha), 146–48; concept of, 146–47

narrative communication model, 176

"Narrative Forms" (Fludernik), 200

narrative identity, 19

narrative instance, 19; disintegration of boundaries in *A Place Within* (Vassanji), 63

narrative progression, 256–57

narrative qua narrative, 17

narrative voice. *See* voice

narrativization, Fludernik on, 257–59, 260

narratological criticism, 3–5; "both . . . and" model, 4–5; postcolonial narratology and, 8–18, 22–23; separatist perspective on, 5; theoretical narratology vs., 3–5

narratological toolbox, 4–5, 18

narratology: Bal on point of, 4; classical typologies of, 194; conceptual framework of, 18; Fludernik's definition of, 194; formalism in, 2–8, 203; form vs. function debate in, 194; general and particular in, 5–8; history of ideology in, Fludernik on, 195–202; ideology in, 2–8; ideology in, Bakhtin on, 195, 196–99; ideology in, Fludernik on, 193–212; ideology in, Uspensky on, 195–96, 199; inductive vs. deductive methodology in, 3–4; issues for postcolonial texts, 18–22; natural, 57, 69, 252, 257–59; postclassical, 194; postcolonial literary studies and, 8–18, 22–23; Prince's restrictive definition of, 3–4; separatist perspective on, 5; synthesis and dialogic reciprocity of theory and criticism in, 8; theoretical scrutiny in, 16–17; theoretical vs. applied, 3–4. *See also specific types and literary works*

narrator, voice vs. character voice, 16

narratorial ductus, 200

narrator's telepathy, in *Midnight's Children* (Rushdie), 126–29, 127n10

Nasta, Susheila, on Forster's preface to Anand's *Untouchable*, 104n4, 105n6, 108–9, 114, 116

nation, cognitive models of, 40, 40n3

national allegory, 40–41, 40n4

nationalism, emplotment of: cognitive models of nation and, 40, 40n3; criminal investigation prototype and, 40; family separation and reunion prototype and, 38, 39; heroic prototype and, 38–39; Hogan on, 25, 37–52; Kashmir, by Kashmiris (disfigured), 41–52; Kashmir, by non-Kashmiris, 37–41; plot prototypes and, 25, 38–41; revenge prototype and, 40; romantic prototype and, 38, 39, 41; sacrificial prototype and, 38, 39

nationhood: allegory in *Midnight's Children*, 26; Bhabha on, 11–12, 38; decoupling postcolony from, 28, 213–14; Kashmiri, plot prototypes on, 25; postcolonialism and concept of, 11–12, 24

NATION IS A FAMILY, 40

NATION IS A PERSON, 40, 45

NATION IS THE LAND AND ITS CITIZENS ARE PLANTS WITH ROOTS IN THE LAND, 40

naturalization, 57; in "The Third and Final Continent" (Lahiri), 173–75

natural narratology, 57, 69, 252, 257–59

Nature of Blood (Phillips), 201n5

Navarro, Hernández, 231n1

Nehru, Jawaharlal, 124, 124n5

neo-imperialism, 24, 27

Neumann, Birgit: on *Midnight's Children* (Rushdie), 123; on postcolonial narratology, 121; on *Running in the Family* (Ondaatje), 65n12

New History of India, A (Wolpert), 132

Ngugi wa Thiong'o, 98n6

Niederhoff, Burckhard, 81n3

Nielsen, Henrik Skov, 22, 126n9

Nietzsche, Friedrich, 215n6

Nixon, Rob, 146

Njoroge, Paul Ngigi, 97n4

nonfiction, generality and particulars in, 6–7
non-focalization, 196
Notebook of a Return to My Native Land (Césaire), 105n5
novels: Anand's choice of genre, 102–4; Lawrence on starting flow with, 102; objects and realism of, 74–75. *See also specific works*
Nünning, Ansgar: on implied reader, 254n5; on multiperspectivity, 196; on semanticized narrative structures, 55; on signals of unreliability, 162
Nünning, Vera: on multiperspectivity, 196; on personhood, 169
Nussbaum, Martha C., 144
Nzabatsinda, Anthère, 97n4

objectified voice, 19
objects: Barthes's concepts of, 74–75; Baudrillard on system of, 75; body as, 87–88; in Bond stories (Fleming), 74; collector's attitude toward, 84–86; commodity exchange and, 75; differentiation of characters with, 76; in Flaubert's work, 75; as functions, 74; as historical experience, 77; historical resonance of, 86; as indices, 74; in *Indulekha* (Menon), 76–77, 79–80; as informants, 74–75; instrumentalities of, 74; in *Lakshmikesavam* (Menon), 77, 79–80; in *Litanies of the Dutch Battery* (Madhavan), 76, 80–88; and new regime of literature, 78–79; non-allegorical reading of, 85; in postcolonial context, 75–76, 79–80; reality effect of, 74–75, 85; remembrance and location, 81–82; as repository of traces, 86–88; status in narratives, Kumar on, 25, 74–90; as talismans of modernity, 76–77, 79–80; in *The Wild Ass's Skin* (Balzac), 78, 79
O'Brien, Susie, 150
Ojo, S. Ade, 99n8
Olson, Greta: on biopolitics, 162–63; on colonial discourse, 166–67; on dominant representation strategies of 9/11 texts, 157–58, 157n2; on history, politics, and power in unreliable narration, 27–28, 163–70; on Kantian ethics, 164–66; on models of unreliability, 156, 163–70; on need for new models of unreliability, 170; on neo-imperialism and globalization, 24; on politics of form, 170; on resistance to ideology of reliability, 169; on unreliable narration as strategy of ideological critique, 156–57; on unreliable narration in *The Reluctant Fundamentalist* (Hamid), 27–28, 156–72
Olsson, Karen, 158
Ondaatje, Michael: anarchic quality of text, 65n13; *Anil's Ghost*, 64; background of, 63–64, 63n9; *The Cat's Table*, 64; creation and multiplicity of self, 64–67; creation of "authenticity," 64–65; double temporality of text, 66; fictionalized memoir approach of, 56, 56n1, 64–65, 64n10; focus on father, 64–65, 64n11; proximity vs. distance of, 66; questioning of established notions of authorship, 65; rejection of traditional autobiography, 66; *Running in the Family*, 56–58, 63–67, 69–71; undermining of conventional self-narration, 64–67, 70–71
Osella, Caroline, 263n11
Osella, Filipo, 263n11
"other," colonized as, 10
Oxfeld, Ellen, on return journeys, 57

Pakistan, and Kashmir, 37–52; depiction in "The Burnt-Out Sun" (Hamadani), 45; disfigured stories in Kashmiri fiction, 37, 41–52; emplotment of nationalism by non-Kashmiris, 37–41; heroic prototype and, 38; sacrificial prototype and, 39
Palmer, Alan, 262
panfictionality doctrine, 21–22
Paraśurām, satires of: aftermath of crisis in, 217; apocalypse, decolonization, and postcolony in, 28, 213–28; coming community (postcolony) in, 28, 223–28; dispositifs in, 214, 221, 227–28; as distinct phase in literary modernity, 214, 215; *Galpakalpa*, 214–15, 214n3; incredible order of history in, 218, 219; magical order of history in, 218; meaning and ambiguity of kalpa in, 214–15; mundane order of history in, 218; projected crisis in, 216–17; prolepsis in, 215; stories or almost stories, 214–17; thematization of postcolony in, 215; unusual resolution of crisis in, 216–17
paratext, 20–21, 22; Copland on, 26; Forster's preface to Anand's *Untouchable* as, 105, 107, 107n9; of *The Reluctant Fundamentalist* (Hamid), 158, 168; "zone between text and off-text," 158

Parry, Benita, 12
particular: alignment with ideology, 7; in fictive and nonfictive rhetorics, 6–7; relationship with general, 5–8
Passage to India, A (Forster): gesture of spatiotemporal deferral in, 118; and preface to *Untouchable* (Anand), 108–11, 113–14; representations of untouchability in, 114–16
pathos, Forster's appeal to, 111, 112
pedagogy: Dwivedi on, 29, 251–72; Spivak on, 235–40, 267–71
Peer, Basharat, 42, 50
peritext, 21
person, nation as, 40, 45
personal voice: in *Animal's People* (Sinha), 149–50, 153–54; in Lanser's typology, 147
personhood, and reliability, 165–66, 169
perspectivalism, focalization and, 19–20
perspective, Bal's critique of, 28–29
perspective structure (Perspektivenstruktur), 196
Pfister, Manfred, on perspective structure, 196
Phelan, James: on addressee function, 269; on authorial audience, 255–57, 269; on authorial disclosures, 180, 180n4, 181, 186; on character-character dialogue, 27, 175–87; on convergent narration, 179, 184–86; on conversational disclosures, 179–80, 180n4; on crossover narration, 186–87; definition of narrative, 103n3, 175–76, 255; on flesh-and-blood readers and authorial audience, 106–7; on mask narration, 179, 187–88; on narrative progression, 256–57; on narrative voice, 255, 260, 269; on power dynamics, 27, 173–74; on reliability and unreliability, 27–28, 163, 165, 177–79, 181, 184; on restricted narration, 178, 180–84; on rhetorical narratology, 20–21, 22, 27, 175–79; on rhetorical reading, 113; taxonomy of unreliability, 177, 255; on "The Third and Final Continent" (Lahiri), 27–28, 173–89
Phillips, Caryl, 201n5
"Philosopher's Stone, The" (Paraśurām), 221–23
Pilapitiya, Kishani, 130
Place Within, A (Vassanji), 56–63, 69–71; alignment of "I" and "eye" in, 60; disintegration of narrative instance boundaries in, 63; experiential nature of, 60; meta-narrative dimension of, 61; multiplicity of histories in, 62; search for identity in, 58–59; significance of subtitle, 58; as social autobiography, 62; subversion of conventional first-person discourse in, 60–61, 63, 70–71; "the journey is endless," 70; as travelogue, 56, 60
plot, in postcolonial literature, 201
plot prototypes: criminal investigation, 40, 47–48; family separation and reunion, 38, 39, 48–51; heroic, 25, 38–39, 44, 46; in Kashmiri fiction, disfigured or fractured, 41–52; in narrative negotiation of Kashmiri nationhood, 25; in non-Kashmiri portrayals of Kashmir, 38–41; revenge, 25, 40, 41, 48; sacrificial, 25, 38, 39, 41–42, 44, 46, 48–51; trauma and distortion of, 41–45
point of narratology, Bal on, 4
politics of form, Olson on, 170
polybridity, 62, 62n7
polyperspectivity, 196
polyphony: Bakhtin on, 196–99; in Dostoevsky's works, 196–97; in *Little Dorrit* (Dickens), 197–98; in *Midnight's Children* (Rushdie), 125, 131; in Pfister's perspective structure, 196
Pontes, Hilda, 104n4, 111n10, 116n12
postclassical narratology, 194
"Post-Colonialism" (Williams), 199–200, 201, 201n5
postcolonialism: Brennan on porous nature of, 9; colonial discourse and, 9–12, 27; Dalit studies in, 11; definition of, 9; emergence of term, 11; interpretive turn in, 12; Marxist characterizations of, 9; relationship of literary studies to, 8–9, 22–23; universalism and, 10
postcolonial narratology: Alber on, 121; "both . . . and" model of, 4–5; co-determination in, 15–16; Fludernik on, 121, 199–209; focalization in, Bal on, 28–29, 231–50; formalism and ideology in, 2–8; goal of, 121; imperative vs. problem in, 1–2; issues for texts, 18–22; literary criticism and, 8–18, 22–23; in *Midnight's Children* (Rushdie), 121, 135–36; native narrative traditions vs. European patterns in, 201–2; negotiation with literary paradigm, 17–18; Prince's model of, 3; relation of content and form in, 24;

South Asian texts as focus in, 23–24; we-narratives in, 202; "writing back" in, 28, 200–201
"Postcolonial Remains" (Young), 141
"Postcolonial Writer: Myth Maker and Folk Historian, The" (Vassanji), 62
post-traumatic stress, emotional memory in, 42
"poverty porn," 152, 152n10
"practised spaces," 58
Prasad, Chandra Bhan, 14
Pratt, Mary Louise, 5
Prendergast, Christopher, 7
Price, Francis, 97n5
primary speech genre, 15–16
Prince, Gerald: on *Les Bouts de bois de Dieu. Banty mam Yall* (Sembène), 26, 94–100; inductive approach in feminist narratology, 3; on languages in postcolonial context, 24, 25–26; on metanarrative signs, 24, 25–26, 93–101; model of postcolonial narratology, 3; on postcolonial narratology, 121; on reader (implied reader), 254n5; restrictive definition of narratology, 3–4; on specificities of postcolonial texts, 200
private voice, in *Animal's People* (Sinha), 153
proairetic code: definition of, 93; metanarrative signs of, 93
problem, framing contextualist narratology as, 1–2
Problems of Dostoevsky's Poetics (Bakhtin), 196–97
prolepsis: completing *vs.* repeating, 215n7; definition of, 215n7; external *vs.* internal, 215n7; in Paraśurām's satires, 215
"Proteus Principle," 203
pseudomimetic approach, 17
pseudo-objective motivation, 197
psychoanalytic view, of trauma, 42
public history, objects in *Litanies of the Dutch Battery* (Madhavan) and, 80–88
public voice, in *Animal's People* (Sinha), 153
Pushkin, Eugene, *Eugene Onegin*, 196

Rabinowitz, Peter: definition of narrative, 103n3, 255; on flesh-and-blood readers and authorial audience, 106; on hypothetical audience, 256

Rai, Alok, 270
Ram, Atma, 104n4
Ramadas, Cherayi, 82n5
Ramayana (Hindu epic), 132
Rancière, Jacques, on objects and new regime of literature, 78–79
Rao, Raja, 202
rationalist methodology, 3
reader: addressee function and, 252–55; conceptualization of, 253; Dwivedi on, 29, 251–72; illusion of narrator, 257–59, 258n9; implied (*see* implied reader); "interpretative moves" of, 257–59; narratological concept of, 251–52; potentiality of, 270–71; subjectivation of, 253–55, 258–59, 261; theory of mind, 259, 267
reading: constitutive role in narrativity, 251; defining, 251–52; dissident, 193–94; Dwivedi on ideology and narratology of, 29, 251–72; Fludernik on process of, 194, 203–9, 257–59, 260; interactive, absent focalization and, 235–40, 245, 266–67; narrativization in, 257–59, 260; Spivak model for, 235–40, 254–55, 266–71; theory of, 258; unreading and, 14
Reading the American Novel (Phelan), 106–7, 113
realism: norms of, 22; object status in narrative and, 74–75, 85; refusal of, 22
reality effect, of objects, 74–75, 85
receiver, and addressee function, 254
reflecting, as cognitive frame, 57
refugee studies, 17
Rehbar, Avtar Krishna, "Anguish," 46–47
reliability, in narration: authorial audience and, 255–56; Booth on, 163–65, 167, 170, 175n2; communicative norms and, 164; essence of, 178; Jameson on, 167; Kantian ethics and, 164–66; need for new models of, 170; Olson on, 27–28, 173–89; personhood, race, and gender in, 165–66, 169; Phelan on, 27–28, 163, 165, 177–79, 181, 184, 255–56; resistance to ideology of, 169; spectrum and subtypes of, 178–79; in "The Third and Final Continent" (Lahiri), 27–28, 175, 181, 184. *See also* unreliable narration
Reluctant Fundamentalist, The (Hamid): ambivalent love story of, 160–61; biopolitics in, 162–63; as counter-narrative to "9/11" texts, 156–63; economics and

American Dream in, 158–59; ethnic stereotypes in, 161–62; impersonal use of "you" in, 160; intertextual references in, 160, 162, 168; paratext of, 158, 168; plot instability of, 159; resistance to ideology of reliability, 169; reverse ethnic profiling in, 161; signals of unreliability in, 159–60; subversion of expectations in, 158–59; "talking back" to power in, 162; unreliable narration in, 27–28, 156–72
reporting, unreliable, 177, 255
restricted narration, 178; in *Huckleberry Finn* (Twain), 178; in "The Third and Final Continent" (Lahiri), 180–84
return journeys, 55–73; analysis using Fludernik's cognitively based model, 57–58, 63, 66, 69, 70; chronological parameters of, 57; concept of self in, 55–58, 69–71; conventions of authorship challenged in, 60–61, 63, 64–67, 70–71; experiential dimension of, 56–57, 69–70; identitary parameters of, 57–58; as modern-day pilgrimages, 57; *A Place Within* (Vassanji), 56–63, 69–71; *Running in the Family* (Ondaatje), 56–58, 63–67, 69–71; spatial parameters of, 57–58; *Tales From Firozsha Baag* (Mistry), 56–58, 67–71; vision vs. narrative in, 69–70
revenge prototype: in Kashmiri fiction, 41, 48; in narrative negotiation of Kashmiri nationhood, 25; in non-Kashmiri portrayals of Kashmir, 40
reverse ethnic profiling, 161
rhetorical model of unreliability, 27–28, 156, 163–64
rhetorical narratology: addressee function in, 29; Copland's contextual analysis of Forster's preface to Anand's *Untouchable*, 26, 102–19; Phelan on, 20–21, 22, 27, 175–79; in *The Sound and the Fury* (Faulkner), 176–77, 178; in "The Third and Final Continent" (Lahiri), 27–28, 173–89
rhetorical reading: definition of, 113; modeling, in Forster's preface to Anand's *Untouchable*, 113–14
Rhetoric of Fiction, The (Booth), 163, 165, 175n2
Rhetoric of Irony, A (Booth), 164, 165
Richardson, Brian, 15, 160, 200, 202, 202n6
Rickward, Edgell, 104, 108, 109

Ricoeur, Paul, threefold model of mimesis, 7
Romans, Bernhard, 166
romantic prototype: disfigured, in Kashmiri fiction, 41, 46–47; in non-Kashmiri portrayals of Kashmir, 38, 39
Rothberg, Michael, 234
Running in the Family (Ondaatje), 56–58, 63–67, 69–71, 70–71; anarchic quality of, 65n13; "authenticity" in, 64–65; chronology of, 64; conventional self-narration undermined in, 64–67; creation and multiplicity of self in, 64–67; double temporality of, 66; as fictionalized memoir, 56, 56n1, 64–65, 64n10; focus on father in, 64–65, 64n11; metamnemonic dimension of, 65n12; proximity vs. distance in, 66; questioning of established notions of authorship in, 65
Rushdie, Salman: on emotional memory, 43–44; *Midnight's Children*, 26, 120–38 (see *Midnight's Children*); on oral narrative, 122; unreliable narrators of, 156, 167–68
Russian Formalists, 194
Ryan, Marie-Laure, 21

sacrificial prototype: disfigured, in Kashmiri fiction, 41, 46, 48–51; in narrative negotiation of Kashmiri nationhood, 25; in non-Kashmiri portrayals of Kashmir, 38, 39; trauma and distortion of, 41–42, 44
Sahgal, Nayantara, *A Time to Be Happy*, 194, 203–5, 208
Said, Edward: on colonial discourse, 9; on construction of self, 69; on Marxist approaches to narrative, 199; on vision vs. narrative, 69
Sandhu, Sukhdev, 200n4
Santosh, Ghulam Rasool, "The Voice," 50–51
Sarangi, Satinath, 143
Satchidanandan, K., 261
satire, ahistorical structure of, 217
satires, Bengali. *See* Paraśurām, satires of
satirical practices, 217–23
Scanlan, Margaret, 159
Schank, Roger C., 6
Schmid, Wolf, 198n3, 256
Schmidt, Siegfried J., 62

Schultheis Moore, Alexandra, on *Animal's People* (Sinha), 142, 145n5, 148, 149
Schwenger, Peter, 246n17
Scott-James, R. A., 103, 104
secondary speech genre, 15–16
"Second Meeting, The" (Mohi-ud-din), 46
"Second-Person Narrative as a Test Case" (Fludernik), 202n6
self: experiential dimension of, 56–57, 69–70; migration/return stories and, 55–58, 69–71; Mistry's concept of (*Tales From Firozsha Baag*), 69; narrative and creation of, 58; Ondaatje's creation and multiplicity of (*Running in the Family*), 64–67; Said on construction of, 69; spatial associations of (center vs. margin), 55–56, 62–63, 66–67, 70; subject positions and, 56; transcultural or cosmopolitan, 55; Vassanji's search for identity (*A Place Within*), 58–59, 62–63
self-fashioning, 57
Self-Help (Moore), 205
Seltzer, Mark, 127n10
Sembène, Ousmane: *Les Bouts de bois de Dieu. Banty mam Yall*, 26, 94–100; concern with legibility, 95
Senegal: metanarrative signs in *Les Bouts de bois de Dieu. Banty mam Yall* (Sembène), 26, 94–100; railroad strike in, 94
"Sexing Narratology" (Lanser), 146
Shakespeare, William: *Hamlet*, 50; *A Midsummer Night's Dream*, 132n15
Shamsie, Muneeza, 162
Shen, Dan: on contextualism, 1; on implied author, 255n7, 257; on unreliability, 163–64
Sherwani, Mohd Maqbool, 39
Sikoumo, Hilaire, 97n4
Silverman, Kaja, 242n11, 243, 244
Silverman, Max, 241
"Simple Heart, A" (Flaubert), 75
Sinfield, Alan, 193–94
Singh, Amardeep, textual analysis of Forster's preface to Anand's *Untouchable*, 108
Singh, Rahul, 39
Sinha, Indra, *Animal's People*, 27, 141–55. See also *Animal's People*
skaz, 198
Slumdog Millionaire (film), 152n10

Smith, Barbara Herrnstein, 5
Smith, Sidonie, 66
Snell, Heather, on *Animal's People* (Sinha), 145
social mind, 262, 262n10
Solomon, Deborah, 161
Sommer, Doris, 38n2
Sommer, Roy: on "both . . . and" model, 4; on contextual narratology, 2; on goal of postcolonial narratology, 121
Sommerfield, John, 103, 104
Sontag, Susan, 151
Sorensen, Eli Park, 14
Sound and the Fury, The (Faulkner), rhetorical analysis of, 176–77, 178
South Asian texts: as focus of postcolonial narratology, 23–24; ideologies in, Fludernik on, 194, 203–9; paradigmatic concepts in, 23. See also specific authors and texts
spatial associations of self (center vs. margin), 55–56, 62–63, 66–67, 70
spatial parameters, of return journeys, 57–58
speech, as narratological issue, 195–99
speech genre, 15–16
Sperber, Dan, 164
Spinks, Lee, 67
Spivak, Gayatri: on access to languages, 269–70; on colonial persistence in language, 10; on counterfocalization, 29, 236, 266–67; on critical intimacy, 238–40; on *Disgrace* (Coetzee), 15, 235–37, 266–67; on double bind, 267; on focalization and its absence, 15, 235–40, 245, 266–67; on implied reader, 15; memorial, personalizing mode of, 239; on narrating disaster, 144; narrative pedagogy of, 235–40, 267–71; on paradigmatic concepts in South Asian texts, 23; philosophical underpinnings of work, 237–38; reading process of, 235–40, 254–55, 266–71; teacher mode of, 238–40; on vernaculars, 270
Sri Lanka, Ondaatje's return journeys to (*Running in the Family*), 56–68, 63–67
Stadler, Florian, on *Midnight's Children* (Rushdie), 134
Stanzel, Franz Karl: classical narratology of, 194; on figural narrative situation, 255
statistical reader, 260–61

Stengers, Isabelle, 246n18
Sternberg, Meir, "Proteus Principle" of, 203
Sterne, Laurence, *Tristam Shandy*, 132–33, 132n16
Story and Discourse (Chatman), 176
Su, John J., on *Midnight's Children* (Rushdie), 135
subalternity, 23, 68; in *Animal's People* (Sinha), 144–45, 149; Young on concept of, 144n4
subjectivation of readers, 253–55, 258–59, 261
subjectivity networks, 245–46
Sukumari (Muliyil), 83
"Swimming Lessons" (Mistry), 67–69
system of acceptability, Foucault on, 265, 265n13
System of Objects, The (Baudrillard), 75

Tagore, Rabindranath, *Gitanjali*, 105n5
"Tale of the Gamman Tribe, The" (Paraśurām), 216, 227–28
Tales From Firozsha Baag (Mistry), 56–58, 67–71; construction of self in, 69; hegemonic discourse in, 68; ideological implications of, 68–69; metalepsis in, 68
"talking back" to power, 162
Tapa, Tariq, *Zero Bridge* (film), 51n9
telling, as cognitive frame, 57
"The Tell-Tale Heart" (Poe), as intertextual source in *The Reluctant Fundamentalist* (Hamid), 162
Theory of African Literature, The (Amuta), 199
Theory of Drama (Pfister), 196
Theory of Literary Production, A (Macherey), 199
theory of mind (ToM), reader's, 259, 267
theory of reading, 258
"Theses on the Philosophy of History" (Benjamin), 234
Thinking in Film (Bal), 236n5
"Third and Final Continent, The" (Lahiri): allegory for naturalization in, 174; arranged marriage as metaphor in, 174; authorial disclosure in, 181, 186; character-character dialogue in, 175; convergent narration in, 184–86; crossover narration in, 186–87; diasporic citizenship in, 174; as epic short story, 174, 187; instabilities in, 173; Jackson on, 174, 181; Koshy's analysis of, 174–75, 181, 187; mask narration in, 187–88; mediation between individual subjectivity and social structures in, 174–75; minority cosmopolitanism in, 174; Phelan on postcolonial and rhetorical perspectives in, 27–28, 173–89; politically oriented criticism of, 175; reliability and unreliability in, 27–28, 175, 181, 184; restricted narration in, 180–84; Splendid Ritual in, 173, 180–87; synergies in, 180–87; turning point scene of, 174
"Third Space": Bhabha's definition of, 129; in *Midnight's Children* (Rushdie), 121, 129–31
"Third World Literature" (Jameson), 199
Thomas, Bronwen, 175n2
thought representation, as narratological issue, 195–99
"Through a Glass Darkly" (Fludernik), 202n6
Tiffin, Helen, 12, 55, 98n6
time: crystallization of, focalization and, 234–35; dual temporality of narrative, 19, 66; in postcolonial literature, 201, 201n5
Time to Be Happy, A (Sahgal): Fludernik on ideology of, 194, 203–5, 208; irony in, 203–5, 208; time structure of, 204
Tomkins, Jane, 194
top-down methodology, 3–4
Touching the World: Reference in Autobiography (Eakin), 58
transcultural self, 55
transnational narratology, Friedman on, 2–3
Tratner, Michael, on hybridity in *Midnight's Children* (Rushdie), 130
trauma, and narration: distortion of plot prototypes, 41–45; Hogan on emotional memory and, 25, 41–45; in Kashmiri fiction, 25, 37, 41–52; Kumar on, 24
trauma theory, 42
traumatic stimuli, 42
traveling concepts, 241
Travelling Concepts in the Humanities (Bal), 238n7
Tristam Shandy (Sterne), as intertextual source in *Midnight's Children* (Rushdie), 132–33, 132n16
Trivedi, Harish, 252n2
Turner, Mark, 44

Twain, Mark: authorial audience of *Huckleberry Finn*, 106; restricted narration in *Huckleberry Finn*, 178

Two Thousand Seasons (Armah), 201n5

Understanding Nationalism (Hogan), 38, 41–42

universalism: false, 2–3, 10; Friedman's transnational narratology vs., 2–3; Hogan's cross-cultural narratology and, 2–3; postcolonialism vs., 10

unnatural narratology, 22

Unnatural Voices (Richardson), 200

"unreading," 14

unreliable narration: assumptions about human nature in, 156; authorial audience and, 255–56; Boothian model of, 163–65, 167, 170; cognitive model of, 156, 163–64; in colonial discourse, 166–67; communicative norms and, 164; communion between preferred reader and implied author in, 157; detection of, 157, 163; estranging, 178; focalization and, 169–70; Jameson on, 167; Kantian ethics and, 164–66; misevaluation and underevaluation, 177, 255; misinterpreting and underinterpreting, 177, 255; misreporting and underreporting, 177, 255; need for new models of, 170; Olson on history, politics, and power in, 27–28, 163–70; personhood, race, and gender in, 165–66, 169; Phelan on, 27–28, 163, 165, 177–79, 181, 184, 255–56; Phelan's taxonomy of, 177, 255; in postcolonial narratology, 19, 27–28, 156–57; in *The Reluctant Fundamentalist* (Hamid), 27, 156–72; rhetorical function of, 157; rhetorical model of, 27–28, 156, 163–64; signals of, 162; in "The Third and Final Continent" (Lahiri), 27–28, 175, 181, 184

"untimely" history: Nietzsche on, 215n6; in Paraśurām's satires, 215, 217–23

untimely interjections, 267–68

Untouchable (Anand): appropriation of Dalit voices in, 117n14; barriers to readership, 104; critical edition of, need for, 116–17, 117n14; Fludernik on, 202; genesis of narrative, 102–4; intended readership for, 104; representations of untouchability in, 114–16; reviews and praise for, 103

Untouchable (Anand), Forster's preface to: appeal to ethos, 110, 111, 112; appeal to logos, 111–12; appeal to pathos, 111, 112; colonizer-colonized dynamic in, 105, 107–8; Copland's contextual rhetorical analysis of, 26, 102–19; disclosure of ending in, 105, 113; establishment of "us" group of readers in, 110–11, 111n10; flesh-and-blood reader and authorial audience, 106–11, 107n8; "highjacking and interception" in, 105, 118; modeling of rhetorical reading in, 113–14; Nasta on, 105n6, 108–9, 114, 116; opening anecdote of, 108–11; paratext of, 105, 107, 107n9; positioning of readers relative to *Passage to India*, 108–11, 113–14; as precondition for publication, 104, 108; "protection and patronage" in, 105, 118; responses to potential objections and criticisms in, 112; rhetorical appeals of, 107, 110, 111–12; Singh's textual analysis of, 104–5, 108; Sommerfield's comments on, 104

"U. S. Ethnic and Postcolonial Fiction" (Richardson), 200

Uspensky, Boris: on character, 195; on ideology in narratology, 195–96, 199; on lexical choice, 195–96

Vakunta, Peter W., 97n4

van Alphen, Ernst, 244n13

Vassanji, M. G.: alignment of "I" and "eye," 60; Canada as vantage point for, 60; as "experiential" traveler, 60; motivation for rediscovering India, 59; multicultural element of Indian ancestry, 61–62, 61n6; personal, affective response to India, 59–60, 59n4; *A Place Within*, 56–63, 69–71; "The Postcolonial Writer: Myth Maker and Folk Historian," 62; search for identity, 58–59, 62–63; subversion of conventional first-person discourse, 60–61, 63, 70–71; travelogue approach of, 56, 60

Verhoeven, Wil, 64

vernaculars, 270

Vervaeck, Bart, 260

Vietnam Syndrome, 43

viewing, as cognitive frame, 57

Vijayan, O. V., *The Legends of Khasak*, 252, 261–67, 270

vision, narrative vs., 69–70

visuality, gaze and focalization in, 241–48

Viswanathan, Gauri, 9, 204, 252n2

voice, 26–28; in *Animal's People* (Sinha), 27, 141–55; authorial, 147, 147n6; auto-rial audience and, 255–56; communal, 147–50, 153–54; complexity of concept, 19; double-voiced discourse, 16; Fludernik on, 201; focalization, 15, 19–20; gender-based critique of, 3; in *How to Get Filthy Rich in Rising Asia* (Hamid), 205; interpellation of narratee or reader, 19; Lanser on, 3, 147–50; lay readers and projection of, 257–59, 260; objectified, 19; personal, 147, 149–50, 153–54; Phelan on, 255, 260, 269; private, 153; public, 153–54. *See also* unreliable narration

"Voice, The" (Santosh), 50–51

von Contzen, Eva, 202n6

voyeurism, in narratives about disasters, 152, 152n11

Waheed, Mirza, 41

Wakhlu, Bharat, 41

Walsh, Richard, 22

Ward, Ian, 161

Warhol, Robyn, 4

Watson, Julie, 66

we-narratives, postcolonial, 202

Westwell, Guy, 161

"What Can We Learn from Contextualist Narratology?" (Chatman), 5

"what if?" questions, Bal on, 236–40, 236n5, 239, 245

"What Is an Author?" (Foucault), 253

"When the Self Is an Other" (Fludernik), 15, 200

White, Hayden, 21

"Who Changed the Face of '47 War?" (Singh), 39

Wide Sargasso Sea (Rhys), 167–68

Widmalm, Sten, 43

Wild Ass's Skin, The (Balzac), 77, 79

Williams, Patrick: on Marxist approaches to narrative, 199–200, 200n4; on postcolonialism, 135–36, 201, 201n5

Wilson, Deirdre, 164

witness literature, 21

Wizard of Oz, The (film), 132

Wolpert, Stanley, *A New History of India*, 132

Wood, Leonard, 166–67

"writing back," 28, 200–201

"Writing Back" (Gymnich), 200, 201

Yahaan (film), 39

Yeats, W. B., preface to Tagore's *Gitanjali*, 105n5

Yelle, Robert A., 13, 14

Young, Robert: on concept of subaltern, 144n4; on postcoloniality, 9, 13; "Postcolonial Remains," 141

Zero Bridge (film), 51n9

Zipfel, Frank, 164

Zunshine, Lisa, on reading, 259, 267

THEORY AND INTERPRETATION OF NARRATIVE

JAMES PHELAN, PETER J. RABINOWITZ, AND KATRA BYRAM, SERIES EDITORS

Because the series editors believe that the most significant work in narrative studies today contributes both to our knowledge of specific narratives and to our understanding of narrative in general, studies in the series typically offer interpretations of individual narratives and address significant theoretical issues underlying those interpretations. The series does not privilege one critical perspective but is open to work from any strong theoretical position.

Narratology and Ideology: Negotiating Context, Form, and Theory in Postcolonial Narratives
EDITED BY DIVYA DWIVEDI, HENRIK SKOV NIELSEN, AND RICHARD WALSH

Novelization: From Film to Novel
JAN BAETENS

Reading Conrad
J. HILLIS MILLER, EDITED BY JOHN G. PETERS AND JAKOB LOTHE

Narrative, Race, and Ethnicity in the United States
EDITED BY JAMES J. DONAHUE, JENNIFER ANN HO, AND SHAUN MORGAN

Somebody Telling Somebody Else: A Rhetorical Poetics of Narrative
JAMES PHELAN

Media of Serial Narrative
EDITED BY FRANK KELLETER

Suture and Narrative: Deep Intersubjectivity in Fiction and Film
GEORGE BUTTE

The Writer in the Well: On Misreading and Rewriting Literature
GARY WEISSMAN

Narrating Space / Spatializing Narrative: Where Narrative Theory and Geography Meet
MARIE-LAURE RYAN, KENNETH FOOTE, AND MAOZ AZARYAHU

Narrative Sequence in Contemporary Narratology
EDITED BY RAPHAËL BARONI AND FRANÇOISE REVAZ

The Submerged Plot and the Mother's Pleasure from Jane Austen to Arundhati Roy
KELLY A. MARSH

Narrative Theory Unbound: Queer and Feminist Interventions
EDITED BY ROBYN WARHOL AND SUSAN S. LANSER

Unnatural Narrative: Theory, History, and Practice
BRIAN RICHARDSON

Ethics and the Dynamic Observer Narrator: Reckoning with Past and Present in German Literature
KATRA A. BYRAM

Narrative Paths: African Travel in Modern Fiction and Nonfiction
KAI MIKKONEN

The Reader as Peeping Tom: Nonreciprocal Gazing in Narrative Fiction and Film
JEREMY HAWTHORN

Thomas Hardy's Brains: Psychology, Neurology, and Hardy's Imagination
SUZANNE KEEN

The Return of the Omniscient Narrator: Authorship and Authority in Twenty-First Century Fiction
PAUL DAWSON

Feminist Narrative Ethics: Tacit Persuasion in Modernist Form
KATHERINE SAUNDERS NASH

Real Mysteries: Narrative and the Unknowable
  H. PORTER ABBOTT

A Poetics of Unnatural Narrative
  EDITED BY JAN ALBER, HENRIK SKOV NIELSEN, AND BRIAN RICHARDSON

Narrative Discourse: Authors and Narrators in Literature, Film, and Art
  PATRICK COLM HOGAN

An Aesthetics of Narrative Performance: Transnational Theater, Literature, and Film in Contemporary Germany
  CLAUDIA BREGER

Literary Identification from Charlotte Brontë to Tsitsi Dangarembga
  LAURA GREEN

Narrative Theory: Core Concepts and Critical Debates
  DAVID HERMAN, JAMES PHELAN AND PETER J. RABINOWITZ, BRIAN RICHARDSON, AND ROBYN WARHOL

After Testimony: The Ethics and Aesthetics of Holocaust Narrative for the Future
  EDITED BY JAKOB LOTHE, SUSAN RUBIN SULEIMAN, AND JAMES PHELAN

The Vitality of Allegory: Figural Narrative in Modern and Contemporary Fiction
  GARY JOHNSON

Narrative Middles: Navigating the Nineteenth-Century British Novel
  EDITED BY CAROLINE LEVINE AND MARIO ORTIZ-ROBLES

Fact, Fiction, and Form: Selected Essays
  RALPH W. RADER. EDITED BY JAMES PHELAN AND DAVID H. RICHTER.

The Real, the True, and the Told: Postmodern Historical Narrative and the Ethics of Representation
  ERIC L. BERLATSKY

Franz Kafka: Narration, Rhetoric, and Reading
  EDITED BY JAKOB LOTHE, BEATRICE SANDBERG, AND RONALD SPEIRS

Social Minds in the Novel
  ALAN PALMER

Narrative Structures and the Language of the Self
  MATTHEW CLARK

Imagining Minds: The Neuro-Aesthetics of Austen, Eliot, and Hardy
  KAY YOUNG

Postclassical Narratology: Approaches and Analyses
  EDITED BY JAN ALBER AND MONIKA FLUDERNIK

Techniques for Living: Fiction and Theory in the Work of Christine Brooke-Rose
  KAREN R. LAWRENCE

Towards the Ethics of Form in Fiction: Narratives of Cultural Remission
  LEONA TOKER

Tabloid, Inc.: Crimes, Newspapers, Narratives
  V. PENELOPE PELIZZON AND NANCY M. WEST

Narrative Means, Lyric Ends: Temporality in the Nineteenth-Century British Long Poem
  MONIQUE R. MORGAN

Understanding Nationalism: On Narrative, Cognitive Science, and Identity
  PATRICK COLM HOGAN

Joseph Conrad: Voice, Sequence, History, Genre
  EDITED BY JAKOB LOTHE, JEREMY HAWTHORN, JAMES PHELAN

The Rhetoric of Fictionality: Narrative Theory and the Idea of Fiction
  RICHARD WALSH

Experiencing Fiction: Judgments, Progressions, and the Rhetorical Theory of Narrative
  JAMES PHELAN

Unnatural Voices: Extreme Narration in Modern and Contemporary Fiction
  BRIAN RICHARDSON

Narrative Causalities
  EMMA KAFALENOS

Why We Read Fiction: Theory of Mind and the Novel
  LISA ZUNSHINE

I Know That You Know That I Know: Narrating Subjects from Moll Flanders to Marnie
  GEORGE BUTTE

Bloodscripts: Writing the Violent Subject
  ELANA GOMEL

Surprised by Shame: Dostoevsky's Liars and Narrative Exposure
  DEBORAH A. MARTINSEN

Having a Good Cry: Effeminate Feelings and Pop-Culture Forms
  ROBYN R. WARHOL

Politics, Persuasion, and Pragmatism: A Rhetoric of Feminist Utopian Fiction
  ELLEN PEEL

Telling Tales: Gender and Narrative Form in Victorian Literature and Culture
  ELIZABETH LANGLAND

Narrative Dynamics: Essays on Time, Plot, Closure, and Frames
  EDITED BY BRIAN RICHARDSON

Breaking the Frame: Metalepsis and the Construction of the Subject
  DEBRA MALINA

Invisible Author: Last Essays
  CHRISTINE BROOKE-ROSE

Ordinary Pleasures: Couples, Conversation, and Comedy
  KAY YOUNG

Narratologies: New Perspectives on Narrative Analysis
  EDITED BY DAVID HERMAN

Before Reading: Narrative Conventions and the Politics of Interpretation
  PETER J. RABINOWITZ

Matters of Fact: Reading Nonfiction over the Edge
  DANIEL W. LEHMAN

The Progress of Romance: Literary Historiography and the Gothic Novel
  DAVID H. RICHTER

A Glance Beyond Doubt: Narration, Representation, Subjectivity
  SHLOMITH RIMMON-KENAN

Narrative as Rhetoric: Technique, Audiences, Ethics, Ideology
  JAMES PHELAN

Misreading Jane Eyre: A Postformalist Paradigm
  JEROME BEATY

Psychological Politics of the American Dream: The Commodification of Subjectivity in Twentieth-Century American Literature
  LOIS TYSON

Understanding Narrative
  EDITED BY JAMES PHELAN AND PETER J. RABINOWITZ

Framing Anna Karenina: Tolstoy, the Woman Question, and the Victorian Novel
  AMY MANDELKER

Gendered Interventions: Narrative Discourse in the Victorian Novel
  ROBYN R. WARHOL

Reading People, Reading Plots: Character, Progression, and the Interpretation of Narrative
  JAMES PHELAN

www.ingramcontent.com/pod-product-compliance
Lightning Source LLC
Chambersburg PA
CBHW020639230426
43665CB00008B/233